Hoover Institution Publications

WESTERN TECHNOLOGY AND
SOVIET ECONOMIC DEVELOPMENT
1930 TO 1945

Western Technology and Soviet Economic Development

1930 to 1945

Second volume of a three-volume series

By

ANTONY C. SUTTON

HOOVER INSTITUTION PRESS

STANFORD UNIVERSITY, STANFORD, CALIFORNIA

1971

The Hoover Institution on War, Revolution and Peace, founded at Stanford University in 1919 by the late President Herbert Hoover, is a center for advanced study and research on public and international affairs in the twentieth century. The views expressed in its publications are entirely those of the authors and do not necessarily reflect the views of the Hoover Institution.

Hoover Institution Publications 90

Standard Book Number: 8179-1901-5

© *1971 by Antony C. Sutton*

Library of Congress Catalog Card Number: 68-24442

Printed by Cathay Press, Hong Kong

TO MY WIFE

Betty Janet

Preface

THIS is the second volume of an empirical study of the relationship between Western technology and entrepreneurship and the economic growth of the Soviet Union.

The continuing transfer of skills and technology to the Soviet Union through the medium of foreign firms and engineers in the period 1930 to 1945 can only be characterized as extraordinary. A thorough and systematic search unearthed only two major items—SK-B synthetic rubber and the Ramzin 'once-through' boiler—and little more than a handful of lesser designs (several aircraft, a machine gun, and a motorless combine) which could accurately be called the result of Soviet technology; the balance was transferred from the West.

Once again I must express sincere appreciation to those who have helped me—and absolve them from responsibility for my errors. The Relm Foundation granted research funds and a fellowship tenable at the Hoover Institution, Stanford University. In addition the Hoover Institution provided research assistance from its Special Fund. Among those at Hoover who have given their personal assistance, particular recognition is due Dr. W. Glenn Campbell, Director of the Hoover Institution, for his unfailing support; Mr. Alan Belmont, Associate Director for Administration, for his prompt solutions to my varied problems; and Miss Carolyn Conrad, for research and secretarial work well and conscientiously performed. To these and others, thank you; without your understanding assistance, this study could not have been completed.

Acknowledgment is also due Congressman John E. Moss (Democrat, Sacramento) and his staff for assistance in locating some 600 boxes of Lend-Lease cargo manifests and letter files which had been temporarily mislaid by the Executive Branch of the Federal Government.

Finally, I must express my appreciation to the Douglas Aircraft Company (now McDonnell-Douglas) of Santa Monica, the Warner & Swasey Company of Cleveland, and the Kern County Land Company (now a division of

TENNECO) of San Francisco, and also to Dr. Roger Freeman of the Hoover Institution, and Colonel Samuel F. Clabaugh and Mr. Joseph Gwyer (both of Washington, D.C.) for various forms of assistance. London G. Green handled the editorial chores with his customary expertise.

None of these is, of course, in any way responsible for my errors, arguments, or conclusions.

A. C. S.

Stanford, California
November 28, 1968

Contents

Tables

Figures

Glossary

Aluminstroi:	Aluminum Plant Construction Trust
Amburo:	American Bureau
Azneft:	Azerbaidjan Oil Trust
Burtsvetmet:	Non-ferrous Drilling Trust
CAXO:	Central Asia Cotton Union (strictly Sakho, but spelt thus in Gorton Papers)
Dalles:	Far East Lumber Trust
Donugol:	Don Coal Trust
Elmashstroi:	Electrical Machinery Construction Trust
GET:	State Electro-Technical Trust
Gipromez:	State All-Union Institute for Planning of Metallurgical Works
Giproshakht:	State Institute for Design of Coal Mines
Giprotsvetmet:	State Institute for Planning of Non-Ferrous Metals
Glavkhlopkom:	Chief Cotton Committee
Glavkontsesskom:	Chief Concessions Committee
Goelro:	State Commission for the Electrification of Russia
Gosplan:	State Planning Commission
Grozneft:	Georgian Oil Field Administration
GUAP:	Main Administration of the Aircraft Industry
Hectare:	2.47 acres
Khimstroi:	Chemical Industry Construction Trust
Kokstroi:	Coke Industry Construction Trust
Kombinat:	Combine
Kramkombinat:	Kramatorsky Combine
Lenmashstroi:	Leningrad Machine Building Trust
Mashinoimport:	All Union Association for Import of Machinery
Mekhanobr:	State Institute for Planning Ore-Treatment Plants

Moskhimkombinat:	Moscow Chemical Combine
Moskvugol:	State Association for Coal Industry in the Moscow Region Basin
Mosstroi:	Moscow State Construction and Installation Trust
Narkomvneshtorg:	People's Commissariat for Foreign Trade
OGPU (also GPU):	All-Union Political Administration of the Council of People's Commissars (Secret-Police)
Orgametal:	Institute for Organization of Production in Machinery and Metalworking Industries
Pood:	36.1128 pounds
Resinotrest:	Rubber Trust
Selmash:	All-Russian Syndicate of Agricultural Machines and Implements
Shakhtostroi:	Shaft-Sinking Trust
Sharikopodshipnikstroi:	Ball Bearing Industry Construction Trust
Sovnarkom:	Council of People's Commissars
Soyuzstroi:	All-Union Construction Trust
Sredazvodproiz:	Central Asia Water Authority
Stal':	Steel Trust
Skeklofarfor:	Glass and Ceramics Trust
Svirstroi:	Svir Dam Construction Unit
TsAGI:	Central Aero-Hydrodynamic Institute, im. Zhukovski
Tsvetmetzoloto:	All-Union Association for Mining, Processing and Sale of Non-Ferrous Metals, Gold and Platinum
Udarnik:	Shock Worker (Leader in establishing new production norms under Party instruction)
Uralgol:	Urals Coal Trust
Uralmash:	Urals Machine Combine
Uralrud:	Urals Ore Trust
VATO:	All-Union Automobile and Tractor Trust
VEO:	All-Union Electrical Trust
Vesenkha (VSNKh):	Supreme Council of the National Economy
VINITI:	All-Union Institute of Scientific Information
Vostokugol:	Far East Coal Trust
Vsekhimprom:	All-Union Trust for the Chemical Industry
Vsekomvodgosplan:	All-Union Committee for Planning of Water Projects
Yugostal:	Southern Steel Trust

CHAPTER ONE

Introduction

METHODOLOGY AND SOURCES

THE first volume of this study[1] concluded that foreign concessions and technical transfers were the most significant factor in Soviet economic development between 1917 and 1930. Concessions were abandoned in the early 1930s and replaced by technical-assistance agreements with Western companies. Later, as Soviet technical cadres became more skilled, the technical-assistance agreements were in turn partly, but never completely, replaced by purchases of complete Western plants built by Western companies, imports of Western equipment, and domestic duplication of this equipment. The technical-assistance agreement and the sale (or gift, under Lend-Lease or reparations arrangements) of Western equipment, in short, replaced the concession as the major transfer mechanism for the period 1930 to 1945.

Early Soviet recognition of the value of these transfer processes was well stated in *Za Industrializatsiiu* in a comment on Soviet industrial achievements prior to 1933: 'A combination of American business and science with Bolshevik wisdom has created these giants in three or four years. . . .'[2] Such frank recognition of the Western contribution has now been expunged from official Soviet history, although the existence of advanced technology within capitalist systems can be explained in Marxian terms. N. Bukharin held that a 'modern capitalist economy is *pregnant with a new technical revolution*. But this technical revolution *cannot develop* unless it breaks through its capitalist shell. . . .'[3] Thirty years later both Khrushchev and Kosygin urged their planners and engineers to look westward in the perennial effort to 'overtake capitalism'

---

[1] A. C. Sutton, *Western Technology and Soviet Economic Development, 1917 to 1930* (Stanford: Hoover Institution, 1968).

[2] *Za Industrializatsiiu*, August 14, 1933.

[3] N. Bukharin, *Socialist Reconstruction and Struggle for Technique* (Moscow: Co-operative Publishing Society of Foreign Workers in the U.S.S.R., 1932), p. 10.

and utilize the capitalist 'technical revolution' for the building of socialism. This Bukharinist argument may still be found in present day Marxist writing.[4]

The inability of the Soviet Union to carry out, with its own internal technical resources, the gigantic construction plans envisaged was in the 1930s frankly recognized in the Soviet press. For example, *Pravda*, in discussing the important Solikamsk potash project, admitted that 'the attempt of the Potash Trust to carry on work without foreign technical assistance proved futile. Thus in 1927–28 several large foreign companies were hired for technical assistance in the construction of the first potash mine. . . .'[5]

Of primary interest was the Soviet attempt in the 1920s to develop even more extensive and technically advanced projects without foreign assistance; such attempts were abandoned in 1929–30 and hundreds—perhaps thousands—of foreign companies[6] were called in to supervise construction of the First Five-Year Plan. This phenomenon, substantially supported by evidence concerning construction dates from Soviet sources alone, is in this book called the 'inability hypothesis.'

Most of this first group of foreign engineers entered Russia in 1929 and left in 1932–3 as a result of the valuta crisis. The benefits of the huge industrial capacity developed under their supervision gave considerable hope to the Communist Party. A rude awakening came in 1936–7 when the product of the enormous capacity developed in the early 1930s reached a plateau, to be followed by four to five years of stagnation during the purge era. Between 1936 and 1941 a number of highly important, but unpublicized, agreements were made with American companies in aviation, petroleum engineering, chemical engineering, and similar advanced technological sectors in which the Soviets had been unable to develop usable technology.

The Nazi-Soviet trade agreement of August 1939 gave the Russians another significant technological boost, although this has been overlooked in literature on the subject. The Soviet view of the pact was well expressed by Molotov: 'This agreement is advantageous to us because of its credit conditions (a seven-year credit) and because it enables us to order a considerable additional quantity of such equipment as we need. . . .'[7]

---

[4]   Even today there is partial admission of continued dependency on the West. For a recent example, see *Pravda* of October 23, 1968, on increasing the effectiveness of technology. This article contains a straightforward directive from the Central Committee to use 'foreign licenses or technical documentation' as a basis for achieving higher technical levels, and also instructs Gosplan and other organs not to plan industrial production on the basis of Soviet experience alone.

[5]   *Pravda*, January 16, 1930.

[6]   The Stalingrad Tractor Plant alone called on the resources of 80 American firms and a lesser number of German companies.

[7]   V. Molotov, *Statement at the Session of the Supreme Soviet of the U.S.S.R. on the Ratification of the Soviet-German Non-Aggression Pact* (New York: Bookniga, August 31, 1939).

Similarly, American Lend-Lease after 1942 gave a massive injection of modern technology which carried the Soviet economy well into the 1950s. Although Congressional intent was to limit Lend-Lease to the military prosecution of the war against Germany and Japan, at least one-third of the shipments had reconstruction potential,[8] and shipments continued through 1947, formalized in the 'pipeline agreement' of October 15, 1945.[9]

Complete corroboration for the general argument of this study comes from an excellent source: Josef Stalin. In June 1944, W. Averell Harriman, reporting to the State Department on a discussion between Eric Johnston and Stalin, made the following significant statement:

> Stalin paid tribute to the assistance rendered by the United States to Soviet industry before and during the war. He said that about two-thirds of all the large industrial enterprises in the Soviet Union had been built with United States help or technical assistance.[10]

Stalin did not add (it would have been irrelevant to his purpose) that the remaining third of large industrial enterprises had been built with German, French, British, Swedish, Italian, Danish, Finnish, Czech, and Japanese 'help or technical assistance.'

This heavy assistance has been briefly recognized heretofore in Western economic literature—the brevity due, of course, to a lack of systematized supportive data. Schwartz, for instance, observes that large numbers of foreign engineers went to Russia in the 1920s and 1930s, and that:

> Many of the Soviet Union's major new plants erected in the late 1920's and early 1930's were equipped with foreign-made machinery. . . . It seems correct to say that every or almost every major branch of the Soviet productive system received substantial aid from abroad and had much of its rapidly expanding corps of native engineers and technicians of all kinds trained directly or indirectly by foreigners.[11]

Bergson suggests that, 'in transforming its production methods under the five-year plans, the U.S.S.R. has been able to borrow technology from abroad on an extraordinary scale.'[12] Later Bergson provides the astute comment that

> . . . there is little necessary correlation between the quantity of imports and the quantity of technology imported; a prototype machine, a blue-

---

8 U.S. State Dept., *Report on War Aid Furnished by the United States to the U.S.S.R.* (Washington, D.C.: Office of Foreign Liquidation, 1945), pp. 19–28.

9 See Schedules 1 and 2 of the Agreement between the Governments of the U.S. and the U.S.S.R. on the Disposition of Lend-Lease Supplies in Inventory or Procurement in the United States, October 15, 1945 (Washington, D.C., 1945).

10 U.S. State Dept. Decimal File, 033.1161 Johnston, Eric/6–3044: Telegram June 30, 1944. (For references to Decimal File, see Appendix D.)

11 Harry Schwartz, *Russia's Soviet Economy* (New York: Prentice-Hall, 1950), p. 132.

12 Abram Bergson, *Economic Trends in the Soviet Union* (Cambridge: Harvard University Press, 1963), p. 34.

print, a technical book, or a technician can (but may not) suffice to transfer the 'knowhow'.[13]

Finally, however, Gershenkron in 1962 pointed out the unusual research gap: 'A serious study of the economic aspects of Soviet technology is still searching for its author or authors. . . .'[14]

Thus, although it has been quite correctly assumed by Western economists that the Soviets have borrowed technology from the West on a large scale, the assumption has not been empirically demonstrated. This study is designed to close the empirical gap. The conclusions suggest that Western scholars have been duly cautious and conservative concerning the impact of Western technology on Soviet development (as indeed they should be in the absence of complete data) and have underestimated the importance of the technological transfers, although their educated guesses have been in the right direction.

On the other hand, this technological impact does not appear to have been investigated by the U.S. State Department, although such an investigation would clearly come within the province of the Intelligence and Research Office of that Department.

Apart from Werner Keller's book *Ost minus West = Zero* (Droemersche Verlagsanstalt: Munich, 1960) which does not meet the methodological standards of the economist, the only previous research specifically related to the empirical aspects of Soviet technical transfers consists of several articles by D. Dalrymple of the U.S. Department of Agriculture.[15] The State Department Decimal File was found to be a superlative source of material in the form of reports from attachés and diplomatic offices, but the Department has not used this data for its own assessments; indeed, public statements by the Department are completely at variance both with previous academic assumptions and with the empirical findings of this study, itself based heavily upon the Decimal File.

For example, Edwin M. Martin, Assistant Secretary of State for Economic Affairs, made the following statement in 1961:

> I don't think there is convincing evidence that the net advantage to the Soviet Union of the continuation of trade is a major factor—or a particul-

---

[13]   *Ibid.*, p. 311.

[14]   Alexander Gershenkron, *Economic Backwardness in Historical Perspective* (Cambridge: Harvard University Press, 1962), p. 265.

[15]   Dana G. Dalrymple, 'American Technology and Soviet Agricultural Development, 1924–1933,' *Agricultural History*, XL, No. 3 (July 1966), pp. 187–206; 'American Tractors and Early Soviet Agriculture,' *The Smithsonian Journal of History*, II (1967), pp. 53–62; 'Joseph A. Rosen and Early Russian Studies of American Agriculture,' *Agricultural History*, XXXVIII, No. 3 (July 1964), pp. 157–60; and 'The Stalingrad Tractor Plant in Early Soviet Planning,' *Soviet Studies*, XVIII, No. 2 (October 1966), 164–8.

arly significant factor in the rate of their overall economic development in the long term.[16]

A State Department publication briefly reviewing 40 years of Soviet economic development between 1920 and 1960 concluded that the U.S.S.R. has a 'self-developed technology.'[17]

This viewpoint was reflected by Secretary of State Dean Rusk in 1961 before the House Select Committee on Export Control: ' . . . it would seem clear that the Soviet Union derives only the most marginal help in its economic development from the amount of U.S. goods it receives. . . .'[18]

There is then a problem of credibility similar to one suggested in the first volume.[19] It was suggested previously that the concession as a development vehicle underwent a significant change in historical interpretation. Recognized as an important development mechanism in the 1920s, it was heavily downgraded by economic historians and almost completely forgotten in the years after 1930. The events covered by this study have also been ignored or given contrary analysis by the State Department. A prime requirement, therefore, is to establish acceptability for the data and credibility for the conclusions. This is particularly necessary because, as noted, academic assessments, although accurate, have not been based on precise empirical findings but on more or less unsystematic reports and general statements.[20] Further, the writer has used State Department files to establish a thesis apparently refuted by the State Department itself. Under such circumstances a high degree of precision and extensive and accurate detail are obviously necessary. For these reasons, fully documented detail, including names of individual foreign engineers and operating characteristics of specific items of equipment, is included within this volume.

---

[16] Edwin M. Martin, Assistant Secretary of State for Economic Affairs, before the House Select Committee on Export Control, December 8, 1961. This statement is surprising in the light of specific data found in the State Dept. files. For example, there is a European Affairs Division memorandum concerning an Ingersoll-Rand order for 100 gas-engine-driven compressors for Soviet oil fields, to cost $1.5 million. It is clearly estimated in the memorandum that this would increase production by 100,000 barrels per day. (See U.S. State Dept. Decimal File, 861.6363/364, December 12, 1939.) A glance at the footnote references in this volume will verify that the Decimal File alone, excluding the specialized Departmental collections, is replete with detailed information, contrary to Secretary Martin's statement.

[17] U.S. State Dept., *Background Notes—U.S.S.R.* (Washington, D.C.: Office of Media Services, Bureau of Public Affairs, 1965).

[18] U.S. House of Representatives, *Hearings before Select Committee on Export Control*, 87th Congress, 1st Session, October 25, 26, and 30, and December 5, 6, 7, and 8, 1961.

[19] Sutton, *Western Technology . . ., 1917 to 1930*, pp. 9–11.

[20] One of the most quoted sources (see Schwartz, *op. cit.*, p. 132) is Hans Heymann, *We Can Do Business with Russia* (Chicago: Ziff Davis, 1945). As the title suggests, this book is not a critical survey of technical transfers.

It is almost certain that this book heavily understates the volume of technical transfers. The State Department files, although excellent, are not complete. The Douglas Aircraft Company granted the writer access to its records (see chapter 14) and these yielded data on important technical assistance in far more detail than has been found in the State Department files. Some companies, such as Caterpillar Tractor and General Electric, which were involved in many important transfers, have not retained their records. In brief, there are at least two gaps in information: they occur when companies made agreements (as they legally could if they did not infringe the Espionage Act of 1917) without informing the State Department and when files have been destroyed. In addition, this study does not include widespread unofficial —or illegal—Soviet acquisitions: no doubt the object of Federal Bureau of Investigation and Congressional study.

METHODOLOGY AND DATA SOURCES

Details were obtained from several sources to determine both the technology used in Soviet manufacture and plant construction and its place of origin in the period 1930–45. For example, the Soviet standard blast furnace of 930 cubic meters has been identified as a Freyn Company, Inc., design. The turbines at the Baku Power Plant were built and installed by Metropolitan-Vickers, Ltd., of the United Kingdom. The merchant rolling mills at Kuznetsk were made and installed by Demag A-G of Germany. The coke ovens at the same plant and at Kertch were built and installed by Disticoque S.A. of France. The Karakliss cyanamide plant was built by Superfosfat A/B of Sweden. These and thousands of similar facts are precisely recorded and verifiable; the sources are always stated. Consequently those who wish to challenge the arguments have the initial burden of disproving recorded statements of fact.

These statements of verifiable fact are then aggregated. When individual plant construction of this period is analyzed, it is found that almost all major units, with only a few isolated exceptions, utilized a technology originating in the West; before 1933 most were built by[21] Western companies or at least had foreign equipment installed by Western engineers. No significant new plant built before 1933 without some major Western technical and construction effort has been identified. Indeed, as Josef Stalin himself stated, two-thirds of all large enterprises built before 1944 were built with U.S. assistance.

By far the most important source of data is section 861.5 of the U.S. State Department Decimal File, from 1928 to 1946. Some of the most useful information concerning technology, engineering, and construction was, however,

---

[21]   See p. 13 for definition of 'built by.'

filed by the State Department Index Bureau under '861.5017—Living Conditions,' with few meaningful Document File cross-references, although 'living conditions' have no obvious connection with engineers' reports. This source was unearthed by a systematic search of all documents listed in section 861.5 purport lists which the Department was willing to declassify.[22] A few documents (no more than about 1 percent) have not been declassified. The purport list description of those still classified suggests they may support the case. The point to be made is that the reader should not be dissuaded by the *title* of the document reference (i.e., 'Living Conditions').

Unfortunately, a few reports (perhaps 5 percent or so) submitted by American companies to the State Department and supposedly at one time in the Decimal File are now listed as missing and are no longer to be found. These reports would contribute detail rather than substance to the argument; information on almost all technical-assistance agreements has been traced somewhere in the files. Blueprints and equipment specification lists are, however, invariably missing; this is particularly unfortunate, as blueprints are a means of tracing technological diffusion *within* the Soviet Union.

This official primary source is supplemented by three serial publications of Soviet trade delegations resident abroad: *Economic Review of the Soviet Union*, published by Amtorg in New York: *La Vie Economique des Soviets*, published by La Représentation Commerciale de l'U.R.S.S. en France in Paris; and *Sowjetwirtschaft und Aussenhandel*, published by the Soviet trade delegation in Berlin.

The German Foreign Ministry, Oberkommando der Wehrmacht, and Oberkommando des Heeres files provide data for the period between 1936 and 1945, as does the Nazi Party Hauptarchiv, at the Hoover Institution. This latter source contains lists of German equipment for which negotiations were made under the Nazi-Soviet pact of 1939.

Relatively little data (compared to that for 1917–30) originated in Soviet internal sources. The Trotsky and Smolensk archives are almost bare of industrial engineering papers. Gosplan (State Planning Commission) publications on the various plans are useful only as a check on anticipation; even the 'not to be distributed' *Gosudarstvennyi plan razvitiya narodnogo khozyaistva*

---

[22] The State Dept. had two main sources of interview information: returning American businessmen and American engineers. Several hundred reports of both types were read closely by the author to determine distortions and inaccuracies. In the final analysis much greater weight has been given to the engineers' reports. Engineers had the advantage of being in day-to-day communication with Soviet construction sites, had less reason to make thinly disguised pleas to the State Dept., and were by training more objective observers. Rarely did businessmen contribute anything of substance to State Dept. knowledge. However, the engineers consistently provided hard information; for an example, see the Ufa refinery flow diagram on p. 83. The original in the State Dept. files was obviously drawn during the interview with the State Dept. officer. The version in the text was redrawn by the writer.

SSSR na 1941 god (the 1941 annual economic plan) was rarely useful. Soviet newspapers concentrate on operating problems which came about as foreign engineers handed over facilities to Soviet personnel. Although technical-assistance agreements were briefly announced in the Soviet press in 1929–31, few details are given, except in the case of the 1929 Ford Motor Company agreement. However, a number of Soviet technical books are surprisingly open about foreign technology,[23] and some contemporary Soviet technical journals are helpful.[24]

The Fish Committee Hearings on Communist propaganda in the United States, held in New York in 1930,[25] provide an unexpected fund of information. Amtorg, under criticism for its espionage activities and anxious to show that it had some legitimate trade functions, submitted documentation concerning the activity of Russian nationals in the United States. This information was analyzed and yields an excellent picture of Soviet technical assistance from the U.S. in 1929–30.

IDENTIFICATION OF FOREIGN TECHNOLOGY

A consistent policy of positive identification of foreign technology is retained throughout this volume. In other words a unit, process, or technology must be clearly identified from acceptable sources as being of Western origin before it is so named. In cases in which this cannot be done, the assumption is that the technology is Soviet. For example, the Pengu-Gurevitch process used in construction of a small lubricating oil unit at Baku in 1931–2 has not yet been positively identified as Western, although, given the nonexistence of Soviet developments in petroleum refining, it is unlikely that the process was purely Soviet; it was probably 'copied.' However, in the absence of evidence to the contrary, it is noted as a Soviet development. A unit is thus always assumed to be Soviet-designed and Soviet-constructed in the absence of positive information to the contrary. *In brief, identification is always biased toward Soviet design and Soviet construction.* Identification sometimes becomes a complex matter. One cannot say, for example, that the Ufa refinery complex built between 1936 and 1941 was completely Western *or* completely Soviet

---

[23]   See, for example, L. Aisenshtadt, *Ocherki po istorii stankostroeniya, SSSR* (Moscow: 1957).

[24]   For example, *Za Standardizatsiiu, Za Industrializatsiiu,* and *Stal'*. The most useful (and the rarest) are newspapers produced by individual factories: *Industrial Spark,* produced (in English) by the Stalingrad Tractor Plant and *Informatsionnyi Biulleten,* produced by the Magnitogorsk Iron and Steel Combinat.

[25]   U.S. Congress, Special Committee to Investigate Communist Activities in the United States, *Investigation of Communist Propaganda,* 71st Congress, 2nd session, Part 3, Vol. 3 (Washington, D.C.: 1930).

in origin.[26] Four units were built by Soviet organizations using Western processes, and ten units were built by Western companies: Alco Products, Lummus, and Universal Oil Products. Thus, Ufa can be claimed by both Soviet organizations and Western companies.

Derivation of the origin of equipment is not altogether a simple matter. In practice there is only one way to ensure that a process or piece of equipment is of Western origin: one must trace its physical transport from Western manufacturer to Soviet plant. It is possible, given sufficient time and data, to do this when the equipment is large or unique: for example, the General Electric generators for the Dniepr Dam or a Davy Brothers flywheel for the Kuznetsk rolling mill. It is a slow and complex but highly accurate method. In a few cases, Soviet sources report the origin of equipment; for example, the excavation work for the Magnitogorsk Iron and Steel Plant was handled completely by identifiable foreign draglines and excavators—Bucyrus, Marion, Oren-Koppel, etc.—and production statistics were reported on an individual machine basis.[27]

On the other hand it cannot be assumed that use of a Western name by the Soviets is necessarily an indicator of immediate Western origin for a specific item. There are cases in which a Western technological process was used, with or without assistance or permission, and given the Western name in cyrillic characters. Thus Sulzer, MAN, and Deutz diesel systems are listed by cyrillic equivalents of these names in Soviet literature in addition to Soviet model numbers.[28] By about 1930 small and medium diesel engines were being manufactured in the U.S.S.R. and still listed by Western diesel system names.

When equipment was unique or had a world-wide reputation, it was often duplicated in the U.S.S.R. and known simply by its Western name in cyrillics. Thus we find 'stoneya mashina' for Stone's machine in foundries, 'rokvell' for Rockwell hardness testing, 'kruksa trubka' for the Crookes X-ray tube, 'shtauffera maslenka' for the Stauffer lubricator, and 'blyming' for blooming mill; and the ubiquitous Stillson wrench is known as 'stil'sona klych.'

In still another category, completely Western technology was used, but with no indication of its Western origin in the Soviet name. For example, the Ford Model A automobile was 'Gaz AA' from the start of production, and the Hispano-Suiza aircraft engine was designated 'M 100'. In neither case was the Western name ever utilized. Thus use of a particular name, either Russian or Western, is not a clear indicator of origin; there must be supporting evidence for accurate identification.

[26] See pp. 83–4.
[27] Magnitostroi, *Informatsionnyi Biulleten*, Magnitogorsk, No. 1 (January 1931).
[28] *Izvestia Vsesoyuznogo Teplotekhnicheskogo Instituta*, No. 5 (1930), pp. 84–5.

A QUANTITATIVE FRAMEWORK FOR
TECHNICAL ASSISTANCE DISCUSSION

This section provides summary statistics concerning the number of foreign concessions, technical-assistance agreements, and individual engineers and consultants in the U.S.S.R. from 1930 to 1945, as a framework for subsequent discussion.

Concessions were the main vehicle for technical transfers from 1920 to 1930. A fairly large number were in operation at the end of the decade. The official Soviet figures are as follows:[29]

Table 1–1   FOREIGN CONCESSIONS IN U.S.S.R., 1927–9

Date	Concessions in Operation	
	All Types	Pure Concessions
October 1, 1927	110	73
October 1, 1928	146	68
October 1, 1929	162	59

Source: A. Gurevitch (Chief, Bureau of Information and Statistics, Glavkontsesskom), in *Moskauer Rundschau*, No. 5 (February 2, 1930).

The decline of the concession is described in chapter 2. By 1935–6 only the Standard Oil, Danish telegraph and Japanese Sakhalin fishing, coal and oil concessions remained; the latter were liquidated in 1944.[30]

Technical-assistance agreements replaced the concession. Firm figures have been published by the Soviets for a few years only, but such agreements were actually in force throughout the period under discussion.[31]

Table 1–2   TECHNICAL-ASSISTANCE AGREEMENTS IN
U.S.S.R., 1928–30

Date	Number of Agreements
1928–9	25
October 1929	70
March 1930	104

Source: La Vie Economique des Soviets, No. 116 (May 20, 1930), p. 20.

[29]   See also Sutton, *Western Technology . . ., 1917 to 1930*, p. 9. When that volume went to press, these figures were not available; they supplement the data in table 1–1 of that volume.

[30]   See p. 28 fn. 47.

[31]   Indeed, they continue down to the present day; the Soviet Government has not since 1930–1 publicized its great dependence on foreign countries. Today, in late 1968, there are about 100 technical-assistance agreements in force between Western firms and the Soviet Union. (See *Business Week*, October 5, 1968, p. 124.) There are also periodic instructions from the Communist Party for more effective application of foreign science and technology. For a Soviet description see A. Kolomenskii, *Kak my ispol'zeum zagranichnuiu tekhniku* (Moscow: 1930).

Of the 104 technical-assistance agreements in force in 1930, approximately 81 were with German and American companies and were distributed among the following Soviet industries:

Table 1–3 TECHNICAL-ASSISTANCE AGREEMENTS IN U.S.S.R.,
1930 DISTRIBUTION

Industry	*Number of Agreements*
Metallurgical	37
Chemical	25
Electrical	13
Minerals and fuel	12
Textiles	5
Clay and glass	3
Miscellaneous	9

Source: La Vie Economique des Soviets, No. 116 (May 20, 1930), p. 20.

This study identifies about 200 technical-assistance agreements between the Soviet Union and foreign companies in force between 1929 and 1945. These are listed in Appendix C; the list is almost certainly incomplete.

In considering aggregate numbers of individual foreign workers hired on a contract basis, two points should be borne in mind: first, that plant construction during the period from 1930 to 1945 took place mainly in the years 1930–2, so that most of the balance of the period to 1945 was taken up with absorbing this enormous capacity, expanding existing plants, and building smaller subsidiary units; and second, that foreign individuals travelling to the Soviet Union were usually highly skilled workers—the only groups of unskilled workers were American Communist Party members and Finnish Americans in the lumber areas. Engineering consultants and experts comprised the great majority.

How many were there? A Soviet source reported in 1936 that some 6,800 foreign specialists of all types worked in heavy industry in 1932.[32] Another Soviet source reports that 1,700 American engineers worked in heavy industry.[33]

These figures can be broken down further. In 1932 there were 200 Germans at Magnitogorsk.[34] About 400 to 500 Finnish Americans were reported working on the First Five-Year Plan.[35] More than 730 American engineers and specialists worked inside the U.S.S.R. at one time or another on the Stalingrad Tractor Plant.[36] There were about 20 U.S. engineers and 20 Germans at

[32]　American-Russian Chamber of Commerce, *Handbook of the Soviet Union* (New York: John Day, 1936), p. 347.

[33]　Amtorg, *Economic Review of the Soviet Union*, VII, No. 10 (May 15, 1932), p. 225.

[34]　U.S. State Dept. Decimal File, 861.5017—Living Conditions/569.

[35]　*Ibid.*, 861.50—FIVE YEAR PLAN/200.

[36]　See p. 185. Some sources say 300 to 400; it depends on what one means: the total employed at any one time, the total at all times, or the peak employment figure.

Kramatorsk in 1931–2 and half a dozen Americans and more Germans in 1936–40 under a different contract.[37] The Metropolitan-Vickers Company of the United Kingdom had, prior to 1933, 350 erectors in the U.S.S.R.[38]

Numbers by themselves can, of course, be misleading. A single engineer with the right qualifications, used in the right place at the right time, even briefly, can have a fundamental influence on a plant or even an industry. Thus we find a Soviet source reporting, in reference to a small group: 'In a term of two or three months the American engineers investigated in detail all of the southern and Ural steel plants. . . .'[39]

We can, therefore, focus profitably upon individual engineers. L. A. Swajian, construction engineer for the Ford Motor Company River Rouge plant, was in turn Chief Engineer for construction of the Stalingrad Tractor Plant (1929 to July 1930) and the Kharkov Tractor Plant (after July 1931).[40]

John Calder's work epitomized American engineering practice in the U.S.S.R. At one time connected with construction of the River Rouge plant as well as the Packard plant in the U.S., he was from 1929 to 1933 the chief Soviet trouble-shooter, sent by Soviet authorities to any project in trouble or behind schedule. Calder held numerous official positions—Chief Construction Engineer at Stalingrad Tractor Plant (before Swajian), a similar position at Chelyabinsk, Technical Supervisor of 90 steel plants under the Stal' Trust, Technical Director at Magnitogorsk, Chief Consultant at the Lake Balkash copper project, and so on. Called by Maurice Hindus 'Russia's miracle man,'[41] he received the Order of Lenin (the highest Soviet order) and is generally known as the hero of the Soviet play *Tempo*, by Nikolai Pogodin.[42]

In 1940 we find individual American engineers in such high regard that the Soviets appealed through diplomatic channels to ensure continuation of their work in the Soviet Union. For example, the Soviets expressed to the American Embassy in December 1939 an 'urgent desire' to keep a Mr. Rasmussen (who was bringing into operation at Grozny a new aviation gasoline-cracking plant built by the Max B. Miller Company) on the job until work was completed.[43]

Those foreign engineers who worked for the Soviet Union between 1930 and 1945, whether under the First Five-Year Plan, during the 1936–9 period,

---

[37]   U.S. State Dept. Decimal File, 861.5017—Living Conditions/568.
[38]   See p. 170.
[39]   A. Zaviniagin, 'U.S.S.R. Favors American Engineers and Equipment,' *Freyn Design*, No. 11 (March 1934), 19.
[40]   Amtorg, *op. cit.*, VI, No. 18 (September 15, 1931), p. 412.
[41]   Maurice Hindus, 'Pinch Hitter for the Soviets,' *American Magazine*, CXIII, No. 4 (April 1932), pp. 31–3, 134–6.
[42]   Eugene Lyons, ed., *Six Soviet Plays* (Boston: Houghton Mifflin, 1934), pp.157–224.
[43]   U.S. State Dept. Decimal File, 700.00116 M.E./24, Telegram, December 29, 1939.

under the Nazi-Soviet pact, or under Lend-Lease, were usually top-flight consultants, without whom the projects would have remained on paper only. The Soviets were adept at selecting, in almost every field from irrigation to metallurgy, first-rank foreign construction companies and the finest individual talent. This should not obscure the fact that the Soviets did hire a few grossly unqualified engineers—even outright frauds: e.g., garage mechanics posing as mechanical engineers. These occasionally survived their contracts by practising local politics in lieu of engineering.

DEFINITION OF THE PHRASE
'BUILT BY WESTERN COMPANIES'

In order to gage accurately the contribution of Western firms to the Soviet Union under technical-assistance contracts and similar mechanisms, a clear interpretation of the phrase, 'built by Western companies,' used extensively in the text, is necessary.

A few technical-assistance agreements called only for the transfer of a process technology and the provision of such drawings, specifications, and literature as were necessitated by the transfer. These were, however, uncommon in the period under discussion. Sometimes, as in the Douglas Aircraft agreement,[44] the Soviets started with this limited kind of contract and then expanded it to include the supply of construction materials, subassemblies, specialized tooling, engine-test results, and operator training. As used in this study, the term 'technical assistance' has the widest interpretation. It normally includes not only the supply of technology, patents, specifications, and laboratory results for an agreed period, but also the supervision of construction and equipment installation, including initial operation of at least the first plant. In other words there was at least one (and sometimes several) 'turn key' plant installation in almost every contract. On this account, many equipment sales contracts are viewed as technical-assistance agreements. When a foreign firm sells a complete plant, prints training and maintenance manuals in Russian, trains the operators, and provides backup service, this certainly constitutes technical assistance.

Thus engineers, specifications, and drawings would be sent from the United States, and the foreign engineers would organize and direct, through interpreters, the Soviet engineers and workers. For example, Stuck, at Magnitogorsk, stationed 27 American engineers at strategic points around the blast-furnace site to direct operations. The Soviets supplied raw labor, interpreters, and Soviet engineers, whose function was primarily to learn; these systems

---

[44] See p. 232.

were always advanced, and not only beyond the experience of tsarist engineers tolerated as holdovers or as 'prisoner engineers,' but also certainly far outside the experience of hastily trained but politically reliable Soviet engineers. Almost to the last man, American engineers in their reports and interviews made the comment that the contribution of the Soviet engineers was detrimental rather than useful. Theirs was a hastily acquired theoretical textbook training, and modern construction practice does not follow theoretical textbook lines.

Initial operation (start-up procedures) was almost always included in technical-assistance contracts. The training of operators and the provision of operation and maintenance manuals in Russian were commonly included. However, there are not a few cases reported in which the Communist Party intervened when a plant was superficially ready and brought the plant into operation with Soviet engineers and operators for propaganda purposes before the schedule established by the Western company. This resulted, of course, in serious damage to the plant; for example, the furnace linings at Magnitogorsk were burned out and the rolling mill bearings at Zaporozhe were damaged in this way. The Communist director usually placed the blame on his Russian technical assistants,[45] although the latter had no part in the decision and foreign engineers bitterly protested such practices. The French Chief Engineer for Disticoque S.A. coke-oven construction projects, for example, finally lost his temper, burned the construction drawings, and returned with his engineers to France. By 1935–6 foreign companies were including in their contracts a clause requiring control of start-up procedures and inspection of all equipment to be installed (even when parts originated in the Soviet Union) before taking responsibility for a project.

Thus 'built by' includes provision of technology and equipment, plus responsibility for satisfactory operation in a 'turn key' installation during an agreed initial period. Provision of labor (including middle-grade engineering talent), raw materials, and, increasingly, semi-fabricated materials (i.e., structural steel) was a Soviet responsibility.

THREE POINTS OF CLARIFICATION

Once again it must be emphasized that the argument is not that technology is the only factor in economic development, although the study is limited to this aspect and the writer himself considers it the most important factor.

---

[45]   See S. Frankfurt, *Men and Steel* (Moscow: Co-operative Publishing Society for Foreign Workers in the U.S.S.R., 1935).

Other elements play their role: one of particular significance in the Soviet Union has been forced labor.[46]

Further, the distinction must be made between the Soviet system and the Russian people. It is easy to confuse an examination of this type with adverse reflections on Russian abilities. Such confusion would be grossly unfair. The Russian people have as much technical and scientific ability as any other people; indeed in certain areas of science and mathematics they appear to excel.

In short, the Soviets have been extraordinarily successful in presenting a façade of indigenous 'socialist' technological progress which they compare to continuing 'capitalist crises.' The statistical presentations of 'expanding socialism' and 'declining capitalism' emanating from Soviet and Western Marxist sources have been ingenious in their use of statistics, graphs, and reasons why capitalism, allegedly in decline for 50 years, still needs to be overtaken. Technical extravaganzas, such as Sputnik and Lunik, involving heavy investment in a narrow sector, are periodic stimuli intended to remind us that Soviet science and technique are, of course, far ahead of that of decadent capitalism.

Those readers who have not forgotten the fallacy of composition might, however, ponder on the alleged quip from one Muscovite to another: 'Why, if things are so good, are they always so bad?'

---

[46] See S. Swianiewicz, *Forced Labour and Economic Development* (London: Oxford University Press, 1965) and D. J. Dallin and B. I. Nicolaevsky, *Forced Labor in Soviet Russia* (London: Hollis and Carter, 1947). The State Dept. files contain considerable data on forced labor, including numbers and locations of the specific camps.

CHAPTER TWO

Soviet Liquidation of the Foreign Concessions

LIQUIDATION of the more than 350 foreign concessions which operated in the Soviet Union during the 20 years after the Bolshevik Revolution is a neglected topic of some importance. No comprehensive examination of the circumstances and methods of liquidation has been made, and this chapter, for reasons of space, can only outline some of the major factors.

By the end of the 1920s the Soviets were convinced they had found a more effective vehicle than the pure concession or the mixed company for the transfer of Western skills and technology. After 1928 the technical-assistance agreement (called the Type III concession in Volume I) and individual work contracts with foreign companies, engineers, skilled workers, and consultants replaced the pure and mixed concessions. These assistance agreements were more acceptable to the Soviets because under them the Western operator had not even a theoretical ownership claim and the Soviets could control more effectively both the transfer of technology and operations inside the U.S.S.R.

However, even while concessions were in the process of liquidation, proposals for new concessions were being solicited and some were even granted. For example, in 1930 the emphasis in Soviet trade journals was on public-utility concessions to develop power plants and water, gas, sewage, and city-transport supply systems.[1] Housing construction concessions were also offered from 1928 onwards to relieve the severe housing shortage.[2] After 1930, however, few concessions were granted—the last known, in March 1930, was to Leo Werke for production of dental products.[3]

---

[1] Amtorg, *op. cit.*, V, No. 3–4 (February 15, 1930), p. 62; also V, No. 11 (June 1, 1930), p. 233.
[2] *Ibid.*, V, No. 5 (March 1, 1930), p. 83.
[3] *Ibid.*, V, No. 6 (March 15, 1930), p. 114.

The formal end of the concessions policy came in a resolution of the All-Union Soviet of People's Commissars on December 27, 1930, repealing all former concession legislation and reducing Glavkontsesskom (chief Concessions Committee) to merely informational and advisory functions. Technical-assistance agreements, however, were specifically omitted from repeal.[4]

Liquidation of pure and mixed concessions had started as early as 1923 and continued throughout the 1920s, but the final stage began only with this resolution in 1930. At the end of the decade only 59 concessions, 6 joint-stock companies, and 27 'permissions to operate' remained in effect.[5] By 1933 no manufacturing concessions remained and the few trading concessions were closed down by the mid-1930s. Only the Danish telegraph concessions, the Japanese fishing, coal and oil concessions, and the Standard Oil lease remained after 1935.

The liquidation of foreign concessions followed the Communist plan. The political theory of such a system demands ejection of capitalist elements at some point, although Leninist tactics may promote temporary compromises such as concessions or joint ventures with capitalists for immediate goals or to solve pressing problems. The concessions were, as Lenin dictated, the means of obtaining 'the basics.' When their Western operators had been cozened into transferring as much capital, equipment, and skill into the Soviet Union as their credulity would allow, the concessions were expropriated. In 1930 Yugoff[6] concluded that the whole concessionary policy and practice of the Soviet Government had been guided by such a principle: to make war upon capitalism.

Let us examine the expropriation of foreign concessions by the Soviet Government in more detail. It was the economic and not the political factor in a concession which usually determined its duration. The only recorded attempt to use the concession as a purely political weapon occurred after the assassination of the Soviet diplomat Vorovsky in Switzerland in June 1923. As a result of the acquittal of the alleged murderers, the Soviets announced that no further concessions would be granted to Swiss citizens and that all offers would be rejected. As there were no Swiss concessions, and few Swiss commercial dealings of any kind, the announcement was merely a gesture.[7]

In all cases a period of duration was agreed upon and written into the concession agreement. In the case of a trading concession, the contract was

---

[4] A translation of the resolution is in U.S. State Dept. Decimal File, 861.602/237, Riga Consulate Report No. 8019, September 4, 1931.

[5] *Za Industrializatsiiu*, February 4 and 16, 1930.

[6] A. Yugoff, *Economic Trends in Soviet Russia* (New York: Smith, 1930), p. 223.

[7] Veridicus (pseud.), *Suisse and Soviets: Histoire d'un Conflict* (Paris: Delpeuch, 1926), pp. 103–4.

for one year and renewable; in the case of a manufacturing concession, the contract was for a much longer term, as would indeed be necessary to induce a foreign entrepreneur to invest his capital. For example, it was agreed that the Swedish General Electric (A.S.E.A.) concession, started in 1927, was to run to 1962. The Bryner and Company concession was to run for 36 years, or until 1960. The Japanese Hokushinkai oil concession on Sakhalin and most of the British Lena Goldfields concession were to run until 1975.

In no case, however, was a manufacturing or mining concession allowed to operate its full agreed-upon length, with the possible exception of the Japanese fishing concessions on Sakhalin and the telegraph concessions, which had clauses allowing revocation by either party on six months' notice. Two other concessions—with the Anglo-Russian Grumant and the Netherlands Spitsbergen Company, both operating coal mines on Spitsbergen—are reported to have been purchased from their operators in 1932,[8] but such purchases were rare.

By early 1930 the Soviet intention to close out the remaining concessions was clear, and Western government officials were remarkably united in their interpretation as to the reasons for, and the circumstances surrounding, closure. The Polish Foreign Office noted that only six Polish concessions remained in February 1930, and that, although they had been quite successful in the past, now 'with the exception of the Serkowski, most Polish concessions in the U.S.S.R. are faring very poorly, for two reasons; namely, the difficulty which the Soviets place in the way of shipment abroad by the concessionaires of their profits and the question of labor. . . .'[9]

By 1931 the German Government, which had previously encouraged concessions, was now urging its nationals that German concessions be closed out and no further capital invested, the principal difficulty being the transfer of cash balances to Germany. At this point the Stock Company, a large Leningrad concession, had already closed down and the Resch concession in the Ukraine, the Tiefenbacher button concession in Moscow, the German Building Construction Company, and the Krupp concern had applied for permission to close. The German Foreign Office pointed out that 'the difficulties of these firms in the past have been the subject of almost continuous diplomatic correspondence.'[10]

The American legation in Warsaw suggested in January 1930 that the Soviets were no longer interested in pure concessions and that the Soviets

---

[8] *Izvestia*, No. 294, October 23, 1932.
[9] U.S. State Dept. Decimal File 861.602/211, Warsaw Legation Report, February 8, 1930.
[10] U.S. State Dept. Decimal File, Report 936, Berlin Embassy, May 26, 1931.

'have even gone as far as sabotage in order to discourage the operators.'[11] Further, it was added that this interpretation was 'universal' among foreign diplomats in Moscow.

While officially the Soviets stated that disagreement with the British concession Lena Goldfields was over violation of the contract, the real reasons, according to well-informed circles in Moscow

> lay in the fact that the time had now come when the enterprise was about to yield profits for the concessionaires and that difficulties had arisen in connection with the transfer of these profits to foreign countries.

Similar problems beset the Estonian concessionaires. As long as concessions were being developed

> and as long as Estonian funds were being invested in these enterprises all was well. When, however, the moment arrived when the Estonian merchants began to secure returns from these investments, such difficulties were placed in their way by the Soviet authorities that the projects had to be abandoned. In this way great losses were incurred by the Estonians who had attempted to carry on business in the Soviet Union.[12]

Thus as each concession became profitable, it also became a target for expropriation.

METHODS OF EXPROPRIATION: PHYSICAL FORCE

Physical force was used in very few instances. Indeed, force was not necessary; the Soviet had ample economic weapons—unions, credit policy, customs, currency-export restrictions—which could be utilized without resorting to crude physical ejection of concessionaires.

However, physical force was used in at least one instance at an early date, before many—indeed most—concession agreements had even been made. What is curious is that the U.S. State Department had affidavits and detailed reports on file in 1924 relating to the forcible expropriation of the Caucasian-American Trading and Mining Company in 1923, but did not subsequently warn other venturing American businessmen.[13]

---

[11]   U.S. State Dept. Decimal File 861.602/210, Warsaw Legation Report, January 13, 1930. The legation also reported a Rykov speech at a session of the Central Executive Committee in which he was reported as saying that foreign firms should invest capital, not capitalists—meaning profit-earners.

[12]   U.S. State Dept. Decimal File, 861.5017—Living Conditions/163.

[13]   See National Archives Microcopy T 640 (Claims against the Soviet Union by the United States), Roll 2 (end) and Roll 3 (start) for extensive material including maps and photographs, and particularly the following document addressed to the Dept. of State: *In the matter of the Application for the Support of a Claim—Caucasian-American Trading & Mining Co., a Delaware Corporation—against—Soviet Government of Georgia (Russia)*, February 9, 1924.

The Caucasian-American Company, registered in Delaware with the objective of developing the use of American agricultural equipment in Russia, signed a concession agreement with the Soviet Government on April 20, 1921. This was agreed to run until 1970. Agricultural equipment, including 70 Moline plows, was imported, and two American engineers were sent with it.[14] The company claimed that it was the first to introduce tractors into Russia, that it spent half a billion rubles, erected buildings, reclaimed marshes, trained workers, and introduced advanced methods in Georgian agriculture.

Two years later the company was physically ejected from its property. The description of the ejection contained in a memorandum to the U.S. State Department is worth quoting extensively. After stating that on February 26, 1923 a group of 'Bolsheviks,' including the top Party officials from Tiflis, came to the company property at Nakalakevie, the memorandum continues:

> . . . they were heavily armed, ordered [the company] to stop the work, arrested the apprentices, assaulted them, intimidated the American engineer, called a meeting at which it was resolved to take over the estate and to offer to the company land somewhere else. After the meeting they organized looting and destruction (pogrom) of the Company's property, much against the wishes of the terrorized population. The estate was looted, buildings, orchards and other property destroyed in the most barbarous manner, beautiful trees cut down, live-stock stolen, employees and books seized, goods supposed to have been given as promised, taken away. . . . Orachelashvili, who is now President of the Republic of Georgia seized the offices of the Company in Tiflis, including furniture. . . . Finally, the President of the Company, D. P. Abashidze was sentenced to death, to save his life he had to escape from the Caucasus and from Russia through Siberia which he did partly on foot. All this had been done in order to secure the documents in his possession, and which are proving that the Company fulfilled all terms of the agreement. . . . All this was done at the very time when after six years of Revolution, the Soviet Government advertised, that it was not as bad as described, and was inviting the outside world to have business dealings with it.[15]

METHODS OF EXPROPRIATION: BREACH OF CONTRACT

Few contracts have been found in which the Soviets fulfilled all the conditions agreed upon; the only exceptions were the short-term one-year renewable trading contracts and those covered by the 'arm's-length' hypothesis.[16] There

---

[14]   *Agreement, Moline Plow Company and Caucasian-American Trading & Mining Company*, dated 6 February, 1922, National Archives Microcopy T 640-3.

[15]   *Ibid.* The documents mentioned in the quotation are now in the National Archives files; these include translations, bills of lading of goods moved into the U.S.S.R. by the company, and signed agreements with the Soviet Government. See Microcopy T 640-2/3.

[16]   See Sutton, *Western Technology . . ., 1917 to 1930*, chap. 17.

are numerous complaints recorded by concessionaires that the Soviets interpreted concession agreements only to suit their own purposes, and abided by neither the letter nor the spirit of the agreements.

One case involving breach of contract and economic pressure is recorded by the German courts: that of I.V.A. (International Warenaustausch Aktiengesellschaft).[17] I.V.A. was a concession devoted to assembling and packing eggs and exporting them to Germany. In late 1929 the Soviets arbitrarily denied I.V.A. the right to continue to export eggs and began to build up a Soviet egg-export organization. This dispute was submitted by I.V.A. to a Moscow court of arbitration, as allowed in its concession agreement. The Soviets then removed the only German member of the three-man court and replaced him with a third Russian member. The court found against I.V.A.

The Soviet Union then brought suit in the German courts to enforce its own decision against I.V.A. The German court decided in favor of I.V.A. 'on the grounds that the elimination of the German member of the Court of Arbitration had taken place illegally and without due course.'[18] The decision was upheld in the Kammergericht in Berlin, sitting as a court of appeals. A damage suit by the Soviets against I.V.A. in the Landgericht in Berlin was also decided in favor of I.V.A. However, the Soviets appealed these decisions within the German courts and the company, 'despairing of a definite settlement within a reasonable time,' went into bankruptcy.[19]

METHODS OF EXPROPRIATION: TAXATION

When concessions were profitable, domestic taxes were used to force expropriation. A prominent example is the Richard Kablitz Company, a Latvian concession which operated six plants in the U.S.S.R. from 1921 to 1930. Kablitz manufactured stokers, economizers, and boilers, and was the only manufacturer of this equipment in the Soviet Union. Although working conditions were not good, the company undertook a very large quantity of work, installing, for example, boilers in more than 400 Soviet factories. Until 1926 Kablitz made significant revenue and, although taxes limited profits, some earnings were exported.

In June 1926 Kablitz was forbidden to send currency abroad—a breach of the concession agreement. After negotiation, Kablitz was granted permission to export 40,000 rubles per year, but the necessary export certificates were not

---

[17] U.S. State Dept. Decimal File, 861.602/204, Report 373, Berlin Embassy, July 14, 1930. The file includes copies of the German court summaries.

[18] The German court held this was a 'positive violation of contract' (U.S. State Dept. Decimal File, 861.602/216, April 1930).

[19] Data from *Sevodnia* (Riga) No. 39, February 8, 1931. Copy in U.S. State Dept. Decimal File, 861.602/233, February 16, 1931, and Report No. 7506 (Riga).

forthcoming in either 1928 or 1929. An explicit demand by the company to export 40,000 rubles in 1929 was countered with a Soviet demand for a 'normative tax' of 300,000 gold rubles.[20] This tax forced the company into liquidation.

While admitting loss of its six factories and all invested capital, Kablitz requested compensation only for exploitation of its patents. This is in itself a revealing episode. One year previous to the imposition of the 'normative tax,' the OGPU had ordered Ramzin, a first-rate Russian engineer,[21] to work out designs to replace those of Kablitz. This was done, but the Ramzin-Kotloturbin designs developed were found to be useless and, in spite of protests of the now-expropriated firm, the Soviets continued to use the Kablitz patents without compensation.

Other concessions suggest that taxation was a common weapon used either alone or with other means to force out the foreign operator. The Czenstochova celluloid factory in Leningrad was burdened with a poorly prepared contract which the Soviets consistently interpreted to allow only a minimum of profits. The coup de grâce was applied in early 1930 when tax difficulties forced the firm to close down.[22] The Vint concession was forced out by continual increases in taxation from 1923 to 1928.[23]

The Soviet monopoly of foreign exchange meant that denial of permission to export proceeds could be coupled with taxation as a weapon. Tiefenbacher Knopfkonzession, employing 1,100 persons, is one example in which both methods were used.[24]

METHODS OF EXPROPRIATION: HARASSMENT

Harrassment, less open than physical ejection, was used as a weapon for expropriation. Drusag, the German agricultural concession owned 90 percent by the German Government, is an example in which Soviet harassment was countered by unsuccessful peace offerings by the German Government.

In 1929 and 1930 a series of labor incidents involved the German management of Drusag. These were climaxed in the trial of Director Ditlow on minor charges involving labor regulations. Ditlow was accused of allowing shepherds to work more than eight hours per day and of not supplying work clothes

---

[20]   The U.S. Riga Consulate did not know of the 'normative tax.' Kablitz provided a jocular explanation: 'The telephone number of the respective concessionary is multiplied by the age of his wife. If the amount thus calculated looks insufficient, one or two ciphers are added to it.'

[21]   Later tried on charges of industrial sabotage.

[22]   U.S. State Dept. Decimal File, 861.602/221, May 6, 1930.

[23]   Sutton, *Western Technology . . ., 1917 to 1930*, pp. 101–2.

[24]   U.S. State Dept. Decimal File, 861.602/216, April 1930.

(which were in any event unobtainable). The 'evident object in view was to undermine the discipline at the concession.'[25] The Soviet authorities then seized and auctioned off the Drusag automobiles and typewriters. A levy of 3 percent was placed on the salaries of all German workers. Messages to the outside world were confiscated.[26]

A search of the U.S. State Department Decimal File produced numerous statements concerning such harassment. For example, the Tetuikhe Mining Corporation concession (after Lena, the largest such concession), was liquidated December 26, 1931, as the following attests:

> ... in 1930 the Soviet Government having forced the Lena Goldfields concessionaires out of the U.S.S.R. began a campaign against the Tetuikhe Corporation, and published reports alleging that it had been in conflict with its workmen. Eventually, at the end of last December, the corporation suspended operations. . . .[27]

The Novik concession, for manufacture of felt products near Moscow, was liquidated in November 1929, 'due to the impossibility of the concessionaires to work in face of the opposition put in its [*sic*] way by the Soviets on labor questions.'[28]

In the case of the Standard Oil lease of a Batum refinery, we find the local press stirring up trouble. For example, *Zaria Vostoka* ran an article critical of the American management of the plant and took exception to the way 'the Americans talk to the Russian workers.'[29] Despite the criticism, Standard Oil was still operating its Batum refinery in 1935.

HISTORY OF THE LENA GOLDFIELDS, LTD., CONCESSION

The experience of Lena Goldfields, Ltd., largest of the concessions, is well worth exploring as a case history. The company was required to make specific investments in properties transferred to its care and to produce stipulated quantities of various minerals and metallurgical products.

An investment of not less than 22 million rubles was required. The Moscow *Izvestia*[30] reported early in 1929 that total investments by the company had reached 18,129,000 rubles, of which 15 million for mining equipment had

---

[25] U.S. State Dept. Decimal File, 861.602/212, Report No. 25, Berlin Embassy, February 20, 1930. The director of the Zellugol concession was fined 10,000 rubles and the director of the Leo Werke concession was fined 5,000 rubles on similar charges.

[26] *Ibid.*

[27] U.S. State Dept. Decimal File, 861.602/244, Report No. 89, Riga Consulate, February 26, 1932.

[28] U.S. State Dept. Decimal File, 861.602/211, Warsaw Legation Report, February 8, 1930.

[29] *Zaria Vostoka* (Tiflis), 'The Smoke of the Fatherland,' No. 268 (September 29, 1931), p. 3.

[30] No. 69, March 26, 1926.

been provided by a banking consortium including the Deutsche Bank of Germany and Blair & Company of New York.

The agreement further required a minimum annual production of 420 poods of gold, 1,000 poods of silver, one million poods of copper, 600,000 poods of zinc, and 180,000 poods of lead. According to *Ekonomicheskaya Zhizn*,[31] the 1926–7 output of gold was 499 poods, an amount which exceeded the required minimum by 79 poods. No reports of failure to meet stipulated production totals have been traced. The company paid royalties of two million rubles in 1926–7.

Although the Soviets breached the agreement from the start by not turning over to Lena Goldfields all properties included under Articles 1 and 2 and, more importantly, by not allowing the free sale of gold on the London gold market, signs of trouble did not appear until early 1928. In April of that year *Ekonomicheskaya Zhizn* printed an article, 'There Must Be an End to It,'[32] objecting to the Lena Goldfields policy of allowing mineral exploration to be undertaken by private prospectors (starateli), although this was allowed under the agreement and indeed was the system used by the Soviets themselves in the Alden fields. Some 18 months later the Soviet Government complained that 1928–9 royalties amounting to one million rubles had not been paid. Lena was unable to pay, as the fixed price paid by the Soviets for Lena's gold was approximately one-fourth the world price. Free export of Lena's gold, although permitted under the concession contract, was in practice prohibited. This forced default was followed on October 22, 1929 by an article criticizing trade unions for 'leniency' toward the company: 'The concessions stand as a sort of appendix, apart from the rest of our life. This part of class warfare has been neglected and all kinds of weeds grow there. . . .'[33]

This Soviet pressure coincided with completion of Lena's technical reconstruction and plant-expansion program. Herbert Guedella, Chairman of the company, reported in late 1928 that three years of intense reorganization and investment were producing results.[34] The large Bucyrus dredge was installed at Lenskoie in 1928. The new plant at Seversky was completed in September 1929. The Revda Iron and Steel Plant additions and renovations were completed in early 1929. A considerable amount of work had been done in opening up the Degtiarsky copper mines and 12,000 tons of copper per year were scheduled to be produced in 1930. The Altai district mines were completely re-equipped by the end of 1929. All this was facilitated by credits provided by Western bankers on the Lena Goldfields account.

[31]   No. 283, December 11, 1927.
[32]   No. 93, April 21, 1928.
[33]   *Izvestia*, October 22, 1929.
[34]   *Times* (London), November 20, 1928.

The actual ejection of Lena Goldfields personnel, as distinct from preliminary propaganda skirmishes, was a multi-pronged effort involving the OGPU, the Central Committee of the Party, the trade unions, and Glavkontsesskom. The latter requested payment of royalties within four months. Simultaneously, the OGPU raided and searched all units of Lena's widespread operations; these raids were not publicized in the Soviet press. Alexei Rykov, a prominent Bolshevik leader, then made a speech to the Central Committee suggesting that concessionaires were welcome if they operated on imported capital, did not expect unlimited profits, and did not indulge in counter-revolutionary activity. The Soviets sabotaged some Lena operations, and company personnel were ejected from other properties.[35] *Ekonomicheskaya Zhizn* then accused the company of delaying wage payment to workers for up to six days.[36]

These acts were followed by a propaganda campaign in both the domestic and foreign press concerning alleged nonpayment of royalties, nonfulfillment of the construction program, and demands for compensation to the Soviet Union for 'uneconomic work.' These accusations were then 'proven' by finding four Lena employees guilty of espionage.

An arbitration court, with Dr. Otto Stutzer as chairman, met at the Royal Courts of Justice, London, in the summer of 1930. Their decision was published on September 2, 1930.[37] The court found the main factors in the failure of the Lena Goldfields concession to be a series of unilateral actions taken by the Soviet Government.

It was determined that Lena had fulfilled its agreement by producing 1,844 poods of gold in four and a half years and by making the specific investments stipulated under the concession agreement.

A number of Soviet acts, explained below, were identified by the arbitration court as breaches of the contract. Article 20 gave Lena the absolute right to sell freely on foreign markets all gold produced. If the gold was sold to the Soviet Union, Article 20 stipulated that the prevailing London market price be paid. The Soviets breached Article 20 by instituting the penalty of death for selling gold abroad, by purchasing Lena's gold only for rubles and at an exchange rate fixed, not in relation to the London gold price, but arbitrarily at about one-quarter of the London price. Thus Article 20 was found by the court to be a 'nullity.'

The Soviet Government, it was found, had not provided police protection as required in Articles 35 and 80. Thefts of gold, estimated at between 30

[35]　U.S. State Dept. Decimal File, 861.63—LENA GOLDFIELDS LTD./18, January 13, 1930, Warsaw Report.

[36]　No. 20, January 25, 1930.

[37]　*Times* (London), September 3, 1930.

and 40 percent of total output, were encouraged at least partly by this refusal of protection.

The Soviets did not transfer to the concession all properties specified in Article 2: particularly certain gold mines, iron-ore mines and the Altai fire-clay deposits. This forced Lena to import fire clay at great cost from Germany. The company had also been physically ejected from the marble-limestone field granted to it under Article 1. Limestone was essential as a smelter flux, and Lena was then forced to buy inferior limestone at great cost.

The civil rights of Lena employees had been removed and simultaneous OGPU raids had been made at nearly all the company's numerous establishments, spread over 2,400 miles. The OGPU had seized and searched 131 company personnel; 12 were arrested and 4 placed on trial and sentenced to prison terms for espionage.

The Soviets did not put in an appearance at the arbitration court, which awarded damages of £12,965,000 sterling (about $65 million) to the Lena Goldfields, Ltd.[38]

The question of compensation was immediately taken up by the British Government, and it is clear that only continued assistance from official sources, five years of negotiation, and the possibility of closing off trade between Britain and the U.S.S.R. brought any compensation at all to Lena.

An agreement was reached in November 1934 under which the Soviet Union agreed to compensate Lena Goldfields to the amount of £3 million ($12 million at 1934 rates of exchange) over 20 years. These payments, in the form of non-interest-bearing notes, were to comprise £50,000 on ratification by Lena shareholders, and 20 installments of £92,500 each, followed by another 20 installments of £55,000 each, paid at 6 monthly intervals beginning in May 1935.[39] This settlement was ratified by the Soviet of People's Commissars in March 1935.[40]

A routine inquiry by the Commodity Credit Corporation to the State Department in early 1937 reopened the Department's file and brought forth information about the notes given by the Soviet Government for Lena

[38]   *New York Times*, September 3, 1931, p. 12, col. 3.
[39]   Details from 861.63—LENA GOLDFIELDS LTD./36, quoting House of Commons, *Parliamentary Debates*, November 12, 1934, col. 1502. Lt. Col. J. Colville (Secretary, Overseas Trade Department): 'the company recognizes that the prospects of any settlement at all without the assistance they received from His Majesty's Government would have been slight.' This settlement was not received enthusiastically in the Commons. For example, Sir William Davison asked, 'Do I understand that this British company has been obliged, on the recommendation of the British Government, to settle for a sum of £3,000,000 which is to be paid over 20 years, in lieu of an arbitral award of £13,000,000?'
[40]   *Za Industrializatsiiu*, March 22, 1935.

Goldfields and the Tetuikhe mining properties. These notes had been distributed to shareholders and privately traded in London. The Commodity Credit Corporation was offered a quantity of Lena Goldfields notes by Cookson Produce & Chemical Company, Ltd., of London in exchange for 15 million pounds of American tobacco.[41] The Departments of Commerce and State, in determining whether to accept such notes, concluded that payments had been made promptly by the Soviet Government and that there was no open market in the notes, although there had been a number of private sales at varying discount rates, one authority quoting 9 percent.[42]

From this source we also learn that the Soviets paid £940,000 in similar non-interest-bearing notes for the Tetuikhe claims. One-third of these fell due before 1938 and two-thirds before 1949. This agreement was concluded in 1932.[43]

The end result was that in the few cases in which the Soviet Union did pay compensation, it was below arbitrated value and did not bear interest, and thus gave the Soviet Union an advantage equivalent to long-term no-interest loans.

SOVIET EXPLANATIONS FOR LIQUIDATION

The reasons for liquidation given in the Soviet press can be summarized under three headings.[44] First, it was argued that concessions were losing their 'monopoly' or 'semi-monopoly' position and consequently the possibility of making 'enormous profits.' This explanation is consistent with Leninist teaching that private capital can only exist in monopoly circumstances. Second, the concessions were said to be unable to compete with 'more advanced' Soviet enterprises coming into production. Third, it was said that capital investment by foreign concessionaires was absolutely inadequate, and that in any event working capital was coming from State banks and not from capital imports; this was coupled with statements that British and American banks had refused credits.

These statements are only partially true and are not by any means full explanations. They ignore the acts of harassment, breaches of contract and trade-union pressure. The 'loss of monopoly' argument was hardly relevant

[41] U.S. State Dept. Decimal File 861.63—LENA GOLDFIELDS LTD./40.

[42] U.S. State Dept. Decimal File 861.63—LENA GOLDFIELDS LTD./41. However, the reader should not infer that all sales took place at this discount. The Soviets inserted some unusual redemption clauses and there were several methods of working out the discounts, giving quite different end results.

[43] See Sutton, *Western Technology . . . , 1917 to 1930*, p. 286, concerning Tetuikhe and the 'arm's-length hypothesis.' Tetuikhe obviously received more favorable treatment than Lena Goldfields.

[44] See, for example, *Izvestia*, March 2, 1930.

in a goods-short economy such as the Soviet Union. The concessionaires were always more efficient than the new Soviet enterprises and sold their products with little difficulty. It is true that foreign banks were reluctant to advance credits for internal operations, yet Drusag, for example, was amply financed by the German Government for many years and was, nevertheless, expropriated.

A standard propaganda ritual was practiced before expropriation of each concession. This ritual consisted of increasingly stronger criticism of errors or supposed errors committed by the concessionaire. Nothing appears to have been too remote or insignificant to escape attention. For example, the Control Company concession gave its employees small sums of money as Christmas gifts. *Izvestia* reported that these gifts were indignantly refused by the workers because 'tips have been abolished' and that Christmas was 'a new weapon for deceiving the workers.'[45] The point, of course, was brought up to prepare the way for expropriation.

Sometimes the ritual became a trifle forced, particularly when the operator had substantially fulfilled his agreement. For example, the Japanese coal concession, Kita Karafuto Kugio Kabusiki Kaisha, signed in 1925 for operation of three coal fields on Sakhalin, was criticized on insignificant grounds. The company built a 300-kilowatt electric-power station, a 361-meter cableway and a 1,500-ton conveyor system, but, it was said, brought in only 'obsolete new machines' with nothing for Soviet engineers to learn. This became the basis for criticism.[46] The company was expropriated in 1944.

In the case of a Japanese oil concession, the Soviets accused the concession of wasting oil because it allegedly utilized 16.5 percent of its output in operating the concession. The future of the concession, warned *Za Industrializatsiiu*, would depend on the ability of the Japanese concessionaires to 'supply sufficient capital.'[47]

Statements by the Hammer concession (the Moscow Industrial Concession) on its own liquidation reflect the official Soviet argument, but the Hammers were in an 'arm's length' relationship with the Soviet Union.[48] The official reasons for liquidation were that inadequate capital had been imported by the Hammers and that further credit had been denied by British and American banks. Thus expansion into new lines was curbed by inadequate capitalization.

[45] January 15, 1930.

[46] *Za Industrializatsiiu*, May 16, 1930.

[47] February 23, 1930. The Japanese coal and oil concessions on Sakhalin, the last surviving concessions, were liquidated in 1944. Harriman reports that Vyshinsky replied to a question concerning compensation for their expropriation: '. . . the Soviet Government would pay a small sum for a large property.' U.S. State Dept. Decimal File 861.b.6363/191: Telegram.

[48] Julius Hammer was a founding member of the U.S. Communist Party.

The concession was in debt to Gosbank, and there was competition from new State enterprises. As a result Hammer was reported as willing to sell, and the factory was put into the Moscow Chemical Trust.[49] Unlike those of other concessions, the Hammer debts, internal and external, were paid by the Soviet Government, and the Hammers were allowed to export their profits. Shortly after leaving the U.S.S.R., they opened the Hammer Galleries in New York and became the sales outlet for confiscated tsarist art treasures.

This favorable treatment, however, was unusual; most concessions were expropriated without meaningful compensation. However, the propaganda ritual was used to preserve a façade of legality over expropriation of the concession. Censorship of the operating results of concessions, coupled with the propaganda ritual, ensured that the historical record would be favorable to the Soviets. This objective has been almost completely achieved.

An excellent review of concession operations and liquidations before 1926 was made by W. Kokovzoff,[50] who concluded that others would suffer the fate of liquidation. He foresaw correctly, for example, the demise of the Harriman concession and that Harriman would one day be faced with 'insurmountable difficulties.'[51] Kokovzoff also noted that in 1926, of the 110 concessions granted, 22 had been liquidated, of which only 13 had not assumed their contractual obligations.[52] This means that 97 concessionaires had already made their investments as required in the contract. Kokovzoff pointed out that the most innocent report by any concession director to his home office was considered an act of 'economic espionage' and cited the case of Professor Clair, a Swiss citizen condemned to 10 years in prison for such activity; on this basis Kokovzoff correctly forecast the circumstances surrounding the expropriation of Lena Goldfields.

The Soviets themselves warned explicitly of the ultimate fate of the concession. Kokovzoff quotes several examples. One from *Le Messager de Paris* reports a speech by Bukharin:

> On the one hand, we admit capitalist elements, we condescend to collaborate with them; on the other hand our objective is to eliminate them completely ['radicalement'] to conquer them, to squash them economically as well as socially. It is a type of collaboration which presumes a furious battle, in which blood may necessarily be spilled.[53]

That this message was not seen and correctly interpreted by Western businessmen is almost incredible. About 250 agreements had yet to be

---

[49] *Izvestia*, March 2, 1930.
[50] 'Les Soviets et les concessions aux étrangers,' *Revue des Deux Mondes*, XXXV (1926), p. 158.
[51] *Ibid.*, p. 168.
[52] *Ibid.*, p. 162.
[53] *Ibid.*, p. 161. *Le Messager de Paris* was an official Soviet publication in Paris.

concluded; yet no warning was given by Western governments to their businessmen.

THE LESSONS OF THE FOREIGN CONCESSION

The concession was a Leninist tactical maneuver consistent with the announced plan to acquire the fruits of Western economic and technical strength. The policy began as the foreign counterpart of the New Economic Policy and continued long after the domestic Russian entrepreneur had been expropriated for the second time in 1924. As Lenin pointed out to the Russian Communist Party on November 27, 1920, 'Concessions—these do not mean peace with capitalism, but war upon a new plane.'[54]

Thus the ultimate fate of the concession was never in doubt. When his skills and his last dollar, pound, mark, or franc had been squeezed from the foreign concessionaire, the door would be slammed shut and his assets inside the Soviet Union expropriated.

In the final stage of this policy, the Russians employed an exquisite combination of tactics. The argument used in 1928–31 to encourage even more Western investment and designed to maximize economic benefits to the Soviet Union was also utilized as the main reason for expropriation. The Soviet theme in 1928–31 was 'either supply more capital or we will expropriate.' This threat worked well, for example, with Drusag, in which the German Government itself made further investments from 1926 to 1931, until it owned 98 percent of the concession. When the foreign businessman discovered such investment was endless, he withdrew and suffered his losses in silence. It is noteworthy that expropriation was given a façade of legality, usually preceded by a propaganda ritual designed specifically for foreign consumption.[55] A policy of rigid censorship concerning concession operation, particularly after the 1927 law which made the publication of concession news a crime of espionage, prevented widespread Western knowledge of the fate of the concession. This policy was aided by the silence of Western businessmen anxious to hide their failures and by the grant of compensation in several key cases in which the concessionaires had considerable political influence in the West.

The Polish, Estonian, Latvian, Lithuanian, Czechoslovakian, and Hungarian concessionaires came off worst, in the final analysis. After helping the Soviets develop Russia, they were ejected not only from their concessions but, in another 15 years, from their own homelands as well.

---

[54]   V. I. Lenin, 'Report on Concessions to the Bolshevik Fraction of the Eighth Congress of Soviets,' December 21, 1920, in *Dokumenty vneshnei politiki SSSR*, III (Moscow: Gospolitizdat, 1957).

[55]   It should be noted that ultimate expropriation was predicted by the United Kingdom and the United States foreign offices when the concession policy was first announced. See Sutton, *Western Technology . . ., 1917 to 1930*, pp. 295–6.

In brief, the lesson for the West is that any joint economic enterprise with a Communist nation is inexorably destined for seizure when the advantages to the Communist nation have ceased or when no further financial or technological investment can be extracted from the foreign partner.

Regrettably, a further lesson for Western businessmen is that his own government, for reasons of policy, may not always be in a position to provide prompt and accurate information on Soviet intentions. The U.S. State Department and the British Government had policies of 'noninterposition' and the German Government a policy of concession encouragement even when it was evident from material on file that concessions were a temporary tactic, and indeed had been predicted as such by all Western foreign offices.[56]

---

[56] Some British Members of Parliament went so far as to encourage investment in concessions for reasons of ideological sympathy with the Soviet Union rather than concern for the interests of British businessmen; see Anglo-Russian Parliamentary Committee, *Possibilities of British-Russian Trade* (London: 1926). Moreover, although most Western businessmen have been able to learn from their experiences, the same cannot be said for Western politicians. For example, the J. G. White Corporation of New York had unpaid claims against the Soviet Union totalling $387,000 and commented to officers of the State Dept., 'We believe it would be a great mistake for the Government of the United States to recognize the Government of Russia, for if our government did, there would probably be the same history of relations on a larger scale that we have had on a smaller scale.' (U.S. State Department Decimal File, 861.602/252, December 31, 1930.) Four years later President Roosevelt recognized the Soviet Union. The Soviets broke every one of their political commitments within a few months of signature.

CHAPTER THREE

Technical Assistance to Irrigation Construction

THE TURKESTAN IRRIGATION PROJECT OF A. P. DAVIS

THE Russian cotton-manufacturing industry was organized into factories about 1825. By World War I it was the third largest in Europe, with over eight million spindles in 745 factories and employing 388,000 workers. Domestic cotton growing, which supplied about one-half the raw material requirements, was concentrated in the Ferghana district of Turkestan and cultivated by an extensive irrigation system.[1]

After the October Revolution both cotton growing and cotton manufacturing almost ceased. Production of cotton textiles was restarted with German assistance and imported American raw cotton financed by the Chase National Bank.[2] These imports were a major drain on limited foreign exchange, and consequently there was a major drive to restore the old irrigation systems, add further irrigated acreage, and increase domestic cotton production. Irrigation of areas in Turkestan and Transcaucasia offered more promising solutions.

In tsarist times Russia had had 4,222,000 hectares under irrigation. Gosplan anticipated expending more than one billion rubles between 1928 and 1932 to increase this irrigated area by 1.5 million hectares: 50 percent in Central Asia, 20 percent in Kazakstan and Transcaucasia, and the remainder in the North Caucasus area.[3]

In 1913, Arthur P. Davis, construction consultant for the Panama Canal, former Director of the United States Reclamation Service, and one of the best-known of American irrigation engineers, had surveyed the feasibility of irrigating the Kara Kam desert of the Golodnaya Steppe (Hungary Steppe)

---

[1] W. Busse, *Bewasserungs Wirtschaft in Turan* (Jena: 1915).
[2] Sutton, *Western Technology . . ., 1917 to 1930*, p. 297.
[3] Amtorg, *op. cit.*, IX, No. 5 (May 1934), pp. 116–7.

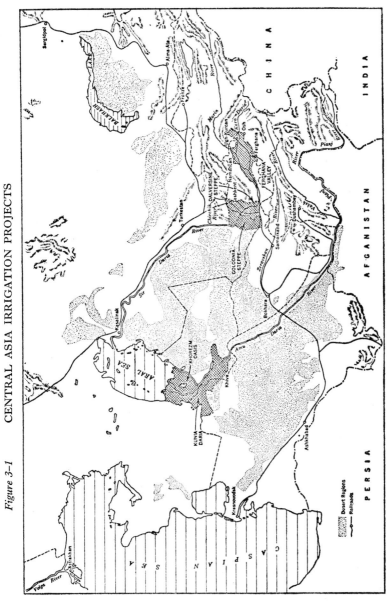

Figure 3–1 CENTRAL ASIA IRRIGATION PROJECTS

Source: Civil Engineering, II, No. 1 (January 1932), p. 2.

in Central Asia. He finally recommended further surveys and preliminary planning work. For 15 years he heard nothing more about the project; then in June 1929 he was invited to Moscow and informed as he reported later, that his recommendations for Golodnaya Steppe had been adopted and that 'it had been ready for construction for several years and was then awaiting my criticism and approval. . . .'[4]

Davis concluded a preliminary technical-assistance contract with the Soviets, re-examined his earlier proposals and all available surveys and plans, inspected the ground, and agreed to remain in the Soviet Union as a consultant, 'giving advice as to necessary changes and further work to be undertaken.'[5] Davis was given complete engineering responsibility for the irrigation program in Central Asia. The organizational structure of Glavkhlopkom (Chief Cotton Commission) and its irrigation construction departments is outlined in figure 3–2, based partly on the original Soviet chart. Amburo (American Bureau) was the all-American engineering consultant organization within Glavkhlopkom and was responsible for new irrigation construction and operations. Davis was chief of Amburo in Tashkent, and a Major Olberg was chief of a similar office in Tiflis.[6] Although the American contingent was by far the most important, other foreign irrigation specialists were used. In 1930, for example, Amtorg reported, 'Twenty-three Japanese and Korean specialists have arrived to assist in the irrigation and sowing work.'[7]

THE AMERICAN BUREAU (AMBURO) IN TASHKENT

This is a sector of the Soviet economy in which the Western technical contribution can be precisely identified. Willard Gorton, a U.S. irrigation consultant employed by the Soviets as Chief Consulting Engineer for the Vaksh irrigation project and C. C. Tinkler of the Seabrook Engineering Corporation (which had road-building contracts in the Turkestan irrigation areas) smuggled their working papers and reports out of the U.S.S.R.[8] These papers throw

---

[4]   A. P. Davis, *The University Hatchet* (Washington, D.C.: May 1932). See also: A. P. Davis, 'Irrigation in Turkestan,' *Civil Engineering*, II, No. 1 (January 1932).

[5]   Davis, 'Irrigation in Turkestan,' *Civil Engineering*, II, No. 1 (January 1932).

[6]   The Amburo office at Glavkhlopkom in Tashkent had two engineers from the United States in addition to Davis. The staff also included one interpreter, two translators, and two Russian-English typists.

[7]   Amtorg, *op. cit.*, VI, No. 12 (June 15, 1931), p. 285.

[8]   Both document collections are in the vaults of the Hoover Institution on War, Revolution and Peace at Stanford University. The Gorton Papers owe their survival in the West to a negligent OGPU border guard. Tinkler's collection is smaller and does not contain original Soviet memoranda, orders, and reports, but is useful, as it covers the same time periods and locations as the Gorton Papers. The success with which the Soviets have thus been able to bury the record of foreign technical-assistance is illustrated by the observation that, if reliance were

considerable light on the actual, rather than the propagandized, processes of Soviet economic development in the 1930s. The difference between the propaganda image, which has unfortunately been reflected in most Western writing on Soviet economic development, and the actual construction process is almost unbelievably great. The work of this single American consultant is therefore described in detail. Willard Gorton's problems and functions were more or less similar to those of other foreign engineers and technicians.

Glavkhlopkom Order No. 220,[9] issued in Tashkent on November 22, 1930, placed Amburo under direct control of Glavkhlopkom Chairman Reingold. Instructions passed from Reingold to the Chief Consulting Engineer of Amburo (A. P. Davis) either directly or through the Liaison Officer (V. V. Tchikoff), also known as the Technical-Administrative Officer, or through the Chief of the Irrigation Department, F. Skorniskoff-Nelson.

A. P. Davis was director of Amburo work, with Liaison Officer Tchikoff in charge during his absence. It was specifically stated in Order No. 220 that the Liaison Officer had no authority over technical activities of the various *consulting* engineers without the prior authorization of Reingold, but all

Figure 3-2 ORGANIZATIONAL STRUCTURE OF GLAVKHLOPKOM
(CHIEF COTTON COMMITTEE), 1930

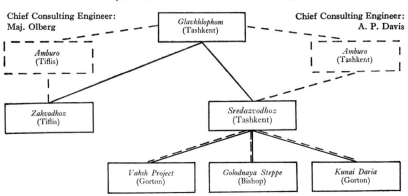

————Soviet nominal control

– – – –American advice and technical responsibility

Source: Gorton and Tinkler Special Collections, Hoover Institution, Stanford University. The Gorton papers include an original Soviet 'Administrativnaya skhema Amburo' (Administrative Chart of Amburo).

---

placed only on Soviet-released information, this chapter would be limited to one sentence: 'The Zakvodhoz (Transcaucasian Water Economy Service) engaged two irrigation engineers.' [S. Bron, *Soviet Economic Development and American Business* (New York: H. Liveright, 1930), p. 145.]

[9] Order No. 220 is in the Gorton Papers.

Russian employees of Amburo were placed under direct charge of the Liaison Officer, who was a naturalized U. S. citizen.

Paragraph five of Order No. 220 begins, 'The American engineers of the Trusts (W. L. Gorton, L. E. Bishop, and others) although directly under orders of the Chairman of the Trust are at the same time members of the American Bureau. . . .' The paragraph then details instructions for the work of these engineers. The Amburo office had to co-ordinate its work, including that of employees of individual consulting engineers. Foreign engineers were required to present a verbal report every 15 days and submit written reports in duplicate not later than the fifth day of each month; these reports were to include the work of interpreters and others working under the consultants. All translations, memoranda, reports, minutes, and official correspondence had to be turned over to Glavkhlopkom in duplicate.

The objective of Order No. 220 was clearly to subordinate the American engineers to detailed central direction and maintain a check on implementation of Glavkhlopkom instructions by means of verbal and written reports. This betrayed Soviet misunderstanding of the abilities of a capable engineering consultant; these engineers had world-wide experience and were accustomed to developing large-scale government projects on a responsible individual basis.[10]

THE WORK OF FOREIGN IRRIGATION ENGINEERS

Gorton's experience is typical for a foreign consulting engineer in the Soviet Union in the 1930s and 1940s. Shortly after arriving he was appointed Chief Consulting Engineer for design and construction of the Vaksh irrigation project, the largest irrigation project implemented between 1930 and 1945.[11] A design and development program for Vaksh was drawn up by an engineering commission comprising engineers Khrustalev, Vassiliev, Yaltenovsky, and Rabinovitch, with Willard Gorton as Chairman. The charge to this commission was to consider: (a) the number of engineering designs to be established and the extent to which each design was to be developed, (b) the type and size of the important structures of the project, (c) the time objectives for the various plans, (d) co-ordination of investigations and preparatory work, and (e) any other technical matters. Any engineering disputes were to be settled by A. P. Davis through the chairman of Sredazvodproiz (Central Asia Water Authority). All Soviet engineers on the irrigation projects were to work under the super-

---

[10] The detailed check may have been due to lack of trust, or the need for bureaucratic 'make-work;' or perhaps the Russians believed that absolute central direction was more efficient in both the economic and the engineering phases than decentralized planning and individual responsibility.

[11] Gorton Papers, Glavkhlopkom Order No. 99, May 9, 1930.

vision of the American consulting engineers, and *Gorton was given full technical and economic responsibility for the Vaksh project.*[12]

It is this charge of responsibility by the Soviet authorities that counters any possible claim that the contribution of American engineers may have been negligible or secondary. This question of engineering responsibility was much in the minds of Reingold, Chairman of Glavkhlopkom, and his Party assistants. The top men in the trust were Communists with no engineering training and only a superficial knowledge of either cotton, irrigation, or construction.[13] They protected themselves from the omnipresent OGPU threat by placing full responsibility on foreign consultants. Gorton's appointment letter from Reingold contains the significant phrase, 'said engineer is entrusted, upon his full responsibility with the direction of designing the Vaksh project and its subsequent construction . . . [underline in original].'[14]

The direction is clear: 'full responsibility' for both design and construction. This is, of course, consistent with Gorton's position as Chairman of the Engineering Commission for the Vaksh project.

Choice of design was a separate and equally important task. The Russian and American engineers each developed designs for these irrigation projects. All designs then underwent evaluation by Amburo. Wilbur, assistant engineer to Davis, made initial evaluations and recommendations. A major part of Davis's work was to choose between competing designs according to Wilbur's evaluations. For example, on the design of the Vaksh head regulator, Wilbur wrote Davis that the Gorton design 'is satisfactory in every respect,' and, after proposing a few changes, concluded that 'the Gorton design is cheaper and better than the type B-7 proposed by Sredazvodproiz.' Thus a private American consulting engineer had the responsibility of deciding which of two designs, one American and one Russian, was to be used.[15]

Gorton's reports to the trust CAXO (Central Asia Cotton Union) give an excellent indication of the nature and extent of his work. A program was turned in covering each six-month period; a copy is available for the period March to December, 1931. During the first two weeks in March he was required to give written conclusions on the Vaksh project. This was followed by a two-week field trip to examine canal-cleaning methods. The next two weeks were spent examining earth work under progress at large projects and

---

12 Gorton Papers, letter from Gorton to Yanchur, November 29, 1930.

13 A. P. Davis, *The University Hatchet*, May 1932.

14 Gorton Papers, Letter No. 4074, Reingold to Davis, May 4, 1931.

15 Gorton Papers, memorandum from Wilbur to Davis, February 13, 1931. There is insufficient data to determine which parts of these irrigation projects, as finally built, were Soviet designed and which were American. It should not be assumed that they were all American-designed, as Russia had a history of irrigation projects originating in the nineteenth century.

indicating specifically, the ways in which imported equipment could be more profitably utilized. From May 15 to June he examined the tsarist-built Palvan and Gazavat canal systems and made proposals for redesign. June was spent on the problem of mechanizing canal cleaning, earth-work removal, and canal construction, and on proposals concerning the simplest type of mechanical equipment for use in Central Asia. After a month's leave, he spent August on the mechanization of large-project construction and made recommendations for the best use of existing equipment, the organization of labor, the choice of standard types of machines, and the production of parts for small irrigation structures. September was spent studying the use of local building materials in irrigation structures. October was utilized in determining the final design and construction schedule for the small Golodnaya Steppe project, and November on compiling conclusions concerning the 1932 construction schedule for the Vaksh project.[16]

For the six-month period covered by the next work program we also have copies of reports submitted by Gorton. On November 12, 1931, Gorton submitted to the manager of the Irrigation Department of CAXO a report entitled 'Conclusions with Reference to the Kunai Daria Project in Turkmenistan.' Three weeks later, on December 2, 1931, he submitted another report to the same department entitled 'Construction of the Lower Khan Main Canal Structures across Angren River.' Written answers to five questions submitted by CAXO were given on December 13, 1931, and a report on the Vaksh project is dated January 3, 1932. The next report was dated January 11, 1932. This was to the chairman of CAXO and entitled 'Methods of Doing Work and the Type of Canals in Ground with Considerable Settlement and Particularly in Ground Which Has Quicksand,' and was submitted with another report concerning the 'Cheapest Rational Method of Lining Farm Ditches in Cobbles and Loess Grounds.'[17]

The basic function, then, of a Western consulting engineer working for a Soviet irrigation construction bureau was to consider and report on problems, plans, and ideas submitted. Gorton's practice was to underscore deficiencies. For example, in his report to the chairman of CAXO concerning the Vaksh construction plan and proposed work for 1932 (January 3, 1932), Gorton points out the importance of transportation to the success of the project. This detailed report, the 'Vaksh Construction Plan, 1932,' emphasizes the key role of transportation and the probability that inadequate transportation would delay the project.

[16]   Gorton Papers, 'Rabot Program.'
[17]   Gorton Papers, Envelope 2.

There were also reports on soil problems: one on the results of soil analyses in the Vaksh River Valley (October 6, 1931); one to the Laboratory of the Water Institute concerning use of copper sulfate to remove algae (September 21, 1931), and others.

RELATIONS BETWEEN AMERICAN IRRIGATION ENGINEERS AND THE SOVIETS

Apart from normal engineering problems, there were two major areas of conflict between American engineers and the Soviet authorities. The Soviets did not, except in a very few favored cases, provide the living accommodations, transportation, or personal assistance specified in their agreements. Further, salary payments were almost always late and in most cases final terminal payment was either not made or made only in part after protracted argument.

The more experienced engineers learned to cope with bureaucratic procedures and shortchanging from Party officials. Gorton, for example, arranged his travel program according to the expense amount actually advanced to him. He decided that prepayment was essential, as travel expenses were 'forgotten' if claimed after actual expenditure. Before one trip to Ferghana Valley he wrote as follows:[18]

> April 8, 1931
> Tashkent

To Mr. Lezinoff
Manager, Irrigation Department

Dear Sir;

I estimate that I need 1000r for my coming trip to the Ferghana Valley. On my last request for advance funds of 1000r only 500 was supplied. Any shortage of funds supplied less than that requested meets with no objection from me but I must advise that when the money supplied is expended it will be necessary for me to return to Tashkent. I must further advise that expenses for meals and foods are at least 50% higher than they were when I was traveling in 1930.

> Very respectfully,
> W. L. Gorton
> Consulting Engineer

[18] *Ibid.* Gorton retained a sheaf of copies of letters, labeled 'bellyaches,' which he had sent to various Soviet authorities. They are worth reading to illustrate the pettiness of Soviet officialdom. For example, they walled up Gorton's apartment so that he could not fuel the stove; this could only be done from the next-door apartment, occupied by a Party functionary concerned with fuel conservation.

Gorton's complaints were numerous. There was no interpreter. He was not paid for two months. His apartment had no heat. On other occasions the house needed repairs, the water was cut off, there was no coal and no electric power, and the well-pump was broken.[19]

In early 1931 Gorton finally exploded in a letter to Reingold:

> In view of all the above, I think the time has come to terminate the contract. For the Vaksh project you have your workers' enthusiasm, your exemplary brigades, and your socialistic competition and a highly trained corps of Soviet engineers all of which you pointed out yesterday. Furthermore, you pointed out to me that you had men capable of filling the position on the Vaksh which you had proposed to me to occupy. Under such conditions it appears to me that my services are unnecessary and that my work is not considered important enough to allow me what I require in order to perform my duties. Moreover, by dispensing with my services you will be able to carry the Vaksh construction to a conclusion with a 100% Soviet force.'[20]

However, it was Reingold, Chairman of the Cotton Commission—and not Gorton—who was finally replaced.

Gorton had trouble getting salary checks on time and was never completely paid for his work in the Soviet Union. Letters to Amtorg in New York from his wife, and letters between Amtorg in New York and Amtorg in Moscow illustrate a continuing problem of irregular salary payment.

At one point Gorton's checks were two months in arrears; no check was ever paid at the time required by the contract. The terminal payment was never made. Gorton received only 23 out of the 24 monthly payments, and received no payment for the $500.00 balance of his travel expenses. The exchange of letters with other engineers in the irrigation projects (Bremer, Fisher, and Major Olberg) indicated they did not receive full payment either. In effect, engineers' services were acquired at a discount, by breach of contract.[21]

This group of road and irrigation engineers, as a result of their excellent interpersonal communications, became hard bargainers where the Soviets were concerned.[22] Although they were shortchanged on their contracts, they certainly did considerably better than engineers in other sectors.

---

[19] *Ibid.*

[20] *Ibid.*

[21] Appendix A is a copy of the Gorton-Sredazvodhoz contract with the method of payment specified. It is often claimed in the West that the Soviets have never failed to live up to a commercial contract. This is demonstrably not so.

[22] A letter from Lyman Bishop to Tinkler (in Moscow) enclosed a check for $50 to cash on his return to the United States and requested him to 'see if I have any money in the bank.' The inference is obvious. April 1, 1930. (Tinkler Papers.)

IRRIGATION PLANNING AND CONSTRUCTION

At the end of two years in irrigation construction, Gorton had made two trips to the Vaksh valley, one trip to the Middle Anu Daria, two trips to the Ferghana valley, and three trips to the Dalverzin valley. He was then requested to report his conclusions. Gorton's report indicates that two things strongly impressed him: the necessity for good roads preliminary to construction and the necessity for proper maintenance and operation of equipment.[23] Neither recommendation was being followed. Further, he said, housing, storage, water, and sanitation facilities should be emplaced *before* construction started:

> It may appear that time will be lost if all such preparations are made in advance, but experience has demonstrated that both time and money as well as human lives are saved in the long run by adequate preparatory work.[24]

Gorton commented on the extreme shortage of capital equipment. He noted, for example, that a simple 18-inch circular saw operated by a 5- to 7-horsepower diesel engine by 'two unskilled but intelligent workmen will saw easily as much lumber in a day as 25 men using hand saws. . . .'[25]

Construction did not follow design; at the four-compartment square opening underdrain near Macoshkent, the walls were being built 8½ centimeters thick, although the design called for 10 centimeters.

> The reinforcing rod was being placed in such a way that the bars were twice as far apart in some places than in others. As a matter of fact the reinforcing was placed in such a manner as to be indescribable on account of the lack of uniformity in spacing. In some places where the reinforcing was supposed to be 5 cm. from the wall it was 1 cm. and in other places it was in the middle of the wall. . . .[26]

There were poor concrete pouring and form work, no machine mixing, no accurate measurement of the concrete mix, and no inspection of finished work. Gorton singled out the Dalverzin main canal where 'Large stretches . . . were of such poor quality as to be a shocking waste of money. . . .'[27] The concrete lining of the canal was 'badly defective' and the canal could not stand a full head of water.

Gorton then pointed out that the Soviet six-month and one-year plans were 'mostly a waste of time' unless certain data were known, and these

[23] Gorton Papers, W. L. Gorton, 'Report on the Assignment: General Conclusions and Recommendations on Questions Concerning Irrigation Construction on the Basis of Your Two Years Work in the American Consulting Bureau' (Tashkent: January 1932).

[24] *Ibid.*

[25] *Ibid.*, p. 6.

[26] *Ibid.*, p. 10.

[27] *Ibid.*, p. 12.

generally were not known. It was not necessary, wrote Gorton, to wait until final design decisions were made before ordering equipment and materials. It was possible to order materials for 10 million cubic meters of earth excavation, for instance, without knowing whether the final excavation total would amount to 18 or 19 million cubic meters.[28]

CONCLUSIONS ON IRRIGATION AND COTTON DEVELOPMENT

Soviet planners correctly recognized the principle of import substitution as an aid to internal economic development, and planned construction of irrigation networks and domestic production of cotton to replace cotton imports from the United States. Prerevolutionary irrigation projects were revived. A. P. Davis, one of the world's foremost irrigation experts, was hired, and a group of top American irrigation engineers percolated into the organizational structure of Glavkhlopkom.

Although most sectors of the early Soviet economy had a shortage of trained Russian engineers, this was not the case in irrigation. However, those Russian engineers who had developed and operated the prerevolutionary irrigation network could not, from the political viewpoint, be trusted. The function of the American engineers was partly as consultant, partly as technical watchdog.

Planning, as well as choice and development of design, was an American responsibility between about 1928 and 1933. Only the shortage of valuta forced the Soviets to dispense with this assistance.

Table 3–1   EXPANSION OF ACREAGE UNDER IRRIGATION,
1928–50

Time Period	Planned Construction	Estimated Actual Construction
Pre-1917, built under tsars	—	4,222,000 hectares
1928–1932	1,500,000 hectares	1,140,000 hectares*
1933–1937	1,012,200 hectares	1,000,000 hectares*
1937–1941	608,000 hectares	None
1945–1949	656,000 hectares	None (all rehabilitation and completion of earlier projects)
Estimated Total, 1950		6,362,000 hectares

Source: Naum Jasny, *The Socialized Agriculture of the U.S.S.R.* (Stanford: Stanford University Press, 1949), pp. 483–4.

* Jasny takes his figures from the official plans and points out that 'part of this had been irrigated previously.' According to Kh. M. Dzhalilov, *Golodnaya step' i perspektivy ee osvoeniya* (Tashkent, 1957), only about 200,000 hectares were under irrigation in Golodnaya Steppe by the late 1950's; this suggests the First Five Year Plan was only about 20 percent fulfilled as late as 1956.

[28]   *Ibid.*, p. 13.

Table 3–1, based on Naum Jasny's data, suggests that the period of American engineering responsibility (1929–33) was also that period in which construction of the greatest irrigation area since tsarist times was initiated.

In the irrigation sector, transfer of Western process technology, as distinct from engineering skills, was not a significant factor. Irrigation is not a complex technology; it relies on applying a set of well-established engineering principles to solution of agricultural problems. The construction problems are those met in canal construction, i.e., soil mechanics and concrete work. Although a number of American gate and regulator designs were introduced, and American terminology came into general use—for example Shiti Staneya (Stoney Gate) and Shiti Teintera (Teintera Gate)—the American technical design contribution was probably not of major significance.

In plans for mechanization of canal construction and manufacture of excavating and operating equipment, however, the American engineers had a central role. The bases for mechanization of canal construction in Central Asia were calculated and reported on by Gorton. This work included a survey of existing equipment manufacturing facilities and recommendations of Western equipment models for introduction and duplication. There is every indication that he put the interests of his Soviet client first: the recommendation to purchase single models of Western equipment for examination and duplication was hardly in the interests of the U.S. manufacturer.

From other reports we learn that irrigation projects faced major difficulties in 1932. The valuta crisis led to cancellation of the contracts with most Western engineers. The Soviets were entitled to do this under the terms of most contracts. Heavy inflation boosted costs. Gorton estimated that on Vaksh, up to 1932, the Soviets had spent more than 30 million rubles to do $300,000 worth of work and comments that 'they are going to have a sad awakening some day. . . .'[29] The project almost collapsed in the summer of 1931 owing to transport difficulties. At the same time there were 26 imported draglines ready for work, but neither operators nor fuel were available.[30]

The general waste and inefficiency were enormous. Gorton estimated he lost 251 working days in two years through inefficient travel arrangements, workers' holidays, and lack of a skilled interpreter.[31]

In irrigation then, we find a sector in which the Western contribution in engineering alone was not as significant as in other sectors, but in which the use of Western technical skills enabled organizational difficulties inherent in the socialist form of 'planned construction' to be partially overcome.

---

[29] Gorton Papers, letter from Gorton to Davis, November 28, 1932.
[30] *Ibid.*
[31] These calculations are on the back of the small envelope in Envelope 2.

CHAPTER FOUR

Technical Assistance to the Non-Ferrous Metals Industry

IN 1930 the engineering and metallurgical position of the Russian non-ferrous metals industry was extremely weak. The entire industry, including gold and rare metals, in all its phases from mining to refining, utilized only 346 Russian engineers and 458 Russian technicians. Moreover, three-quarters of these had less than one year of experience and only seven percent had more than three years of experience.[1] In short, almost all experienced Russian engineers had left Russia; only 20 with more than three years of experience remained. This handful of remaining engineers could by no means undertake the ambitious plans proposed for the industry, nor indeed even keep it operating. The only solution was to import experienced foreign engineers.

The scattered nature of non-ferrous mining and metallurgical activities makes this reconstruction of Soviet technological acquisitions more than usually complex and frustrating. There are, however, two clues which provide a quantitative framework. Soviet sources report that there were approximately 200 American engineers employed in their non-ferrous mining and metallurgical industries in addition to technical-assistance programs with foreign companies and consulting engineers. Further, John Littlepage, an American engineer and Deputy Director of Tsvetmetzoloto (Non-Ferrous Metals Trust), reported that he had four or five American engineers in each mine in the trust.[2] This suggests there were 10 American engineers in the Soviet Union for every Russian engineer of equivalent skill between 1929 and 1933.[3]

---

[1] I. P. Bardin, ed., *Metallurgy of the U.S.S.R. (1917–1957)* (Moscow: 1958), p. 598.

[2] John D. Littlepage, *In Search of Soviet Gold* (London: George G. Harrup and Co., 1939).

[3] Just over 10 percent of these 200 Americans replied to an enquiry by H. H. Fisher of the Hoover Institution in 1934. This was remarkable, as mining and metallurgical engineers, because of the confidential nature of their work, do not usually discuss their clients. Moreover, many anticipated the possibility of further Soviet

Figure 4–1　LOCATION OF URALS COPPER MINES,
SMELTERS, AND REFINERIES

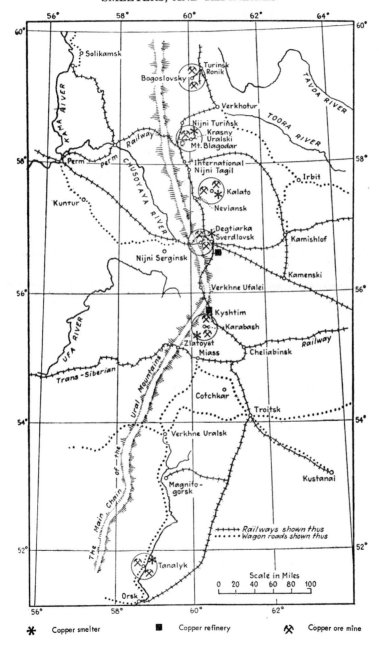

Railways shown thus ++++++
Wagon roads shown thus •••••

Scale in Miles
0 20 40 60 80 100

✳ Copper smelter　　■ Copper refinery　　⚒ Copper ore mine

The influx started in December 1929, when J. L. Thomson, an American mining consultant, arrived in Moscow to conduct an inspection of the Urals copper mines in behalf of Tsvetmetzoloto. Thomson's first survey trip was to Sverdlovsk, with instructions to determine how many foreign engineers and how much equipment was required to re-establish the copper mines in the Urals area. After visiting the Kalata and Karabash districts, he returned to Sverdlovsk and reported:

> What I saw was appalling—the waste, the slackness, the inefficiency, the divided authority, the disregard for human life, the consumptive faces of the workmen, the women performing the most grinding manual labor, the crooked shafts, the frayed cables, the worn out and obsolete equipment. . . .[4]

Extraordinary mining practices were observed by Thomson. For example, accepted mining practice is to sink the main working shaft in country rock, and then tunnel across to the ore veins. In this manner ground settling does not affect shaft alignment and the shaft guides remain true. In the Urals, shafts were being sunk right on the vein so that ore could be taken out on the way down. The ore is mined a little quicker but only at a heavy long-run cost. However, Thomson observed that 'if the technical man doesn't believe in this method, the Communist does and that's where the shaft is sunk. . . .'[5] In the United States dry drilling is banned by law in all states: it leads to silicosis. In the Soviet Union in 1930 no one had heard of wet drilling.[6]

Thomson recommended immediate hiring of 48 American mining engineers, mill-construction men, and plant operators for the Urals copper mines and smelters.

A reconstruction of the management organization between August 1931 and April 1933 is contained in figure 4–2. There was a thorough percolation of American engineers into all levels of the organizational structure. Leading positions in all units of the non-ferrous metals industry were held by Americans,

---

contracts and were unwilling to prejudice the possibility of future employment. This factor was reinforced by the depression uncertainty and a clause in their contracts prohibiting discussion of work in the U.S.S.R. The response came from the middle layers of personnel: i.e., the key operating, design, and consulting personnel. Only rarely did individuals at the top level or the foreman level respond.

[4]   *The Saturday Evening Post*, June 27, 1931.

[5]   *Ibid.* Thomson also noted that at least one-third of the Kalata smelter had been built over mine workings and was in danger of caving in.

[6]   Similar Western newspaper reports in the 1930s gave rise to claims of exaggeration, as well they might. However, even reports of the more absurd practices check out. For example, Warren, an American engineer, was called in to straighten out the Kalata smelter; of 21 pumps in the smelter, 16 had been rigged to pump *downhill*. There is no question that these things happened; too many independent reports cross-check for them to have been completely false. The only logical explanations are sabotage or complete incompetence.

including the position of Assistant Director of Tsvetmetzoloto, held by John Littlepage under Serebrovsky, the Russian Director. At lower levels, positions of director and technical director at combinats and mine managerships were commonly held by American engineers with Russian assistants.

This use of American engineers in everyday working positions was supplemented by several technical-assistance agreements with leading American companies which introduced their own consultants and methods. Between 1929 and 1933, then, the Soviet non-ferrous industry was almost completely run by American engineers. Between 1933 and 1936 these engineers were gradually withdrawn and hastily trained Russian engineers substituted; from 1936 to 1945 very few foreign engineers were employed.

THE KARABASH AND KALATA MINES AND SMELTER

The largest copper smelter in prerevolutionary Russia was the Karabash in the Urals, producing about 8,000 tons of black-fired copper per year. It was closed until 1925 and reopened with American technical assistance.[7]

Karabash was supplied by four mines: the Stalinsky, the American (later called the First of May), the Dzerzhinskya, and the Rikovsky. G. Jermain was the mine manager in 1931[8] under Milo Krejci, who was Technical Director of the Karabash Combinat, which included the Karabash smelter. Krejci had 11 American engineers, of whom three were Party members, working in the mines and smelter. There was considerable friction in the Karabash complex. Russian engineers, almost all non-Party men, resented the presence of Americans, and there is some evidence of sabotage.

In the early 1930s the Karabash smelter was under the supervision of Krejci and at that time produced about 80 percent of planned production, although 'it [was] an old project built before the war, [and] most of the original machinery [was] English, although the plant [had] some new German machinery.'[9] By 1939 the Karabash smelter was equipped with four Nichols-Herreshoff ovens, a Martin oven, and four Pierce-Smith converters.[10]

The Kalata mines were also under U.S. supervision in the early 1930s. The district is 80 kilometers north of Sverdlovsk in the Urals. After being flooded during the Revolution, it was reopened in 1923. The main mine—the Kalata—produced about 300 tons a day of 2.25-percent copper ore, but in 1933 the mine was on fire and only the neighboring Lovochka mine was producing ore.

---

[7] Sutton, *Western Technology . . . 1917 to 1930*, p. 81.
[8] Later Chief Engineer of Tsvetmetzoloto.
[9] U.S. State Dept. Decimal File, 861.5017—Living Conditions/643, Report No. 115, Riga, April 4, 1933.
[10] National Archives Microcopy T 84, Roll 27, Frame 663.

Figure 4-2 ORGANIZATIONAL STRUCTURE OF SOVIET
COPPER MINING, SMELTING, AND REFINING
INDUSTRY (1931) WITH WESTERN TECHNICAL ASSISTANCE

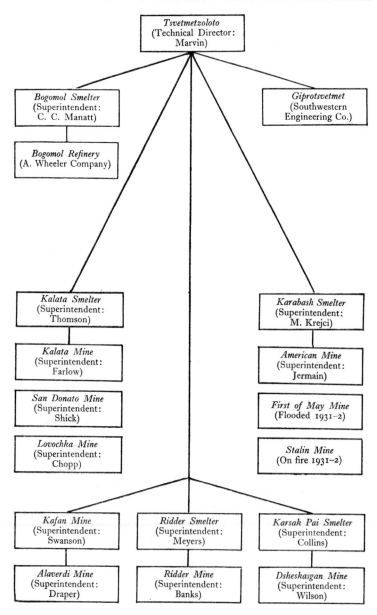

Table 4–1   SOVIET COPPER SMELTERS, 1941

Plant	Location	Capacity 1937 (Tons/ Concentrate)	Production 1936	1942 (Planned)	Western Technical Assistance
Karabash	Chelyabinsk	25,500	20,128	25,000	Expanded tsarist plant with U.S. and German
Kalata (later Kirovgrad)	Sverdlovsk	38,500	22,996	40,000	equipment and U.S.
Karsak Pai	Karaganda	10,000	6,388	10,000	technical assistance
Krasnoural'sk (Ordzhonikidze)	Sverdlovsk	40,000	22,840	40,000	Arthur Wheeler Corp. project
Lake Balkash	Karaganda	50,000	—	—	German technical assistance and John Calder as consultant
Baymak	Bashkir	5,000	4,759	10,000	Southwestern
Alaverdi	Armenia	5,000	4,744	10,000	Engineering Corp.
Kafan	Armenia	3,000	1,501	10,000	projects

Source: Die Kupfererzeugung der UdSSR (Berlin: Der Reichsminister der Luftfahrt und Oberbefehlshaber der Luftwaffe, 1941), pp. 24–5. Geheim Report No. 788, Microcopy T-84, Roll 127, Frame 1427764.

A description of an incident at Kalata offers some insight into the problems involved. The mine manager in the early 1930s was Hawkins, and his final act, as recounted by Thomson, was roughly as follows:

> Something else that the Russians do not believe in is leaving pillars to support the roof. Hawkins did succeed in having a pillar left in place in a certain station, and he posted a placard forbidding that it be shot. Furthermore, he gave pointblank orders to everyone to leave it alone. One morning it was gone. And when the level caved a loud cry went up that the Amerikanski was to blame. Hawkins blew up with a loud bang.
>
> The Trust heads did not want to lost Hawkins, and a meeting of executives was called to find out what he was angry about and soothe his ruffled feelings if possible. He was offered more money, more food, a better house but rejected them all. Two other Yankees and I heard him tell them, in good old Texas language that they were 'absolutely hopeless' and incapable of learning the first principles of good mining. No American miner he declared could be of any help to them or himself.[11]

This, by the way, dramatizes the problem of choosing between sabotage and incompetence as possible explanations. The incident could have been sabotage; it could just as well have been caused by a Russian miner on the night shift trying to make his ore quota the easy way by loading a close-at-hand pillar of ore.

[11] J. L. Thomson, 'Red Metal Mining in Russia,' in *American Engineers in Russia* (manuscript collection in Hoover Institution, Stanford University), p. 18.

Kalata had a prewar smelter supplied by these local mines and 'equipped with English and some German machinery.'[12] The capacity of the smelter was 100 tons per day, with one reverbatory furnace, three Great Falls 10-ton converters, and one Pierce-Smith 40-ton converter. The smelter and mines together employed 22 American engineers and technicians between 1930 and 1933, but later became a completely Russian-operated enterprise.[13] New installations included a Cottrell plant and an American 1,000-ton flotation mill.

GIPROTSVETMET: NON-FERROUS PLANNING INSTITUTE

Giprotsvetmet had responsibility for the design of non-ferrous mining and metallurgical installations. The bureau was headquartered in Moscow with field offices in Sverdlovsk and Leningrad.

In March 1930 the design bureau concluded a technical-assistance contract with the Southwestern Engineering Corporation of Los Angeles, which would act, according to Amtorg, 'as consultants in the preparation of projects, and the construction and operation of new and existing concentration plants in the Soviet Union.'[14] After pointing out that the company had designed milling plants in the United States, Mexico, and Canada, Amtorg added that the company would 'make available to the Soviet non-ferrous industry the latest developments and patents with regard to the concentration of ores.'

The Southwestern party of engineers was headed by E. R. Cullity[15] and was in Russia from June 1930 to January 1932, with responsibility for the supervision of design, installation, and initial operation of ore-dressing plants. The Southwestern projects were in Dzhezhakgan district, previously known as the Atabasarski concession, and the Caucasus and Urals. The company designed extensive concentrating facilities and complete plans for a 6,000-ton-per-day flotation mill.[16]

An agreement with the Radiore Company of Los Angeles was signed at the same time as that with Southwestern Engineering. Radiore, a front-rank geophysical exploration concern, contracted to locate non-ferrous and precious-metal ores by geophysical means.[17] Several exploration engineers left imme-

---

[12]   U.S. State Dept. Decimal File, 861.5017—Living Conditions/643, Report No. 115, Riga, April 4, 1933.

[13]   *Ibid.*

[14]   Amtorg, *op. cit.*, V, No. 7 (April 1, 1930), p. 131.

[15]   *American Engineers in Russia*, Fisher, Folder 4. S. E. Hollister was a Southwestern engineer working on projects in the Don, South Kazakstan, Urals, and Leningrad. Other engineers in the Southwestern group were E. R. Kinney, T. H. Oxnam, and A. J. Bone.

[16]   *Engineering and Mining Journal*, CXXXVI, No. 2 (February 1935), p. 4.

[17]   Amtorg, *op. cit.*, V, No. 7 (April 1, 1930), p. 131.

diately for the Soviet Union.[18] Little is known of their work except for one brief reference to indicate that the Radiore Company reported unfavorably on a copper deposit south of Kafan in Armenia.[19]

ARTHUR WHEELER ENGINEERING CORPORATION TECHNICAL ASSISTANCE AT COPPER SMELTERS AND REFINERIES

The Wheeler Engineering Corporation specialized in design and construction of non-ferrous metal plants, with experience not only in the United States and Canada but also in Chile and the Belgian Congo, where they had undertaken large copper-development projects. Extensive interviews with Frederick W. Snow, Chief Engineer of Wheeler, and other company engineers by U.S. State Department officials in the early 1930s have left a detailed picture of the development of the Soviet copper industry during the first 20 years after the Revolution.[20] As Snow had access to Tsvetmetzoloto records, his information is of great value and, as his salary was $25,000 per year, his services were no doubt highly appreciated.

The Snow memoranda suggest immense copper deposits in Russia. These were little prospected, and many were of low grade and required extensive construction of transportation facilities. In 1932, about 70 percent of the copper metal mined was coming from old re-equipped tsarist plants in the Urals, with Bogomol as the only Soviet-era development. Although the production plan for 1931 called for 150,000 metric tons, the total reported production in 1930 had been 47,000 tons, and in 1931, 48,423 tons. However, production actually *fell* in 1931, as more copper in that year came from scrap rather than mining operations. Accidents and the failure to open Bogomol were cited by Snow as reasons for the decline. The forced pressure of the Five-Year Plans created cave-ins at Kompaneinsk and fires at both Kalata and Karabash.

Although Wheeler then tried hard to get the proposed Lake Balkash development project, which opened about 1940, the company was unable to compete with credit terms offered by German and British firms. In September 1932 Wheeler retired completely from Russia. Chief Engineer Frederick Snow, however, returned to Tsvetmetzoloto as a consultant on individual contract at $25,000 gold (plus ruble payments) per year.[21]

---

[18]   *Ibid.*, V, No. 13 (July 1, 1930), p. 281. Geolkom (Geological Committee) hired nine geologists, geophysicists, and engineers, of whom five were connected with the Radiore Company.

[19]   U.S. State Dept. Decimal File, 861.5017—Living Conditions/691, Report No. 174, Riga, July 11, 1933.

[20]   Based on several lengthy reports at 861.6352/15 and 861.5017—Living Conditions/471. These reports contain a great deal of information not available elsewhere on conditions in Soviet copper mines.

[21]   U.S. State Dept. Decimal File, 861.6352/15.

THE BOGOMOL (KRASNOURAL'SK) COPPER COMBINE

Bogomol was the first Soviet copper combine; it required development of new copper ore mines, mills, a smelter, and a town. Designed by the Arthur Wheeler Engineering Corporation and started in 1926–7, it was not only a copy of the Noranda smelter in Quebec, Canada, but was also designed and supervised in the construction phase by the same company and many of the same engineers.[22] On completion of construction in 1931, it was taken over by the Red Army and renamed first Krasnoural'sk, and then Ordzhonikidze.

Construction records of the Bogomol copper smelter present a unique opportunity to compare the building of similar plants in free-enterprise and socialist environments. The writer knows of no other case where the parallels can be drawn so closely from the engineering, economic, and social points of view. This comparison is given in table 4–2.

Table 4–2   COMPARATIVE CONDITIONS AND RESULTS IN CONSTRUCTION OF SIMILAR COPPER SMELTERS IN CANADA AND U.S.S.R.

	Noranda Smelter (Quebec, Canada)	Bogomolstroi Smelter (Urals, U.S.S.R.)
Smelter design	Arthur Wheeler Engineering Corp. (New York)	Arthur Wheeler Engineering Corp. (New York)
Construction supervision	Wheeler Engineering and Noranda Mines, Ltd. (Canada)	Wheeler Engineering and Tsvetmetzoloto (U.S.S.R.)
Superintendent of construction	J. Gillis	Frederick W. Snow
Start of construction	Spring 1926	Spring 1926
Start-up of smelter	Dec. 16, 1927	Late 1931
Construction time	18 months	5 years
Cost (including mines development)	$3 million	Estimated 350 million rubles
Climate	Winter: −50°F	Winter: −50°F
Railroad link required	40 miles	Already built
Road link required	45 miles	Already built
Power supply required	Installed by Dec. 27, 1926	Supplied from existing Kushva plant
Labor employed	Average: 400 (maximum: 600)	Average: 6,000–7,000
Production	End 1929: passed 1,000 tons/day 1930: passed 2,000 tons/day 1931: passed 2,500 tons/day	1931: 3 tons/day
Incentives	(1) Management: profit (2) Labor: wages	(1) Soviet management: fear and ideology (2) Labor: coercion, wages and propaganda (3) U.S. consultants: profit

Sources: Noranda: L. Roberts, *Noranda* (Toronto: Clarke, Irwin and Co., 1956). Bogomolstroi: U.S. State Dept. Decimal File, 861.6352/15.

[22]   U.S. State Dept. Decimal File, 861.6352/20, in which a report by George F. Kennan says that Bogomol was developed with the help of 'hundreds of foreign engineers and thousands of Russian engineers and workmen.'

Although climatic and engineering conditions for both smelters were substantially the same (except for the fact that road and rail links for Bogomol were already built), there was a significant difference in results. Noranda was built in 18 months by only 400 workers, while Bogomol required 5 years and 6,000 to 7,000 workers. Labor efficiency was far lower in Russia but the larger amount of labor available was used in an attempt to compensate for this disadvantage.

The Krasnoural'sk smelter was described by Jermain as 'new and beautiful, being equipped entirely with American machinery.'[23] There were four roasting furnaces, two reverbatories, and two Pierce-Smith 20-ton converters. The plant was equipped almost entirely with new American machinery, the bulk of which was from the Allis-Chalmers Company, with the balance from the Nichols Copper, General Electric, and Western Electric companies.[24]

Twenty-five Americans were employed at one time in construction. When completed, Krasnoural'sk employed 350 in the smelter, 2,000 in the mines, and 1,475 in the offices.[25]

Chief Engineer Snow of Wheeler Engineering recounted the difficulties attending the start-up of Bogomolstroi (Krasnoural'sk) to the State Department, but concluded:

> Red Urals is a good plant and will eventually produce. Particularly since the Red Army officials are now taking a distinct interest in it because of its military significance. It is a splendid illustration of all the weaknesses of the Soviet methods. Built as a rush plant of great military and industrial significance, it has taken five years to complete it, whereas a similar plant was built in one year as an ordinary commercial undertaking in Canada. Provided with a tremendous supply of labor and all modern equipment, it has failed to produce for a year after being in a theoretical position to do so. . . .[26]

In addition to the Bogomol smelter and mines, there was a 'gigantic copper refinery' at Sverdlovsk, also built under the Wheeler contract. It was similar in design to the Phelps Dodge refinery in Texas, and designed to produce 100,000 metric tons of refined copper with provision for expansion to 400,000 tons by the mid-1930s. This plant took about three years to erect, whereas the Phelps Dodge plant had been erected in 11 months as a regular job. Snow suggested that 'the delays at this plant and at Bogomolstroi have recently had

---

23   U.S. State Dept. Decimal File, 861.63/92, Report No. 174, Riga, July 11, 1933.
24   U.S. State Dept. Decimal File, 861.5017—Living Conditions/643, Report No. 115, Riga, April 4, 1933.
25   *Ibid.*
26   U.S. State Dept. Decimal File, 861.6352/15, which includes a report by Frederick W. Snow, Chief Engineer of Arthur Wheeler Engineering Corp. for the Bogomolstroi project.

a salutary effect in convincing the military and other authorities that something is wrong with the Soviet construction system.'[27]

THE KARSAK PAI AND KAFAN COPPER SMELTERS

In the years between 1910 and 1930, metal extraction procedures moved towards flotation of ores into concentrates followed by smelting in reverbatory furnaces. The first copper smelter in the Soviet Union to use such flotation methods with reverbatory furnaces was Karsak Pai, where flotation yielded a 30-percent concentrate converted by Bonnett system reverbatory furnaces into a 50-percent-plus matte and acid slag. The matte was then treated in converters to obtain blister copper.

The Karsak Pai plant needed only completion; the equipment was pre-revolutionary.[28] In the early 1930s the Technical Director was a Russian trained in the United States, and the Chief Engineer an American, as was the flotation plant superintendent, who increased mill capacity from 250 to 400 tons per day. Karsak Pai was also assisted by Milo Krejci, attached to Giprotsvetmet to solve field problems. As part of his work he produced a training manual which was translated, printed, and distributed to plant workers.[29]

The Chief Engineer between 1930 and 1932 was H. R. Wilson. He had the prime responsibility for bringing the mines up to standard, although two months after he left output was down to 15 percent of capacity.[30]

One of the two copper smelters in Armenia was the Kafan, formerly a French concession and almost completely rebuilt in the 1930s. T. F. Collins, an American mining engineer employed at the Kafan mines for 22 months in the years 1930 and 1933, commented that 'the new plant was planned by an American engineer and is entirely built according to American plans,' with a 1,000-ton-per-day flotation mill and two 150-ton smelters.[31] In 1933 the smelters were operating to capacity but there were still difficulties with the flotation plant. According to the Luftwaffe files, the plant operated only at 50 percent of capacity in 1941.[32]

THE LAKE BALKASH PORPHYRY COPPER DEPOSITS

Very large deposits of low-grade (1 percent and less) copper ore were prospected in the late 1920s near Lake Balkash. A mine was sited at Kounrad,

[27] U.S. State Dept. Decimal File, 861.6352/15.

[28] Sutton, *Western Technology . . ., 1917 to 1930*, p. 83.

[29] Milo W. Krejci, 'The Korsak [*sic*] Pai Enterprise,' *Case Alumnus*, XII, No. 3 (December 1933), pp. 12–3, 25–7.

[30] U.S. State Dept. Decimal File, 861.5017—Living Conditions/323 and 861.50—FIVE YEAR PLAN/189.

[31] U.S. State Dept. Decimal File, 861.5017—Living Conditions/854.

[32] *Die Kupfererzeugung der UdSSR* (Berlin: 1941).

and a refinery at Bertish Bay on the northern shores of Lake Balkash, a power plant, and a rail line to the coal deposits at Karaganda were also built. Construction laborers were predominantly expropriated kulaks. The Balkash project was typical in the extraordinary brutality utilized in Soviet construction:

> I saw them die at Balkashstroi by the tens of thousands. . . . We were doing a lot of grading and excavation work and having no machines we needed much labor. . . . But they were poor workers. So the chief of construction—a brutal drunkard named Ivanov, who was the husband of the sister of Stalin's first wife, Aleluyeva—enforced piecework rate, making not only the men's wages but their rations dependent on their work. There was never enough food. . . . They died like mice in the winter.[33]

The Wheeler Engineering Corporation made strong efforts to get the Lake Balkash development contract, but lost out to strong competition from European firms who were willing to take ruble payments and grant extensive credit.[34] Although New York banks offered to back Wheeler, his offer was not as favorable as those of the European group. Thus Wheeler himself remained on an individual contract, and development work was taken over by German firms. We know very little about the actual German development work at Balkash; there is a report in the Hoover files concerning a 'trainload' of German workers on their way to erect a plant at Lake Balkash in 1933.[35] John Calder was chief adviser to Ivanov and took over when Wheeler withdrew completely from Russia.[36] By October 1941, the Lake Balkash plant had two converters and two ovens producing 85 tons of copper per day, and employed some 5,000 workers. The equipment was chiefly of American origin.[37]

DESIGN AND OPERATION OF ZINC AND LEAD PLANTS

American engineers designed all Soviet zinc and lead plants. W. C. Aitkenhead worked for Giprotsvetmet from August 1930 to June 1932 and worked on the design of three electrolytic zinc plants, of which one was built and put into operation. Another metallurgical engineer, J. H. Gillis, worked from May 1930 to 1936 on the design and construction of 15 metallurgical plants. In one project he worked on the initial plans and then was promoted to a position as technical director, and then moved on to another plant as technical director. As Gillis specialized in electrolytic zinc plant design, it can be assumed that he had a dominant influence in the zinc industry. A 1937 State Department report indicated that most of his work had been 'with

[33] *Fortune*, April 1949, p. 82.
[34] U.S. State Dept. Decimal File, 861.6352/15.
[35] *American Engineers in Russia*, Fisher, Confidential Report.
[36] U.S. State Dept. Decimal File, 861.6352/15.
[37] National Archives Microcopy T84, Roll 127, Frame 665.

design, construction and operation of electrolytic zinc plants of which two have been completed and are in successful operation.'[38] His conclusions were that the plants as constructed were capable of efficient operation but that the irregularity of ore supply and fluctuating power supplies handicapped zinc output.[39]

Several large zinc concentrators, smelters, and refineries were built between 1930 and 1945. One was the Ukrtsink, at Konstantinovka in the Ukraine, with a 35,000-ton input of concentrate to produce 12,000 tons of refined zinc and 30,000 tons of sulphuric acid from roaster gases. Another was the Ordzhonikidze in the North Caucasus, to produce electrolytic zinc. According to Chamberlain[40] the plant produced 5 tons of zinc per day and for this required 300 office workers and 1,600 plant workers. In St. Louis a similar refinery producing 50 tons of zinc a day required only 16 in the office and 170 in the plant.

The Ridder lead-zinc smelter and refinery in Leninogorsk was completely Western in equipment. The concentrator had Blake crushers and Dwight-Lloyd roasting machines. The refinery had Parkes kettles with a Howard mixer, and a small Cottrell furnace copied from the one located at Port Pirie, Australia. There were five Faber du Faur retort furnaces, all Soviet-made but

Table 4–3　　　LEAD AND ZINC SMELTING AND REFINING WORKS, 1930–45

Location	Plant Name	Capacity (1941) (Metric Tons)	Type of Plant
Ukraine	Konstantinovka (Ukrtsink)	12,000 zinc	Zinc distillation
Transcaucasia	Elektrosink (Ordzhonikidze) (formerly Vladikavkaz)	30,000 electro-zinc 7,500 zinc 14,000 lead	Electrolytic zinc Zinc distillation Lead smelting
Chelyabinsk	Zinc plant	20,000 electro-zinc	Electrolytic zinc
Leninogorsk	Ridder lead works	14,000 lead	Lead smelting
Tschimkent	Kalinin lead works	60,000 lead	Lead smelting
Novosibirsk	Belovo	18,500 zinc	Zinc distillation
Primorsk	Tetuikhe	15,000 lead	Lead smelting
*Altai	Ust' Kamenogorsk		Electrolytic zinc

Source: Oberkommando der Wehrmacht (OKW/Wi Rü Amt/Wi), March 1941. Miscellaneous German Records, National Archives Microcopy T 84–122.
* Built during World War II.

[38]　U.S. State Dept. Decimal File, 861.5017—Living Conditions/795, Report No. 1172, Paris, June 11, 1937.

[39]　Both Aitkenhead and Gillis have reports in *American Engineers in Russia.*

[40]　William H. Chamberlain, *Russia's Iron Age* (Boston: Little, Brown, and Co., 1934), p. 57.

copied from a Belgian 500-kilogram type.[41] The Belovo zinc plant at Novosibirsk, opened in 1931, had U.S. equipment.[42]

DEVELOPMENT OF AN ALUMINA-ALUMINUM INDUSTRY

A great deal of research was undertaken in tsarist Russia in aluminum technology. Bayer worked at the Tentelev chemical plant (St. Petersburg) perfecting the Bayer process, patented in 1887 and still the world's standard process for alumina reduction. Six years later Penyakov patented a dry process for converting bauxite into alumina. This process was used in France and Belgium before World War I. Work by other Russian scientists, including Fedotiv on the reduction cell, helped put prerevolutionary Russia in the forefront of aluminum technology, although the country was weak in production facilities.

The basic problem, which also presented itself to the Soviets, was that Russian bauxite deposits were small and of low grade. The Tikhvin bauxite deposits were initially explored in 1882 and in detail during World War I. Nevertheless, Russia did not manufacture alumina, but only a few aluminum goods from imported aluminum metal. The Alcoa concession[43] in the mid-1920s explored and drilled known bauxite deposits and confirmed these prerevolutionary findings.[44] The basic Soviet choice then was either to build an aluminum industry on the low-grade, limited Tikhvin bauxite deposits or to use nonbauxite raw materials. Nonbauxite material had not been used elsewhere in the world and required development of a new technology. A military demand for self-sufficiency dictated the choice of the nonbauxite option as well as use of the Tikhvin deposits.

Development of the aluminum industry in the late 1920s and 1930s was 'under the direction of Mr. Frank E. Dickie.'[45] Dickie, previously with Alcoa, was attached as consultant to Tsvetmetzoloto. A commission from Aluminstroi (Aluminum Plant Construction Trust) also visited Germany in 1929 to study the German aluminum industry.[46]

The first plant built in the Soviet Union, for production of 40,000 tons of alumina and 13,500 tons of aluminum per year, was at Volkhov, 75 miles east of Leningrad. Construction was begun in 1930, and the plant was brought

[41] *Engineering and Mining Journal*, CXXXVII, No. 10 (October 1936). This issue contains an extensive article on the Ridder plant.

[42] Amtorg, *op. cit.*, VI, No. 3 (February 1, 1931), p. 64.

[43] Sutton, *Western Technology . . . 1917 to 1930*, pp. 106–7.

[44] Alcan Hirsch, *Industrialized Russia* (New York: Chemical Catalog Co., 1934), pp. 89–90. Hirsch reported that even by 1934 only 7 million tons of bauxite had been located at Tikhvin.

[45] *Ibid.*, p. 90.

[46] Amtorg, *op. cit.*, V, No. 2 (January 15, 1930), p. 43.

into partial operation in mid-1932. Technical assistance was provided by Cie. de Produits Chimiques et Electrométallurgiques Alais, Troques et Camargue, of Lyons, France, and covered both design of the plant and supervision of erection by French engineers. Soviet operating engineers were trained in plants (Sabart et St. Jean de Maurieme) belonging to the company in France.[47] The alumina plant received bauxite from the Tikhvin deposits and converted it to alumina by the old Deville-Péchiney process, called the Mueller-Yakovkin process in the Soviet Union.

Another aluminum plant, also started in 1930, at Zaporozhe in the Ukraine, began to produce aluminum in June 1933 and alumina in early 1934 from Tikhvin bauxites. This was also designed and built under the technical-assistance agreement with Cie. de Produits Chimiques and included plants for the manufacture of synthetic cryolite and carbon electrodes—not part of the Volkhov project. Dneprovsk used the Pedersen process,[48] called the Kuznetsov-Zhukovski process in the U.S.S.R. The equipment for the plant was reported by a member of the U.S. Embassy in Moscow as coming from Italy.[49]

Kamensk, finished in 1939 to produce 108,000 tons of alumina and 30,000 tons of aluminum per year, used the standard Bayer wet alkaline process.

The Kandalakskii plant, using nepheline and not bauxite, was started in 1934 but not completed until 1955: a measure of the advantage of transferring known foreign techniques.

THE UNITED ENGINEERING CONTRACTS FOR ALUMINUM ROLLING MILLS

The United Engineering and Foundry Company contracts of January 1938 exemplify the advanced nature of the technology supplied by Western firms to the Soviet Union: indeed some of these projects strained the research and development abilities of the most advanced Western firms and were far beyond the abilities of the Soviet Union at that time.[50] The contracts do suggest, however, that the Soviet Union has had a remarkable ability to recognize advanced technology and enlist front-rank foreign firms in the acquisition process.

[47] Oberkommando der Wehrmacht (OKW/Wi Rü Amt/Wi), March 1941. Miscellaneous German Records, National Archives Microcopy T 84–122, Bericht No. 10, p. 14; R. J. Anderson, 'Russian Aluminium,' *The Mining Magazine* (London), February 1938.

[48] The Pedersen process was developed by Prof. Harold Pedersen in Norway and patented in 1926. The work was financed by Norsk Aluminum (Norway) and Alcoa.

[49] U.S. State Dept. Decimal File, 861.6463/66, Dispatch No. 183, American Embassy in Moscow, September 28, 1934.

[50] The wide-strip mill used in the steel industry may even today (1968) be beyond Soviet capabilities. Only one such mill has been produced: a copy of the original United mill, installed in Poland, not the U.S.S.R.

The January 1938 agreement involved the sale of $3 million worth of equipment and technical assistance for aluminum mills at Zaporozhe. These were 66-inch (1680-millimeter) hot and cold mills complete with auxiliary equipment: the most modern mills in the world. Jenkins, the United Chief Engineer in the U.S.S.R., said of the Zaporozhe mill that 'not even the Aluminum Company of America has machinery as modern as it is.'[51] Both mills were 'completely powered and controlled by General Electric apparatus. . . .'[52]

The Stupino mill (Plant No. 150) near Moscow, by far the most important Soviet aluminum development project, was also the subject of an agreement in May 1939 between Mashinoimport and United Engineering and Foundry for the installation of hot and cold rolling mills. These were mills of extraordinary size, and, if erected in the West, would certainly have been the subject of interested discussion in the trade literature.

The Stupino installation comprised two sections: a hot mill and a cold mill. The hot mill had two units. One was a 2-high 66-inch hot rolling mill for rolling cast duraluminum, including Type 17-S and 24-S ingots. On a basis of 300 working days with two shifts operating at 70 percent efficiency, its capacity was rated at 45,000 metric tons of aluminum sheet per year. The 66-inch mill came into regular operation about February 1, 1940 and the 112-inch mill a few weeks later.

The cold mill contained two mills of similar size for cold working sheets produced in the hot mill. The 66-inch cold mill started about March 1940 and the 112-inch cold mill late in 1940. All finishing equipment was supplied and placed in operation by United Engineering for the Soviets.[53] The complete contract was worth about $3.5 to $4 million to United Engineering; for this amount the Soviets acquired an installation capable of rolling 2,000-foot-long aluminum sheets for aircraft. United Engineering said of it that 'nothing of such a size has ever been produced before.'[54] The electrical equipment for Stupino was supplied by General Electric, as was the equipment for a third (name unknown) aluminum mill.[55]

The Brown-Boveri Company supplied equipment for annealing and hardening aluminum (almost certainly associated with the above rolling mills) to an unknown plant operated by Tsvetmetzoloto.[56] The company commented on this equipment as follows:

---

[51] U.S. State Dept. Decimal File, 861.6511/37, Report No. 902, Moscow Embassy, January 31, 1938.

[52] *The Monogram*, November 1943. Although the source does not mention Zaporozhe, it does refer to the 'first rolling mill,' which was probably Zaporozhe.

[53] U.S. State Dept. Decimal File, 861.25/420, Report No. 298, February 5, 1940.

[54] *Ibid*. The Stupino plant also manufactured Hamilton 2-blade and 3-blade variable pitch propellers for aircraft.

[55] *The Monogram*, November 1943. Location of the third mill is not known.

[56] *Brown-Boveri Review*, January 1932, pp. 24-6.

The large output required from this plant, the exceedingly large dimensions of the pieces to be treated, and the resulting high power requirements made necessary designs which considerably exceeded in dimensions and type of construction the scope of our furnace designs as used up to date.[57]

Twenty-one furnaces were constructed for a continuous process system with electrically driven conveyors. Two pusher-type furnaces were made for the 600-ton press, and another electric furnace with a step-type conveyor was made for the 1,500-ton press. Yet another continuous electric furnace with conveyor chain was installed by Brown-Boveri in the 3,000-ton press shop. The hot rolling mill was supplied with two electric continuous furnaces as well as a pusher-type furnace and a hardening furnace. The sheet and tube rolling mill had two electric annealing furnaces and a hardening furnace. The laboratory was supplied with eight small electric furnaces.[58]

Thus we may conclude that the technically weak Soviet non-ferrous metals industry was essentially designed and constructed by Western companies specializing in this field. In mining operations the assistance was given in the early 1930s only and limited to the provision of foreign equipment and American superintendents, later supplanted by Russian management. However, the design of smelters and refineries was completely American and the Russian operators were trained by foreign construction engineers.

[57]   *Ibid.*, p. 24.
[58]   *Ibid.*, p. 26.

CHAPTER FIVE

Technical Assistance to the Iron and Steel Industry

GENERAL DESIGN OF SOVIET IRON AND STEEL PLANTS

STALIN placed great emphasis on iron and steel as the basis for a socialist economy. His plans included rebuilding and expanding 20 prerevolutionary plants (suitably renamed after favored Bolsheviks) and construction of three gigantic new plants at Magnitogorsk, Kuznetsk, and Zaporozhe.[1] What has escaped Western economists is that the Soviet Union lacked entirely the technical resources to build even tsarist-era metallurgical plants, quite apart from the highly complex systems contemplated. No amount of Soviet investment, within a politically acceptable time period, could have replaced importation of the latest Western smelting and rolling-mill technologies.

Between 1927 and 1932 the responsibility for directing the transfer of modern technology to the Soviet iron and steel industry belonged to Gipromez and the Freyn Engineering Company of Chicago. Mr. Henry J. Freyn, President of the company, described the objectives of his 1928 technical-assistance contract as follows:

> The work of our group of engineers and operators located in Leningrad and attached to Gipromez [State All-Union Institute for Planning of Metallurgical Works], consists in making available to Soviet executives, engineers, and operatives [sic] the American training, knowledge and practical experience of our organization, to the end that the reconstruction and enlargement of the existing plants and the planning and construction of new iron and steel works be predominantly of American design and standards.[2]

---

[1] A. I. Gurevitch, *Zadachi chernoi metallurgii v 1932 g* (Moscow: 1932), pp. 8–9.
[2] Henry J. Freyn, 'Iron and Steel Industry in Russia,' *Blast Furnace and Steel Plant*, XVIII, January 1930, p. 92. See also Sutton, *Western Technology . . .*, *1917 to 1930*, pp. 74–5.

The degree of his involvement in the actual planning process may be judged from Mr. Freyn's comment that 'one of the principal tasks of our Leningrad force is the allocation of the steel production demanded by the five-year plan, and provision for the necessary plant capacity. . . .'[3]

Freyn had retained a staff in the U.S.S.R. since 1927 and Kuznetsk was one of the projects designed with this assistance. The company agreement to build the Kuznetsk plant,with a pig-iron capacity of one million tons per year, was signed on June 4, 1930 with Novostal. A contemporary wrote: 'Between fifty and sixty American engineers will constitute the organization which will direct the execution of design, specifications, fabrication, and superintend the erection and initial operation of the Kuznetsky Steel Works.'[4]

In 1928 a Soviet commission of four members visited the offices of Arthur G. McKee and Company in Cleveland. These Cleveland discussions resulted in broad agreement on the type and location of another major unit, the Magnitogorsk plant, although the drawing completed in early 1928 was 'one small general plan showing the proposed plant layout that had been agreed upon by our engineers and the Russian Commission. . . .'[5] This McKee design was based on the Gary, Indiana, plant of United States Steel, at that time the largest integrated iron and steel plant in the world. The proposed project was then reduced to drawings by 450 American engineers working day and night. Design work alone on Magnitogorsk cost the Soviet Union two million gold rubles. R. W. Stuck describes this McKee design as complete 'to the last nut and bolt' before construction started; 'nothing of this size and magnitude had ever been done before . . . it is the finest design of a steel plant that was ever reduced to drawings. . . .'[6]

Design work completed, a group of McKee engineers then outlined the mill layout and specifications to an audience of 75 to 100 Russian planners, bureaucrats, and steelworks engineers in Moscow. This design became the largest project in the First Five-Year Plan, and the showpiece of 'socialist construction.'[7]

Most competent Russian construction engineers had left Russia, and the tsarist metallurgical equipment plants such as Sormovo and Kramatorsk,

---

[3]   *Ibid.*

[4]   Arthur J. Whitcomb, 'Soviet Union to Build Steel Plant,' *Blast Furnace and Steel Plant*, XVIII, July 1930, p. 1135.

[5]   *American Engineers in Russia*, Stuck MSS, Folder 5. R. W. Stuck was Chief Engineer in charge of blast-furnace construction at Magnitogorsk and later head of the McKee group in the Soviet Union.

[6]   *Ibid.*, p. 26.

[7]   John Scott has remarked, 'It was necessary to give this contract to a foreign contractor because of the obvious incapacity of any Soviet organization then in existence to do the work.' [*Behind the Urals* (Cambridge: The Riverside Press, 1942), p. 68.]

which in the late nineteenth century had produced some types of iron and steel plant equipment, had been stripped of their technical forces. The remaining competent engineers were in and out of OGPU camps. German engineers running the metallurgical plants in 1927–8 were politically suspect, and the hastily trained 'red engineers' more apt to talk than to do. Accordingly, Gipromez was initially charged with the transfer of American metallurgical technology to Soviet industry, rather than with the development of new designs. This transfer was achieved by employing American (and some German) engineers to simplify and standardize this foreign technology. This technology was then duplicated by metallurgical equipment plants such as the new Uralmash and the greatly expanded Kramatorsk plants. It is a mistake to assume that the Freyn Company, the McKee Corporation, and similar Western contractors acted only as consultants in the development of the industry.[8] Individual American engineers managed Gipromez departments, and the technical staff of Gipromez was for some years heavily Americanized. One engineer, W. S. Orr, at work in Leningrad Gipromez headquarters from 1929 to 1933, has provided a description of this technical penetration:

> When we first joined Gipromez we were only asked questions—the Russians made the layouts, reports and decisions. In about six months we were asked in on the layouts and decisions, in about nine months we were made Chief Engineers of steel plant projects and at the end of the first year some of our men were heads of departments. Last year one was the Assistant Chief Engineer of the entire bureau. Naturally we instituted American short-cut methods, weeded out a lot of unnecessary work and when we left we considered that Gipromez was the most efficient organization in Russia.[9]

The Americanization of Gipromez is significant as it coincides with a Sovnarkom (Council of People's Commissars) decision, in line with a McKee Corporation specification, to change Magnitogorsk from a plant 20 percent the size of the United States Steel plant at Gary, Indiana, to a plant equal in size to the Gary plant and with a pig-iron output of 2.5 million tons per year.

Koptewski,[10] Chief Engineer at Soviet steel plants in the early 1930s and with Gipromez at that time, recalls these significant German and American technical contributions, and suggests that both made 'a tremendous contribution towards facilitating the manufacture of standard metallurgical equipment. . . .' Koptewski also suggests that not only the standardization of the

---

[8] For example, see M. Gardner Clark, *The Economics of Soviet Steel* (Cambridge: Harvard University Press, 1956), p. 56. This is not intended as a criticism of Clark's excellent study. The data has not been previously forthcoming.

[9] *American Engineers in Russia*, Fisher material, Folder 3, Report 15.

[10] Sergei Koptewski, *The Costs of Construction of New Metallurgical Plants in the U.S.S.R.* (New York: East European Fund, Inc., 1952), p. 9.

blast furnace but also the advances in construction simplification and maintenance methods were initiated by Westerners. Blast-furnace equipment was standardized on foreign models by Gipromez to simplify production at the new machinery plants being built and equipped by foreign companies. For open-hearth departments, standard plans were drawn up for stripping, scrap yards, mixers, and 150-ton fixed and 250-ton tilting furnaces. Cast-iron teeming equipment, single- and multi-stage electric gas purifiers, and turbo air-blowers were standardized in drawings. In rolling mills the significant standard model was a blooming mill with an annual capacity of 1.5 million tons, based on a Demag 1150-millimeter design. Koptewski states that great effort was made to incorporate latest Western techniques into these standard designs. The procedure was much like converting a military aircraft from the development stage to mass production by freezing design at a particular point; in the case of Soviet industrial development, design was frozen on the most suitable of foreign designs.[11]

In the reports of foreign delegations and observers visiting those iron and steel plants, there is consistent evidence of the widespread use of foreign equipment and methods. The Hanczell Industrial Delegation from Finland, for example, reported as follows:

> Organization methods and most of the machinery are either German or American. The steel mill MORNING near Moscow, which was visited by the delegation is said to be one of the most modern establishments of its kind in the world. Constructed, organized and started by highly paid American specialists, it employs 17,000 workers and produces steel used by motor plants, naval shipyards and arms factories.[12]

We may then assert that Soviet iron and steel technology, a favored development sector, was wholly dependent on foreign design and engineering ability. This assertion is now examined in detail.

DEVELOPMENT OF IRON-ORE MINES BY THE OGLEBAY, NORTON COMPANY

Historically, Krivoi Rog is the base of Russian iron-ore production and was operated in the 1920s by mining engineers of Rawack and Grunfeld A-G of Germany. Early reports by the German firm were adopted and expanded by an Oglebay, Norton Company technical-assistance contract with Novostal.

---

[11]   The saving in drafting costs alone was substantial. About 30,400 engineering drawings are required for an integrated iron and steel plant. Koptewski estimates these to have cost about 16 million (1934) rubles (*op. cit.*, p. 12). Scott estimates that the McKee Corp. had over 100,000 such blueprints in the cellar of the combinat building. (*Op. cit.*, p. 67.)

[12]   U.S. State Dept. Decimal File, 861.5017—Living Conditions/456, Report No. 665, Helsingfors, April 2, 1932.

In January 1928 a group of American mining engineers specializing in iron-ore development reported on the Krivoi Rog ore mines and formulated plans for their rehabilitation, expansion, and future operation.[13] Their objective was to prepare operating and development plans and schedules for Vesenkha (Supreme Council of the National Economy). Between 1928 and 1934 the firm worked on all the major iron-ore deposits in the U.S.S.R. but concentrated its efforts on Krivoi Rog, the four major Urals iron-ore deposits, and those supplying Kuzbas. (See table 5–1.) J. M. Price was manager and a corps of American mining engineers was retained in the U.S.S.R. until 1934. Their work covered all phases of open-pit and underground iron mines and was the key element in modernization and mechanization. Initial implementation of modern methods and the introduction of imported mining equipment were supervised, and assistance was given in developing early Soviet models of Western equipment. Magnitogorsk, for example, was equipped with the largest current model of Traylor and Gates ore-crushers.[14]

Rodin[15] has pointed to the absolute and relative gain in *per capita* output of iron ore in the U.S.S.R. in the face of a 'marked deterioration' of two naturally determined factors: a decline in the proportion of open-pit-mined ore from 68 to 31 percent and a fall in yield of mined crude ore from 100 to 88 percent. Increased production was due to counterbalancing advantages: the amount of power equipment available per unit of output, the size of the average mine, and improvement in mining practices and mining equipment. These three advantages can be specifically traced to Western origins, while the disadvantages, as Rodin pointed out, were 'naturally determined.' The size of a mine is primarily determined by type of mining desired: open-pit or underground. Open-pit mines tend to be larger and, in the U.S.S.R., labor productivity at the best open-pit mines is three to four times greater than at

---

[13] *American Engineers in Russia*, E. S. Dickinson, Folder 4, No. 6. Oglebay, Norton Company is a large independent iron-ore producer based in Cleveland, Ohio. The company supplied (letter of April 12, 1934) a list of 21 engineers who had worked in the U.S.S.R. Some stayed on with individual contracts after expiration of the company agreement. Engineers were hired on one-year or two-year contracts. At least five have left detailed accounts of their work. F. W. Uhler was Chief Engineer at Sverdlovsk, directing the work of the Urals group of mines from June 1930 to July 1931. C. M. Harry was on a two-year contract to project new operations for Krivoi Rog. K. H. Donaldson was based at Sverdlovsk and traveled to mines at Zlatoust, Turin, and Samsky. H. H. Angst was on a two-year contract specializing in mining techniques, and worked at Lipetsk, Tula, Sverdlovsk, and the Urals mines. An anonymous engineer was based in Leningrad and made consulting trips for specific problems to Kharkov, Lipetsk, and Kerch'. See also U.S. State Dept. Decimal File, 861.5017—Living Conditions/347, for interviews with returning engineers.

[14] *American Engineers in Russia*, 'Statement of J. S. Ferguson Covering Personal Experiences in Russia over a Period of Eighteen Months,' April 30, 1933, p. 26.

[15] N. W. Rodin, *Productivity in Soviet Iron Mining, 1890–1960* (Santa Monica: The RAND Corp., 1953), Report RM-1116, p. 2.

the best underground operation (Krivoi Rog). The amount of ore mined by open-pit methods, however, has declined heavily since tsarist times (from 68 percent in 1913 to 31 percent in 1940), a reversal of the trend in the United States. The reasons are not clear. There is no reason to believe that iron-ore deposits with heavy overburden, requiring underground mining, are concentrated in the Soviet Union. In any event the U.S.S.R. has a much greater land surface, and iron ore is a commonly occurring mineral. These problems suggest inefficient iron-ore exploration methods.

Rodin concludes that there is a technological lag not explainable in terms of deficient power capacity. Rodin's conclusion is consistent with reports of Oglebay, Norton engineers working on development of these deposits. Modernization between 1928 and 1935 increased technical efficiency but was introduced unevenly and may have taken a long time to penetrate some mining areas.

This suggested technological lag may be exemplified by the much smaller size of power shovels at open-pit iron-ore operations. Introduction of power shovels began only in 1929, but the average shovel capacity remained small throughout the period under study. In 1929 Uralrud (Urals Ore Trust) had 17 power shovels averaging 0.88 cubic meters; in 1940–2 its shovels

Table 5–1   DEVELOPMENT OF SOVIET IRON-ORE MINES,
1928–40

| Mine | District | Million Metric Tons Produced in 1940 | |
		Developed by Oglebay, Norton Engineers (1928–1934)	Not Known to Have Been Developed by Oglebay, Norton
Tula	Central industrial	0.63	—
Lipetsk	Central agricultural	0.49	—
Crimea	Kerch'	1.92	—
Tagil-Kushva	Urals	1.23	—
Kusa	Urals	—	0.25
Bakal	Urals	—	0.63
Magnitogorsk	Urals	7.85	—
Zagazine-Kamarevskaya	Urals	—	0.50
Khalilovo	Urals	—	0.35
Telbess-Temir Tau	Siberia	0.70	—
Krivoi Rog	Ukraine	18.90	—
Others		—	0.19
TOTAL		31.72*	1.92

Source: D. Shimkin, *Minerals: A Key to Soviet Power* (Cambridge: Harvard, 1953), pp. 43, 48–9.
* 95% of iron ore produced in 1940 by Oglebay, Norton-developed mines.

averaged 1.73 cubic meters. Rodin compares this to Lake Superior mines, which in 1924 had 447 power shovels averaging 2.5 to 3.0 cubic meters, and explains the difference on the basis that small-ore bodies are better worked with small shovels. This is, however, a remote argument. Ore-deposit size does not affect shovel size to any extent in the range of 1 to 3 cubic meters, although it might inhibit the use of very large shovels. The technological lag is more likely to have been due to the Soviet inability to duplicate large foreign excavators, thus restricting iron-ore mining operations to the use of smaller shovels.

DEVELOPMENT OF THE STANDARD BLAST FURNACE

Until 1928 Russian blast furnaces were units of comparatively small capacity, although they were well-suited to the widespread geographical distribution of Russian metal-consuming industries. The Freyn-Gipromez design assistance contract of 1928 resulted in a standard blast furnace of 930 cubic meters capacity which could produce 1,000 tons of pig iron per day, with features enabling expansion to 1,200 tons. This standard furnace was a definite innovation. It conformed closely to American Freyn basic design and was patterned for the use of Krivoi Rog ores, which are similar to Lake Superior hematites. The innovatory feature was the use of the same standard design (capable of slight change for different site conditions, raw materials, and pig iron specifications) in multiple locations.[16] Standardization yielded economies

Table 5–2 FREYN STANDARD BLAST FURNACES IN THE
SOVIET UNION, 1934

| Name of Plant | Number of Standard Blast Furnaces | | |
	Operating	Building	Projected
Dzerjinsky	1	1	5
Zaporozhe	1	1	4 or 6
Voroshilov	1	1	4
Azovstal	1	1	6
Lipetsk	0	2	4
Tula	0	2	4
Krivoi Rog	1	1	6
Nikopol	0	0	2 or 3
Tagil	0	0	6
Total	5	9	41 or 44

Source: Adapted from *Freyn Design*, No. 11 (March 1934), p. 6.

[16] Gordon Fox and Owen R. Rice, 'Soviet Standard Blast Furnace,' *Freyn Design*, No. 11, March 1934, pp. 1–6. For another detailed description of the standard blast furnace see: Gordon Fox and Owen R. Rice, 'Soviet Standardizes Blast Furnace Design,' *The Iron Age*, CXXXIII, No. 10, March 8, 1934, pp. 20–4, 58. Fox was Vice-President of Freyn Engineering Co. and Rice a metallurgical engineer at Freyn. The article includes furnace dimensions, details of Freyn-designed equipment, and locations in the Soviet Union.

in the engineering and production costs of equipment; about 22 furnaces were finally built from the Freyn drawings.[17] The first units required imported American (and German) equipment; later units utilized the same equipment design but were manufactured at the new Uralmash and Kramatorsk plants.

In brief; no new blast furnaces were built between 1917 and 1928. From 1928 to 1932 all Soviet blast furnaces were designed and built under supervision of either the McKee Corporation or Freyn Engineering, to U.S. designs. After 1933 the standard Freyn and, to a lesser extent, the McKee design (1,180 cubic meters) were duplicated until 1938, when the Gipromez 1300-cubic-meter or second standard design was introduced.

Turbo-blowers for the hot-blast stoves (Cowpers units) for blast furnaces of 115,000-cubic-foot-minute capacity were supplied for Kuzbas and Magnitogorsk by the Brown-Boveri Company of Switzerland.[18] This was 'one of the biggest modern blower plants' in the world, built at the Brown-Boveri works in Mannheim (Germany) and Baden (Switzerland), and installed and started up by Swiss and German engineers. Altogether five of these gigantic units went to Kuznetsk and six similar units, built at Mannheim, went to Magnitogorsk. Of new design, they were far beyond the technical capability of the Soviet Union at this time.[19] General Electric turbo-blowers were installed in at least six other iron and steel plants.[20]

Soviet plants fabricated some constructional steelwork for the new plants and then, after about 1932–3, ventured into the manufacture of simple blast-furnace equipment items, starting with Dewhurst slag ladles of 10-cubic-meter capacity at Kramatorsk. These were large, heavy ladles mounted on a railroad wagon chassis for removal of hot slag from blast furnaces to adjacent slag dumps. Ferguson, blast-furnace superintendent at Kutnetsk, reported 25 slag ladles of Soviet manufacture: the only Soviet-supplied equipment there, apart from some mill electrical motors of less than 25 horsepower.[21] Shortly afterwards came manufacture by Uralmash (Urals Machine Combine) of larger, Dewhurst-type, pig-iron (i.e., hot-metal) ladles of 12-cubic-meter capacity.[22] Both slag and pig-iron ladles had been manufactured, however, as far back as 1890 at the Sormovo and Briansk works. Then, in the 1930s,

17   Institut promyshlenno-ekonomicheskikh isslodovanni NKTP, *Chernaya metallurgiya SSSR v pervoi pyatiletke* (Moscow: 1935), p. 55.
18   *The Brown-Boveri Review*, XX, No. 1 (January/February 1933), pp. 46–9.
19   'A blower plant of this kind attains the thermal efficiency of a gas engine driven plant but is much cheaper to build and keep up and more reliable in operation.' *(Ibid.)*
20   Amtorg, *op. cit.*, VII, No. 9 (May 1, 1932), pp. 209–10.
21   *American Engineers in Russia*, 'Statement of J. S. Ferguson Covering Personal Experiences in Russia Over a Period of Eighteen Months,' April 30, 1933, p. 3.
22   Koptewski, *op. cit.*, table 19. Koptewski calls Dewhurst 'Duerst,' being unfamiliar with the English spelling.

the Soviets manufactured more and more types of blast-furnace equipment, all to foreign design, until by 1940 they had the capability to produce more or less efficient duplicates of all such equipment.

STANDARD OPEN-HEARTH FURNACES

Open-hearth design was based on American and German models, standardized largely to one basic size: the 150-ton (56-square-meter) model.

Table 5–3   ORIGIN OF EQUIPMENT DESIGN FOR
OPEN-HEARTH STEEL-MAKING

Unit	Country of Origin	Firm
Open-hearth furnaces (150 tons per heat)	U.S.	Freyn Engineering Co.
Charging equipment	U.S.	Morgan Engineering Co.
Electric stripper cranes	U.S.	Morgan Engineering Co.
Pouring equipment	Germany	Demag A-G
Soaking pits	U.S.	Freyn Engineering Co.
Roller bearings for cranes, charging cars and ingot cars	Sweden	SKF

The Kuznetsk plant had 15 American-designed open-hearth furnaces and Magnitogorsk had 14 similar furnaces of 150 tons per heat, installed to operate on either producer or mixed blast-furnace/coke-oven gases. The shops were equipped with Morgan (United States) and Demag (Germany) charging and pouring equipment, all in duplicate.

Of steel-making shops constructed before 1934, five plants (Kuznetsk, Magnitogorsk, Zaporozhe, Kirov, and Dzherzhinsk) are described as having 'modern Martin shops of the American type.' These furnaces were mainly 150-tonners, although there were three 300-tonners of Freyn design. Four other plants had 'modern German shops' with 70-square-meter furnaces. The remainder had tilting or special furnaces of foreign design.[23]

A German study made in 1944 suggests that this foreign influence continued at least through World War II.[24]

DEVELOPMENT OF STANDARD BLOOMING AND SLABBING MILLS

Primary blooming and slabbing mills are used to break down ingots into sizes more suitable for final rolling into various shapes. Such mills are essential

---

[23] Institut promyshlenno-ekonomicheskikh issledovanni NKTP, *op. cit.*, p. 72.
[24] Report No. 68 of the Gmelin-Institute, *Eisenhüttenindustrie*, National Archives Microcopy T 84–127–1428293 *et seq.*

to large-tonnage operations and form part of all modern integrated iron and steel plants. There were no modern primary mills of this type in the Soviet Union before 1932. Each of the metallurgical giants, Magnitogorsk and Kuznetsk, was equipped with a Western-built mill—a Demag 45-inch mill with General Electric control and drive equipment—produced abroad and installed and started up in the U.S.S.R. by Demag and General Electric engineers.

The Soviets then adopted a standard blooming mill based on United and Demag 1150-millimeter (45-inch) design and duplicated at the Izhorsky and Kramatorsky plants, with the help of United Engineering, for installation in other iron and steel plants. Western blooming mills range from 40-inch to 78-inch roll widths; adoption of a standard 45-inch width obviously imposed limitations on the range of rolled products produced by the mills, but was consistent with the planning objective of producing a limited range of steel shapes and sizes with standardized equipment.[25]

Table 5–4   DESIGN CHRONOLOGY OF SOVIET LARGE
BLOOMING AND SLABBING MILLS, 1932–45

Date of Mill Start-Up	Mills of Foreign Design and Manufacture	Mills of Foreign Design and Technical Assistance, Made in Soviet Union	Mills of Soviet Design and Manufacture
Nov. 5, 1932: Kuznetsk	Demag A-G 45-inch mill; G.E. Co. control and drive equipment	—	—
1932: Magnitogorsk (section 1)	Demag A-G 45-inch mill; G.E. Co. control and drive equipment	—	—
Early 1933: Kirov (McKeevsky)	—	Izhorsk 45-inch 'standard'	—
June 1933: Dzherzhinsk	—	Izhorsk 45-inch 'standard'	—
August 1933: Magnitogorsk (section 2)	—	Kramatorsk 45-inch 'standard'	Demag A-G and United Engineering —
1934–1941: Zaporozhstal	—	Kramatorsk 45-inch 'standard'	—
Chelyabinsk	Demag A-G 43-inch	—	—
Zlatoust	—	Probably Kramatorsk	—
Total Mills	3 before World War II	5 before World War II	None between 1917 and 1945

[25]   See chap. 9 for information on assistance by United engineers in building the standardized duplicates.

Izvestia correctly claimed that the blooming mills at Kirov, Dzherzhinsk and Zlatoust utilized 'Soviet materials, Soviet workers and engineers.'[26] What *Izvestia* did *not* state was that these mills were of foreign design and duplicated in the Soviet Union with the help of U.S. steel-mill designers and engineers.[27] Adoption of a standard blooming mill design, although advantageous given the limited technical and innovatory resources available, inhibited adoption of newer rolling improvements. For example, the high-lift blooming mill, to handle wider ingots, was adopted in the United States after about 1940, but not in the U.S.S.R. The choice facing the Soviets, therefore, was to concentrate on duplication of a single standard proven design and achieve large-tonnage production by sacrificing the flexibility and economic advantages of a slower pace of technical adaptation. The road taken enabled training of cadres of mill operators and very rapid increases in production.

Bolshevik haste to meet propagandized deadlines also affected output; Frankfurt relates that the Kuznetsk mill was started up over the objections of Freyn engineers.[28] Output figures in the first four months suggest that a series of mill breakdowns was caused by this impatience. Start-up on November 5 produced 2,934 tons in that month and 6,108 tons in December. Then came two months with a little over 1,000 tons per month: less than 1 percent of capacity. In March the mill was in better shape and in September produced 30,000 tons, or 25 percent of capacity.[29]

THE UNITED ENGINEERING CONTRACT FOR HOT AND COLD CONTINUOUS WIDE-STRIP MILLS

By far the most significant advance in rolling technique in the twentieth century has been the American wide-strip mill producing hot and cold rolled wide steel strip—a prerequisite essential for automobile and appliance production.

The United Engineering and Foundry technical-assistance agreement, signed in February 1935, provided for transfer of both hot and cold stripmill

---

[26] November 26, 1932.

[27] See chap. 9.

[28] S. Frankfurt, *op. cit.*

[29] S. M. Veingarten, *Ekonomika i planirovanii a chernoi metallurgii SSSR* (Moscow: 1939), p. 361. Frankfurt's recollections of the premature start-up of the mill state that the Freyn engineers objected and boasts that 'Soviet people—builders, erectors, the operating staff—succeeded in mastering the complicated machinery without the help of Americans.' (Frankfurt, *op. cit.*, p. 113.) Any reader familiar with the highly skilled procedures of steel-mill operation will readily envisage the chaos that came to pass on November 5, 1932 at the Kuznetsk blooming mill.

Table 5-5   ORIGIN OF MAJOR ROLLING MILLS (OTHER THAN BLOOMING AND SLABBING MILLS) INSTALLED 1930–45

Plant	Flat Strip, Sheet, Skelp, and Plate	Light Structurals and Rod Bar Mills	Rail and Heavy Structural Mills	Continuous Hot Strip Mills	Cold Reduction Mills
Magnitogorsk	Sack skelp mill	Krupp rod mill Demag light bar mill	Demag rail and bar mills	U.S. 66", Siemag	U.S. 66"
Kuznetsk	Schloemann plate mill	Two Schloemann merchant mills	Schloemann rail mills Schloemann structural mills	—	—
Zaporozhe	U.S. equipment in cold mill	—	—	U.S. 66", United Engineering	U.S. 66", United Engineering; Demag skin pass mills
Dzherzhinsk	—	—	—	Universal mill, Krupp-Grusonwerk A-G	—
Dnepropetstal	Tube Reducing Co., Mannesman	—	—	—	—
Nikopol	Tube Reducing Co., Brown-Boveri Co. (Vienna)	—	—	—	—
Lend-Lease (unknown)					
Location I	—	18" merchant mill	—	—	—
Location II	Seamless pipe mill	—	—	—	—
Location III	Seamless pipe mill	—	—	—	—
Location IV	—	—	Rail mill, structural mill	—	—

Sources: American Iron and Steel Institute, *Steel in the Soviet Union* (New York: 1959).
U.S. State Dept. Decimal File, 861.60/325 and 861.6511/34.
U.S. State Dept., *Report on War Aid Furnished by the United States to the U.S.S.R.* (Washington: Office of Foreign Liquidation, 1945).
Iron and Steel Industry, June 1937, pp. 475-7.

technologies to the U.S.S.R.[30] and included a \$3-million equipment order and \$1 million for technical assistance. The contract also provided for installation of a complete electrically driven rolling mill at Zaporozhe. Part of this mill was to be built at Kramatorsk according to United drawings and with technical assistance provided by that company.[31] The mill installation, complete with a blooming mill, was similar to one already completed by United Engineering at the Ford River Rouge plant with an annual capacity of 600,000 metric tons of 60-inch hot and cold strip. At the same time an agreement was signed with American Standard Corporation for \$3 million worth of rolling-mill equipment.[32]

There is in the State Department files an excellent and objective interview of T. W. Jenkins, Chief Engineer for United Engineering in the Soviet Union, concerning the problems of installing the mill at Zaporozhe. The interview took place on February 2, 1937, some two years after signature of the agreement.

Jenkins had arrived in the U.S.S.R. in August 1936. Under the contract some of the equipment was to be built at the Kramatorsk plant. Jenkins and three other American engineers were to spend one year in the U.S.S.R. to install the United equipment, supervise construction in Soviet plants, and train Soviet engineers. One American engineer was stationed at Kramatorsk to ensure the quality of equipment being built there; this apparently presented some difficulties and Jenkins made arrangements, as could be done under the contract, for all Soviet equipment to be approved by the United engineer before shipment to Zaporozhe:

> One of the main difficulties experienced in this connection has been that the Soviet mechanics and engineers do not appreciate or understand the necessity for exact and precise work in connection with the construction of machinery. They do not keep within the allowances specified on the drawings. It is for this reason that many of the parts in the rolling mill which was operated in December did not stand up during the test.[33]

Jenkins suggested that installation might be completed by the end of 1937. By January 1939 the hot-strip mill was installed and operating at about 30 to 35 percent of capacity.[34] By the end of 1940 the mill was producing about

---

[30] See chap. 9. For a detailed description of the design and equipment of the Zaporozhe strip mill supplied by United Engineering and Foundry Co. see M. Stone, 'Continuous Wide Strip Mill Now Being Built in Russia,' *Steel*, December 9, 1935, pp. 32–5, 57. Stone was an engineer with United Engineering and Foundry. Also see U.S. State Dept. Decimal File, 861.64/17 and 861.6511/34, Moscow Embassy, 1937.

[31] U.S. State Dept. Decimal File, 861.6511/34; *New York Times*, February 26, 1935, p. 27.

[32] U.S. State Dept. Decimal File, 861.6511/34.

[33] *Ibid.*

[34] U.S. State Dept. Decimal File, 861.6511/42, Report No. 2008, Moscow Embassy, January 17, 1939.

1,500 tons of steel sheets per day.[35]

Steel tube mills relied exclusively on American (Tube Reducing Company) and German (Pilger, Mannesman) processes. In 1939 Howard Kenworthy, Assistant Chief Engineer for the Tube Reducing Company of New Jersey, stayed for six months at the Nikopol tube plant supervising installation of seven machines for the manufacture of carbon-steel and stainless-steel tubes. Two similar machines were supplied by the Tube Reducing Company for installation by Soviet engineers at the Dnepropetrovski plant. The total contract to supply the 'most modern' tube-manufacturing equipment was estimated to be worth between $750,000 and $1 million.[36]

Several other complete modern steel mills were supplied under the U.S. Lend-Lease program.[37] An 18-inch merchant mill valued at $3.5 million was completed and shipped by February 1945. Two pipe-fabrication mills for production of seamless pipe valued at a total of $1.2 million were shipped in May 1945. Another project valued at $15 million included a blooming mill, rail mill, structural mill, railroad tie and fishplate mill, and soaking pits, and was also exported during 1945 under the Lend-Lease program.

In addition to these complete installations, orders for $13.2 million worth of auxiliary steel-mill equipment (with the potential of increasing Soviet steel output by 2.5 million tons per year) were shipped under the program.[38]

CONSTRUCTION OF THE MAGNITOGORSK COMPLEX BY McKEE CORPORATION [39]

Planned as the largest steel complex in the world, Magnitogorsk is a replica of the United States Steel plant at Gary, Indiana, with an annual capacity of

---

[35]　*Ibid.*, 861.6511/46, Report No. 978, Moscow Embassy, December 4, 1940.

[36]　*Ibid.*, 861.60/325, Report No. 2154, Moscow Embassy, March 7, 1939. The electrical equipment for the Nikopol tube mills was built by the Brown-Boveri Co. in Vienna. This equipment comprised: two 900-kilowatt motors for the boring mills, two 600-kilowatt motors for the forming mills, and four 180-kilowatt motors for the tube-finishing mills. Two other motors were supplied for the reversing rollers in the forming mills (180-kilowatt). In addition two 2000-kilowatt motor generators were supplied for the rolling mill together with the necessary switchboards and circuit breakers. See *Brown-Boveri Review*, January/February 1934, p. 10.

[37]　U.S. State Dept., *Report on War Aid Furnished by the United States to the U.S.S.R.* (Washington: Office of Foreign Liquidation, 1945), p. 17.

[38]　*Ibid.* This discussion has concerned only some of the major iron and steel units. There is a complete detailed listing of 150 or so iron and steel plants dated 1944. (See Report No. 68 of Gmelin Institute, *Eisenhüttenindustrie*, National Archives Microcopy T 84–127–1428293 *et seq.*) This list included numerous installations not mentioned here; for example, a Davy mill in Leningrad, a Thomas Trio at Sormovo, a Bliss mill at Krasnyi Etna, several Lauta trios, a number of Universal mills, and numerous other foreign units. The writer has not found any evidence of a Soviet-designed mill in the period 1930–45.

[39]　*Berliner Tageblatt*, August 4, 1931. In addition to references cited in this section, see: Fred N. Hays, '5 Great Power Plants Rise at Magnitogorsk,' *Power*, August

2.46 million tons of finished steel products. The Soviets started to build the plant with their own resources and then, after almost two years of fruitless effort and a competitive battle between McKee and Siemens of Germany for the contract, handed planning and design over to the McKee Corporation. *Pravda* reported that construction started in early 1928 with plans to expend 84 million rubles by September 30, 1930;[40] in fact, only 20 million was expended and a large proportion of that was for the McKee design work. 'The principal cause of delay,' said *Pravda*, 'is the lazy work of political and professional leaders.'[41]

R. W. Stuck, American superintendent in charge of Magnitogorsk construction for the McKee Corporation, arrived at the site late May 1930 and found that the Soviets had started work on Blast Furnace No. 1. Stuck photographed preliminary excavation work on the No. 1 furnace site and also on the No. 2 site when he had gotten it to a similar stage.[42] At the peak of plant construction in late 1931 there were 250 Americans, as well as a large number of German and other foreign technicians, at Magnitogorsk.[43] Blast-furnace construction alone required 27 U.S. engineers, stationed by Stuck at the most strategic points of the project. The greatest single problem was to restrain Soviet engineers (known among the Americans as '90-day wonders'), who were convinced that a hastily devised three-month training program and revolutionary ardor were adequate substitutes for capitalist engineering experience. According to Stuck, Russian blast-furnace construction techniques were 50 to 75 years out of date, and attempted improvements by Russian engineers reduced, rather than enhanced, efficiency. Another problem was the creation of construction schedules for propaganda, irrespective of engineering feasibility. The Communist Party required start-up of Blast Furnace No. 1 on January 31, 1932: however, at that time the furnace was only three-quarters completed. As Stuck said, 'It was put into operation against our insistent demands not to do such a foolish and rash thing as the furnace was not ready and would be destroyed. . . .'[44]

1932, pp. 79–80, for German power station equipment: W. A. Haven, 'The Magnitogorski Mines and Metallurgical Plant,' *Blast Furnace and Steel Plant*, January 1931. Haven was Vice President of McKee Corp. and includes a layout diagram of the plant. E. C. Kreutzberg, 'Filling Equipment for Blast Furnace Steps-up Output," *Steel*, March 26, 1934, reviews Otis Elevator equipment and skips for Magnitogorsk blast furnaces. Also see W. A. Haven, 'Some Comments on the Design and Construction of a Mining and Metallurgical Plant for the U.S.S.R.,' *Mechanical Engineering*, XLV, 1932, pp. 461–6, 497.

40 *Pravda*, August 16, 1930.
41 *Ibid.*
42 The reader is referred to these comparative photographs: they illustrate the disorder of the Soviet attempt at excavation. See R. W. Stuck, 'First-Hand Impressions of Soviet Russia,' *Case Alumnus*, November 1932.
43 *La Vie Economique des Soviets*, No. 114, April 20, 1930, p. 15.
44 *American Engineers in Russia*, Stuck MSS, p. 41.

Attempts were also made, absurd as it may appear, to carry out construction according to pictorial rather than engineering objectives. According to Stuck, open-hearth stacks were built first, 'as these were very tall and made a nice picture. . . .'[45] There is support for Stuck's assertions: a close examination of early propaganda photographs of the Magnitogorsk plant indicates the absence of certain major components.[46]

Ultimate success in handling this political interference depended on personality. Ferguson, in charge of blast-furnace construction at Kuznetsk, had similar problems, laid down flat directives, and got away with them, while Stuck was rarely able to outwit or beat down the Party propagandists in their battle against engineering logic. Stuck outlined his construction problems at length and was particularly caustic in comments on Soviet planning and engineering practice. The contract provided that Magnitogorsk was to be designed and constructed 'according to the best and most modern metallurgical practice. . . .' There was, according to Stuck, dispute over where the best designs could be obtained; some Soviet engineers contending that 'German, French, British and their own methods were just as good and in most instances better than those prevalent in the United States.' On the contrary, Stuck estimated Russian practice at that time as being 'from half to three-quarters of a century behind the rest of the world.' Soviet engineering practice hardly impressed him; he noted, for example, the following:

> Even the anchor bolts for the building steel were not in line. They were never checked in spite of our pointing out . . . that serious results were bound to occur if the bolts did not line up properly. The steel was erected and the inevitable happened. The steel would not fit, the crane girder rails would not meet by four inches, yet the erectors started riveting the steel together and no one could stop them. The bricklayers started the brickwork around the columns even though they, as well as everyone else, knew that the steel was not set properly. Finally after an effort that almost took armed force to carry out I succeeded in having the work stopped and an attempt made to rectify the mistakes.[47]

Soviet purchasing commissions abroad buying equipment for Magnitogorsk were equally independent. For example:

> In connection with the gas cleaning system, the design called for disintegrators, which are large rotating drums driven at high speeds, causing the gas and water to be in more intimate contact and resulting in better cleaning of the gas. The design of the machines and their capacity were such that they would handle the greatest amount of gas the furnaces would ever produce. The design was approved by the Commission work-

[45]   *Ibid.*, p. 42.

[46]   See various issues of *U.S.S.R. in Construction.*

[47]   R. W. Stuck, 'First Hand Impressions of Soviet Russia,' *Case Alumnus*, XII, No. 2, November 1932, p. 10.

ing with our company, and the specifications sent to the Russian buyer in Germany, since the machines to be purchased were built in Germany. The Russian who was doing the buying felt that since he had not been consulted the design was certainly not correct, and that no one except he knew what they were doing. Therefore he, without consulting anyone else, bought machines of larger capacity. Consider for a moment what this meant. All piping connections, size of water lines, foundations of machines, buildings for the machines, in fact, all details of the design and installation were voided by his action in buying contrary to specification. . . . Of course, we were not let into the secret until the machines were purchased and on their way to the site.[48]

Both gas holders at Magnitogorsk were also imported from Germany and erected by German technicians at a cost of two and a half million gold rubles. Although erected in 1934, they were idle until 1940: operation was guaranteed only to $-15°C$ and the Plan did not allocate money for conversion, so for six years the combinat operated without a gas reserve.[49]

The General Electric Company, however, under its 1928 technical-assistance agreement, made an 'outstanding engineering contribution' by sending a 'special group of highly trained General Electric steel mill specialists who formed the nucleus of a steel mill electrical designing bureau . . . (at) Electroprom.'[50] This group supervised the electrical layout design for Magnitogorsk and other iron and steel plants. General Electric concluded, 'As a result of this co-operation, a large number of Soviet electrical engineers learned and obtained firsthand intimate knowledge of General Electric engineering methods as applied to the rolling mill industry.'[51]

CONSTRUCTION OF THE KUZNETSK COMPLEX BY THE FREYN ENGINEERING COMPANY[52]

Kuznetsk (known as Stalinsk after 1932) was designed and built by the Freyn Engineering Corporation of Chicago. The Freyn contract covered the entire Kuznetsk plant except the by-product coke plant and the chemical plants, which were the responsibility of a French company (Disticoque S.A.)

---

[48]   *Ibid.*, pp. 8–9.
[49]   Scott, *op. cit.*, pp. 182–3.
[50]   *The Monogram*, November 1943, p. 19.
[51]   *Ibid.*
[52]   Based on *American Engineers in Russia*, 'Statement of J. S. Ferguson Covering Personal Experiences in Russia over a Period of Eighteen Months,' April 30, 1933, pp. 2–3. Ferguson was superintendent of blast-furnace construction at Kuznetsk. Also see E. P. Everhard, 'Kuznetsk Steel Plant in U.S.S.R.,' *Blast Furnace and Steel Plant*, December 1932, pp. 889–93, and M. J. Wohlgemuth, 'Building a Steel Plant in Soviet Russia,' *The Electric Journal*, February 1934, pp. 62–7. Wohlgemuth was Assistant Chief Electrical Engineer for Freyn at Kuznetsk, and his article has excellent data on the electrical equipment at the mill.

under contract to Kokstroi (Coke Industry Construction Trust). Freyn also supervised modernization of all tsarist plants scheduled for reconstruction elsewhere in Russia under the First Five-Year Plan. The only iron and steel plant not covered by the Freyn contract was the Magnitogorsk complex, under contract to McKee Corporation and Demag A-G. The rolling mills were built and installed by two German companies: Demag A-G and Schloemann A-G. Individual equipment items were purchased from the supplier offering the best terms and technical specifications, and were selected initially by Freyn, subject to approval by a Soviet commission. The company had contractual responsibility for equipment acceptance and operations during the initial six months. The 115,000-cubic-foot-per-minute capacity turbo-blowers were supplied by Brown-Boveri of Switzerland; the disintegrators were Zschocke. Freyn designed, built and installed the automatic ore-hoppers, the pressure burners and stock-line recorders. Demag A-G built the ore bridge cranes and Pollock-type hot-metal ladles as well as the rolling mills. Charging cars were by Orr, skip and bell hoists by Otis, clay guns by Brossius, stock distributors by McKee, and the automatic hot-blast controls by Bristol: all were manufactured in the United States. The only items for Kuznetsk manufactured in the Soviet Union were Dewhurst slag ladles.

The service units at the Kuznetsk plant were supplied from Europe. A refractories plant (for fire-clay and silica-brick products for the furnaces) utilized German equipment and was built by German engineers. In power plant No. 6, the generator (of the standard type) was made in the U.S.S.R., probably by the Elektrosila plant in Leningrad. The condenser equipment was from Wumag (Germany) and the turbine drives from Rateau (France).

Between 1929 and December 1932, construction of the first section of Kuznetsk was under general supervision of E. P. Everhard, who had 70 U.S. engineers working for him. They supervised construction and initial operation of the plant in December 1932, and when they left, the plant had achieved an annual rate of 450,000 tons, compared to the control figure of 330,000 tons.[53] The director of Kuznetsk while it was under construction was Sergei Mironovitch Frankfurt,[54] a former textile mill operator, while I. P. Bardin, a well-known Russian metallurgist, was Frankfurt's chief engineer. Assistants to Frankfurt were Party men with little knowledge of iron and steel plants. Everhard, senior American engineer on site, apparently had effective control while construction was under way. For example, Everhard comments (with reference to Frankfurt and Bardin):

> I made it a hard and fast rule that no Russian, not even the Red Director or technical superintendent could authorize the changing of the

[53] *American Engineers in Russia*, Folder 4, Report 9.
[54] S. Frankfurt, *op. cit.*

burden or temperature and volume of the blast. This precaution saved us trouble many times later on. . . .[55]

The rolling mills for the first section of Kuznetsk (construction of which was supervised by Americans) had been imported. The blooming mill was a 45-inch Demag with drive and control equipment by General Electric. The rail mill, the 24-inch structural mill, the 70-inch plate mill, and two merchant mills for rods, rounds, bars, sections, and agricultural shapes were made and installed by Schloemann A-G of Germany. All mill cranes were either from Germany or the United States, and all mill motors of over 25 horsepower were imported and mainly of General Electric design. The only Soviet-made equipment in the first section of the Kuznetsk rolling mills were mill motors of less than 25 horsepower made to General Electric design; these powered the 'live rollers.'[56]

The second section of Kuznetsk was begun immediately but with a significant difference. Construction was now under Soviet supervision; foreign participation was limited to the installation and operation of imported equipment, which consisted mainly of rolling mills. An article in *Za Industrializatsiiu* (Moscow) for March 24, 1933, reports on progress of this second section. The Soviet-built equipment consisted of the sixth turbo-generator, boilers number 5, 6, and 7, and 900-millimeter rolling mill, and the model 210 crane. The second unit of Kuznetsk included blast furnaces No. 3 and 4 of the standard type,[57] the last five open hearths, two section mills, a sheet mill, and coke-oven batteries No. 3 and 4. This second section included imported equipment and a larger proportion of Soviet duplicates of foreign equipment made with foreign technical assistance.

CONCLUSIONS

Iron and steel plant construction and reconstruction in the period from 1928 through 1932 was of American design and was built under the supervision of American and some German engineers, utilizing imported equipment from either the United States or Germany but usually manufactured to American design.

Gipromez, the metallurgical design bureau, was charged in 1928 with the transfer of American technology, and for this purpose a number of American engineers took over key positions. Its function was to compare foreign

---

[55] E. P. Everhard, *op. cit.*, p. 25. (See fn. 52 above.)

[56] *American Engineers in Russia*, 'Statement of J. S. Ferguson Covering Personal Experiences in Russia over a Period of Eighteen Months,' April 30, 1933, p. 3.

[57] Blast furnaces Nos. 1 and 2 had capacities of 1,164 cubic meters, and Nos. 3 and 4 had capacities of 1,163 cubic meters.

technologies, select the most suitable, and develop this as a Soviet standard; this standard design was duplicated during the period 1932 to 1945 with U.S. and German engineering assistance.

The standard blast furnaces were initially of Freyn design. The McKee design was not duplicated. The second standard was a 1300-cubic-meter design produced by Gipromez without assistance by 1938, but not widely utilized. The standard open-hearth furnace was a Freyn 150-ton design. The standard hot and cold continuous wide-strip mills were of United Engineering design. Product and merchant rolling mills were of the U.S. type, although originally made in Germany and then duplicated by Soviet machine-building plants. Demag slabbing and blooming mills were also adopted.[58]

Thus between 1928 and 1945 there was complete diffusion of iron and steel technology from capitalist countries (primarily the U.S. and Germany) to the Soviet Union; the Soviets utilized proven foreign designs and adapted them, with foreign help for their standards. No reverse diffusion from the Soviet Union to the U.S. has been found; neither has any indigenous Soviet innovation, apart from the Gipromez 1300-cubic-meter second standard design and several larger open-hearth furnace designs.

[58]   Tube mills will be considered in Volume III. There were in Russia in this period Mannesman and Pilger mills and a Tube Reducing Co. mill (at Nikopol).

CHAPTER SIX

Technical Assistance to the Fuel Industries

'MISTER GRAVER, WHO BECAME COMRADE GRAVER'[1]

IN 1930 the Soviet Union had a refinery capacity of about 95 million barrels per year in shell still units which were built before 1917 and yielded kerosene and oils rather than gasoline. Volume I briefly outlines extensive construction of new shell still and pipe still units during the period 1927–30 by German companies (Borman, Pintsch, and Wilke), and then British (Vickers) and American companies (Graver, Badger, Foster-Wheeler, Max Miller, Winkler-Koch, and Alco Products).[2] This first construction phase (which ended in 1932–3 with the departure of American engineers, although some Germans remained on individual ruble contracts) added a refinery capacity of about 96 million barrels, including lubricating and Winkler-Koch cracking units, not previously known in Russia.

Even the propaganda magazine of the First Five-Year Plan acknowledged this enormous debt to American technology. Under the title, 'Mister Graver, Who Became Comrade Graver' this acquisition was described:

> Baku and Grozny adopted Graver—an American; following in Graver's footsteps came 'Badger'—a kerosene and oil still; then came 'Foster' and then a cracking still of the 'Winkler, Cokh & Jenkins' [sic] system. This year another foreign child adopted by the Soviet petroleum workers —the 'Max Miller' still which produces high-grade cylinder oils, will be put into operation.[3]

In 1932–3 the Soviets started to build their own refinery equipment, based on imported designs. Machine shops at Baku, Grozny, Podolsk and other locations were assigned to the oil industry for this purpose. Little progress

---

[1] *U.S.S.R. in Construction*, No. 12, 1931.
[2] Sutton, *Western Technology . . ., 1917 to 1930*, pp. 35–40.
[3] *U.S.S.R. in Construction*, No. 12, 1931.

was made, as both the shops and the personnel were unsuited to the heavy work involved in refinery construction.

THE RETURN OF U.S. FIRMS FOR CONSTRUCTION OF THE 'SECOND BAKU'

In 1936 American refinery construction companies were called back and remained in the Soviet Union until 1945. Badger, Alco Products, Universal Oil Products, Winkler-Koch, McKee, Petroleum Engineering, Lummus Company of New York, and Max Miller expanded older locations at Baku, Grozny, and Batum and built the refineries at the 'Second Baku.'

On July 10, 1936 a contract was signed by the Petroleum Engineering Company of Tulsa, Oklahoma and by the McKee Corporation for expansion of the Baku petroleum refinery.[4] Technical assistance, drawings, material, and equipment were sold for a total of $178,780 to build an absorption plant, crude stabilizer, gasoline-stabilizing units, butane-fractionating unit, and propane-fractionating unit. Capacity of the complex was 5,000 barrels per day with an input of 24 million cubic feet per day of natural gas. The Brown Instrument Company supplied the control equipment.[5] By 1939, however, the complex was reported only 80 percent complete.[6] It is a reasonable inference that similar contracts were let and units built at Batum. An Embassy official toured the Batum complex in 1938 and reported that it had four Winkler-Koch, four Jenkins, and four Foster-Wheeler stills.[7] This is a greater number than had been built in the period 1928–31. Since no Soviet construction has been reported, it is a reasonable inference that six units were built by American companies between 1932 and 1938. In the late 1930s the Universal Oil Products Company installed high-octane gasoline plants at both Grozny and Saratov. These were polymerization units about equal in size, and they were about 60 percent complete in 1940 when the American engineers were withdrawn.[8]

However, the major focus of American refinery-construction effort after 1936 was not in the Baku-Batum-Grozny region, but farther north, along the Volga River in the 'Second Baku.'

In 1938 another contract was made with the Universal Oil Products Company for installation of a hydrogenation and iso-octane plant (see figure 6–1)

[4]   U.S. State Dept. Decimal File, 861.602/299, Report No. 1419, Moscow Embassy, June 27, 1938.
[5]   *Ibid.*, 861.6363/345. These were original Brown control units, not copies made under the company's technical-assistance agreement. (See p. 165.)
[6]   *Ibid.*, 861.6363/351, Report No. 2024, Moscow Embassy, January 19, 1939.
[7]   *Ibid.*, 861.6363/341, Report No. 1327, Moscow Embassy, June 1, 1938. This is a lengthy but rather vague report; no other technical details are included.
[8]   *Ibid.*, 861.6363/370, Report No. 263, Moscow Embassy, January 18, 1940.

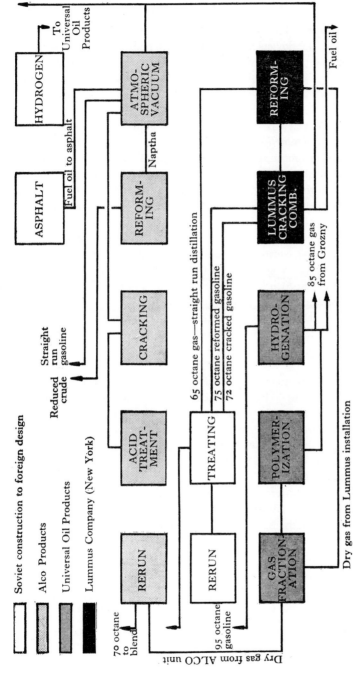

Figure 6-1 FOREIGN AND SOVIET CONSTRUCTION OF THE UFA PETROLEUM REFINERY COMPLEX, 1938–40

Soviet construction to foreign design

Alco Products

Universal Oil Products

Lummus Company (New York)

HYDROGEN

To Universal Oil Products

ASPHALT

ATMO-SPHERIC VACUUM

Fuel oil to asphalt

Naptha

REFORM-ING

REFORM-ING

Fuel oil

Straight run gasoline

Reduced crude

CRACKING

LUMMUS CRACKING COMB.

65 octane gas—straight run distillation

75 octane reformed gasoline

72 octane cracked gasoline

85 octane gas from Grozny

ACID TREAT-MENT

TREATING

HYDRO-GENATION

POLYMER-IZATION

RERUN

RERUN

GAS FRACTION-ATION

70 octane to blend

95 octane gasoline

Dry gas from ALCO unit

Dry gas from Lummus installation

Source: U.S. State Dept. Decimal File, 861.602/285.

at Chernikova, 35 kilometers from Ufa, in the 'Second Baku.'[9] This was the first installation of its type in the Soviet Union and of some importance, since to this time the Soviets had been unable to make 87 or 94 octane gasoline for aviation use. The hydrogenation units built by Universal Oil Products received 85 octane gasoline from Saratov and Grozny and polymerization charge stock from the Alco and Lummus units, and converted this into 95 octane aviation gasoline.[10]

The refinery at Ufa was built by Alco Products (the oil-refining division of American Locomotive) and consisted of an atmospheric vacuum unit, reformer, cracking plant, rerun unit, and acid-treating plant.[11] The value of the equipment supplied was $1 million, 50 percent payable when the equipment was delivered to the dock in New York and 50 percent when the plant was completely in operation. Alco provided supervision of construction and technical assistance, and supervised initial operation of the refinery. Until the plant began to produce in 1937, the Alco Company kept five engineers on the Ufa site to supervise construction and train Russian workers in operation. It was reported by Alco engineers that the OGPU was in 'absolute control.'[12] The total cost of the Alco Products contract, including services, was $2.5 million.

The third part of the Ufa complex was built by the Lummus Corporation of New York and consisted of cracking and reforming units to produce 500,000 tons of 66 octane gasoline per year, to feed into the rerun and treating units.[13]

In April 1939 only four of the six units under construction were actually in operation.[14]

There were numerous problems at Ufa; one reported by several engineers concerned attempts by Soviet engineers to change the original designs. Meredith commented, 'I was surprised to learn upon my arrival that the preliminary work already done by Soviet engineers had changed the original design and line-up of equipment as provided for in the plans.'[15] Soviet engineers had decided to discard the centrifugal refining process and 'to install in its stead a new chemical process which had recently been developed by a firm in Kansas.' Meredith suggested that this process was still in the experimental stage and not well-adapted to the type of crude oil intended to be run through the Ufa refinery. Later he added that 'during my entire stay in Ufa I

[9]   *Ibid.*, 861.6363/340, Report No. 1292, Moscow Embassy, May 20, 1938.
[10] *Ibid.*, 861.6363/370, Enclosure to Report No. 263, January 18, 1940.
[11] *Ibid.*, 861.6363/348, Report No. 1651, Moscow Embassy, September 15, 1938. Also see 861.602/285, Report No. 2203, Moscow Embassy, January 16, 1937. For Soviet attitudes toward Alco Products and E. B. Badger and Sons during negotiations, see pp. 264–6 and U.S. State Dept. Decimal File, 861.602/263.
[12] *Ibid.*, 861.6363/348.
[13] *Ibid.*, 861.6363/340, Report No. 1292, Moscow Embassy, May 20, 1938.
[14] *Ibid.*, 861.6363/353, Report No. 2240, Moscow Embassy, April 10, 1939.
[15] *Ibid.*, 861.602/285.

was continually obliged to insist that the Soviet engineers construct the plant according to plan and not try to put in so-called improvements.' Meredith indicated to the Soviets that if the plant was not constructed exactly according to the plans as provided for in the contract, Alco would take no responsibility for the final results.

Crude oil for the Ufa plant came from fields about 200 kilometers to the southeast; Soviet organizations had nearly completed construction of the pipelines while the refinery was being built. From partial examination of the lines and from reports from other engineers, Meredith concluded that there would be considerable difficulty in maintaining the lines; there were no boosting stations anywhere along the 200-kilometer length and, despite the extreme Russian climate, no provision had been made for expansion joints, 'so that there will undoubtedly be continuous leaks and breakdown.'[16] The Alco Company was not able to acquire samples of the crude oil for analysis, but Meredith suggested that if it had the high sulphur and water content rumored, it would be 'extremely difficult to refine it by the chemical process which has been adopted.'[17]

That great value was attached by the highest political authorities to the work of these American engineers and the installations supplied by these firms was demonstrated in 1939, when the Soviets refused to allow the employees of the Max B. Miller Company to travel from Grozny to the U.S. Embassy in Moscow to have their passports renewed. The Soviets apparently thought the Americans were planning to leave the Soviet Union.[18]

Mashinoimport telegraphed the Miller Company in the United States, stating 'that the Company's engineers for "unknown causes" insist upon leaving and request[ed] the Company to instruct them to continue their work until the plant is in operation.'[19] In the meantime the Soviet authorities, according to the U.S. Embassy, stalled the engineers, first promising them transportation, then insisting it was not available, and finally stating that the trip to Moscow was not necessary, as 'arrangements' had been made with the U.S. Embassy. The Embassy commented that 'this misrepresentation could only have been made for the purpose of misleading the engineers into believing the trip to Moscow to be unnecessary.'[20]

---

[16] *Ibid.*

[17] *Ibid.* It appears extraordinary that the Alco Products Company would have received a contract to design a refining unit without samples of the crude oil to be used. It would be possible to do this from the Russian specifications but certainly not in the best interests of efficient operation. This is an example of the deep-seated Soviet distrust of foreign organizations: a completely unfounded distrust, as there is no question that the American firms were providing excellent equipment.

[18] U.S. State Dept. Decimal File, 361.11 Employees/360, December 28, 1939.

[19] *Ibid.*

[20] *Ibid.*

Later, after some negotiation, the Russians acquiesced to the principle that American citizens had freedom to travel to Moscow to renew passports but expressed concern over the departure of Rodman, Rasmussen (in charge of construction at Grozny for a Universal Oil Products polymerization unit), Miller, Hanson, and Owens:

> Potemkin [the Russian ambassador] expressed great concern over the serious effect which their withdrawal would have on the large investment of the Soviet Union in the respective plants the construction of which they have been supervising and particularly emphasised the urgent desire of the Soviet Government to retain the services of Rasmussen whose work appears to be most vital until the period specified under his contract shall have expired.[21]

Table 6–1   PERCENTAGE OF SOVIET REFINERY AND
CRACKING CAPACITY WITH FOREIGN
DESIGN AND CONSTRUCTION, 1932 AND 1945

	Foreign Design and Construction		Soviet Construction Using Foreign Design	
	*1932**	*1945***	*1932**	*1945***
Refineries	77.5%	n.a.	22.5%	n.a.
Lubricating oil plants	96.4%	99.3%	3.6%	0.7%
Cracking plants	91.6%	94.7%	8.4%	5.3%

Sources: 1932 data calculated from *The Petroleum Times*, February 13, 1932, p. 173. 1945 data calculated from data in U.S. State Dept. files.

* The data used were incomplete. This was by far the most difficult industrial sector to reconstruct, because of numerous name changes of individual refineries and the almost complete lack of usable Soviet data. Although these percentages do cross-check, for example, with the unpublished 1935 plan for refinery construction in the Smolensk archives, they are not presented as definitive. The general order of magnitude is, however, quite acceptable.

** Excludes tsarist construction.

These units were supplemented by four complete refineries supplied under Lend-Lease and shipped during 1943. A total of 100,000 tons of equipment comprised these four units.[22] In early 1944 the Soviets approached seven United States manufacturers of refinery equipment concerning equipment deliveries in the postwar period,[23] and equipment deliveries were made under the 1945 pipeline agreement.[24] In late 1944, when Soviet troops entered Rumania they dismantled large quantities of refinery equipment (including Romana Americana and Astra Romana refineries) from the Rumanian oil fields and shipped it to the U.S.S.R. It is interesting to note, in light of continuing U.S. and British Lend-Lease assistance and the alliance against Nazi Germany, that

[21] U.S. State Dept. Decimal File, 700.00116 M.E./24, Telegram, December 29, 1939.
[22] *Ibid.*, 861.24/1473, Telegram, Moscow to Washington, D.C., May 24, 1943.
[23] *Ibid.*, 861.50/2944, Memorandum, WEA to AA (State Dept.), May 29, 1944.
[24] To be covered in Volume III.

'removal of equipment [was] limited to companies owned by Americans and British and others have not yet been disturbed.'[25]

LUBRICATING-OIL UNITS BY MILLER AND ALCO PRODUCTS

At the end of 1931 the Soviets had about 11 million barrels per year of lubricating-oil capacity, one-half of which had been built before 1917 and the other half by German and U.S. companies at the end of the 1920s. The largest single unit added between 1932 and 1945 was a Max Miller bright-stock plant at Baku, designed to produce almost 3 million barrels per year of high-grade lubricating oils.[26] This was supplemented by a 700,000-barrel Russian-built Pengu-Gurevitch vacuum unit.

The Max Miller unit at Baku was erected under the supervision of Miller Company Chief Engineer Werner Hofmann. Twice during its construction Hofmann left the Soviet Union and was interviewed on the progress of his work. In December 1931 he reported problems with refinery construction; for example, on one job, he said that there were 'one thousand leaks where there should not have been more than ten or twenty.'[27]

In November 1932, leaving for the last time, he was more caustic in his comments on the Soviet Union in general and the Max Miller plant in particular. After dismissing the Soviet Union with the statement that 'the entire present regime is one big lie,'[28] he said that the Miller plant had cost $5 million but that only $25 worth of maintenance tools were available, adding that one shop had a half million dollars invested in one type of machine but that he couldn't get rags to wipe off the oil. Hofmann himself bought cloth in the foreigners' store to make wiping rags, but the workers took it to make children's clothes. These workers, he added, had neither protective clothing nor work clothes.[29]

Another lubricating-oil unit, with a capacity of 1.4 million barrels, was built at Batum by Foster-Wheeler. Three other units were built at Grozny (another Foster-Wheeler 1.4-million-barrel unit and two Alco Products units: one in 1933 and one in 1938–9), with an aggregate capacity of about 3.8 million barrels. In 1939 it was reported that the Max Miller Company had another lubricating-oil unit under construction at Grozny.[30]

[25] U.S. State Dept. Decimal File, 871.6363/11–244, Telegram 1106, November 2, 1944. Reparations as a development mechanism will be explored in Volume III.

[26] *World Petroleum*, May 1932.

[27] U.S. State Dept. Decimal File, 861.5017—Living Conditions/389, Report No. 755, Vienna, December 12, 1931.

[28] U.S. State Dept. Decimal File, 861.5017—Living Conditions/389, Report of November 9, 1932.

[29] *Ibid.*

[30] *Ibid.*, 861.6363/351, Report No. 2024, Moscow Embassy, January 19, 1939.

WINKLER-KOCH GASOLINE-CRACKING TECHNOLOGY

The Soviet Union continued to be dependent on Western technology (primarily American) for cracking petroleum into light gasoline fractions. Lend-Lease equipment deliveries were sufficient to bring the output of aviation gasoline from only 110,000 metric tons per year in 1941 to 1.67 million metric tons in 1944, despite the fact that several Lend-Lease cracking units were not delivered until after the end of the war.

In 1931–2 the Winkler-Koch Engineering Corporation of Wichita designed and furnished to the Soviets 15 cracking units to produce gasoline from fuel oil and gas oil derived from Russian crudes; these units comprised about 85 percent of the total cracking capacity in the U.S.S.R. in the 1930s.[31] *The Petroleum Times* reported: 'These units were erected by Russian labour and Russian engineers supervised by Winkler-Koch construction engineers. The operation and instructions to the Russian operators during the test runs of the units were in charge of Winkler-Koch operators.'[32]

This cracking capacity of almost 20 million barrels a year was erected in only two years; 'only 14 months elapsed from the time the first unit was completed and put on stream until the last of the 15 units was erected, tested out and fully accepted with all guarantees fulfilled.'[33]

Three Vickers (United Kingdom) units were erected at Baku and Grozny in 1928–9. It was apparently from the Vickers cracking system that the Soviets derived their own standard system. An article by Professor Andreyev in *The Petroleum Times* stated that 'the ability to conduct liquid-phase cracking— a technical process new to the U.S.S.R.—was in the main acquired at the Vickers refinery, the first industrial cracking plant to appear in the Soviet Union.'[34] This process was then called the Shukov-Kapelyushnikov system and was used to build two cracking units in 1931 at Baku with a total capacity of 2.1 million barrels a year. No further units were built to this system.

Winkler-Koch and Alco Products systems were used for those units built in the middle and late 1930s, at which time the Houdry catalytic plants were received under Lend-Lease; this certainly suggests that the 'Soviet-Vickers' process was not as effective as either the Winkler-Koch or the Alco Products system.

The U.S. responded in 1939 to the Soviet attack on Finland and decided that 'there should be no further delivery to certain countries of plans, plants, manufacturing rights, or technical information required for the production of

[31]   *The Petroleum Times*, February 13, 1932, p. 173.
[32]   *Ibid.*, p. 174.
[33]   *Ibid.*
[34]   December 29, 1934, p. 700.

Table 6-2   CRACKING UNITS BUILT IN SOVIET UNION, 1932–45

Location	Built 1930–32[1],[2] (Units)	Capacity (Barrels/Day)	Built 1932–41[3],[4] (Units)	Capacity (Barrels/Day)	Built 1941–5[5] (Units)	Capacity (Barrels/Day)
Batum	4 Winkler-Koch 2 Jenkins	14,000	Universal Oil Products*			
Baku	4 Winkler-Koch 2 Vickers 2 Kapelushnikov	14,000	Petroleum Engineering Co.* McKee Corp.*			
Grozny	6 Winkler-Koch 1 Jenkins 1 Vickers	21,000	Alco Products[3]* Max Miller[7]* Universal Oil Products[9]*			
Tuapse	4 Winkler-Koch	7,000				
Yaroslavl	1 Winkler-Koch	2,000	1 Winkler-Koch	6,000		
Konstaninovka	1 Winkler-Koch	3,500 (estimate)[1]				
Khabarovsk	—		2 Winkler-Koch	7,000[1]		
Saratov	—		Universal Oil Products[9]	6,000[1]		
Cherson	—		1 Winkler-Koch	2,800[4]		
Berdyansk	—		1 Winkler-Koch	2,800[4]		
Ufa	—		Alco Products, Inc.[6]* Universal Oil Products[8]* Lummus Company[8]*			
Syzran	—				4 units Lend-Lease	7,000 each

Sources: [1] *World Petroleum*, May 1932, pp. 200–1; July 1931, p. 436.   [2] *The Petroleum Times*, February 13, 1932, p. 173. [3] Generalstab des Heeres. Microcopy T-78, Roll 491, Frame 647382–759. [4] Oberkommando der Wehrmacht (OKW/Wi Rü Amt/Wi), March 1941, *Erdölfund-und Erdölverar im Kaukasischen R* (incomplete title in original). [5] U.S. State Dept., *Report on War Aid Furnished by the United States to the U.S.S.R.* (Washington: Office of Foreign Liquidation, 1945), p. 16. An additional seven refinery and cracking units were supplied to the Soviet Union under U.S. Lend-Lease. As these were shipped after the end of World War II and did not come on-stream until the late 1940s and 1950s, they will be treated in Vol. III. [6] U.S. State Dept. Decimal File, 861.602/285 (January 16, 1937).   [7] *Ibid*, 361.11 Employees/360, December 28, 1939. [8] *Ibid*, 861.6363/310.   [9] *Ibid*, 861.6363/370.

* Exact numbers of units unknown.

high quality aviation gasoline.'[35] This left the Soviets unprepared for the demands of World War II, so that one-quarter of all aviation gasoline had to be imported under Lend-Lease, together with four complete Houdry catalytic cracking and alkylation plants, totaling some three million metric tons of capacity.[36]

As part of Lend-Lease assistance, and at the request of 'government agencies,' the Standard Oil Company of New York was said either to have supplied or to be preparing to supply the Soviet Union with technical information, plant designs, and pilot manufacturing plants for the following processes: sulfuric acid alkylation for production of 100 octane gasoline, 'voltolization' of fatty oils for production of aviation lubricating oils, the manufacture of hydrogen from methane, the production of alcohol from refinery gases, and the production of Buna-S.[37]

The assistance in production of Buna-S is interesting in that the Soviets, as will be described later, had had an initial advantage in synthetic-rubber production by building on tsarist-era research and by establishing manufacturing facilities predating those in the West. Their requirement for foreign Buna-S technology would suggest that in the conversion from laboratory production to practical manufacture the system had failed in some respects.

WESTERN ASSISTANCE FOR MECHANIZATION OF COAL MINES

The first technical-assistance agreements concluded in 1926 were with U.S. and German engineering consultant firms for the coal-mining industry. Agreements with Stuart, James and Cooke, Roberts & Schaefer, and Allen & Garcia in the United States were renewed in the early 1930s,[38] so that these three companies operated continuously in the Soviet Union for at least five to six years, reorganizing and expanding coal mines in the Donbas and the Urals. Up to 1930–1 almost all equipment used in coal mines was imported, but in that year a few domestic machines based on Western designs and produced under technical-assistance contracts were first used in Russian coal mines.

Stuart, James and Cooke, Inc., made its first agreement, with Donugol (Don Coal Trust), in October 1926 and started work on March 25, 1927.[39] This agreement was for schematic projects for two mines in the Donbas. The work accomplished must have been acceptable, as the company was given a

[35]   U.S. State Dept. Decimal File, 861.796/98a, Telegram, December 24, 1939.
[36]   U.S. State Dept., *Report on War Aid Furnished by the United States to the U.S.S.R.* (Washington: Office of Foreign Liquidation, 1945).
[37]   U.S. State Dept. Decimal File, 861.6363/439, Letter: Standard Oil of New York to State Department, April 5, 1943.
[38]   See Sutton, *Western Technology . . ., 1917 to 1930*, chap. 3.
[39]   Amtorg, *op. cit.*, VI, No. 6 (March 15, 1931), pp. 135–8.

more extensive contract to make schematic projects for the Yugostal (Southern Steel Trust) coal mines and five mines for Moskvugol (State Association for Coal Industry in the Moscow Region Basin). This contract was followed by another three-year contract for technical assistance to Donugol, Moskvugol, and Uralugol. Ten company engineers were assigned to this contract, which expired in November 1931. Other Stuart contracts in the coal industry (there was one for the iron-ore mines as well) included a two-year agreement with Donugol, signed March 24, 1930, for five additional engineers to rehabilitate Donbas coal mines, a contract with Shakhtostroi (Shaft-Sinking Trust) for five key technical men to plan coal mines west of the River Volga, and a contract for an additional five engineers to give technical aid to coal mines of the Vostokugol (Far East Coal Trust), east of the Volga. In all, the company had 11 separate contracts for technical assistance to the coal mines of the Soviet Union between 1926 and early 1931.[40]

The Allen & Garcia Company had two forces in Russia: 20 engineers at Kharkov and 15 at Tomsk. This company had previously built the largest mine in the world: the Orient, at Franklin, Illinois,[41] and in 1929 signed a second contract for technical assistance in the design and construction of new shafts in the Donbas and in Siberia.

One function of Allen & Garcia was to design coal-cleaning plants, but this work apparently was ignored by the Soviet planners. According to J. A. Garcia, writing in 1934:

> We made a good many designs for coal cleaning plants both in the Don Basin and Siberia, but none of them were built, and the other American engineering firms had the same experience from 1926 to date. However, the Germans did build one large cleaning plant for them in the Don Basin at Gorlovka, and Mr. Appleyard of England built a dry cleaning plant of about 100 tons per hour in 1933. Outside of these two plants our fellows know of no cleaning plants built in the entire Soviet Union since we started working with them in 1927.[42]

As a result of this planning decision, the Soviet Union transported two million tons of ash and dirt attached to coal in 1931 alone.

The use of individual foreign technical personnel (as distinct from those imported by formal agreement with foreign firms) in the coal mines probably peaked about 1931,—at least until German occupation of the Don. In 1931 there were about 2,000 foreign specialists in the Don coal mines, about 80 percent of them German.[43] In 1931 some German personnel started to return home as a result of bad working conditions, but other reports suggest that

[40] *Ibid.*

[41] *Ibid.*, IV, No. 18 (September 15, 1929), p. 302.

[42] *American Engineers in Russia*, Letter, J. A. Garcia to H. H. Fisher, March 28, 1934.

[43] U.S. State Dept. Decimal File, 861.6362/48.

a large number did remain throughout the 1930s, and even while some German miners were reported leaving the Donbas, American miners—perhaps as many as 1,500—were reported arriving in the Leninsk mines in Siberia. Five groups arrived by August 1931 and others were expected to follow.[44] Also, Isaac Goldfein, a chemical engineer at the Kemerovo coke plant for 10 years, reported that in late 1932 a group of 50 German engineers and technicians were sinking new shafts for an 800,000-ton-per-year coal mine in Kemerovo.

> The Russians sank the first shafts themselves, but they had difficulty in preventing the flow of water from underground water courses, and by following their own methods permitted large portions of the mine to fill with water. German engineers are engaged in damming up the flow of water by a freezing method.[45]

It was the larger mines that were designed and brought into production by American consultant firms between 1928 and 1933 and operated by German technicians after about 1931. The largest of these was the OGPU mine in the Shakhty district, with an investment of eight million rubles, closely followed by the Amerikanka, also with an investment of eight million rubles. Others were the Nikitovka, Lutiaino, and Karl No. 7–8. While not as large in initial development, these were far larger than existing operations. They all became the show mines for visiting Communists and foreign tourists. Astute observers, however, noted that women still comprised 50 percent of the underground labor force[46] and that 'prisoner-engineers' were used.[47] In the Kuznetsk Basin, the largest mine was the Capital Coke Mine, started in 1929 with a capacity of one million tons of coking coal per year; J. W. Powell was consulting engineer.[48]

The emphasis on concentrating existing coal mines into fewer large shafts (designed by the United States firms) while at the same time opening up new areas behind the Urals was continued from 1930 until 1945.[49] The concentration in the Donbas areas is shown in table 6–3.

There were no shafts producing in excess of 500,000 tons per year before 1928, while in 1941 more than 17 percent came from such large-capacity shafts; almost 83 percent of output came from shafts producing more than 100,000 tons per year in 1941, compared to only 31 percent in 1928–9.

Foreign technical assistance in coal mining expired before that in any other industry, and by 1932–3 Soviet industry was on its own, although still

---

[44]   *Ibid.*, 861.6362/50.
[45]   *Ibid.*, 861.5017—Living Conditions/536, Riga, September 28, 1932.
[46]   K. Legay, *Un Mineur Français chez les Russes* (Paris: Editions Pierre Tisne, 1937), p. 58.
[47]   E. G. Grady, *Seeing Red* (New York: Brewer, Warren and Putnam, Inc., 1931), pp. 50–1.
[48]   Amtorg, *op. cit.*, IV, No. 10 (May 15, 1929), p. 201.
[49]   See Sutton, *Western Technology . . ., 1917 to 1930*, p. 56.

receiving substantial quantities of imported equipment. The reorganization underway since 1926 under these contracts began to pay off. Whereas the average annual increase in labor productivity was 6.3 percent between 1928 and 1932, it rose to 10.7 percent between 1932 and 1937, although it subsequently dropped to 4.4 percent in the purge years 1937–40. In the same manner the capital-labor ratio changed dramatically as the mines were mechanized; from a base of 100 in 1928 the ratio rose to 205 in 1932 (a doubling in four years) and 409 in 1940 (a further doubling in eight years).[50]

Table 6–3   CONCENTRATION OF COAL MINING IN
THE DONBAS, 1928–41

Annual Production of Shaft (Thousands of Tons)	1928–9	1933	1941
	(Percentage of Total Output)		
Under 10	4	3	0
10–50	33	18	—
50–100	31.6	31	17.4
100–200	20	26	20.2
200–500	11	19	45.1
Over 500	0.4	3	17.3

Source: I. M. Budnitskii, *Ugol'naya Prom'shlennost'* (Moscow: 1958), p. 7.

However, some doubt is thrown on such official claims by the comments of engineers working for American consulting firms. For example, William von Meding, of the Allen & Garcia Tomsk group, suggested that while the coal industry did show an increase in the early 1930s 'it was not nearly in proportion to the increase in capital investment or in the number of workers.' Von Meding specifically pointed to transportation deficiencies.[51]

Similarly, although Soviet plants started to produce coal cutters and mine equipment in the early 1930s under the Goodman and Casablancas technical-assistance agreements, they were still using large quantities of imported equipment in the middle and late 1930s. We have precise figures for the Kisel mines, producing 4.5 million tons of coal per year; in 1936 the Kisel district mines employed 54 coal cutters. Of these, 12 were of German make (Eickhoff), 24 were American, and 18 were the Soviet DTK-2.[52] The DTK-2 cutters

[50] Figures from C. E. Butler, *Productivity in Soviet Coal Mining, 1928–64* (Harvard University Economics Dept.: 1965–6), unpublished Ph.D. thesis, p. 478. The Butler thesis, by far the most comprehensive work on the Soviet coal industry generally available in the West, notes the increase in Soviet output and productivity, and concludes that 'part of the Soviet advantage in growth rates was due to great initial technological backwardness and the opportunity to borrow technology from other countries.' (P. 385.)

[51] *American Engineers in Russia*, Folder 3.

[52] Gmelin Institute, *Russland: Die Kohlenlagerstatten des Urals*, Bericht No. 66c; National Archives Microcopy T 84, Roll 127 (about 1940).

were copies of the Sullivan Machinery model,[53] and other coal-cutting equipment was made under the Goodman assistance agreement at the Gorlovka plant.

Thus the years between 1930 and 1941 witnessed the development of large-scale coal mines designed by American coal-mining consultants and the phasing out of small mines. These new mines were highly mechanized, at first with imported equipment and then after 1931–2 increasingly with Soviet-made equipment based on the most suitable of Western models. However, even by 1940 a large proportion of underground equipment was still imported. No indications of indigenous Soviet development have been found, either in coal-mine development or in mine equipment.

This American assistance was apparently well appreciated: in January 1944, upon an inquiry by Averell Harriman concerning postwar construction plans, Molotov indicated nothing specific except to inquire concerning the possibility of sending a U.S. expert for the Don Basin coal mines.[54]

THE RAMZIN 'ONCE-THROUGH' BOILER: AN INDIGENOUS DEVELOPMENT

In boiler construction we find an example of an indigenous Soviet development—the 'once-through' high-pressure boiler—adopted in 1936 for the bulk of the new construction program.

In 1936 there were four high-pressure boilers operating in the U.S.S.R.: two Czech Loeffler boilers with a capacity of 330,000 pounds per hour working at a pressure of 1,850 pounds per square inch,[55] and two once-through boilers—the experimental Ramzin boiler of 1931 and the commercial model of the Ramzin built in 1933 with a capacity of 440,000 pounds per hour at 2,000 pounds per square inch.[56]

Numerous other foreign high-pressure boilers, including the La Mont, Velox, Babcock and Wilcox, Ladd-Lakeside, Hanomag, and Borsig-Ilse No. 3, had been tested and data had been developed,[57] but the adoption of the

---

[53]   U.S. State Dept. Decimal File, 861.797/35, Report No. 165, Moscow Embassy, September 7, 1934.

[54]   *Ibid.*, 861.51/3019, Harriman to Hopkins, January 7, 1944.

[55]   Built by Wiklowitzer Bergbau und Eisenhütten Gewerschaft of Czechoslovakia. Technical details are in Browlie, 'The Loeffler Boilers at Moscow,' *The Steam Engineer*, XXI, No. 5 (February 1933), pp. 216–8.

[56]   The experimental Ramzin is described in *The Steam Engineer*, VII, No. 73 (October 1937), pp. 26–8. The commercial version is described in No. 76 (January 1938), pp. 160–1 and 168, and in T. Saur, 'The Ramzin Once-Through Boiler,' *Combustion*, X, No. 1 (July 1938), pp. 35–6. For a report on operating experience with a 'once-through' boiler after several years, see P. G. Kaufmann, 'Operating Experience with a Pulverised Fuel-Fired "Once-Through" Boiler,' *The Steam Engineer*, XIII, No. 156 (September 1944), pp. 358–64.

[57]   *Genie Civile*, CIII, No. 25 (December 16, 1933).

Ramzin was advantageous, although it required extensive development of heat-resistant steels, high-pressure fittings, and automatic regulating instruments, as it avoided the heavy cost of the drums which for high-pressure use required expensive and complicated steel-working equipment.

Table 6–4 gives the weight of raw material inputs for several types of contemporary boilers and suggests a real savings advantage in terms of material for the Ramzin over the two-drum TKZ and single-drum TKZ, both based on Western designs.[58]

Table 6–4   COMPARATIVE MATERIAL INPUTS FOR
VARIOUS SOVIET BOILERS, 1936

Input Material	Boiler Type		
	Two-Drum TKZ Single-Drum TKZ *(Based on Western Design)* *(tons)*		*Ramzin 'Once-Through'* *(Soviet Design)* *(tons)*
Rolled steel	362	232	158
Tubes and headers	139	88	140
Boiler plates	30	16	9.5
Cast iron	26	5	15
Heat-resistant steel	—	—	14
Other materials	33	5	3
Total	590	346	339.5
Steam generating capacity: specific weight per lb./hr.	3.98	2.31	2.21

Source: The Steam Engineer, XIV, No. 167 (August 1945), p. 332.

However, in spite of concentration of design effort in the C.K.K.B. (Central Boiler Design Institute), development of a standard boiler, and introduction of the successful Ramzin 'once-through' boiler, Soviet development achievements by 1945 were limited. The position has been summarized by Paul G. Kaufmann in an article in the August 1945 issue of *The Steam Engineer* and based on Soviet source material: 'With regard to small boilers . . . there is no appreciable development evident in the Soviet technical literature. Nor was there any development in high pressure steam engineering before the war, apart from the introduction of the "once-through" boiler.'[59]

[58] P. G. Kaufmann, 'Development of Steam Boiler Design in Russia,' *The Steam Engineer*, XIV, No. 166 (July 1945), p. 292.

[59] P. G. Kaufmann, 'Development of Steam Boiler Design in Russia—II,' *The Steam Engineer*, XIV, No. 167 (August 1945), p. 333. There is also some evidence that the Soviets had boiler fabrication difficulties; for example, in mid-1938 the Republic Steel Company sold a quantity of welded seamless boiler tubes to the U.S.S.R. (See U.S. State Dept. Decimal File, 861.602/298, Report No. 1446, Moscow Embassy, June 6, 1938.)

CONCLUSIONS

This chapter has examined technical development of two natural fuels and the boilers used to convert fuel into energy.

In petroleum refining we find an extraordinary degree of dependence on American technology right through to 1945. Not only was almost all the Soviet capacity actually built by American firms but, even as late as 1940, duplication of this technology by the Soviets was not successful. This is confirmed by the diplomatic appeal, at the highest levels, to retain a single American engineer—Rasmussen—in the Soviet Union to complete a single cracking plant.

On the other hand, in coal production, also an early recipient of technical assistance, we find Soviet-built equipment in operation. The three U.S. consulting companies had left by 1933, and by 1934–5 Russian mines began receiving Soviet-made equipment—duplicates of foreign equipment already in use, perhaps, but still Soviet-made. By 1942–3 probably half of the equipment in Soviet coal mines had been domestically manufactured to foreign design. There are no signs of indigenous technical advance before 1945.

The third sector—boilers—suggests greater, albeit unsuccessful, technical advance. Although in 1945 there had been no appreciable advances in either small-, medium-, or high-pressure boilers, there had been—in the Ramzin 'once-through' boiler—an example of a purely indigenous Soviet development. This was put into operation but then discarded. It must be presumed that the Ramzin boiler was not used further because Western design effort was more satisfactory.

In brief, the three sectors provide somewhat different conclusions. Although all three were essentially dependent on the West, we find in petroleum refining no indigenous development and in coal mining a degree of success at copying Western equipment but no indigenous development. In the boiler industry we find that the Soviets copied Western designs and also produced an original design, adopted it, and finally discarded it as unusable.

CHAPTER SEVEN

Technical Assistance to the Chemical Combinats[1]

THE Soviet Union, normally secretive about its industrial structure, is unusually secretive concerning development of the chemical and allied industries. This has posed problems in tracing the use of Western technology. Two approaches have been used to help overcome the paucity of accurate data. First, the structure of several large combinats based on comparatively small tsarist plants and expanded between 1930 and 1945 is examined. Second, major chemical processes are examined for the origin of Soviet technology in these combinats. Cross-checking processes against the industrial structure provides additional information.

Construction of chemical combinats was irregular and progress was directly related to Western assistance. For example, the Berezniki combinat had extensive Western assistance and equipment in all units. In full operation by the mid-1930s, it was by 1941 the largest Soviet chemical complex, employing 25,000 persons and producing large quantities of explosives and military chemicals.[2] Similarly, Shostka, where Du Pont built a nitric-acid plant, employed 13,750 by 1936.[3] On the other hand, although much equipment at Bobriki (Stalinogorsk) was imported, greater reliance was placed on Soviet technical cadres and domestically produced duplicates of Western apparatus,

---

[1] This chapter is based on Oberkommando der Wehrmacht (OKW/Wi Rü Amt/Wi), March 1941, Miscellaneous German Records, National Archives Microcopy T 84-122, supplemented by U.S. State Dept. reports from returning engineers, articles in the Western engineering literature, Alcan Hirsch's *Industrialized Russia* (New York: Chemical Catalog Co., 1934), B. S. Blinkov's *Khimicheskaya promyshlennost' SSSR* (Moscow: 1933), and *Bolshaya Sovietskaya Entsiklopediya* (Moscow: 1945).

[2] Oberkommando der Wehrmacht (OKW/Wi Rü Amt/Wi), March 1941, Miscellaneous German Records, National Archives Microcopy T 84-122.

[3] *Ibid.*

and progress was very slow. We know that efforts were made in 1931 to build Bobriki on a 24-hour 'crash' basis, but by 1937 only about 1,500 operating workers were employed in the combinat.

The Berezniki-Solikamsk project was by far the largest chemical project attempted between 1930 and 1945. The basic project for Berezniki, a synthetic-ammonia plant, was designed, supervised, and initially operated by the Nitrogen Engineering Corporation of New York under its President, Colonel Frederick Pope. The agreements between Nitrogen Engineering, Du Pont and Westvaco Chlorine and the Soviets are considered below in detail, and the construction of the more important chemical combinats is then examined.

THE NITROGEN ENGINEERING CORPORATION AGREEMENTS OF 1928 AND 1931[4]

The first agreement between Nitrogen Engineering and Khimstroi (Chemical Industry Construction Trust) was signed on November 11, 1928. The main provision covered

> ... the erection and putting into operation, under NITROGEN'S technical advice and direction, of a plant or plants for producing synthetic ammonia within the territory of U.S.S.R., and the grant to KHIMSTROI by NITROGEN of the right to use within such territory the methods, principles and processes of NITROGEN for the construction and operation of such plants.

The first project under this agreement was a synthetic ammonia plant at Berezniki.

The 1928 agreement was extended and modified by a second contract, dated June 29, 1931. (See Appendix B.) Exhibit C of this 1931 agreement specified in detail the project contribution to be made by Nitrogen Engineering, and was quite similar to specifications contained in other technical-assistance agreements.[5] A project, according to Exhibit C, consisted of two parts: a preliminary and a final section.

The preliminary section was to contain a general plan drawn on a scale of not less than 1:1000, with a 'schematic indication of sewage, steam, water and gas pipes, electric lines, transport lines and sidings.' Drawings for buildings with equipment locations and foundations, economic and technical calculations

---

[4]   A copy of the second (1931) contract is reproduced as Appendix B. The original is in the State Dept. files, together with a memorandum of discussion between Col. Pope and officials at the U.S. Embassy in Moscow in 1934. (See U.S. State Dept. Decimal File, 861.602/259, October 3, 1934. The first page has been removed; otherwise the documents appear to be intact, except for missing appendix containing a list of equipment supplied under the contract.)

[5]   For example, the Douglas Aircraft agreement, p. 232.

for the various energy components with variations and calculations of costs and inputs, descriptions of processes (with calculations and methods of estimating energy and heat-power requirements), specifications and cost of equipment, labor requirements, and cost-of-production figures were also required.

The final section required a series of drawings on a scale of 1:50 or 1:100, covering the boiler house, gas plant, conversion plant, compression plant, purification plant, synthesis plant, catalyst plant, and general piping layout; detailed working drawings of the equipment 'of such scale and detail reasonably necessary to enable a first-class shop to manufacture the same'; and, in addition, detail drawings of piping, loads, apparatus, and the electrical layout, as well as detailed calculations concerning economic balance, raw material inputs, heat balance, and design assumptions.[6]

The June 1931 agreement extended this assistance to 1936 and also attempted, according to Colonel Pope, President of the company, to give Nitrogen engineers more protection while working in the Soviet Union. Under the 1931 agreement Vsekhimprom (All-Union Trust for the Chemical Industry) was granted 'in perpetuity' exclusive rights to 'build, extend, operate and transfer' chemical plants for the manufacture of synthetic ammonia according to Nitrogen Engineering (NEC) processes. All NEC patents had to be transferred to the U.S.S.R. for five years. Under Clause IV, consulting, technical, and engineering services were to be provided and NEC was to maintain a staff of engineers in the U.S.S.R., provide drawings and data on improvements, and give assistance in transferring technology. For five years the Soviet Union also had the right to send its engineers into any NEC factory in the United States. Further, NEC had to send 'detailed written instructions for the use of its technical staff in starting and operating the synthetic ammonia plants and all departments thereof constructed by Vsekhimprom.'

Disagreements arose between the Soviets and Nitrogen Engineering, and these were the subject of discussion between Colonel Pope and members of the U.S. Embassy in Moscow in mid-October 1934.[7] Colonel Pope pointed out that in the six years since the first agreement there had been numerous organizational changes in the chemical industry and 'new Soviet officials appear to consider it incumbent upon themselves to criticize the acts of their predecessors.'[8] Difficulties mounted as the Soviets 'began to copy our machines and patented apparatus.'[9] Pope negotiated the second agreement, hoping to alleviate these problems by providing for Swedish arbitration and

---

[6] See Appendix B.
[7] U.S. State Dept. Decimal File, 861.602/259, October 3, 1934.
[8] *Ibid.*
[9] *Ibid.*

... since the Soviet Government was already copying equipment patented by NITROGEN and adopting various processes worked out by NITROGEN and since, in view of the peculiar nature of Soviet patent laws, no effective steps could be taken to prevent them from so doing, I assented to a provision in this contract which gave the Soviet Government the right to employ the processes of NITROGEN and to use its patents for a period of five years.

By 1934 the Soviets had become obligated to NEC to the extent of $1 million and refused a payment of $60,000 then due. Vsekhimprom 'gave a number of frivolous reasons for its refusal,' and this brought Pope to Moscow, where he was met by yet another board of directors who 'have resorted in their dealings with me to all of those small artifices generally practiced by dealers in second-hand clothes.' Colonel Pope indicated he had no intention to discuss the $60,000 but would refer it to arbitration. Vsekhimprom suggested that arbitration would cost $10,000 and 'I might find it preferable merely to reduce my bill by that amount.' When this was refused it was suggested that NEC give Vsekhimprom 'as a token of goodwill an instrument or two which was difficult to procure in the Soviet Union and which they sorely needed.' A list was drawn up containing $15,000 worth of instruments 'which they insisted should be donated to them by NITROGEN.' Vsekhimprom finally agreed to a donation of $8,000.

The Colonel added that he refused to discuss (with another trust) a further technical-assistance agreement and concluded as follows to the Embassy officials: 'I am disgusted with Soviet business and do not intend to waste my time and ruin my temper in engaging in other transactions with Soviet agencies.'[10]

THE DU PONT NITRIC-ACID CONTRACTS

The Du Pont Company built two nitric-acid plants in the Soviet Union under its 1929 agreement. These were at the Kalinin combinat and at Shostka in the Ukraine. Not very much information about these units is recorded except in reports from two Du Pont engineers after their return from the U.S.S.R.[11] One, J. K. Jenney, worked first at Kalinin and then, from August 1930 to February 1932, at the Shostka installation. His concluding comment was: 'After putting the plants into operation, one was conducted to what promised to be early ruin. The second was operated and maintained excel-

---

[10] Presumably the Soviets then paid the $60,000 overdue and met another commitment of $60,000 due in June 1935. This tactic of refusing to pay bills while attempting to get something else of value, or reduce the amount owed, was not confined to Nitrogen Engineering. See: Douglas Aircraft, page 235, for another example.

[11] *American Engineers in Russia*, Fisher, Folder 3, Item 22. See also U.S. State Dept. Decimal File, 861.5107—Living Conditions/241, Report No. 240, April 17, 1931, Berlin.

lently.'[12] Jenney also commented that there were no delays in construction because of transportation problems; this coincided with the priority given to chemical industry construction.[13]

Another Du Pont engineer, F. H. McDonald, also worked at both nitric-acid plants but added very little to this except that one unit was of 50-ton and the other of 20-ton capacity. However, McDonald did indicate that the technical director of one unit (not specified) was a Russian about 25 years old who had spent four to five months in the United States, was currently writing books on chemical problems, and, he suggested, had little knowledge of chemical engineering.

In 1932 negotiations were conducted for construction of a gigantic nitric-acid plant with a capacity of 1,000 tons per day, enormous when compared to previous plant capacities of 20 and 40 tons per day. This approximates 350,000 tons annually; 25 years later, in 1957, the largest Du Pont process nitric-acid plant in the United States at Hopewell had an annual capacity of 425,000 tons. Under its earlier contract Du Pont was obliged to supply such technical assistance to the U.S.S.R. for a period of five years and consequently inquired of the State Department whether this plant of 'excessively large capacity'[14] would meet with objection from the U.S. Government.

The State Department position is summarized in a memorandum dated April 6, 1932[15] which reviewed the matter of the export of military shipments to the Soviet Union and concluded that the Department would have no objection to construction of such a large nitric-acid plant.[16]

THE VSEKHIMPROM-WESTVACO CHLORINE PRODUCTS, INC., TECHNICAL-ASSISTANCE AGREEMENT

During the early twentieth century the production of caustic soda by the ammonia-soda process was replaced by a process utilizing the electrolysis of salt brine solution; this process yields chlorine and hydrogen in addition to caustic soda.

In February 1930 a technical-assistance agreement was concluded between Vsekhimprom and Westvaco Chlorine Products, Inc., of Virginia for technical assistance 'in the production of liquid chlorine and the manufacture in the Soviet Union of Vorce chlorine cells for salt brine electrolysis.'[17] The Soviets chose well; the Vorce cell, heart of the electrolytic method, is one of several

[12] *American Engineers in Russia*, Fisher, Folder 3, Item 22.
[13] *Ibid.*
[14] U.S. State Dept. Decimal File, 861.659—DU PONT DE NEMOURS & CO/5.
[15] *Ibid.*, 861.659—DU PONT DE NEMOURS & CO/9.
[16] *Ibid.*, 861.659—DU PONT DE NEMOURS & CO/9 to /11. See also chap. 15.
[17] Amtorg, *op. cit.*, V, No. 5 (March 1, 1930), p. 81.

methods of producing chlorine and caustic soda by electrolysis. The Vorce design, however, is compact, efficient, simple, and accessible, and utilizes strong, inexpensive construction of steel and cement with inexpensive anodes.[18]

The agreement provided for use of Westvaco patents on the Vorce cell. American engineers were sent to the U.S.S.R. and Soviet engineers studied cell production methods at Westvaco plants. It was anticipated that 'the first chlorine plant of the several to be constructed in the U.S.S.R. is to be conpleted in about six months.'[19]

THE BEREZNIKI-SOLIKAMSK CHEMICAL COMBINAT

The major construction effort in the chemical industry between 1930 and 1945, and also the focal point of the Nitrogen Engineering and other technical-assistance agreements, was this chemical combine, located behind the Urals comprising 10 integrated units and requiring an expenditure in excess of 100 million rubles.

The raw materials for the Berezniki complex came in part from the extensive Solikamsk potash deposits. These were the largest potash mines in the world, with a capacity some two and one half times that of the largest German mine. They were developed by the German firm Deilmann Bergbau und Tiefbau in the late 1920s.[20] In partial operation by September 1931, the Solikamsk mines were completely mechanized, to a great extent with Demag A-G equipment.[21] Coal was obtained from the Kisel fields to the south.

The site for the chemical combinat itself (to the south of Solikamsk) was the Luibimoff-Solvay soda plant, built in 1883. To this early enterprise were added plants to produce intermediate products—chlorine, synthetic ammonia, nitric acid, catalysts, and finally fertilizers and explosives. Power was supplied from a power station of 80,000 kilowatts' capacity, itself requiring an expenditure of 60 million rubles.[22] The water reservoir supplied 26,000 cubic meters per hour—twice the quantity supplied to the city of Moscow.[23]

Construction of the Berezniki chemical complex got under way in fall of 1929. By May 1930 foundations were completed, and in the fall of 1930 the walls of the first units were up. As will be seen in table 7–1, construction of this complex was a completely Western undertaking. The basic unit was a

[18]   C. L. Mantell, *Industrial Electrochemistry* (New York: McGraw-Hill, 1950, third ed.), pp. 430–6.

[19]   Amtorg, *op. cit.*, V, No. 5 (March 1, 1930), p. 81.

[20]   Sutton, *Western Technology . . ., 1917 to 1930*, pp. 215–7. Also see Amtorg, *op. cit.*, VI, No. 18 (September 13, 1931), p. 145.

[21]   Amtorg, *op. cit.*, IX, No. 11 (October 1934), p. 233.

[22]   *Ibid.*, VII, No. 3 (February 1, 1932), p. 57.

[23]   *La Vie Economique des Soviets*, VII, No. 143 (October 5, 1931).

Table 7–1   WESTERN TECHNICAL ASSISTANCE TO THE
BEREZNIKI-SOLIKAMSK COMPLEX

Product or Production Unit	Source of Technology or Construction
Soda	Tsarist Luibimoff-Solvay process
Chlorine	Westvaco Chlorine Products, Inc.
Synthetic ammonia	Nitrogen Engineering Corp., under supervision of Col. Pope
Catalyst	Nitrogen Engineering Corp., under supervision of C. O. Brown
Nitric acid	Du Pont (not confirmed)
Boiler house for complex	German and U.K. boilers
Gas generator plant	Power-Gas Corp., Ltd. (United Kingdom)
Caustic soda II	Westvaco Chlorine Products, Inc.
Caustic soda III	Siemens-Billiter
Sulfuric acid	Petersen (tower system)

Sources: U.S. State Dept. Decimal File, 861.5017—Living Conditions/653, May 10, 1933; and 861.602/259, October 3, 1934.

U.S.S.R. in Construction, No. 5, 1932.

Alcan Hirsh, *Industrialized Russia* (New York: Chemical Catalog Co., 1934).

synthetic-ammonia plant built by Nitrogen Engineering. The 90-ton-per-day plant was designed, erected, and put into operation under Colonel Pope. The catalyst plant was designed, erected, and put into operation by the same company under supervision of Dr. C. O. Brown. Most of the ammonia was shipped to Perm for fertilizer and explosive manufacture; the balance was retained at Berezniki for the manufacture of nitric acid and ammonium nitrate. The nitric-acid unit, with a capacity of about 75 tons per day, was probably built according to Du Pont designs, while the ammonium-nitrate plant had a capacity of about 20 to 25 tons per day. The sulfuric-acid department, using the 'latest type of tower system' process was the first of the new units, opening in December 1932.

THE BOBRIKI CHEMICAL COMBINAT

The Bobriki (Stalinogorsk) chemical combinat was established 200 kilometers south of Moscow and comprised a group of plants somewhat similar to those at Berezniki, but larger and more varied in chemical production.[24]

The history of its construction is intriguing. Excavation was under way on a 'crash' basis in 1931; later that year a Linde oxygen process plant was in operation, and imported equipment for a silicate-ceramics plant and gas-generator station had been assembled.[25] In 1933 work was started on a

---

[24]   U.S. State Dept. Decimal File, 861.5017—Living Conditions/653, Riga, May 10, 1933, Interview with Atherton Hastings, employed by Vsekhimstroi.

[25]   Amtorg, *op. cit.*, VII, No. 3 (February 1, 1932), p. 65.

synthetic-ammonia plant and on units for production of nitrogenous fertilizers, sulfuric acid, nitric acid, and sodium nitrate.[26] In January 1934 it was indicated that the turbines would soon be in operation, and in September the synthetic methanol plant—the first in the U.S.S.R.—was reported in operation.[27]

However, troubles were reported by several sources.[28] The Oberkommando der Wehrmacht also records that in 1937 less than 2,000 workers were employed at Stalinogorsk: less than 10 percent of the Berezniki employment figure.[29] From this low employment figure and the paucity of output statistics it is inferred that Soviet construction organizations ran into considerable trouble after the erection of imported equipment or parts copied from foreign models in the Stalinogorsk chemical equipment manufacturing department.

The feature distinguishing Bobriki from Berezniki is that the former depended far more (although by no means completely) on Soviet technical resources than Berezniki, and was probably intended as a training ground for chemical construction and operating technicians.

Table 7–2   WESTERN TECHNICAL ASSISTANCE TO THE
BOBRIKI (STALINOGORSK) CHEMICAL COMBINAT

Product	Western Technology
Synthetic ammonia	Nitrogen Engineering Corp.
Nitric acid	Most equipment from Germany and U.K.; some U.S. Probably assembled by Soviet organizations.
Sulfuric acid	Most equipment from Germany and U.K.; some U.S. Probably assembled by Soviet organizations.
Nitrogen fertilizers	Most equipment from Germany and U.K.; some U.S. Probably assembled by Soviet organizations.
Silicate ceramics	Foreign equipment assembled by Soviets.
Methanol	Probably Hastings (U.S.) design.
Chlorine	Westvaco Chlorine Products design; possibly Soviet-manufactured.
Oxygen	Linde process.
Chemical equipment manufacturing plant	Equipped with German, American, and English machinery.
Power station	Origin probably Western; assembled by Soviet organizations.

Sources: See text.

[26] *Ibid.*, IX, No. 1 (January 1934), p. 18.
[27] *Ibid.*, No. 11 (November 1934), p. 241.
[28] Alcan Hirsch, *op. cit.*, and U.S. State Dept. Decimal File, 861.5017—Living Conditions/653. Interview with Atherton Hastings, employed by Vsekhimstroi.
[29] Oberkommando der Wehrmacht (OKW/Wi Rü Amt/Wi), March 1941, Miscellaneous German Records, National Archives Microcopy T 84–122.

Atherton Hastings, who worked at both combinats in the early 1930s, makes the point that although mistakes were made in construction and operation of Bobriki, great progress was made by learning from experience and the plant was producing a nucleus of chemical industry workers.

Another distinguishing feature of Bobriki was its chemical equipment manufacturing plant, the first in the U.S.S.R., for construction of heavy chemical machinery. This, according to Hastings, was efficient: 'It is equipped with German, American and English machinery and constructs heavy machinery not only for Bobriki plant but for all Russian chemical plants. . . .'[30]

Most of the equipment for Bobriki was, however, imported. For example, in reference to the gas generator station, Amtorg comments: 'The assembling of the equipment for the station was accomplished by Soviet engineers and workers alone.'[31] The same article also makes reference to 'assembling' the ceramic plant. If the equipment had been *manufactured* in the Soviet Union, it is almost certain that reference would have been made to this point.

This observation is confirmed by Alcan Hirsch, Chief Consulting Engineer to the chemical industry in the early 1930s, who states: 'Some of the equipment at Stalinogorsk has been imported from the United States, but most of it came from Germany and England.'[32]

THE KALININ CHEMICAL COMBINAT[33]

The Kalinin chemical combinat was based on the prerevolutionary Raspiapino lime and sulfuric-acid plants. The Tenteleev-process sulfuric-acid plant was entirely rebuilt, expanded, and fitted with new equipment. With the addition of Gay-Lussac and Glover tower units, it produced 40,000 tons per year, including fuming acid, by 1944.[34]

The synthetic-ammonia plant bought from Casale in Italy[35] utilized a water-gas process with a capacity of 16,500 short tons of nitrogen per year. There was also some direct American engineering assistance to the combinat, as it was reported in 1938 that an American engineer had been employed there since 1935.[36]

---

[30] U.S. State Dept. Decimal File, 861.5017—Living Conditions/653, Riga, May 10, 1933, Interview with Atherton Hastings, employed by Vsekhimstroi.

[31] Amtorg, *op. cit.*, VII, No. 3 (February 1, 1932), p. 65.

[32] Alcan Hirsch, *op. cit.*, p. 85.

[33] Formerly Raspiapino, also called Dzherzhinsky or Chernoreznitsky at Nizhni-Novgorod (Gorki).

[34] Wirtschaftsgruppe Chemische Industrie, *Die Schwefelsäureindustrie in der Sowjet-Union*, January 1944, National Archives Microcopy T 84-122-1421980.

[35] Sutton, *Western Technology . . ., 1917 to 1930*, p. 214.

[36] U.S. State Dept. Decimal File, 861.659—CHEMICALS/10, Report No. 883 from Moscow Embassy, January 21, 1938.

At Karakliss, in Armenia, a plant was finished in October 1931 to produce 10,000 tons of cyanamide a year, and later, when power was received from the new Leninakhan power station, output was raised to 20,000 tons of cyanamides and 4,000 tons of carbonates, with oxygen as a by-product. The complex was built with technical assistance from the Swedish company Stockholms Superfosfat Fabriks Aktiebolaget.[37]

Table 7–3   WESTERN TECHNICAL ASSISTANCE TO THE
KALININ CHEMICAL COMBINAT

Plant	Origin
Lime plant	Tsarist plant
Sulfuric acid	Tsarist plant; Russian Tenteleev process plus Western tower units (Gay-Lussac and Glover)
Synthetic ammonia	Casale (Italy)
Nitric acid	Du Pont design and supervision with German equipment
Chlorine	Westvaco Chlorine Products (probable)
Calcium carbide	Stockholms Superfosfat Fabriks Aktiebolaget
Cyanamide	Stockholms Superfosfat Fabriks Aktiebolaget
Liquid oxygen	Linde process
Superphosphate	Stockholms Superfosfat Fabriks Aktiebolaget

Sources: V. I. Ipatieff, *Life of a Chemist* (Stanford: Stanford University Press, 1946), p. 413.
Die Chemische Fabrik, No. 9, (1928), p. 107.
Amtorg, *op. cit.*, 1930–3.
Vneshtorgizdat, *Economic Conditions in the U.S.S.R.* (Moscow: 1931), p. 22.

At Konstantinovka a chemical complex was built based on roaster gases from the zinc smelter. The sulfuric-acid plant comprised a Tenteleev contact system[38] and a tower system with a capacity of 25,000 tons. Arsenic was also produced. The superphosphate plant at Konstantinovka was started in 1927, but for some unknown reason construction was delayed for two years and probably completed sometime in the mid-1930s.[39]

One apparent exception to the rule of heavy Western assistance was the tsarist Moscow plant of Dorogomilov; five departments were added to the original unit and 'all formulae for the chemicals produced were developed by Soviet specialists, the construction work was supervised entirely by Soviet engineers, and over 90 per cent of the equipment installed was produced in Soviet plants.'[40] The plant probably used prisoner engineers and certainly produced poison gases.[41]

[37]   Vneshtorgizdat, *Economic Conditions in the U.S.S.R.* (Moscow: 1931), p. 22.
[38]   *Die Chemische Fabrik*, II, No. 25 (June 19, 1929), p. 304.
[39]   Amtorg, *op. cit.*, IV, No. 10 (May 15, 1929), p. 202.
[40]   *Ibid.*, VII, No. 1 (January 1, 1932), p. 20.
[41]   V. I. Ipatieff, *Life of a Chemist* (Stanford: Stanford University Press, 1946).

The Gorlovka coke-chemical combinat was the first coke by-product plant to be put into operation. The first part, Ordzhonikidze Works I, consisted of two batteries of coke ovens ($14\frac{1}{2}$ tons capacity per oven) built by Koppers A-G, and equipment to produce by-products (benzol, sulfate, and tar) from the gas. Coal was supplied from several old coal mines and one modern mine known as '8-bis,' which delivered coal right into the coal-washing plant. The latter was built by a German company and was the first coal-washing plant in the Soviet Union.[42]

The Soviets then added Works II, comprising another two coke-oven batteries with by-products departments. It was a copy of the first installation, and in this book is called 'Soviet Koppers.' Simultaneously a complete synthetic-ammonia plant using the Fauser process was built to use the H_2 in the coke-oven gas and nitrogen from the air to make NH_3. Sulfuric-acid and nitric-acid plants laid the base for combining the NH_3 in the manufacture of either fertilizer or explosives. The synthetic-ammonia and related plants were put into operation in 1935 and demolished in 1941 at the time of the German invasion.[43]

We have accurate data on the Magnitogorsk by-product coke-chemical plant, as John Scott (now Senior Editor of TIME magazine) was in 1935–6 operator of the Magnitogorsk benzol department.[44] The by-product coke-oven installation, the largest in Europe, was a Koppers-Becker system installed by the Koppers A-G, although, as Scott points out, the design was developed partly by the McKee Corporation and several Soviet organizations. As finally built it was not nearly as large as originally planned. No departments came into production before the mid-1930s.

In 1936 the plant consisted of a condensation department with four German exhausters and a sulfate department with three imported saturators giving a maximum of 60 tons of ammonium sulfate per day. The benzol department had four stills producing 60 tons a day and a benzol rectification unit (opened in 1936) producing benzol, tuluol, and naphthalene. As John Scott says, 'All pumps and most of the apparatus of the benzol department were imported.'

Another combinat in Moscow was the Voskressensk, of which the sulfuric-acid plant (the largest in the world) had an annual capacity of 160,000 tons with possible expansion to 240,000 tons per year. The Benker-Milberg system was used[45] for production of phosphates and superphosphates.[46] Much of the

---

[42] *American Engineers in Russia*, Folder 4, No. 16.

[43] *Fortune*, October 1949, p. 117.

[44] John Scott, *op. cit.*, p. 155.

[45] *Die Chemische Fabrik*, 1928, p. 454. The mechanical furnace section was the Nichols Engineering and Research Corp. design, called VKhZ and manufactured and widely distributed in the U.S.S.R. [*Bolshaya Sovietskaya Entsiklopediya* (Moscow: 1945), LI, col. 14.]

[46] Hirsch, *op. cit.*, p. 83.

equipment was bought from Germany.[47]

The Grozny Chemical Combinat No. 22 had a butanol-acetone plant, utilizing an adaptation of the Weizmann fermentation process,[48] and a synthetic methanol plant, probably designed by Hastings.

Thus an examination of the Soviet chemical combinats built between 1930 and 1941 suggests a great amount of Western design assistance and equipment at locations of earlier tsarist enterprises. No evidence of significant practical Soviet contribution to chemical engineering is found in this period.[49]

TECHNOLOGY IN ALKALI PRODUCTION

Alkalis form the basis of many other chemical products; production of soda ash (sodium carbonate) and of caustic soda (sodium hydroxide), with or without chlorine as a by-product, are the most important sectors.

Table 7–4   METHODS OF ALKALI PRODUCTION IN THE SOVIET UNION, 1930–44

Plant	Process Used	Capacity (Tons per Day)	Note
SODA ASH			
Donsoda[1]	Solvay	270	Restarted February 1944[2]
Slaviansk[2]			
Old plant	Henningman	50	Restarted February 1944[2]
New Plant I	Solvay	210 ⎫	⎰ Open 1937–41, restarted
New Plant II	Solvay	210 ⎭	⎱ November 1946[2]
Berezniki[1]	Solvay	90	Expansion of old plant (1890?)
Karabugaz[2]	Le Blanc	150	Expansion of old plant (1897)
Zapadonosibirsk[1]	Le Blanc	100	Expansion of Luibimoff-Solvay works (1898)
CAUSTIC SODA			
Donsoda[1]	'Levig' (Löwig)		
Slaviansk	Wet lime		
Berezniki	'Levig' (Löwig)		

Sources: [1] B. S. Blinkov, *Khimicheskaya promyshlennost' SSSR* (Moscow: 1933), p. 196.
[2] G. E. Lury, *50 let sovetskaya khimicheskaya nauka i promyshlennost'* (Moscow: 1967), pp. 158–62.

[47] *Die Chemische Fabrik*, 1931, pp. 2–38.
[48] Hirsch, *op. cit.*, p. 86.
[49] See chap. 18. Under the technical-assistance contract with the French firm Société Electrométallurgique de Montricher, nine furnaces were installed at Donoi-Postroi (each of 10,000-kilowatt capacity) to produce calcium carbide according to the Miguet system. Three copies of these furnaces were later built by the Soviets and installed in Leningrad. The 10,000-kilowatt capacity was the largest economical size for this process and gave the Soviets an estimated 250,000-ton capacity for the production of calcium carbide. W. G. McBurney, *et al.*, *German Carbide, Cyanamide and Cyanide Industry*, C.I.O.S. Report No. XXVII-92, p. 28.

Soda ash was produced in three plants in tsarist Russia, using the Solvay and Henningman processes. In the 1930s these plants were re-equipped and considerably expanded, and two new Le Blanc plants were added at Karabugaz and Zapadonosibirsk. (See table 7-4.) The process used at the Le Blanc plants is of interest. The Le Blanc soda process, although never used in the United States is historically most important. It was succeeded in about 1870 by the Solvay ammonia-soda process in Europe as well as Russia. However, in the new Soviet plants a return was made to the Le Blanc process,[50] which was no longer in use elsewhere in the world.

In caustic-soda manufacture we find the same use of an obsolete process. The Löwig process, originating in nineteenth-century Germany and not used in the West in the twentieth century, was the process selected for caustic-soda plants.[51]

THE RUSSIAN TENTELEEV PROCESS FOR SULFURIC-ACID PRODUCTION

The Soviet Union does not offer, even 50 years after the Revolution, an example of an indigenous technology utilized on a world-wide basis. However, tsarist Russia does offer an excellent example: the Tenteleev contact process for production of sulfuric acid. Developed in the Tenteleev St. Petersburg works (now called the Krasnyi Khimik), it was used in more than half the sulfuric-acid plants of prerevolutionary Russia, patented in Russia and throughout the West, and used in a number of Western countries.

Of the more than 40 Russian sulfuric-acid plants in existence before 1917, over 20 units utilized the Tenteleev process,[52] while the others used the Grillo-Schroder and Mannheim systems. In 1913 the Tenteleev process was used in the United States (by the Boston-Merrimac Chemical Company in

---

[50] B. S. Blinkov, *op. cit.*, p. 202. Whether the explanation lies in factor resource patterns occurring in Russia and not elsewhere, faulty planning decisions, or a static technology has not been explored. The writer hopes to re-examine this problem in a later study.

  It should be noted that the use of a long-established process is not, of itself, an indication of inefficiency, at least in the chemical industry. There are many examples in the West in which an old process has been improved, redesigned or adapted to take advantage of new equipment, and so has competed successfully with newer methods. For example, in the acid-pickling process for removing scale from steel, the only change in centuries has been in the design of larger continuous units and improved equipment; the basic principle remains the same.

[51] M. B. Zelikin, *Proizvodstvo kauticheskoi sody khimicheskimi sposobami* (Moscow: Goskhimizdat, 1961), p. 14.

[52] An excellent summary of the Russian sulfuric-acid industry in 1917 is given in *Chemical and Metallurgical Engineering*, XXX (1924), pp. 384–8. The position in 1944 is described in Wirtschaftsgruppe Chemische Industrie, *Die Schwefelsäureindustrie in der Sowjet-Union*, January 1944, National Archives Microcopy T 84–122–1421980.

New York and by the General Chemical Company), Germany (by Dynamite Nobel in Hamburg), and the United Kingdom (by the Dynamite Trust in London), as well as in other Western countries. In all, 24 Tenteleev units were at work in Germany, Rumania, Sweden, the United States, and Japan at the end of 1911.[53]

By 1945 the Soviet sulfuric-acid industry was operating either on tsarist processes or standard Western processes. Reference to *Bolshaya Sovietskaya Entsiklopediya* for 1945 supports this statement. Seven pages are devoted to a discussion of sulfuric-acid production. Standard Western equipment (the Nichols-Herreshoff mechanical furnaces—called VKhZ designs—at Voskressensk[54] and the Lurgi revolving furnace) and standard chamber, tower, and contact methods are indicated on the diagrams. The contact method described in most detail is the German Herreshoff-Bauer method.

THE CHAMBER PROCESS FOR PRODUCING SULFURIC ACID

This process utilizes Glover towers, used throughout the world since 1859, to concentrate acid and remove nitrogen oxides. Gay-Lussac towers, also utilized, are arranged in series to recover nitrogen oxides from the spent gases.

Figure 7–1   SOVIET CHAMBER SYSTEM FOR MANUFACTURE
OF SULFURIC ACID, 1945

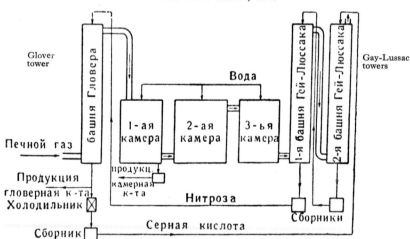

Diagram of Chamber System

Source: Bolshaya Sovietskaya Entsiklopediya (Moscow: 1945), LI, col. 18.

[53]   George Lunge, *The Manufacture of Sulphuric Acid and Alkali*, I, Part iii (London: Gurney & Jackson, 1913), p. 1359.

[54]   See *Bolshaya Sovietskaya Entsiklopediya* (Moscow, 1945), pp. 7–14.

They are similar to Glover towers but taller and of smaller diameter. The many variations of this process in use throughout the world include Mills-Packard, Gaillard-Parrish, Opl, Petersen, and Kachkaroff-Guareschi (French).

This method was utilized in the U.S.S.R. between 1930 and 1945 in its varying forms, including the Gaillard-Parrish for two units in the Urals[55] and the Petersen at a large new plant at the Krasnyi Khimik in Leningrad.[56] In 1944 more than one-fifth of all sulfuric acid was being made by some variation of this chamber process.[57]

THE CONTACT PROCESS FOR THE MANUFACTURE OF SULFURIC ACID

Two basic processes used in Russia have been sulfur-burning contact system for converting SO_2 to SO_3 and for the manufacture of sulfuric acid based on utilization of roaster gases from metallurgical plants and coupled with use of towers. It is reported that in 1937 about 8 percent of Soviet sulfuric acid was obtained from the roaster gases of metallurgical plants,[58] leaving a balance of about 70 percent (allowing 20 percent for chamber processes) produced by contact processes using sulfur and pyrites.

Figure 7–2   SOVIET HERRESHOFF-BAUER CONTACT
SYSTEM FOR SULFURIC ACID PRODUCTION, 1945

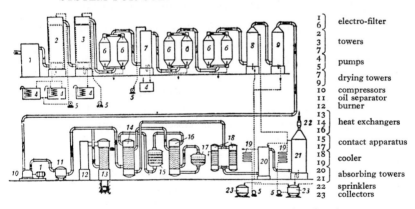

1, 6	electro-filter
2, 3, 7	towers
4, 5	pumps
7, 9	drying towers
10	compressors
11	oil separator
12	burner
13, 14, 16	heat exchangers
15, 17	contact apparatus
18, 19	cooler
20, 21	absorbing towers
22	sprinklers
23	collectors

Source: Bolshaya Sovietskaya Entsiklopediya (Moscow: 1945), LI, col. 22.

55   *Chemical and Metallurgical Engineering*, CXXXVII, No. 8 (August 1930), p. 472.
56   *Die Chemische Fabrik*, II, No. 40 (October 2, 1929) p. 442.
57   Calculated from Wirtschaftsgruppe Chemische Industrie. This is a minimum; incomplete data prevents more accurate calculation.
58   *Chemical Age*, July 28, 1945, p. 81. These figures are very approximate and are subject to revision.

Units for production of sulfuric acid from roaster gases were located at the Ridder lead-zinc smelter (using an adapted Glover process), in several Herreshoff-Bauer systems, at a Lurgi plant at Baku, and in the Benker-Milberg system at the Moskhimkombinat, and in other similar systems.

Figure 7–3 SOVIET SIX-TOWER SYSTEM

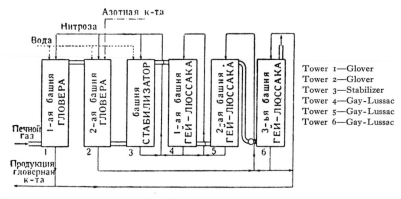

Tower 1—Glover
Tower 2—Glover
Tower 3—Stabilizer
Tower 4—Gay-Lussac
Tower 5—Gay-Lussac
Tower 6—Gay-Lussac

Source: *Bolshaya Sovietskaya Entsiklopediya* (Moscow: 1945), LI, col. 19.

PRODUCTION OF CHEMICALS FOR MILITARY USE[59]

The large production of explosives and 'war chemicals' in the Soviet Union at this time supports the argument that the nation had a war-oriented economy. Oberkommando der Wehrmacht Intelligence listed 52 chemical plants, including many old, small units manufacturing explosives and allied chemicals in 1936–9 for war use. The largest of these plants was the Okhtinsky chemical combinat in Leningrad, employing 14,000 workers in 1938, with the Du Pont-built plant at Shostka following closely with approximately 13,750 employees in 1936. The Nitrogen-Engineering-designed complex at Berezniki employed 25,000 workers in 1937 and manufactured thermit, powder, and nitroglycerin. In aggregate the Soviets probably had a quarter of a million workers in plants producing explosives and war chemicals in the years 1936–8.[60] The larger of these plants had been built by Western companies nominally for the manufacture of fertilizers; but conversion to explosives is a comparatively

[59] Based on Oberkommando der Wehrmacht (OKW/Wi Rü Amt/Wi), March 1941, Miscellaneous German Records, National Archives Microcopy T 84, Roll 122, Frames 1421291–6, Pulver und Sprengstoffwerke.

[60] Based on figures for the 24 works where employment was known; figures for the remaining 28 works are not given.

straightforward procedure, and the facts were suspected by the companies involved and the State Department.[61]

The Olgin chemical works in Moscow was fully equipped for production of poison gases during World War I. After the Revolution it was shut down until 1928, when it was re-equipped with imported German Hoffer compressors and an autoclave for high-pressure experiments, together with other equipment for gas production.[62] The plant was then operated by prisoner engineers, including Kravets, head of the Glavkhim planning department, at least until 1941 for the production of arsenic and cyanide compounds.[63]

Several sources reported great interest in poison gases and noted that absolute priority had been given to production of arsenic, an ingredient of poison gas. One excellent source is E. G. Brown, a metallurgical engineer and the only foreigner employed in the Tsvetmetzoloto laboratories which made analyses of ore specimens and designed reduction processes. The Soviet chemists made the analyses and Brown determined the reduction process to be used. He reported that every effort was made to increase the production of arsenic. For example, in the case of complex ores (containing, for instance, lead-silver and arsenic) he was ordered to design a plant to free the maximum amount of arsenic even if that meant losing other by-products.[64]

TECHNICAL ASSISTANCE FOR MINOR CHEMICAL AND PHARMACEUTICAL PRODUCTION

Chemical products required only in comparatively small quantities also received foreign assistance.

An ultramarine plant was built in Rostov with a capacity of 1,000 tons per year, utilizing foreign equipment and technical assistance.[65] A carbon disulfide plant with a seven-ton-per-day capacity was built by the Berlin firm of Zahn, utilizing the company's patents.[66] In 1930 the major British chemical producer, Imperial Chemical Industries, Ltd., agreed to sell 30 million rubles worth of chemicals to the Soviet Union on a credit basis; 'the agreement also provided for technical-assistance to the Soviet chemical industry in the

---

[61] U.S. State Dept. Decimal File, 861.659—DU PONT DE NEMOURS & CO./5, Du Pont to Secretary of State Stimson, February 19, 1932, which states: '. . . while we have no knowledge of the purpose of the proposed plant, yet the excessively large capacity contemplated leads us to believe that the purpose may be a military one.'

[62] Ipatieff, *op. cit.*, pp. 469, 487.

[63] Oberkommando der Wehrmacht, *op. cit.*, Plant No. 321.

[64] U.S. State Dept. Decimal File, 861.5017—Living Conditions/415, Riga, January 19, 1932. In a similar report, Steffenson indicated the emphasis on arsenic.

[65] *Die Chemische Fabrik*, II, No. 25 (June 19, 1929), p. 304.

[66] *Ibid.*, II, No. 42 (October 16, 1929), p. 461.

production of commodities manufactured by the British concern. . . .'[67] It was reported by Amtorg in the same year that 'several technical-assistance agreements have been concluded with large French construction firms, especially for the building of chemical enterprises. . . .'[68]

Technical assistance was also provided by I. G. Farben[69] and other German firms: Dürkopp-Werke, Charlottenburger Wasser und Industriewerke and Lenz. American firms providing technical assistance included Parke, Davis in pharmaceuticals, Moren and Company, and Chain-Belt;[70] also under contract were the Dutch firm Electro and the French firm Cellulose de Bourges.[71] H. D. Gibbs (U.S.) furnished plans and supervised the installation and initial operation of a small chemical plant in 1934 to manufacture phthalic anhydride, aluminum chloride, and antraquinone.[72]

CONCLUSIONS

The largest production complex (Berezniki) and the most important technologies (synthetic-ammonia, nitric-acid, and, to a lesser extent, sulfuric-acid and alkali production) originated in the West. Reproduction of foreign equipment for part of the Bobriki combine was coupled with imports but does not appear to have been immediately successful, although it no doubt provided useful training for technical cadres.

Findings on the Soviet chemical industry suggest that a great effort has been made to withhold details of this development from the outside world. This was essentially a military sector which reflected intense Soviet interest in chemical warfare and military preparations in general. The combination of technical backwardness and military necessity ensured that great efforts would be made to obscure both the development of individual plants and the processes utilized. However, despite military pressures, by 1945 the Soviet chemical industries provided no examples of indigenous Soviet technology.

[67]   Amtorg, *op. cit.*, V, No. 11 (June 1, 1930), p. 226.
[68]   *Ibid.*, V, No. 12 (June 30, 1930), p. 226.
[69]   *Ibid.*, III, No. 19 (October 1, 1928) pp. 331–2.
[70]   *Die Chemische Fabrik*, II, 1929, p. 47.
[71]   *Ibid.*
[72]   *American Engineers in Russia*, Fisher, Folder 1, Letter from Gibbs to Fisher.

CHAPTER EIGHT

Technical Assistance to the Coke-Oven, Synthetic-Rubber, Cement, Alcohol, and Wood-Distillation Sectors

KOPPERS-BECKER DESIGNS IN THE COKE-CHEMICAL INDUSTRY

COKE, derived from coking-quality coals, is an essential input for metallurgical industries. Russian coking capacity in the mid-1920s consisted chiefly of tsarist-era French and Belgian Coppe and Piette ovens; there were no modern vertical pusher ovens (also known as by-product ovens) of the Koppers or Koppers-Becker type which enabled by-products of the coking process to be utilized for chemical production. The United States had developed several types of efficient by-product ovens: the Wilputte, Hemet-Solvay, Cambria, and Simon-Carves, but by the 1920s Koppers and Koppers-Becker had the dominant position and their ovens were being installed in three-quarters of new plants in the United States. These designs were adopted by the Soviet Union. Almost all iron and steel plants built between 1928 and 1932, including the gigantic Magnitogorsk and Kuznetsk complexes, received imported Koppers-built by-product vertical pusher ovens; plants built since 1932 have used either 'Soviet Koppers' or 'NKVD Koppers' systems.

A complete list of these coke-chemical plants was compiled by merging data given in *Fortune* of October 1949 by Louis Ernst, a former engineer at Soviet coke-chemical plants (he lists 27 plants in operation in 1941 and others under construction by the NKVD), with data from the OKW files (which contain a list, dated March 1941, of 25 plants, some of which do not appear on the Ernst list.)[1]

'Soviet Koppers' designs are defined by Ernst in the *Fortune* article as 'built under Soviet supervision, according to Soviet design based on Koppers

[1] Oberkommando der Wehrmacht (OKW/Wi Rü Amt/Wi), March 1941, Miscellaneous German Records, National Archives Microcopy T 84–122–1421229.

original designs with equipment partly imported, partly increasingly manufactured by Soviet factories.' The NKVD Koppers designs were Soviet Koppers ovens produced and installed under NKVD supervision by forced labor. These ovens were usually also operated by the NKVD using forced labor.

CONSTRUCTION OF COKE-OVEN BATTERIES AT MAGNITOGORSK AND KUZNETSK

The largest coke-oven and by-products installation built in the period 1930–45 was at the Magnitogorsk iron and steel complex. This plant was planned to contain eight batteries, each consisting of 69 ovens, with a late-1931 completion date. The Koppers Corporation of Pittsburgh won the contract for installation and at the end of 1930 sent 16 American engineers, together with a number of German Koppers A-G engineers, to Magnitogorsk. Only one battery of 61 ovens was completed by late 1931; another was completed in mid-1932, and two others in 1933. By November 1932 only one American and five or six German Koppers engineers were left at the Magnitogorsk coke plant.

Louis Gerhardt, the Koppers Chief Construction Engineer in the U.S.S.R., has described the organization of the construction effort and the utilization of foreign engineers and their place in coke-oven construction. Gerhardt was in charge of Koppers construction and had four American construction engineers working directly under him. Each American was teamed with one Soviet engineer and two Russian foremen. Each foreman supervised four subforemen, each of whom in turn supervised a gang of about 30 to 50 laborers.[2]

The greater part of the machinery and piping, and 13,000 tons of firebrick, came from Germany. Special castings came from the United States. Only the structural steel work was manufactured in the Soviet Union.

Although Magnitogorsk was initially projected to have eight batteries of Becker ovens, all with Koppers by-product recovery plants, and a four-battery complex was erected by Koppers under its technical-aid contract, only the original four batteries were in operation in 1945. The remaining four batteries planned were not built.

The Koppers engineers were very pessimistic about the future of the batteries constructed. They were designed to last 20 years, but it was considered doubtful that they would last four to five years, owing to inefficient operation by unskilled labor. Louis Gerhardt mentioned to a State Department

---

[2] U.S. State Dept. Decimal File, 861.5017—Living Conditions/569.

official that the ovens were already about '12 years old' after operating only a few months.

The chemical plant, based on coke-oven by-products, was allowed to lag in construction. It has been described by John Scott as 'shoddily projected but [having] a fairly good condensation department with four German exhausters.'[3] The sulfate department went into operation in 1935 and had three saturators producing 60 tons daily of ammonium sulfate. The benzol department, with four imported stills, went into operation in 1936, producing 60 tons daily of tar, benzol, tuluol, naphthalene, and other chemical products.[4]

The coke-oven batteries at the Kuznetsk iron and steel plant, the second giant of 'socialist construction,' were erected by French engineers working for Distocoque S.A. (the Koppers French licensee). They designed two batteries, each with fifty-five 17-inch ovens of the Koppers type.[5] About 20 French engineers under Chief Engineer Louis completed the first battery by March 1932 and put it into operation. At this point continuing friction between the French and Russian engineers came to a head, and sometime later in March, 'after a heated interview with the administration, Chief Engineer Louis returned to the foreign engineers' quarters, gathered together all the plans for the coking plant, and burnt them in the stove.'[6] The French engineers were ordered to leave and the second battery was completed by the Soviets with assistance from German engineers.[7]

CHANGES IN COKE-OVEN TECHNOLOGY

The technological structure of Soviet coke ovens changed completely between 1928 and 1947. In 1928 more than one-half of Russian coke was produced in tsarist-era ovens with little chemical by-products capacity. The balance of the capacity was German- and French-built, on Koppers, Otto, and Distocoque systems. During the period from 1928 to 1932, a decision was made to standardize on the basis of the Koppers system. By 1932 tsarist ovens accounted for less than one quarter of an output which had more than doubled (3.2 to 7.1 million tons). The balance of the capacity was split between Soviet Koppers ovens and Koppers systems imported and installed by the American, German, and French Koppers companies.

---

[3] Scott, *op. cit.*, p. 154.

[4] *Ibid.*

[5] U.S. State Dept. Decimal File, 861.5017—Living Conditions/434, March 4, 1932, interview with Aaron J. Winetz, coke oven engineer at Kuznetsk.

[6] U.S. State Dept. Decimal File, 861.5017—Living Conditions/454, Report No. 291, Riga Consulate, April 22, 1932, p. 8, interview with T. A. Hoffmeyer, Freyn Co. construction engineer at Kuznetsk.

[7] U.S. State Dept. Decimal File, 861.5017—Living Conditions/434, March 4, 1932.

By 1940 coke output had again tripled—to 23 million tons, of which more than 60 percent was now produced from Soviet Koppers ovens. The tsarist ovens were closed down and no systems were built after 1933 by foreign construction companies. Also by 1940 the NKVD was building Koppers ovens in more remote northern regions, using forced labor. The German invasion of the Ukraine in 1941 temporarily changed this pattern, but in 1947 almost 60 percent of the output was again being produced in Soviet Koppers systems. In addition, there was a significant increase in NKVD Koppers capacity.

We may therefore conclude that in the 20 years from 1928 to 1947 the Soviets increased coke-oven capacity by a factor of eight and replaced the small-scale prewar ovens almost completely with Koppers systems at first imported (as at Magnitogorsk and Kuznetsk) and then duplicated and built in the Soviet Union.

COKE-OVEN BY-PRODUCT TECHNOLOGY AND THE KOPPERS CORPORATION

The Soviet claim that 'in the years of Soviet power, the Soviet Union developed a new technique of coking through its own efforts'[8] does not stand up under investigation. As we have seen, there was a significant increase in coke-oven capacity, and an even more significant increase in chemical by-products capacity between 1928 and World War II, but both were wholly based on Koppers technology transferred to the Soviet Union.

It is also suggested by the Soviets that 'the experience which was acquired in the process of rebuilding and redesigning old plants was not sufficient for the construction of new plants on a high engineering level,' and that 'the coke-chemical industry which developed in the period of the First Five-Year Plan was on an engineering level which exceeded that of Europe.'[9] Soviet coke capacity was based on Koppers designs and built by Koppers until such time as the Soviets could duplicate the Koppers system in their own machine-building plants at Kramatorsk and Slaviansk and later at Orsk.'[10]

This combination of imported Koppers systems and domestic duplication to a single standardized design enabled the Soviets to acquire a large coking capacity in a short space of time. From 1931 to 1946 the standard Soviet coke oven was the 17-inch Koppers. Apart from one experimental design (the PVR-39, with paired vertical valves and recycling of combustion products)

---

[8] 'Koksokhimicheskaya promyshlennost' SSSR,' in *Metallurgiya SSSR (1917–1957)*, ed. I. P. Bardin (Moscow: 1957), p. 77.

[9] *Ibid.*

[10] See chap. 9 for U.S. assistance in the machine-building industry. See also I. L. Nepomnyashchii, *Koksovye mashiny, ikh konstruktsii i raschety* (Moscow: 1963).

tried at the Kharkov Coke-Chemical Plant in 1940, no attempt at indigenous innovation can be traced. Other types (Evans-Cope, Becker, and Otto) were purchased and installed but not standardized. By 1945 the Soviets had added very little of technical value, if anything, to this transfer; their whole effort had been spent on mastering and reproducing the most effective of foreign designs. The significant rates of growth in the coke industry[11] are explainable in terms of this transfer.

DANISH AND GERMAN EQUIPMENT IN THE CEMENT INDUSTRY

By 1929 all 31 of the tsarist-era cement plants were back in production (after being re-equipped with imported machinery) and were able to produce 13 million barrels of cement that year. All these plants had been expanded and modernized by several German firms and one Danish firm (F. L. Smidth and Company A/S of Copenhagen); the largest project was at Novorossisk in the Caucasus and had been undertaken by Friedrich-Krupp Grusonwerk A-G and designed to produce 400,000 tons of cement a year.[12] Also in 1929 a technical-assistance agreement was concluded with the American firm of

Table 8–1   ORIGIN OF CEMENT PLANTS IN THE
SOVIET UNION, 1938

Revolving kilns		Shaft kilns Ordinary		Shaft kilns Automatic		Total of all types
Manufacturer	No.	Manufacturer	No.	Manufacturer	No.	
Allis-Chalmers	1	Candlo	5	Graber	1	
Amme-Gieseke	7	Dietch	34	Krupp	10	
Feollner	1	Schneider	73	Lundstedt	12	
Krupp	5			Tiele	1	225 foreign*
Miag	4					
Pfeiffer	12					
Polysius	13					
Smidth	46					
Russian	21					21 domestic
Total	110		112		24	246

Source: I. Ershler and S. Stoliarov, 'The Cement Industry in the U.S.S.R.,' *Pit and Quarry*, XXX, No. 8 (February 1938), pp. 61–4.
* Percentage of foreign installations (based on 246 known makes, not including 24 periodic kilns of unknown origin): 91.5 percent.

[11]   G. Warren Nutter, *The Growth of Industrial Production in the Soviet Union* (Princeton: Princeton University Press, 1962), p. 96. The average annual growth rate in the coke industry for the period 1928–55 is given as 9.1 percent.
[12]   *Die Chemische Fabrik*, I, No. 44 (October 31, 1928), p. 640.

MacDonald,[13] and between 1930 and World War II some 16 large Portland Cement plants were added. Table 8–1 summarizes the origin of Soviet kilns (the most important components of a cement plant)—in use in 1938.

In 1927 the Soviets organized a bureau for design and construction of cement plants and from about 1930 onwards some basic equipment (kilns, mills, crushers, etc.) was built in the U.S.S.R., probably at the Leningrad Shipbuilding Works.[14] By 1938 some 21 kilns (of a total of 246, or 8.5 percent) were of Soviet construction to foreign design. Almost 50 percent of the revolving kilns were built by one Danish company—Smidth, manufacturers of the Unidan and Unax designs.[15] However, even the 21 mills built by Soviet organizations contained a great amount of imported equipment. Table 8–2 illustrates this for the Novo Spassk, the largest cement plant in the U.S.S.R. in 1938–9.

It is unlikely that, during the period under consideration, the Soviets availed themselves of the latest advances in American cement technology. This conclusion is gleaned from an article by one of the hired engineering consultants, who, after pointing out that the expectation of American cement engineers going to the Soviet Union had been that recent improvements in equipment would be adopted, was surprised to find an 'extreme conservatism' evident in all designs finally accepted for building.[16]

> The American engineers were closely questioned on all improvements in machinery and process, but very few of these new developments were incorporated into the plants actually built. The tendency to follow the older European types of design was very strong. On the high councils many of those who enjoyed authority showed a practical familiarity with this older type of cement plant and expressed extreme doubt as to the practicability of adopting modern American designs.[17]

The writer then pointed out that American engineers' plans were criticized in 'great detail' by these councils and changed many times, and that foreign engineers were expected to have 'great masses of detail' to prove every design point.

This argument regarding the negligible transfer of American technique is supported by the data in tables 8–1 and 8–2. In 1938 Soviet kilns were dependent on European, rather than American, design. Further, an article by two Soviet engineers,[18] while confirming that only 21 of the 110 revolving kilns

---

[13] *Ibid.*, II, No. 47 (November 20, 1929), p. 501.
[14] Amtorg, *op. cit.*, V, No. 18–19 (October 1, 1930), p. 373.
[15] See table 8–3.
[16] 'Facts about Russian Cement Plants Told by American Engineers,' *Concrete*, XXXIX, No. 5 (November 1931), pp. 53–5.
[17] *Ibid.*
[18] *Pit and Quarry*, February 1938, p. 61.

in 1938 were built in the Soviet Union, limited its claims concerning the Soviet-built kilns to the following statement: 'Several large new factories have been equipped mainly with equipment made in the country.'[19] Nowhere do the Soviet engineers claim provision of a cement mill with all Soviet-built equipment.

On the other hand, the Soviet cement mill design bureau was in 1938 undertaking design work for cement plants and mill equipment for delivery to Turkey, Iran, and the Mongolian People's Republic. The rationale behind constructing cement plants for export while importing equipment for domestic cement plants lies in the relative quality of imported versus domestic equipment. Soviet-built equipment was acceptable, even if less efficient, in barter deals with underdeveloped areas. It also provided a training ground for mill construction. The mistakes fell elsewhere, and at the same time provided an acceptable propaganda package: the U.S.S.R. exports cement mills and *therefore* has the ability to supply its own cement mill requirements.

Table 8–2 ORIGIN OF EQUIPMENT AT THE NOVO SPASSK CEMENT PLANT, 1938

Department	Equipment Item	Soviet-Made, to Foreign Designs	Foreign-Made (Firm)
Limestone Crushing Dept.			
	Preliminary crusher	—	Smidth A/S
	Hammer mill	—	Smidth A/S
Clay-Crushing Dept.			
	Toothed roll crusher	—	Smidth A/S
Raw Material Storage			
	Traveling crane	—	Babcock & Wilcox
Raw Materials Drying Dept.			
	Limestone driers*	Soviet-made	—
	Pulverized coal burners*	—	Peabody
	Pumps	—	Fuller-Kinyon
Raw Materials Grinding Dept.			
	4-compartment mills*	—	Smidth A/S
	Dish plate feeders*	—	Smidth A/S
	Speed-reducers (in mills)*	—	Wuelfel
	3-compartment mills*	Soviet-made	—
	Filters	—	Beta
Mixing Silos Dept.			
	Pumps*	—	Fuller-Kinyon (made by Claudius Peters)
	Filters*	—	Beta
Rotary Kiln Dept.			
	Kilns and coolers*	Soviet-made	—
	Speed-reducers*	—	Wuelfel
	Pumps	—	Fuller-Kinyon
Clinker Storage			
	Traveling crane	—	Babcock & Wilcox

[19] *Ibid.*, p. 64.

Table 8–2   *(Continued)*

Department	Equipment Item	Soviet-Made, to Foreign Designs	Foreign-Made (Firm)
Cement Mill House	4-compartment mills*	—	Unidan (Smidth)
	Plate feeders*	—	Smidth A/S
	Speed-reducers*	—	Wuelfel
	3-compartment mill	Soviet-made	—
	Pumps*	—	Fuller-Kinyon
Gypsum Storage	Tubular drier	Soviet-made	—
Fuel Preparation Plant	Roll crushers*	Soviet-made	—
	Tubular driers*	Soviet-made	—
	Pumps*	—	Fuller-Kinyon
	2-compartment mills*	—	Smidth A/S
	Plate feeders*	—	Smidth A/S
	Coal mills*	Soviet-made	—
Central Compression Plant	2-stage vertical compressors*	—	Five-Lille (France)
	Pumps*	—	Fuller-Kinyon
Power Plant	3,000-kilowatt steam turbines*	Soviet-made	—
	3,300-volt alternators*	Soviet-made	—
	Vertical Garbe boiler	Soviet-made	—
	Pulverized fuel furnace	—	Babcock & Wilcox
	2 boilers (750 square meters each)	Soviet-made	—

Source: *Pit and Quarry*, October 1938, pp. 55–64.
* Exact number unknown.

SOVIET DEVELOPMENT OF SYNTHETIC RUBBER

The Soviets can rightfully claim indigenous progress in development and initial production of synthetic rubber. The Russian chemist I. I. Ostromislensky worked on synthetic rubbers before the Revolution and in 1915 announced the first organic vulcanizing agents: symmetrical trinitrobenzene, m-dinitrobenzene, and benzoyl peroxide, as well as several agents not using elemental sulphur. Butadiene was produced in Russia in 1915 according to Ostromislensky's method, using a catalytic process starting from ethyl alcohol. Although Ostromislensky later went to work for the U.S. Rubber Company, his work was continued in the Soviet Union by B. V. Buizov, who in 1921 announced the vulcanizing properties of diazoaminobenzene, and by S. V. Lebedev, who in 1928 developed a process for producing butadiene from alcohol 'using a catalyst of magnesium hydroxide, with small proportions of kaolin and hydrous silica and much smaller proportions of iron, titanium and zinc oxides at a temperature of about 385°C.'[20] This pioneering Russian work was preceded only by an English patent (No. 24,790 of 1910) using sodium as the

[20]   Harry L. Fisher, *Chemistry of Natural and Synthetic Rubbers* (New York: Reinhold, 1957), p. 85.

catalytic polymerizing agent in production of butadiene synthetic rubber and by a small German production effort using similar methods during World War I.

Commercial production and marketing of synthetic rubber began in 1929 with Thiokol in the U.S.; by 1940 there were a dozen synthetic rubbers in production in the United States and Germany, in addition to Lebedev's SKB, the sodium-butadiene type, in the Soviet Union.[21] During the 1930s the Soviets made some progress with SKB. Production time was halved, and in 1935 'rodless' polymerization was achieved by using disseminated sodium in large trays; by 1939 production reached 90,000 tons per year. However, Soviet synthetic rubber had a low tensile strength of only about 2,000 psi, compared to 4,500 psi for natural rubber and 4,000 psi for Neoprene (the Du Pont chlorophrene synthetic introduced in 1931). In the United States synthetic rubbers with low tensile strengths of this order, such as the U.S. Rubber Company Type AXF, were not introduced onto the market.

Table 8–3   SOVIET SYNTHETIC RUBBER PRODUCTION, 1939 AND 1945

1939: Types Produced		*1945: Types Produced*
1. SKB in three plants (butadiene polymerized with metallic sodium): tsarist research plus Soviet development		1. SKB 2. Resinit (Thiokol)
		⎧ 3. Du Pont Neoprene (Sovprene): 2 plants, 40,000 tons each (polymerization of acetylene)
2. Resinit (Thiokol polysulphide elastomers): U.S. development	Supplied under Lend-Lease	⎨ 4. Houdry butadiene method: 1 plant, 40,000 tons
		⎩ 5. Houdry catalyst plant 6. Dow Chemical Styrene plant
Capacity at 1939		*Capacity at 1945*	
SKB	90,000 tons	SKB	90,000 tons
Resinit	Very small	Neoprene (Sovprene)	80,000 tons
		Houdry	40,000 tons
		Dow	(?)
		Total	210,000 tons (plus)

Sources: U.S. State Dept., *Report on War Aid Furnished by the United States to the U.S.S.R.* (Washington: Office of Foreign Liquidation, 1945).
George Racey Jordan, *From Major Jordan's Diaries* (New York: Harcourt, Brace and Co. 1952), pp. 138–9.

[21] However, even this Soviet product was developed with U.S. technical assistance. In 1930 a Soviet rubber delegation went to the United States; Soviet rubber engineers were sent for training, three 'foreign specialists' were employed by Resinotrest (Rubber Trust), and four contracts for technical assistance were made with U.S. firms. See *Za Industrializatsiiu*, February 22, 1930.

Thus in 1941–2, when the U.S.S.R. was in urgent need of high-tensile strength synthetic rubber for military purposes, domestic production was small, of mediocre quality, and lacking in the oil-resistant and light-resistant qualities necessary for military use. Only two types were being produced: the original SKB (sodium butadiene) and Resinit (the Soviet version of the Thiokol product, made from ethylene chloride and sodium tetrasulfide).

The Soviet rubber position at 1941 is therefore interesting. The Russians had done early work of great significance on synthetic rubbers, and Ostromislensky's research had certainly placed Russia at least on a par with Western countries during World War I, and perhaps even ahead in theoretical work. This development work was successfully continued in the Soviet Union by his associates and finally led to the sodium-butadiene type, SKB. Thus at the end of the 1920s there had been little Western influence on Soviet synthetic rubber development apart from the usual exchange of theoretical knowledge among scientists. A plant was subsequently built on the basis of this internally generated research and by 1939 was successfully producing 90,000 tons a year. However, there was no technological progress from the original butadiene concept except in the slight improvement of manufacturing methods. While Germany produced and abandoned the numbered Bunas (85 and 115) and the U.S. brought out and replaced a dozen synthetic rubbers with varying properties, the Soviets stayed with SKB plus the adopted Thiokol product, Resinit.

The Baruch Committee on Russia recommended during World War II that the United States investigate Soviet experience with Buna rubbers. In the final analysis very little information was forthcoming and the results of this attempted exchange were slow and disappointing. It was found that the Soviets were producing only the original Buna-S (butadiene polymerized by sodium) and had no experience with improved Buna-S or emulsion polymerization methods. However, the Office of Rubber Administration did send a special mission headed by Ernest W. Pittman, President of the Inter-Chemical Company, to the Soviet Union. There is, in the State Department files, an interesting memorandum of conversation in which Colonel Dewey, Deputy Rubber Director, commented on this attempted exchange of information.[22] As synthetic rubber was the only sector in which the Soviets had undertaken technological development on their own on the bases of extensive tsarist-era research, it is worth quoting:

---

[22] Dept. of State, Memorandum of Conversation, 861.645/17, April 1, 1943. Participants were: Col. Dewey, Deputy Rubber Director; Dr. Gilliland, Assistant Deputy Rubber Director; Major General Wesson, Office of Lend-Lease Administration; Mr. John Hazard, Office of Lend-Lease Administration; Mr. Dean Acheson, Assistant Secretary of State; and Mr. Loy Henderson, Assistant Chief, Division of European Affairs.

In response to a suggestion which had been made last year by the Soviet authorities for an exchange of information with regard to the manufacture of rubber, the Office of Rubber Administration had sent to the Soviet Union a mission composed of four of the outstanding experts in the United States on the production of rubber. These men spent six weeks before their departure collecting data relating to American manufacturing processes to take with them. They left the United States in December 1943. When they arrived in Moscow they called immediately upon the appropriate Soviet authorities and had a discussion with them regarding the scope and method of the exchange of information. The Soviet authorities apparently were pleased at the ideas expressed by the members of the mission during this discussion and suggested that these ideas be reduced to writing.

Dr. Pittman, the Chief of the American mission, assisted by the other three members, thereupon prepared a proposal outlining the method of exchange of information and the scope of the exchange. This proposal was handed in the latter part of January to the appropriate Soviet authorities in the form of a letter. No reply to this letter was ever received. The Soviet authorities proceeded for a period of more than two months, however, to engage in sporadic conversation relating to the rubber industry and on two occasions went so far as to take the mission through rubber producing plants. The information which they furnished the mission was of too superficial a character to be of any practical use, and the members of the mission were hurried through the plants at such a fast pace that they derived no technical benefit from their visit.

In the meantime the Soviet Government sent a committee of highly qualified rubber experts to the United States in order to obtain information regarding American processes of rubber manufacture. This commission arrived a number of weeks ago. In view of the manner in which the American rubber mission was being treated, Colonel Dewey gave orders that no information of any practical value should be given to it until he had assurances that the American mission was being given information of value or until the return to the United States of the American mission. The Soviet Government now proposes, Mr. Dewey continues, in a letter to Mr. Stettinius that a formal agreement be drawn up providing for the exchange between the United States and the U.S.S.R. of information with regard to rubber. This proposal was of a more far reaching nature than that made by Mr. Pittman in January. It provided that the Soviet Government should furnish certain technical information to the American Government; that the American Government would furnish technical information to the Soviet Government not only regarding the processes with regard to which Mr. Pittman had suggested an exchange but also with regard to other processes which were in various stages of development in the United States; that for a period of several years the American Government should furnish the Soviet Government full details regarding any new processes or improvements in processes for manufacturing rubber which might be worked out; that the American Government should furnish the Soviet Government with machinery and technical personnel to enable it to build during 1943 and 1944 large rubber producing factories in the Soviet Union.

Colonel Dewey said that a good deal of the information which the Soviet Government demanded could not possibly be put to practical use during the war; that the Russians were asking for some extremely complicated, technical secrets of American manufacturers the utilization of which would require elaborate machinery and equipment which could not be manufactured during the war period without interfering with other important war production; that it would be impossible to set up and begin operating plants containing such machinery and equipment during war time; that, furthermore, the production of this equipment and the explanation of its use to the Soviet authorities would require much time of numerous American technicians whose services are urgently required in the war production field.

On balance then, the Soviets gained far more than the United States in the World War II technical exchange in synthetic rubber, although this was the single area where the Soviets were presumed to be more advanced.

Gaps in Soviet synthetic rubber-manufacturing facilities were filled by Lend-Lease. Two complete plants were acquired for the manufacture of Neoprene by polymerization of acetylene, with a capacity of 40,000 tons each per year.[23] The U.S. also shipped a Houdry-method butadiene plant, a Houdry catalyst plant, and a Dow Chemical Company styrene plant. Table 8–3 summarizes this acquisition of U.S. synthetic rubber manufacturing facilities by the Soviet Union. The Du Pont Company, at the request of the State Department, supplied its Neoprene process, as well as two plants,[24] to the Soviet Union with the right to use patents and processes. Russian engineers visited Du Pont plants and were granted access to technical data. Du Pont engineers erected the plants in the Soviet Union.[25]

Several agreements to transfer allied U.S. technologies were negotiated with the assistance of the State Department. One agreement was with the Standard Oil Company for a process producing synthetic ethyl alcohol from petroleum gases. The Standard Oil agreement gave the Soviets special advantages (apart from designs, specifications, and operating instructions); for example, an inspection party was allowed to inspect the Baton Rouge plant. At first the party, headed by P. S. Makeev, was denied entrance on security grounds, but inspection was later allowed.[26]

---

[23] Now called Narit, in the U.S.S.R.

[24] *New York Times*, July 3, 1944, p. 24, col. 3.

[25] *Ibid.* Very large shipments of Lend-Lease synthetic rubbers confirm the shortages. Some $36 million worth of manufactured rubber goods, $1\frac{1}{2}$ million pounds of synthetic rubber, and more than $115 million worth of tire casings, as well as camelback and rubber cements, were shipped. (Jordan, *op. cit.*, pp. 158–9.)

[26] Frank A. Howard, *Buna Rubber* (New York: Von Nostrand, 1947), p. 241.

RECLAIMED RUBBER TECHNOLOGY[27]

In the early 1930s the proportion of reclaimed rubber to total consumption was about one-half and increasing. Thus reclaim processing was as important as original manufacture. Up to 1932 there were two tsarist plants in Moscow and Leningrad processing reclaim from rubber footwear by the acid process. The Leningrad plant was reconstructed during the First Five-Year Plan and supplemented by a new and much larger plant at Yaroslavl which produced 23 tons of reclaim per day from rubber tires by the alkali process.

The technology used in the new Yaroslavl plant was completely American, and used equipment made in the United States and in the United Kingdom to American design. It was the equal of the most modern plants under construction and the technology was significantly in advance of current European practice. The grinding operation, for example, utilized a 2.5- to 4-ton capacity chopper 'used at the best American plants but little known in Europe, though its capacity is very considerable.'[28] The devulcanizing room was of American layout, using two Louisville presses and three Sargent conveyor dryers. The washing process utilized Anderson moisture-expellers. The recuperating unit utilized a Dorr thickener and an Oliver vacuum filter. The mill room was of American layout but much of the equipment was supplied by the United Kingdom.[29]

CARBON BLACK MANUFACTURE

Carbon black is an important raw material in the manufacture of tires, about five pounds being required for each 10 pounds of synthetic rubber. The Soviets acquired carbon-black technology from three sources before 1945. First, a small, crude plant to manufacture carbon black from gas was designed and built by the Marietta Manufacturing Company in 1930. Then during World War II Soviet engineers acquired a good deal of technical information from United States plants. After World War II the Soviets took as reparations the largest of the German plants manufacturing carbon black from crude anthracene residue.[30]

E. B. BADGER WOOD-DISTILLATION AND CONTINUOUS ALCOHOL UNITS

Two specialized plants for production of chemicals from wood products were erected by the E. B. Badger and Sons Company of Boston. In 1931–2

[27] Partly based on M. I. Farberov and V. N. Komarov, 'Russia's Reclaiming Process,' *The India-Rubber Journal*, CLXXXVII, June 23, 1934.

[28] *Ibid.*, p. 699.

[29] *Ibid.* See p. 699, for details of these units.

[30] U.S. Senate Foreign Relations Committee, *East-West Trade* (Washington, D.C.: November 1964), p. 51.

the Nadezhdinsk and the Ashinsky plants, near Sverdlovsk, were entirely designed by the Badger Company, and according to Alcan Hirsch, Chief Chemical Consultant to the Soviet Union 'closely resemble[d] the great plant they built for the Ford Motor Co. at Iron Mountain, Michigan.'[31] These were the most modern wood-distillation units and, as the Soviets have claimed, the largest in the world outside the United States. They produced 80 percent glacial acetic acid and C. P. Methanol grade wood alcohol, both using Badger Company processes. Alcan Hirsch described the equipment of the Ashinsky as follows:

> The still house is equipped with the latest type triple effect evaporators; acetic acid fractionating and concentrating apparatus, and wood alcohol and methyl-acetone refining equipment of the most modern, continuous type. The equipment is provided with heat exchangers and automatic temperature, pressure and flow regulators, and with the latest type controls and accessories for continuous production.

After stating that it was designed with emphasis on economy, Hirsch added that 'upward of a million dollars was spent on equipment being imported from this country.'[32]

In December 1935 a further agreement was made under which E. B. Badger and Sons agreed to build three complete continuous 97-percent alcohol-distillation and refining units, three complete 99.8-percent anhydrous alcohol units, three complete benzol-refining units, and three 'calandria for heating crude alcohol.'[33] These were completed in 1937 and 1938. The Soviets obviously continued to lag in alcohol technology in 1941, as in that year the Kellogg Corporation advised Amtorg that it was unable to supply an ethyl alcohol plant.[34]

CONCLUSIONS

This chapter has considered eight major chemical or allied industries.

The development of coke ovens—particularly by-product coke ovens—was based wholly on Koppers and Koppers-Becker designs, at first built by the Koppers Corporation or its licensees and then gradually by the Soviets themselves.

[31]   Hirsch, *op. cit.*, p. 82. For a description of the Ford Iron Mountain wood-distillation plant, see W. G. Nelson, 'Waste-Wood Distillation by the Badger-Stafford Process,' *Industrial and Engineering Chemistry*, XXII, No. 4 (April 1930), pp. 312–5. The process was 'a radical departure from established procedure' and the plant was 'probably the cleanest wood distillation plant in the world.' A pilot plant had been built in 1924 after extensive investigation. The Soviets were able to acquire the Badger-Stafford process within one to two years after the Ford Motor Co.

[32]   Hirsch, *op. cit.*, p. 83.

[33]   U.S. State Dept. Decimal File, 861.602/284, Report No. 2209, Moscow Embassy, January 16, 1937.

[34]   U.S. State Dept. Decimal File, 861.659/17, January 16, 1941.

The cement industry was almost completely of European origin; 91.5 percent of the kilns operating in 1938 were of foreign manufacture—chiefly Danish. Those of Soviet manufacture contained a great amount of foreign equipment and were built to foreign design.

Synthetic rubber is of considerable interest as the Soviets started with an initial advantage in the form of tsarist research. SKB rubber was a purely Soviet development, but by World War II Soviet development had slipped behind Western development and this necessitated imports of Neoprene, Houdry, and Styrene processes and equipment for manufacture of special rubbers. Reclaimed rubber technology was wholly American and carbon-black technology was American and German in origin.

Wood-distillation plants were built by E. B. Badger and Sons of the U.S. in 1931–2, and the same company built three continuous alcohol-distillation units in 1936–7.

Thus in these major chemical industries, seven technologies (coke-chemicals, carbon black, cement, high-tensile-strength synthetic rubber, reclaimed rubber, wood distillation, and alcohol distillation) were transferred from the West with no indigenous Soviet development. The eighth technology, synthetic rubber from butadiene, was one in which the Soviets had an initial research advantage; however, the Soviet industry did not develop as rapidly as that in capitalist countries, and in 1941 technology for more advanced synthetic rubbers was imported under the Lend-Lease program.

CHAPTER NINE

Technical Assistance to the Machine Building and Allied Industries[1]

Two plants, Uralmash and Kramatorsk, were of major significance in Soviet development between 1933 and 1945. These plants built machinery for heavy industry, including the iron and steel and non-ferrous smelting and rolling sectors. Both were equipped with the finest obtainable Western equipment and produced standard adaptations of Western designs, enabling multiple production of heavy equipment and machinery of known and reliable capability without investment in research and development.

The key to Soviet development is mass production for capital industries of heavy equipment (furnaces, kilns, compressors, etc.) of a standard type based on a proven Western design. This principle has three essential components: first, flow or multiple-unit rather than single-unit production; second, standardization to avoid the cost of customizing for a particular location and market; and third, avoidance of research and development costs by adaptation of a proven design.

EXPANSION OF THE FITZNER & HAMPNER MACHINE-BUILDING PLANT AT KRAMATORSK

The Fitzner & Hampner plant founded in 1896 at Kramatorsk, about 225 kilometers southeast of Kharkov, manufactured general mining and metallurgical equipment (including cranes, ladles, and slag cars), using iron and steel products made in four small blast furnaces and rolled in mills associated with

---

[1] Sources for this chapter include the U.S. State Dept. Decimal File; Oberkommando der Wehrmacht records in the National Archives; articles in the U.S. trade press for the machine tool industry; L. A. Aisenshtadt's *Ocherki po istorii stankostroeniya SSSR* (Moscow: 1957); and an informative article by Joseph Gwyer, 'Soviet Machine Tools,' in *Ordnance*, November–December 1958. For a different argument, see David Granick, *Soviet Metal-Fabricating and Economic Development* (Madison: University of Wisconsin, 1967). Granick's study is based wholly on Soviet source material.

the plant. This plant was little used by the Soviets until the early 1930s. Then enormous capital investments in the newly formed Kramatorsky combine (Kramkombinat) turned the old plant into the largest machine-building unit in the Soviet Union, with three main sections: the original iron and steel mills at Kramatorsk, the Fitzner & Hampner machine works (both considerably expanded with new imported equipment), and a gigantic new enterprise, Novo Kramatorsk, far larger than the early plant. The latter was opened in sections beginning in 1931.

The first new unit of Novo Kramatorsk was a steel construction shop to manufacture structural steel work for the Dniepr Dam and the Magnitogorsk and Kuznetsk iron and steel plants. A large forge shop followed, 'equipped with modern machinery imported from abroad and partly produced in Soviet factories'[2] to produce forgings of up to one and a half tons. In addition there were two iron foundries: one of 27,700 square meters for large and medium castings and one of 17,000 square meters for small castings. A 60,000-square-meter steel foundry—the largest in Europe—was added. It was supplied by four open-hearth and four electric furnaces.

Figure 9–1   STRUCTURE OF KRAMKOMBINAT, 1930–2

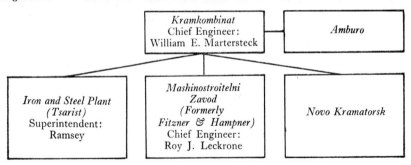

Source: Construction from data in U.S. State Dept. Decimal File, 861.5017—Living Conditions/568, /553.

Later extensions comprised three mechanical shops (A, B, C). Shop A produced rolling-mill equipment; Shop B blast-furnace equipment, open-hearth furnaces, and coke ovens; and Shop C vacuum drums, cylinders, generator shafts, pinions, and turbine rotors. More than 600 machines of the finest Western make were installed in these three shops. The first group of departments opened in 1932. By August 1934 the plant had 13 large departments operating. The balance came into operation by 1936–7.

---

[2]   *U.S.S.R. in Construction*, No. 7 (July 1932). The Soviet machines were the simplest types of lathes and drilling machines, as the machine-tool plants were not producing modern units. All the heavy presses and forges were imported.

Technical assistance supplied to Kramkombinat began on an informal basis; i.e., it was unrelated to specific Western firms, and comprised groups of both American and German engineering designers and specialists. After 1936 it was supplied by contract with United Engineering and Foundry, and possibly by Demag A-G.

The American contribution began with a conversation sometime in 1929 between Meshlauk (in charge of heavy industry) and William Martersteck, a member of the Freyn Engineering Company staff in the U.S.S.R. Martersteck was an experienced steel-rolling-mill designer and suggested to Meshlauk that the Soviet Union should make its own rolling-mill equipment rather than import it. It was suggested that this would provide training for Soviet engineers and in any event help solve the eventual problem of repairing imported equipment. Meshlauk was impressed. He sent Martersteck back to the United States, where, independently of the Freyn Corporation, he gathered a party of 20 U.S. engineers and designers. They returned in December 1930 to the Kramatorsk plant.[3]

Martersteck was Chief Engineer of a group consisting of five machine-shop designers, three foundry experts, one pattern-shop expert, one open-hearth expert, one expeditor for the planning department, two crane designers, five steel-mill machinery designers, and one steel-mill operator. All were employed on a two-year contract payable in U.S. dollars plus rubles. Total wages for the group were $14,350 and 10,600 rubles per month.

After several months spent working on small projects, the group was requested to design a rolling mill: the standard blooming mill later produced at Kramatorsk. In February 1932, concurrently with Soviet financial difficulties, the group was informed that the contract would be terminated March 1, 1932 and replaced with another contract employing only Martersteck, seven designers, and Ramsey, the steel-mill operator—with a 50 percent pay cut. One of the crane designers refused and returned to the U.S.[4] By the end of 1933 only one designer, Puttman, remained in the Soviet Union.

The Martersteck group formed, for about 18 months, a mill-design bureau. Individual American and German engineers were also employed in both the

[3]   U.S. State Dept. Decimal File, 861.5017—Living Conditions/568, Riga Consulate, November 22, 1932, interview with Karl E. Martersteck (his son); and 861.5017/ 553, Riga Consulate Report No. 892, November 4, 1932, interview with Miriam Martersteck, Russian wife of Karl.

[4]   As the group had a two-year contract, this was a clear breach of contract by the Soviets. A somewhat harsher view is given in a letter written by E. G. Puttman, a blooming-mill specialist. Puttman says that half the group was dismissed on 'trumped-up charges' and a month later the others had their dollar allowances cut. After bargaining for 5 months, Puttman was given the Soviet terms: accept or face termination. He accepted and a simple rider covering the changes was added to the contract. He was unable to obtain a copy of this 'voluntary agreement.' (See U.S. State Dept. Decimal File, 861.602/254.)

old and new Kramatorsk plants. The Chief Engineer of Mashinostroitelni Zavod was Roy J. Leckrone,[5] who reported that 26,000 Russian workers were fabricating steel for the Dniepr Dam and making iron and steel plant machinery and 400 gun limbers.

Although Martersteck and Leckrone stayed on until 1933, most American designers and engineers left at the time of the valuta crisis and were replaced with Germans—some 500 at Kramatorsk alone—willing to work for rubles without foreign currency.[6]

The machine-shop equipment at Kramatorsk was evidently British and German. Sir Walter Citrine, General Secretary of the Trades Union Congress of Great Britain, reported in 1936 after a lengthy tour of Kramatorsk, 'I saw many machines by English makers, amongst them Craven, Asquith, Herbert, Igranic and Richards, and these and German machines dominated the shops. . . .'[7]

In 1936 the United Engineering and Foundry Company of Pittsburgh signed an agreement with the Soviet Union to design, construct, and install both hot and cold steel-strip mills. These reflected the very latest in American steel technology. Such wide-strip mills were essential for production of automobile body sheets. The contract included special designs in millimeter measurements and technical assistance to the Kramatorsk works to build such mills. Soviet engineer P. Perepelitsa spent two years in the United States at United Engineering plants and American engineers in turn worked at the Kramatorsk plant. On his return to the U.S.S.R. in 1937, Perepelitsa wrote an objective comparison of work at the United plants and at Kramatorsk[8] and quite clearly had greatly benefited from his lengthy exposure to American production methods.

Preparations for installing the strip mill in the U.S.S.R. were supervised at Kramatorsk by T. W. Jenkins,[9] who summarized the Russian engineering position at that time as follows: 'Soviet engineers are not yet able to execute American blueprints which require great precision and . . . the lack of highly skilled workmen for the execution of such work is a great handicap to Soviet plants.'[10] Even casting for the strip mills required skilled workmen from

---

[5] U.S. State Dept. Decimal File, 861.5017—Living Conditions/542, Istanbul Consulate, October 5, 1932.

[6] *Ibid.*, 861.5017—Living Conditions/553. The Germans were treated as Russians and paid 150 rubles per month, whereas the American designers had been earning up to $1,000 plus 500 to 600 rubles per month.

[7] W. Citrine, *I Search for Truth in Russia* (London: Routledge, 1936), p. 222.

[8] *Za Industrializatsiiu*, No. 10, January 12, 1937.

[9] U.S. State Dept. Decimal File, 861.6511/35, Report No. 19, Moscow, February 3, 1937.

[10] *Ibid.*

the United States.[11] It is interesting to note that the Perepelitsa article is reasonably consistent with Jenkins' criticisms and, coming at the time of the purges, is a remarkably frank commentary.

On the other hand, some progress in learning was undoubtedly being made in the U.S.S.R. In 1936 Kramatorsk turned out the first Soviet coking machine, a copy of a Koppers model, which, while not of the same order of construction complexity as a strip mill, still represented a considerable advance from the 1930–2 period.[12]

During the German occupation, Kramatorsk was turned over by the German occupation authorities to Berg und Hüttenwerke-Gesellschaft Ost m.b.H., which repaired the buildings, plant, and existing machinery, and assembled raw materials. Initial work consisted of the repair of mining machinery.[13] Early in 1943 Alfred Krupp requested a special report on Kramatorsk, submitted on August 13, 1943 by Dr. Hedstueck, deputy plant manager. This report resulted in an order to all Krupp departments in Germany to render all necessary assistance to the renamed Neue Maschinenfabrik Kramatorsk, 'especially as regards placing at their disposal the material and manpower

Table 9–1 ANNUAL CAPACITY OF SOVIET HEAVY-MACHINE-BUILDING PLANTS

Non-Military Heavy Equipment	*Kramatorsk**	*Uralmash**	*Expanded Tsarist Plants***
Standard blast furnaces	6 per year	4 per year	4 per year
Standard (150-ton) open hearths	30 per year	20 per year	20 per year
Standard blooming mills	3 per year	2 per year	2 per year
Other blooming mills	13 per year	10 per year	12 per year
Gas generators	150 per year	50 per year	50 per year
Heavy forgings	24,000 tons	20,000 tons	—
Mining equipment	—	17,000 tons	—
Non-ferrous metallurgical equipment	—	5,000 tons	—
Heavy presses	—	5,000 tons	—

* Output for Uralmash includes all important items. Kramatorsk also produced turning lathes, 125-ton cranes, heavy hoists and gas-blowing machines. Kramatorsk output includes that for the Fitzner & Hampner plant established in 1896 and incorporated into the new Kramatorsk plant next door. Both plants had a considerable military capacity.

** Output estimated.

Sources: American-Russian Chamber of Commerce, *Handbook of the Soviet Union* (New York: John Day Co., 1936), p. 152.

U.S.S.R. in Construction, No. 7 (July 1932).

[11] *Ibid.*

[12] I. L. Nepomnyashchii, *op. cit.*, p. 5.

[13] *Report on Russian Foundries*, April 14, 1943, Nazi Industry Reports, No. 4332 (at Hoover Institution).

urgently required for starting production in the tank maintenance plant which is of vital importance to the fighting troops.'[14]

By August 1943 there were 2,000 Russian workers at Kramatorsk, working mainly on tank and military equipment repairs and producing small tools such as shovels, hammers, and wheelbarrows. Very little complex equipment was manufactured, although one order was for 1,000 cylinder-boring and grinding sets for the Wehrmacht.[15]

THE URALMASH PLANT AT SVERDLOVSK

Uralmash was another giant plant, only slightly smaller than the expanded Kramatorsk complex. Designed to build equipment for the mining and metallurgical industry, Uralmash also produced large quantities of military goods.

Uralmash opened July 15, 1933, but as late as 1936 was working at only 60 percent capacity. The complex contained numerous shops and departments handling production procedures all the way from raw-material conversion through steel manufacture to the production of finished heavy equipment. By 1936 Uralmash could produce prefabricated submarines.

Table 9–2   REPRESENTATIVE LIST OF GERMAN
                EQUIPMENT SUPPLIED TO URALMASH

Description	Cost (Millions of Marks)	Supplier
Generator plant (peat)	1.25	'Machine factory in Berlin'
Boiler plant (550 square meters)	0.75	'West German' plant
Steam turbines	—	'Silesian machine plant'
Cranes	2.0	Several German plants
Tilting furnaces	0.5	'West Germany'
Roll-turning machines	0.6	'West German plant'
Forge ovens	0.4	'Middle Germany factory'
Forge shop cranes	0.7	'Rhineland machine plant'
Forging press and installations	0.8	'Rhineland machine factory'
Drilling banks	1.0	'Berlin tool plant'
Drilling machines, lathes, etc.	3.0	'Rhineland machine factory'

Source: Sowjetwirtschaft und Aussenhandel, Handelsvertretung der UdSSR in Deutschland, Berlin SW., IX–XII, 1930–3.

Construction required some 12,000 workers; 'about 150 foreign specialists and workers were engaged to help in the construction and operation of the

[14] *Report on Neue Maschinfabrik Kramatorsk*, in Nazi Industry Reports, No. 2959 (at Hoover Institution).

[15] *Ibid.*

factory.'[16] The construction and design of several key departments, such as the foundry, were American in concept, and American engineers were hired to design layouts and develop methods of reinforcing concrete for the plant.[17] The complex included foundries, hammer and press shops, forge shops, heat-treating shops, two mechanical departments, and machine fabrication and assembly shops. The equipment came largely but not completely from Germany.

Scott received a conducted tour of the plant in 1935–6 and wrote an enthusiastic description:

> It is one of the best-looking plants I have ever seen. The first mechanical department was a beautiful piece of work. A building a quarter of a mile long was filled with the best American, British and German machines. It was better equipped than any single shop in the General Electric Works in Schenectady. There were two immense lathes not yet in operation. Later I found out that they were used for turning gun barrels.[18]

CHANGES IN THE SOVIET DEMAND FOR IMPORTED MACHINE TOOLS

The Kramatorsk and Uralmash plants were primarily intended for construction of heavy equipment, although they did manufacture heavy machine tools such as presses and forges. Machine tools—lathes, shapers, grinders, broachers, and similar tools—were manufactured in large, specialized plants, some of which were expanded tsarist plants and some completely new Soviet enterprises.

This construction and expansion of giant specialized tool plants did not, as has been suggested by some observers, reduce the total Soviet demand for foreign equipment in the 1930s,[19] although it did change slightly the structure of that demand. In 1931 most American, United Kingdom, and German machine-tool exports in all categories were going to the Soviet Union. (See table 9–3.)

---

[16] *Factory and Industrial Management*, LXXX, No. 2 (1931), p. 637.

[17] Amtorg, *op. cit.*, IX, No. 10 (October 1934), p. 198.

[18] Scott, *op. cit.*, p. 103.

[19] For example, see Harry Schwartz, *Russia's Soviet Economy* (New York: Prentice Hall, 1950): 'But as Soviet machine tool and machinery factories increased their output as Soviet engineers mastered advanced foreign technology, the U.S.S.R.'s imports of machinery and technicians from abroad could be and were reduced.' (P. 241.) On the other hand American engineers working in Russia correctly foretold the need to continue machine tool imports. For example, see A. M. Wasbauer, 'Machine Tools for the Soviets,' *American Machinist*, v. 78, February 1934, pp. 147–9. In 1933–4 Wasbauer was on the Design Commission in charge of heavy-machine-tool design.

Table 9–3   PERCENT OF U.S. MACHINERY EXPORTS
              GOING TO SOVIET UNION, 1930–1

Equipment Item	1930 (Percent)	1931 (Percent)
Drilling machines	51.79	78.05
Foundry and molding equipment	57.56	73.81
Milling machines	42.01	70.26
Forging machinery	51.92	67.54
Vertical boring mills	36.25	65.68
Lathes	50.73	65.61
Planers and shapers	36.61	64.60
Other metal machines	35.98	59.98
Grinding machines	29.56	57.90
Sheet and plate metal working machines	30.93	53.91
Other metal working machines	36.79	35.82

Source: Amtorg, *op. cit.*, VII–VIII, No. 10 (May 15, 1932), p. 223.

In the case of the United Kingdom, the impact of Soviet purchases was almost complete; in 1932 the Soviet Union took no less than 90 percent of all United Kingdom machinery exports.[20] In some machinery categories the Soviets took almost all United Kingdom exports: £161,000 worth of presses were exported, of which £157,000 worth (98.1 percent) went to the Soviet Union. In the same year the U.K. exported £382,000 worth of planers, of which £365,000 worth (95.5 percent) went to the Soviet Union. Of other machine tools such as lathes, drilling machines, and grinders, 90 percent of U.K. exports went to the U.S.S.R.[21]

By 1935–6 production of engine lathes, semi-automatic and single-spindle automatic lathes, planers, and some pneumatic tools had been 'mastered' by the Russians, but objectives for the following year still included such machine tools as axle-turning lathes, six-spindle automatics, internal grinding machines, and radial drills, and many other types.[22]

At the end of the 1930s, the Soviet Union was still importing significant quantities of machine tools, and its trade agreements were negotiated with this as a primary objective. The 1939 trade agreement between Germany and the Soviet Union placed great emphasis on machine tools. After indicating that Germany would grant a 200-million-Reichmark credit, a 'Strictly Confidential' German Foreign Office memorandum adds:

> The credit will be used to finance Soviet orders in Germany. The Soviet Union will make use of it to order the industrial products listed in schedule

[20] *Engineering*, July 27, 1934, p. 86.
[21] *Ibid.*
[22] 'Machine Tool Building in Russia,' *Machinery*, v. 42, October 1935, p. 107.

A of the agreement. They consist of machinery and industrial installations. Machine tools up to the very largest dimensions form a considerable part of the deliveries. And armaments in the broader sense (such as optical supplies, armor plate and the like) will, subject to examination of every single item, be supplied in smaller proportion.[23]

Soviet requests and delivery schedules under the agreement reflect a primary interest in large, specialized machine tools.[24] It appears that German-occupied Czechoslovakia also played an important role in supply of machine tools. Between March 1939 and August 1940, more than 85 percent of Czech exports to the Soviet Union consisted of machines and apparatus of various kinds, and much of the remaining 15 percent consisted of iron and steel products.[25]

Soviet stripping of Manchurian industry in late 1945 confirms their over-riding interest in machine tools; so many machine tools were removed that the productive capacity of the considerable Manchurian metal working industry was reduced by some 80 percent. For example, the Manchurian Machine Tool Company plant at Mukden was completely removed to the Soviet Union. An American engineer from the Pauley Mission visited the plant in June 1946 and reported, 'There was very little to observe in this factory except the absence of equipment. Everything of value was removed.'[26]

Between September and October of 1945, 120 Soviet officers and men had been billeted in the plant; in 40 days, with the help of 200 Japanese employees, they 'stripped the equipment listed, crated it individually and completely, and shipped it out by rail.' This plant produced small lathes, automatic lathes, drilling machines, and milling machines. Similarly, the Manchu Machine Works was stripped of 90 percent of its equipment, and half a dozen similar large plants, each with several thousand machine tools, were removed to the U.S.S.R.[27]

---

[23]   Raymond J. Sontag and James S. Beddie, *Nazi-Soviet Relations, 1939–1941* (Dept. of State, Washington, D.C., 1948), p. 83. (Translation of Foreign Office Memorandum, August 29, 1939.) See also the negotiations between Germany and the U.S.S.R., 1939 to 1941, in the Hauptarchiv, Hoover Institution, Boxes 1137 and 1138.

[24]   Hoover Institution, Hauptarchiv, Box 1138. For example, see Documents 324623–29.

[25]   Hoover Institution, Hauptarchiv, Box 1137, *Ausfuhr-Warenverkehr des Protektorate Böhmen und Mühren mit der U.d.S.S.R. vom 16.3.1939 bis 31.8.1940.* See Tariff Classes 38, 40, and 41.

[26]   Edwin W. Pauley, *Report on Japanese Assets in Manchuria to the President of the United States, July, 1946* (Washington, D.C.: 1946), Appendix 7, 'Plant Inspection Report 1-J-3.' The question of reparations will be covered in Vol. III.

[27]   *Ibid., Appendix 7*, 'Plant Inspection Report 1-J-7.' The Northeast Economic Commission says the plant was 100-percent stripped; the U.S. inspecting engineer says the figure was closer to 90 percent.

A continuing interest in machine tools is also suggested by the recommendations of the Pauley Mission on Japanese reparations,[28] the machine tool
section of which was written by Owen Lattimore.[29] 'Although I do not believe
that the U.S.S.R. should assert a substantial claim for reparations from Japan,
nevertheless certain plants and machine tools may well be made available to
the U.S.S.R.'[30]

The reason given was that low levels of economic development in the Far
East would make absorption of this industrial capacity by other countries
'difficult' and that China and the Philippines were not technically ready to
receive such reparations.[31] Lattimore presented the topic to the Reparations
Committee on January 12, 1946 and suggested that after war damage was taken
into account Japan might have 850,000 machine tools available for reparations.
As China and the Philippines had already been ruled out on the grounds they
were economically backward and therefore had no need for such equipment,
the obvious recipient would be the Soviet Union. China had already lost its
share of reparations by quick Soviet action in Manchuria, where the machine
tools taken by the Soviets were actually a charge against Chinese reparations
claims.[32]

This continued Soviet demand for certain important categories of machine
tools is supported by tabulations compiled by Joseph Gwyer.[33] Between 1932
and 1945 approximately one-half of the steadily increasing machine-tool

Table 9–4   COMPOSITION OF SOVIET MACHINE TOOL
PRODUCTION, 1932–45

Tools Produced	*1932*	*1940*	*1945*
Total machine tools produced	19,978	58,437	38,419
Group A: lathes (not turret or semi-automatic)	7,145	11,523	13,063
Group B: vertical drilling machines	6,838	15,251	7,168
Groups A and B as percent of total	72.8%	45.8%	52.7%

Source: Adapted from Joseph Gwyer, 'Soviet Machine Tools,' *Ordnance,* XLIII,
No. 231, November–December 1958, pp. 415–9.

[28] Edwin W. Pauley, *Report on Japanese Reparations to the President of the United
States, November 1945 to April 1946* (Washington: April 1, 1946).
[29] For background of Owen Lattimore, see Anthony Kubek, *How the Far East Was
Lost* (Chicago: Regnery, 1963), pp. 263–4.
[30] Pauley, *Report on Japanese Reparations . . . 1946,* p. 13.
[31] *Ibid.*
[32] *Ibid.,* pp. 18–9.
[33] Joseph A. Gwyer, 'Soviet Machine Tools,' *Ordnance,* November–December 1958.

production was comprised of just two elementary types: simple lathes (excluding turret and semi-automatic lathes) and vertical drilling machines. (See table 9–4.)

If we analyze Soviet production in complex machine-tool categories, we find that by 1945 the Soviets were hardly beyond the prototype stage. In 1932 no broaching machines were made, and in 1945 only five. In 1932 only 46 slotters were made; this declined to 20 in 1945. No radial drilling machines were made in 1932 and only 43 in 1945. Some 233 planers were made in 1932, but only five in 1945. Finally, only 42 machines described as 'large, heavy, unique' were made in 1945.[34]

Thus the structure of Soviet machine-tool production in 1945 is quite clear. Output was concentrated on producing very large numbers of very simple machine tools. Even tools of moderate complexity (radial drills, broachers, and slotters) were imported. Thus the dependence of the Soviet Union on the West was almost as great in 1945, as far as machine tools were concerned, as in 1932. Only two groups of fairly simple machine tools had been mastered with any degree of certainty by 1945, and this circumstance was brought about only by Western technical assistance to individual machine-tool plants.

TECHNICAL ASSISTANCE TO MACHINE-TOOL PLANTS

The Podolsk plant, about 24 miles from Moscow, employed some 2,000 workers on the production of turret lathes. This plant had a technical-assistance agreement with Frank D. Chase, Inc., and was subsequently reorganized on American lines by John W. Lundin, who installed a large refinery and metal casting plant.[35] The Frank D. Chase consulting organization also undertook three other large foundry projects. The first, in 1929, was for production of sewing-machine castings; for this purpose the company brought back Soviet engineers to the United States and 'made the design, drawings, specification and purchase of equipment in this country.'[36] The very large foundry at the Stalingrad Tractor Plant was built under a Frank Chase contract, as was the foundry at the Putilovets plant; in these, Chase also supervised construction, installation of equipment, and initial operation. The Putilovets plant was

---

[34]   *Ibid.* It could be argued quite accurately that Lend-Lease was supplying Soviet imports of more complex tools. However, if the Soviet Union had the production capability for these tools it is likely that requests would have been for other urgently needed equipment. Lend-Lease was not a bottomless barrel, and the Soviet Union was required, even though the Administration gave first priority to the Soviets, to establish priorities and make choices.

[35]   U.S. State Dept. Decimal File, 861.5017—Living Conditions/274 and /482. See also Sutton, *Western Technology . . ., 1917 to 1930,* p. 72.

[36]   *American Engineers in Russia,* C. R. Cody folder.

'the first modern mechanically equipped foundry completed in Russia [and] also one of the early projects of the Five Year Plan. . . .'[37]

The Prisposoblenie plant of Orgametal in Moscow was stocked in the early 1930s with 'the very latest in American machine tools—rows of milling machines and other machine tools of the most approved design.'[38] This was in addition to a sprinkling of German millers, shapers and lathes. According to Walter Wells,[39] Prisposoblenie had the responsibility of establishing standards, and dies and jigs were built at Prisposoblenie for Soviet tool-manufacturing plants.

The Krasny Proletariat plant in Moscow was an expanded tsarist plant previously known as Bromley Brothers, making small diesels with German technical assistance in the late 1920s and then lathes. The first lathe models produced in 1929–30 were cone pulley types, replaced in 1932 by the new Soviet standard lathe 'which follow[ed] very closely the design of the German standard machine' and was produced in three sizes—150, 200, and 300 millimeters (center height).[40] In 1932, 20 were produced and in 1933 only 550, although 6,000 were planned.[41] By 1937 the plant employed some 7,500 workers, still producing standard lathes.

Another very large Moscow plant was the Ordzhonikidze (Works No. 28), built in 1930–2 and by 1940 employing 5,000 in three shifts. Production started with 65-millimeter turret lathes 'which were direct copies of a Warner & Swasey machine.'[42] In 1934 the Plan added production of a semi-automatic multi-tool lathe: 'a copy of the Fay automatic.'[43] In 1937 another model was added—the first multi-spindle automatic built in the Soviet Union: 'a copy of the Cone machine.'[44] *American Machinist* commented, 'With these machines as the base, Ordzhonikidze built-up experience in the shops and the design office. These were the only three types of machines made until the beginning of World War II when Russia modernized and improved tooling. . . .'[45]

The Leningrad Ilytch works concluded a technical-assistance agreement in 1928 to run for three years with the firm Vereinigte Carborundum und Elektritwerke A-G of Neu-Betanek in Czechoslovakia.[46] This plant was

[37] *Ibid.*
[38] Walter Wells, 'An American Toolmaker in Russia,' *American Machinist*, LXXV, November 26, 1931, p. 816.
[39] *Ibid.*
[40] L. A. Aisenshtadt, *Ocherki po istorii stankostroeniya SSSR* (Moscow: 1957), pp. 171–3.
[41] *Machinery*, September 1931, p. 54. Included is an outline drawing of the lathe.
[42] *American Machinist*, November 19, 1956. (See also chap. 18.)
[43] *Ibid.*
[44] *Ibid.*
[45] *Ibid.*
[46] *Die Chemische Fabrik*, I, No. 18 (May 2, 1928), p. 256.

Table 9-5 SELECTED SOVIET MACHINE TOOLS AND WESTERN ORIGINS, 1930-50

Class of Equipment	Models (basic model in *italics*)	Years Produced	Western Origin of Basic Model	Specialist Plant in the U.S.S.R.	1941 Plan Output
Gear-cutting machine	*Pfauter*, 532, (750 mm)	1931—after 1950	Pfauter (Germany)	Komsomolets (founded 1909)	70
Boring machine	*R-80*, A-80, (80 mm)	1930—after 1950	Union		
Cylindrical grinding machine	*Fortuna*, 316, 316 M (250 mm)	1930—after 1950	Fortuna	Zlatoyet	1,647
Centerless grinder	*3180*, (5–75 mm)	1945—after 1950	Cincinnati		105
Shaper	*Sheping*, 7S35, 735 (500 mm)	1926—after 1950	Pre-World War I model	Samotochka (founded 1898)	
Bench lathe (150 mm)	*Chemnitz*, 162 SP, 1615, 1615 M	1930—after 1950	Chemnitz (Germany)	TZ-K	4,638
Bench lathe (200 mm)	*Standard DIP series*, 1D62, 1D62M, 1A62	1932?	Standard German model (replaced Tn series)		5,387
Gear-cutting lathe			Krause (Austrian)		95
Turret lathe (65 mm)	*136*, 1M36	1935—after 1945	Warner & Swasey Model 2A		1,600

Sources: L. Aizenshtadt, *Ocherki po istorii stankostroeniya, SSSR* (Moscow: 1957); L. Turgeon, *Prices of Metalworking Equipment in the Soviet Union, 1928–1951* (Santa Monica: RAND Corp., 1953), Research Memorandum RM 1112.

expanded after 1934, by an expenditure of more than 30 million rubles, to include production of two models of the German Stock tool grinders (after expropriation of the Stock concession); the plant also produced in 1934 its first Cincinnati universal tool grinder, 'fully equal to the American product.'[47]

Similarly the Frunze plant was reported as 'preparing to produce the German automatic lathe, Index, of the firm Hahn and Kolb, Stuttgart and . . . to produce 45 units in this year [1934] and 500 units up to 1938.'[48]

SPECIALIZED AND AUTOMATIC EQUIPMENT

While the expanded tsarist and new machine-tool plants concentrated on producing large quantities of single models based on Western designs, there remained an unfilled need for specialized equipment of a sophistication far beyond Soviet capability. As each machine model was produced, imports were halted even if the Soviet version was decidedly below the import in quality; machine imports from the early 1930s to the present time have been concentrated in specialized equipment not produced in Soviet plants.

Given the Soviet concentration on mass production of standardized products, automatic machinery was a prime requirement. Such machines came primarily from the United States. One such order was for a shipment of 47 Fay automatic lathes[49] for machining the motor cylinders, pistons, and sprocket shafts of the No. 60 Caterpillar tractor being built at Chelyabinsk.

The use of imports to supplement limited internal production capabilities is well exemplified in the case of gear-cutting machines. In 1933–4 the only gear-hobbing machine produced was the Pfauter model at the Komsomolets plant in Yegorievsk, near Moscow, an old tsarist plant founded in 1909 and specializing in production of this single German machine model. The Pfauter had very limited capacity. Specialized equipment was therefore needed to produce, for example, the high-quality gears used in high-speed rolling mills. For this purpose an engineering delegation was sent to the U.S. in 1934 to investigate available types of gear-cutting equipment. An order was placed with Farrel-Birmingham Co., Inc., of Buffalo, New York for two 'huge Sykes machines.' Although of design similar to others in Farrel-Birmingham's own plant, they were 'considerably larger, the one intended for the Kramatorsk plant having capacity for cutting gears up to 8 meters. . . .'[50] These machines,

[47] *American Machinist*, March 14, 1934.

[48] *Ibid.*

[49] Ralph E. Miller, 'American Automatic Machinery Aids Soviet Reconstruction,' *The Iron Age*, CXXXI, No. 4 (January 26, 1933), pp. 16–24. Miller describes these machines, shipped in 1932, in detail. A comparison of the Fay (in Aisenshtadt) with Miller's description of the machines produced supports the estimate of American and Soviet capabilities.

[50] 'Large Farrel-Sykes Gear Generators for Soviet Russia,' *Machinery*, XLIII, November 1936, pp. 211–2.

weighing 130 tons each, could cut gears weighing up to 50 tons each. One Sykes machine was for Uralmash and one for Kramatorsk.[51] Design of the Sykes machines occupied eight engineers and draftsmen for more than one year and actual manufacture about 15 months. They were probably the largest such machines in the world.

In the field of rolling-mill equipment, a large gear drive was made by the United Kingdom firm of David Brown and Sons (Huddersfield), Ltd., from castings supplied by the English Electric Corporation. This gear drive weighed 24 tons, was designed to encounter peak loads of 10,800 horsepower and was described as 'probably the largest gear wheel of its kind ever cast in one piece.'[52]

Other special designs, supplied by the British firm of Davy Brothers, Ltd., of Sheffield, were for large forging manipulators ranging from 5 to 15 tons capacity. Known as the Davy-Alliance models, they were the result of a special Davy study of forging manipulators.[53] The same company also supplied a 6,000-ton Davy patented forging press for the Stalingrad tractor works.[54]

Similar equipment for steel works was supplied by Craven Brothers (Manchester), Ltd., of Reddish, who in the early 1930s supplied a double 50-inch center lathe with a 112-foot by 9-foot 9-inch bed and 8-foot face plates.[55] German firms supplied similar large specialized equipment; for example, Maschinenfabrik Augsburg-Nürnberg A-G (MAN) supplied a 300-ton overhead traveling crane to serve a 15,000-ton forging press.[56]

Thus for the whole period under consideration the Soviets depended entirely on more advanced countries for imports of machine tools beyond the two simplest types.

THE ACQUISITION OF BALL- AND ROLLER-BEARING TECHNOLOGY

The Swedish SKF Company established a ball-bearing manufacturing plant in Moscow in 1917. After the October Revolution the company was given a concession agreement to continue operation of the original plant and build new facilities for the manufacture of complete ball and roller assemblies.[57] The new plant was opened in 1929. Although the basic agreement was for

[51] See p. 130 *et seq.*
[52] *Engineering*, CXL, July 26, 1935, p. 99.
[53] *The Engineer*, CLII, July 1931.
[54] *Ibid.*
[55] *Ibid.*, CLIV, 1932, p. 253.
[56] *Engineering*, April 27, 1934, pp. 482–3.
[57] Sutton, *Western Technology . . ., 1917 to 1930*, pp. 177–8.

40 years, both SKF plants were taken over in 1930 and renamed Moscow Ball-Bearing Plant No. 2.

Yearly production for the ex-Swedish SKF plants was three million ball and roller bearings. By 1937, under the management of 10 ex-SKF engineers, including the chief engineer (they all remained under individual ruble work contracts), production reached eight million bearings per year. The plant employed 15,000 workers in three shifts.

Table 9–6 TECHNICAL ASSISTANCE TO BALL- AND ROLLER-BEARING PLANTS

Location	Technical Assistance	Production
Moscow, Plant No. 1 (Kaganovitch)	RIV (Italy)	1938: 18 million ball and roller bearings
Moscow, Plant No. 2	Former SKF (Sweden) concession	1937: 8 million ball and roller bearings
Saratov, Plant No. 3	Imported U.S. equipment	Started about 1941 to produce 22 million ball bearings per year

Source: Oberkommando der Wehrmacht, National Archives Microcopy T 84–122–1421222/3.

Construction of Moscow Ball-Bearing Plant No. 1, the Kaganovitch, exemplifies Soviet economic development during the years 1930–45. The only completely new ball- and roller-bearing plant, with a full product range, to be constructed between 1930 and 1941, it covered an area of 1.5 million square feet under one roof. Whereas in 1931 all European anti-friction bearing plants together produced 120,000 pieces per day, the Kaganovitch alone was scheduled to produce 100,000. With an ultimate capacity of 40 million bearings annually, Kaganovitch could have equalled one-third of 1931 world production and one-half the United States production.

The plant cost 116 million rubles, including 35 million for 5,000 imported machines. It was conservatively described by Amtorg as 'one of the largest and most up to date of its kind in the world,'[58] with an output destined to provide all bearings necessary for production of the Amo (Fiat) 3-ton truck, the Yaroslavl (Hercules) 5-ton truck and bus, the Ford Models Gaz A and Gaz AA, the Fordson tractor, two models of the International Harvester tractor (produced at Kharkov and Stalingrad), the Caterpillar 60-horsepower tractor (produced at Chelyabinsk), and the Velo motorcycle and bicycle plant (Birmingham Small Arms Company). The Kaganovitch plant was a vital unit in Soviet industrialization.

[58] Amtorg, *op. cit.*, 'The Moscow Ball Bearing Factory,' VII, No. 9 (May 1, 1932), pp. 197–200.

The history of the Kaganovitch plant began in 1928 when Orgametal attempted to develop a construction plan.[59] In 1929 the plan was sent to Berlin, where a prominent German expert was employed as a consultant. Later in the year a Soviet Bearing Commission went to the U.S. and retained another engineer as consultant. Then followed a complex series of international expeditions, consultations, designs, and redesigns; 'finally a total of five bureaus in four countries, with three working simultaneously, were required to present a final plan. . . .'[60]

The technical-assistance picture was equally complicated. The Italian firm RIV (Officine Villar-Perosa of Turin) signed a technical-assistance contract to 'supervise the job complete from project to finished plant in operation.'[61] The company also accepted a 'large number' of Soviet workers and technicians in its plants for training.[62] RIV was a subsidiary of Fiat, which was partly American-owned; this provided a funnel for the transmission of American bearing technology, which U.S. manufacturers had been reluctant to provide directly. Albert Kahn, Inc., of Detroit designed the buildings.[63] In August 1930 Sharikopodshipnikstroi (Ball-Bearing Construction Trust) was transferred from the Machine-Building Trust to VATO (All-Union Automobile and Tractor Trust) and a number of top-flight U.S. engineers were sent to work in both Sharikopodshipnikstroi and the Kaganovitch plant itself. See table 9–7 for the organizational structure.

The Kaganovitch production program included 120 sizes of bearings: i.e., ball bearings (53 sizes, from E12 to 318), tapered roller bearings (35 sizes, from 40 to 200 millimeters outside diameter), helical roller bearings (20 sizes), cylindrical roller bearings (9 sizes, including the Hoffman type, from 40 to 160 millimeters), and simple ball retainer assemblies.[64]

The specifications and tolerances were based on the International Standard, somewhat more rigorous than the Society of Automotive Engineers standards used in the United States. Specifications also reflected foreign practice in the products using bearings. For example, in helical roller bearings, 'the final

---

[59] A series of five articles entitled 'Bearings for the Soviets,' by Frank Schubert, appeared in *American Machinist* in early 1933 and describes in detail the planning, construction, and output of the Kaganovitch plant. See *American Machinist*, LXXVII: April 12, 1933, pp. 229–32; April 26, 1933, pp. 273–6; May 10, 1933, pp. 296–9; May 24, 1933, pp. 334–7; and June 7, 1933, pp. 369–73.

[60] Schubert, *op. cit.*, *American Machinist*, LXXVII, April 12, 1933, p. 230. These countries were the United States, Germany, Italy, and the United Kingdom. Sweden, foremost in ball-bearing technology, was not a candidate, as the Soviets were in the process of expropriating the Swedish SKF ball-bearing concession.

[61] *Ibid.*, p. 232.

[62] Amtorg, *op. cit.*, V, No. 18–19 (October 1930), p. 386.

[63] Schubert, *op. cit.*, *American Machinist*, LXXVII, April 12, 1933, p. 231.

[64] *Ibid.*, April 26, 1933, p. 273.

Table 9–7   ORGANIZATION OF THE BALL-BEARING
INDUSTRY, 1932

VATO
(Sharikopodshipnikstroi)
Chief Consulting Engineer:
H. S. Trecartin

Plant No. 1	Plant No. 2
(Kaganovitch)	(ex-SKF concession)
Director:	Director:
H. J. Miller	(Swedish engineer)
U.S. engineers in charge of:	
Tapered roller-bearing division	
Ball-bearing division	
Helical-bearing division	
Cylindrical-bearing division	
Russian engineers with U.S. assistants in:	
Stores dept.	Technical management under
Forge shop	ten Swedish engineers
Turning shop	
Heat-treating shop	
Grinding shop	
Ball-making shop	
Roller-making shop	
Press operations	
Assembling and packing	
Tool and die shop	
Repair and maintenance shop	

Sources: H. S. Trecartin, *Iron Age*, October 13, 1932.
F. Schubert, *op. cit.*

decision was based on Ford practice for bearings to be used in Ford type units and on the largest available commercial bearings for those to be used in other units.'[65]

Hoffman specification bearings were used on Yaroslavl 5-ton trucks and buses and International Harvester specifications for tractors produced at Stalingrad and Kharkov.

When the processes and specifications had been decided upon, the task became one of selection, purchase, and installation of equipment. Schubert comments: 'After the general technological processes had been laid out here, in America, the selection of machines became the making of a decision between

[65]   *Ibid.*, p. 275.

two (or perhaps three, if available) different makes of machines for each operation.'[66]

Two Soviet buying commissions were appointed: one for Italy and Germany, and another for the United States and the United Kingdom. A buying plan was established which apportioned equipment purchases as follows:

United States: 185 grinding machines (a key component) valued at over $1 million, together with some helical roller winders[67]

Italy: electric furnaces, ball-making equipment, some ring-grinding equipment, roll-lapping machines, and polishing machines

United Kingdom: grinding machines

Germany: forging equipment, automatic screw machines, chucking machines, presses, gaging, and laboratory equipment

These were unusually large purchases; indeed, some German orders were transferred elsewhere as the firms were unable to handle such large quantities. For example, in Germany the initial 1931 order alone comprised 100 single-spindle chucking machines, 80 multiple-spindle chucking machines, 80 internal grinders, 120 oscillating grinders, and 30 ball grinders.

Altogether, about $30 million worth of equipment for Kaganovitch was made, installed, and initially operated by Western firms.[68] The Soviet machine-building plants, just getting into production, supplied the simpler tools: 'many lathes, some milling machines and some grinders. . . .'[69] Indeed, one of the first machines installed was a simple cylindrical grinder built in the Leningrad Karl Marx factory, a copy of the German model, Fortune. The special steel required was supplied by Elektrostal in Moscow and Zlatoust in the Urals; both plants had Western technical assistance.

For a plant of this size and complexity, construction was remarkably swift. Some site-grading was in progress in November 1930, and the plant was almost complete by September 1931. By January 1932 the first trial batch of bearings had been produced, and by March 1,000 machines were installed. The second

---

[66] *Ibid.*, May 10, 1933, p. 299.
[67] It is a reasonable deduction that a great deal of this equipment—particularly the grinding machines—came from the Bryant Chucking Grinder Company of Springfield, Va. (now part of the Ex-Cello Corp.). In 1931 Bryant shipped 32.2 percent of its output to the U.S.S.R., and in 1934 55.3 percent of its output. Then there were no shipments until 1938, when the Soviets again bought one-quarter of Bryant's annual output. Major shipments were made under Lend-Lease. After that there were none. In 1959 Bryant was prevented by Congressional action from shipping 46 Centalign-B machines for the manufacture of miniature ball bearings, mainly used in missiles. (U.S. Senate, Committee on the Judiciary, 87th Congress, 1st session, *Export of Ball Bearings Machines to Russia* [Washington, 1961], I, p.41.) These shipments, from 1931 to 1959, coincide with the Soviet construction of ball-bearing plants.
[68] *Ibid.*, p. 299.
[69] *Ibid.*

section was opened in November 1933 and in that year the plant produced about 50 types of ball and roller bearings.

Understandably, such an enormous plant had its teething problems.[70] Planned to produce 24 million bearings in 1934, it achieved an annual rate of only 18 million by 1938. The SKF concession (renamed Plant No. 2), planned to produce only 3 million in 1933, was producing 8 million bearings per year by 1937 under its Swedish engineers, despite the severe problems after expropriation, when production fell 50 percent and the rejection rate increased from 2 to 14 percent.[71]

The large imports of ball and roller bearings under Lend-Lease suggest that the Soviets had problems assimilating bearing technology. In 1945 alone, $6 million worth of ball and roller bearings and their parts as well as manufacturing equipment were shipped under U.S. Lend-Lease.[72]

PLANS FOR THE MANUFACTURE OF DIESEL ENGINES

Before the October Revolution diesel engines were manufactured at the Nobel works in Petrograd and at the Kolomna works.[73] Both manufactured engines under license from Diesel. These arrangements ceased with the October Revolution and were replaced in 1927 with a license and technical-assistance agreement to manufacture MAN diesels at the old Nobel works (renamed Russky Diesel) and the Kolomna plant.[74]

During the late 1920s, production of diesels was expanded to occupy four plants: the Kolomna, Sormovo, Russky Diesel, and Krasny Proletariat; and about 20 million rubles was spent between 1926–7 and 1930 on these efforts to expand. Kolomna 'mastered' production of diesels (for the second time) in 1930, and was scheduled to produce two-thirds of Soviet diesels by 1932–3. The other three plants, together with the Dvigateli Revolutsii plant, the

---

[70] Walter Citrine, General Secretary of the Trades Union Council (United Kingdom), toured Kaganovitch in 1935 and was not impressed with plant construction, maintenance or working conditions: 'Not a single door fitted properly, the concrete floor was full of holes and rolled up and down, like the waves of the sea. . . .' (*Op. cit.*, p. 85.)

[71] H. S. Trecartin, 'Industrial Russia,' *The Iron Age*, October 13, 1932.

[72] U.S. State Dept., *Report on War Aid Furnished by the United States to the U.S.S.R.* (Washington: Office of Foreign Liquidation, 1945).

[73] 'The L. Nobel plant in St. Petersburg . . . was founded in 1862. The first diesel of 20 hp. was made in the plant in 1898. . . . In the period 1903–1910 the plant built marine diesels with a total capacity of 54,850 hp.' [E. M. Penova, ed., *Podvodnoe Korablestroenie v Rossii (1900–1917)*, (Sudostroenie: 1965), p. 356.] See also A Cyril Yeates, 'Nobel's Contribution to the Early Development of the Diesel Engine,' *Gas and Oil Power*, XXXII, No. 385 (October 1937), p. 255.

[74] *U.S. Naval Institute Proceedings*, 77, No. 3 (March 1951), p. 273.

Table 9–8   PLANNED MANUFACTURE OF DIESEL ENGINES: 1928–41

Soviet Plant	Sulzer System	Nobel System	MAN System	Otto Deutz System
Russky Diesel (tsarist Nobel Plant)	Marine diesels (1,400–2,700 hp.) Stationary diesels (1,500–3,000 hp.) Compressorless diesels (100–300 hp.)	Small diesels with compressors (150–1,000 hp.)*	—	—
Kharkov locomotive works (tsarist plant)	Marine diesels (100–465 hp.) Marine diesels Type S-47 (800–1,200 hp.) Stationary diesels (1,000–2,700 hp.)	—	—	—
Nikolaevsky im. Marti (tsarist shipyards)	Marine diesels (1,400–2,700 hp.)	—	—	—
Kolomna (tsarist plant)	—	—	Double action MAN (2,250–4,500 hp.) MAN system (165–1,575 hp.) including locomotive engines	—
Sormovo (tsarist plant)	—	—	MAN system (120–2,970 hp.)	—
Krasny Proletariat (formerly Bromley Brothers)	—	—	—	Small Deutz system diesel engines (10–200 hp.)
Dvigateli Revolutsii (Gorki)	—	—	MAN system BK-38 (70–150 hp.), unknown 'B' series with compressors	—

Source: Izvestia Vsesoyuznogo Teplotekhnicheskogo Instituta, No. 5, 1930, pp. 84–5.

* The tsarist plant had a Nobel license to manufacture diesel engines.

Komitern plant at Kharkov, and the Nikolaevsky shipbuilding yards, were planned to handle the building of the remaining one-third.[75]

At the same time, plans were made to expand production of Sulzer and Deutz diesel engine systems, each plant specializing in one foreign system with a limited range of end uses. The Sulzer agreement made in 1927 gave Lenmashstroi (Leningrad Machine-Building Trust) the right to make Sulzer diesels, the firm sending its own engineers and blueprints to assist in the process.[76]

The Kolomna works produced a variety of MAN-system diesels without compressors ('G' series) and with compressors ('B' series), in a range of horsepowers from 165 to 1,575. All were four-cycle engines. Production was scheduled to include locomotive engines for the E el-9 diesel electric locomotives and double-action marine diesels of 2,250 to 4,500 horsepower. The main productive effort in both large-horsepower and specialized models was expended at the Kolomna works on the German MAN system.

The Russky Diesel works specialized in heavy marine diesels and stationary diesels produced on the Sulzer system, together with smaller diesels on the Nobel system (R.D. construction). The Kharkov locomotive works concentrated on medium-size engines for ships and stationary use. The Nikolaevsky Shipyards (im. Marti) handled repair and construction of large marine diesels of between 1,400 and 2,700 horsepower on the Sulzer system. The Sormovo works, a very large tsarist plant, produced small and medium-sized marine diesels on the MAN system. Krasny Proletariat (formerly Bromley Brothers) specialized in small diesels (10–200 horsepower) on the Deutz system. Dvigateli Revolutsii at Gorki produced small and medium horsepower stationary diesels on the MAN system.[77]

Thus, each of the seven Soviet diesel engine plants produced a well-defined, narrow line of engines based on a single Western system. These domestically produced diesels were supplemented throughout by specialized imported engines. For example, the Krasny Oktiabr' electricity-generating plant at Stalingrad was equipped with three MAN 2,230-horsepower engines coupled to AEG 1,610-kilowatt a.c. generators.[78] A large order for 100 marine diesel engines for fishing boats with 96 to 104 horsepower was placed in 1932 with Ruston & Hornsby, Ltd., of England.[79] Even at the end of the 1930s large diesels were still imported; in 1938, for example, National-British Thomson

[75] *Izvestia Vsesoyuznogo Teplotekhnicheskogo Instituta*, No. 5, 1930, p. 78.
[76] Kassell, Lt. Cdr. Bernard M., '1,000 Submarines—Fact or Fiction,' *U.S. Naval Institute Proceedings*, LXXVII, No. 3 (March 1951), pp. 267–75.
[77] *Ibid.*
[78] *Izvestia Vsesoyuznogo Teplotekhnicheskogo Instituta*, No. 1, 1931, pp. 10–28.
[79] *Far Eastern Review*, March 1932, pp. 124–6.

Houston engines of 4,032 horsepower were made in the United Kingdom for Soviet power stations.[80]

The practice of producing Soviet diesels to standard well-known foreign designs, supplemented by selective imports, continued through the 1930s while Soviet research organizations experimented and tested different types, including those for tractor and road use.[81] In 1940, according to a German source, there was still only a limited range of diesel and gasoline motors produced in the U.S.S.R.[82]

---

[80]   *Oil Engine*, No. 1, January 5, 1938, p. 283.

[81]   See, for example, *Diesel Power*, II, No. 2 (November 1933), pp. 702–5; and *The Automobile Engineer*, XXV, No. 336 (September 1935), pp. 333–6.

[82]   'Motorenbau in Sowjet-Russland,' *Brennstoff-und Wärmewirtschaft*, January 22, 1940, pp. 7–10.

CHAPTER TEN

Technical Assistance for Electrical-Equipment Manufacture and Power-Station Construction

MANUFACTURE of electrical equipment, including transformers, switchgear, lamps, and motors, was concentrated in the VEO (All-Union Electrical Trust) with 34 plants: 14 in Moscow, 14 in Leningrad, and the rest in the Ukraine and Urals. This trust included all the tsarist electrical plants as well as several large units constructed after 1930; its principal works were Elektrosila (Leningrad, electrical machinery), Elektrozavod (Moscow, electrical machinery and switchgear), Dynamo (Moscow, traction motors and equipment), and Elektroapparat (Leningrad, switchgear). Technical-assistance agreements were concluded with numerous foreign companies, the most important of which were International General Electric (1929, extended through 1944), Metropolitan-Vickers (extended from the early 1920s to 1935)[1] and Radio Corporation of America (1927, extended to April 1941). These agreements were of enormous benefit to the U.S.S.R.; in 1932–3, for example, a proposal was made to build 150 new types of electrical apparatus under the General Electric and Metropolitan-Vickers agreements alone.[2]

As electrical-equipment manufacture was concentrated in a few plants of great size, the industry can be effectively considered on a plant-by-plant basis.

GENERAL ELECTRIC ASSISTANCE TO THE KHEMZ TURBINE PLANT AT KHARKOV

The second largest unit constructed under the Second Five-Year Plan[3] was a giant new turbine-manufacturing plant located in Kharkov. Begun in 1930,

---

[1] Metropolitan-Vickers engineers were expelled from the Soviet Union in 1933; the agreement may have continued for several years, but not beyond 1935.
[2] *The Electrical Review*, April 15, 1932, p. 555.
[3] Gosplan, *Vtoroi piatiletnii plan razvitiia narodnogo khoziaistva SSSR (1933–1937 gg)* (Moscow, 1934) I, p. 587.

partially opened in 1933, and completed in 1935, it absorbed a planned investment of over 87 million rubles. With an aggregate annual capacity of 2.3 million kilowatts of finished equipment, it had a productive capacity more than twice that of General Electric, which until that time had been the largest producer of turbines in the world.[4] Such a plant was urgently needed to produce large steam-turbine generators for the GOELRO (State Commission for the Electrification of Russia) program; up to 1933 these had all been imported.

VEO contracted with the International General Electric Company and Metropolitan-Vickers for design, construction, and technical assistance to KHEMZ. General Electric was the world's largest builder of steam-turbine generators, and prepared in Schenectady 'the complete architectural and engineering design for this new turbine manufacturing plant in which steam turbine generators of General Electric type in capacities of 50,000 kW and over were built.'[5]

General Electric engineers went to Kharkov to erect the plant and supervise installation of German equipment, and many Soviet engineers went to Schenectady for training. General Electric engineers also became members of Soviet commissions to purchase foreign equipment and tools for installation at KHEMZ. Solomon Trone, a General Electric engineer at KHEMZ, stated that 'the Kharkov plant is equipped with German machinery, but is, as far as possible, modelled after similar American plants.'[6]

The impact of KHEMZ was immediate and significant. Whereas before 1935 all generators and most turbines had been imported, after this date only one turbine was imported—an advanced design for the Union Heat Engineering Institute in Moscow.

The other turbine-manufacturing plant was the Putilovets plant in Leningrad, also a producer of locomotives, tractors, and automobiles. The Putilovets turbine shop had technical assistance from Metropolitan-Vickers, and the turbine shop was completely refitted with British machine tools in 1930-3 under the supervision of British engineers.[7]

---

[4] 'Kharkov Turbo-Generator Works,' *Metallurgia*, October 1932, pp. 187-8.
[5] *The Monogram*, November 1943, p. 19.
[6] U.S. State Dept. Decimal File, 861.5017—Living Conditions/616. Detailed information on General Electric work in the U.S.S.R. is scarce, as the company instructed its large force of engineers and workers not to discuss its work in the U.S.S.R. This instruction was interpreted by some of these personnel to include discussion with the U.S. State Dept.
[7] U.S. State Dept. Decimal File, 861.5017—Living Conditions/635, March 29, 1933. 861.5017—Living Conditions/617 records Metropolitan-Vickers assistance at the KHEMZ plant.

MOSCOW ELEKTROZAVOD[8]

The Moscow Elektrozavod plant employed more than 25,000 in 1941 and produced about one-fifth of Russian electrical equipment; the plant concentrated on transformers, rectifiers, electrical equipment, and accessories for the automotive and tractor industries, including electric light bulbs and special-purpose bulbs.

The transformer shop was stocked with Western equipment during the late 1920s and early 1930s, mostly from Siemens and A.E.G. in Germany. The A.T.E. shop produced electrical equipment, including magnetos and generators, for automobiles and tractors. The bulb shop was established by a group of eight German technicians between 1930 and 1935. There was a searchlight department with technical assistance from Sperry Gyroscope Company of the United States, and possibly there were other military production units. These shops were supplemented by a tool-making shop.

Elektrozavod was a heavy employer of German technicians—especially skilled toolmakers, almost all of whom came from the Berlin area, and were administered under a Foreign Bureau headed by Swassman. In December 1930 there were more than 100 Germans in the plant as heads of departments and in similar key positions. Pose also comments that a 'considerable number of foreign workers were placed in responsible posts.'[9] In the transformer department, German foremen included Müller, Schwartz, Drause, and Heinz, and the inspector was Schippel. In the A.T.E. department, Baument and Lampe were foremen. Horn was head of the bulb department repair shop, and Pose himself was in charge of the 14 imported machines in the rotor workshop.[10]

Not only were Germans scattered among the lower management levels but all-German and mixed German-Russian shock brigades and individual udarniks were created. Socialist competition was developed among German workers at Elektrozavod and at other electrical-equipment plants, such as Elektroapparat and Svetlana, both in Leningrad.[11] There was also General Electric technical assistance at Elektrozavod. Manufacture was begun on 220,000-volt transformers, at first for the Svir system, and then for other electric projects. These were G. E. designs, produced with the technical assistance of General Electric.[12]

---

[8] Details are from F. Pose, *German Workers in a Moscow Factory* (Moscow: 1933).
[9] *Ibid.*, p. 50.
[10] *Ibid.*, pp. 50–1.
[11] For an American view of Electrozavod, see U.S. State Dept. Decimal File, 861.5017— Living Conditions/775, Report No. 399 from Moscow Embassy, February 19, 1935, an interview with Andrew Smith who worked at the plant. Also see Andrew Smith, *I Was a Soviet Worker* (New York: E. P. Dutton, 1936) for a full-length description of life at Elektrozavod.
[12] *The Monogram*, November 1943.

THE UTILIZATION OF HEROULT AND DETROIT
ELECTRIC-FURNACE DESIGNS BY ELEKTROZAVOD

The Technical Director of the electric furnace department of Elektrozavod was an American, C. H. vom Bauer, under whom the production of standard electric furnaces at the rate of 100 per year was attained. By the end of 1933 the Soviet Union had about 450 electric furnaces in operation, accounting for about 2 percent of its total steel output. By comparison, electric furnaces produced 1½ percent in the United States and 1 percent in Germany.

Electric furnaces are used in both ferrous and non-ferrous metallurgical industries where cheap electricity is available and high-quality metals are required. Great emphasis was placed by Soviet planners on electric-furnace steel manufacture and, fortunately, we have precise data for the years 1928 to 1943.[13]

Until 1928 all Russian electric furnaces were imported. The Soviets hired C. H. vom Bauer, a well-known New York consultant on electric furnaces, who became Technical Director of the newly formed electric furnace department of Elektrozavod in Moscow, as noted above. Vom Bauer remained in this post until 1932, instituted electric-furnace manufacture and, after returning to the United States, presented data on his achievements at the Sixty-Third General Meeting of the Electrochemical Society in Montreal. He estimated that between 1914 and 1932 some 149 foreign electric furnaces had been imported into Russia, including 76 Heroult, 26 Detroit, 10 Ajax-Wyatt, and 30 high-frequency furnaces, and three Miguets and a few other special types.[14]

Production under vom Bauer concentrated on three main series: Heroult, Detroit and Ajax-Wyatt, 'all built according to the author's [i.e., vom Bauer's] specifications. The operation of these furnaces was superintended by the author during the years 1931 and 1932.'[15]

Most furnaces, both imported and newly built, were Heroults and were used in the iron and steel industry. The 'Soviet Heroult' was so close to the regular Heroult that vom Bauer does not bother to distinguish between Soviet-made and imported furnaces. After 1933 only large-capacity Heroults were imported. The greater number of new installations were 'Soviet Heroults,' almost all of 3-ton or 5-ton capacity. By the early 1940s the U.S.S.R. had

---

[13]   C. H. vom Bauer, 'The Electric Furnace and Its Products in the U.S.S.R.,' *Electrochemical Society: Transactions*, LXIII, 1933, pp. 305–8. The vom Bauer data is supplemented by the detailed equipment lists of Soviet steel plants in Bericht No. 68, from the Geheim-Archiv of the Oberkommando der Wehrmacht (OKW/Wi Rü Amt/Wi), prepared by the Gmelin Institute (National Archives Microcopy T 84–127–1428132).

[14]   Vom Bauer, *op. cit.*

[15]   *Ibid.*, p. 305.

Figure 10–1 ORIGIN OF ELECTRIC FURNACES IN THE
U.S.S.R., 1934

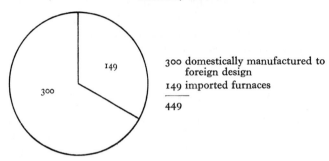

300 domestically manufactured to
  foreign design
149 imported furnaces
———
449

Distribution between imported and domestic electric furnaces

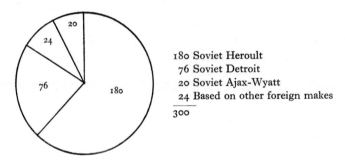

180 Soviet Heroult
76 Soviet Detroit
20 Soviet Ajax-Wyatt
24 Based on other foreign makes
———
300

Design origins of Soviet domestically manufactured electric furnaces

more than 300 Heroult furnaces, of which only about 76, or one-quarter, had been imported.

The standard smaller furnace (less than one ton per heat) was the Detroit. Of these, 26 were imported between 1914 and 1932 and about 50 'Soviet Detroits' made between 1928 and 1933 under vom Bauer's supervision.[16]

The third standard type was the Ajax-Wyatt Type 1–3. Ten were imported between 1914 and 1932; the Soviets made an additional 20 between 1928 and 1931, also under vom Bauer's supervision. Apparently none were built after 1932. While Heroult and Detroit furnaces were manufactured, special types continued to be imported.[17]

---

[16] We cannot estimate construction after 1933, as the OKW lists only steel plants in Bericht No. 68 and use of this type of small furnace is concentrated in non-ferrous plants.

[17] *Ibid.* The OKW records state that several large 10- to 35-ton Heroults were installed in 1935–6.

Electric-furnace manufacture typifies Soviet development during this period. In 1928 all such furnaces were imported. The Soviet Union hired, for a period of four years, one of the top-ranking foreign experts in the field, and vom Bauer organized production of Western models. The Soviet continued this production by concentrating on the two standard foreign models (Heroult and Detroit) most suited to their conditions.

THE DYNAMO (KIROV) PLANT

This was a large prewar plant employing about 10,000 in 1937 and manufacturing electric locomotives, mine locomotives, electric motors, dynamos, generators, and war equipment. The factory started manufacture of the General Electric 3,000-volt d.c. main line electric locomotives based on the G. E. Suram locomotive.[18] These locomotives, eight of which were supplied by the General Electric Company, were of the 125-metric-ton C-C type designed for multiple-unit operation for both passenger and freight work. The first two locomotives were constructed in the U.S. and shipped complete. The balance of six were shipped complete except for the motors, which were manufactured at the Dynamo plant from G.E. drawings under supervision of G.E. engineers.[19] The Dynamo engine became the pattern for further manufacture.

SPERRY GYROSCOPE COMPANY AND THE LENINGRAD ELEKTROPRIBOR PLANT

The Elektropribor was a tsarist-era plant, expanded and modernized under the Soviets, by agreement with Sperry Gyroscope Company of the United States, to manufacture electrical equipment (light bulbs, radios, voltmeters, ampere meters, and batteries). The plant had a separate division for the manufacture of army and navy instruments.

In the fall of 1931 the Sperry Company sent Mr. 'A,'[20] an American mechanical engineer, to the Elektropribor plant with instructions to supervise the assembly of machinery supplied by Sperry and to 'instruct in copying and designing such machines.'[21] Mr. 'A' worked for two years at Elektropribor and then went to the U.S. Consulate in Riga to renew his passport. The interviewing officer commented that 'he was a pathetic figure. He seemed frightened, uneasy and his attitude was one of humility and servility which is unusual in the average American.'

---

[18]   *Ibid.*
[19]   *General Electric Review*, XXXVIII, May 1935, pp. 220–1.
[20]   Name withheld by author in view of the State Dept. comments quoted.
[21]   U.S. State Dept. Decimal File, 861.5017—Living Conditions/680.

Although Mr. 'A' supplied information to the Riga Consulate, he was concerned as to whether it would be treated confidentially; the OGPU had attempted to get him to 'supply . . . secret American military information.' He had refused to do this and put his refusal in writing.

Figure 10–2 FOREIGN TECHNICAL ASSISTANCE TO PRINCIPAL PLANTS UNDER VEO (ALL-UNION ELECTRICAL TRUST), 1930–45*

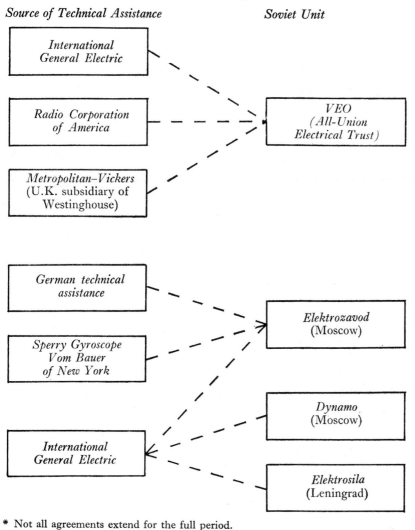

Source of Technical Assistance *Soviet Unit*

* Not all agreements extend for the full period.

Figure 10–2 (Continued)

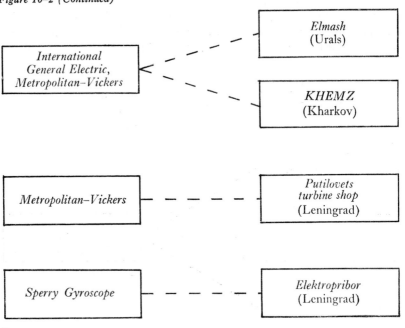

Sources: see text.

Later, after a senior Sperry official had visited the U.S.S.R., the OGPU came back to Mr. 'A' demanding information on bomb sights which the Soviets had begun to import from the Sperry Company. Just before leaving the U.S.S.R., he was again approached by the OGPU, which suggested that there were Sperry products which the company would not sell the U.S.S.R. and that the Russians 'would be pleased to have plans and specifications of these.'[22] Interest was also indicated in questions posed by the 'American Secret Service.' This placed Mr. 'A' in something of a dilemma and no doubt accounted for the attitude noted by the Riga Consulate, particularly as Mr. 'A' was 'sure' that the 'agents of the GPU at the present time [are] in the employ of the company' (i.e., Sperry in the U.S.).

THE URALS ELEKTROMASH COMBINAT

Urals Elektromash has been claimed, probably with accuracy, as the largest electrical-equipment building plant in the world. As planned, it comprised 14 separate but integrated factories with an aggregate annual output value of 2 billion rubles, seven times greater than that of all existant Soviet electrical

[22] *Ibid.*

equipment manufacturing plants. Employment was over 100,000, with about 12,500 engineers and technicians. The combine had its own city of 300,000 inhabitants.[23]

Two of the main shops at Urals Elektromash were the turbo-generator shop, with an annual production of 38 large steam generators of 50,000 to 160,000 kilowatts, and a machine-building shop for production of large modern mechanical equipment for mining and heavy industry, such as rolling-mill motors and generators. The transformer shop specialized in production of equipment in excess of 200,000 volts. A general apparatus shop produced oil switches, circuit breakers, electrical switchgear, crane and motor control apparatus, and similar units. A cable shop produced cable for other shops of the combinat.[24]

Amtorg summarized Western assistance as follows: 'Prominent American and British specialists are participating as consulting engineers in designing the plant. . . . The combine will employ the most modern machinery and technique.'[25]

THE RADIO CORPORATION OF AMERICA AGREEMENTS, 1927-41

In 1927 the Radio Corporation of America concluded an agreement with the Soviet Union for extensive provision of technical assistance and equipment in the radio communications field.[26] RCA was 'frequently consulted by the Soviets in the construction of radio stations' and the Soviet Radio Delegation to the U.S. in 1930 was able to visit a number of American radio stations 'under the auspices of the Radio Corporation of America.'[27]

In 1935 the VEO proposed another general agreement[28] whereby RCA would furnish 'engineering, technical and manufacturing information in those portions of the radio field in which RCA is or may be engaged.'[29] On September 30, 1935, RCA concluded an agreement[30] and approached the State Depart-

---

[23] Amtorg, *op. cit.*, VI, No. 18 (September 15, 1931), p. 426.

[24] 'Der Plan des Elektromaschinenwerks im Ural,' *Sowjetwirtschaft und Aussenhandel*, 1931, pp. 34–6.

[25] The American and British specialists were almost certainly from General Electric and Metropolitan-Vickers (the Westinghouse subsidiary), but the writer has no firm evidence at this point concerning their work at Elektromash in the Urals. Both General Electric and Metropolitan-Vickers are very reticent concerning their work in the U.S.S.R.

[26] See Sutton, *Western Technology . . ., 1917 to 1930*, pp. 250–2.

[27] Amtorg, *op. cit.*, V, No. 21 (November 1, 1930), p. 435.

[28] U.S. State Dept. Decimal File, 861.74 RADIO CORPORATION OF AMERICA/ 19–20.

[29] *Ibid.*, 861.74 RADIO CORPORATION OF AMERICA/20.

[30] A copy of the agreement is in U.S. State Dept. Decimal File, 861.74 RADIO CORPORATION OF AMERICA/30 and in 811.20161/52.

ment for permission, with the argument that if the agreement was not made with RCA then VEO would go to its European competitors. The Departmental reply indicated the 'proposed agreement will not be contrary to any policy of our government.'[31]

The extensive contract emphasized technical assistance and included 'the entire field of manufacturing and experimental activities of RCA and its subsidiaries. . . .'[32] The fields of technology to be transferred included both radio and television transmission and reception, electro-vacuum apparatus, sound recording, sound motion picture equipment, measuring apparatus, and remote control apparatus. RCA made a related agreement with Glavesprom (People's Commissariat of Heavy Industry), and Soviet personnel were sent to the United States for training.[33] A payment of $2.9 million was made to RCA and it was further agreed that the Soviets would purchase quantities of equipment from the company.

In 1938 eight RCA engineers were in the U.S.S.R. supervising installation of this equipment. In exchange for the purchase of $230,000 worth of RCA television equipment and $825,000 worth of related equipment, including some for military use, RCA also supervised erection of a television station.[34] The RCA Chief Engineer, L. F. Jones, was unable to complete installation, however, as Soviet construction organizations had not completed the building and materials supplied by Soviet plants were not delivered in time to complete the project by the agreed date of January 1, 1938.[35]

In particular, work was delayed on the station antenna. Jones did not want to report this to the Soviet authorities for fear the Soviet engineer on the job would be arrested as a 'wrecker.' Previous delays had been reported, however, and the Soviet engineer—not in any way to blame—was arrested a few days later on charges of wrecking activities. This delayed the work even further, as a second Russian engineer had to be trained. Thus in this instance RCA negotiated an extension of this section of the general agreement to avoid repetition of the accusation of wrecking and further delays.[36]

In 1939 the RCA agreement was extended to September 30, 1941,[37] but in

[31]   U.S. State Dept. Decimal File, 861.74 RADIO CORPORATION OF AMERICA/ 21.
[32]   *Ibid.*, 861.74 RADIO CORPORATION OF AMERICA/30, November 26, 1940.
[33]   *Ibid.*, p. 6.
[34]   U.S. State Dept. Decimal File, 861.74 RADIO CORPORATION OF AMERICA/ 26, Report No. 1283, Moscow Embassy, May 14, 1938.
[35]   *Ibid.*, 861.74 RADIO CORPORATION OF AMERICA/25, Report No. 707, Moscow Embassy, November 10, 1937.
[36]   *Ibid.*, Attachment to Report No. 707, Moscow Embassy, November 10, 1937, Memorandum of Statements. See also Metropolitan-Vickers below, p. 171.
[37]   U.S. State Dept. Decimal File, 861.74 RADIO CORPORATION OF AMERICA/ 28, Memorandum, Division of Controls, August 3, 1939.

April 1941 this extension was modified and limited to May 31, 1941.[38] The annual charge for technical assistance had been $120,000; this figure was reduced to $77,777 on July 27, 1939. A further request by Kalinin, a Soviet leader, in April 1941 for a reduction of the fee was turned down by RCA.[39]

THE INTERNATIONAL GENERAL ELECTRIC COMPANY TECHNICAL-ASSISTANCE AGREEMENT OF 1929

On May 24, 1929 the Soviet Union ratified an agreement signed by Amtorg and International General Electric Company—by far the most important single agreement in the development of the Soviet electrical equipment industries.

The contract provided for a 'broad exchange of patents as well as exchange of designing, engineering and manufacturing information' for a period of 10 years. In practice the 'exchange' was a one-way transfer; this is clear from the second and third paragraphs of the formal announcement. The second paragraph stated that:

> American engineers will be sent to the Soviet Union to assist the Soviet Electrotechnical Trust in carrying out its plans of expansion of the electrical industry, in all its phases. The engineering assistance to be rendered by the International General Electric Company will involve the construction of electrical apparatus and machinery for use in electric lighting. . . . Soviet engineers will visit this country to study American methods employed in the manufacture of electrical equipment and its application to industry.[40]

The diffusion of General Electric technology within the Soviet Union from 1929 until the end of World War II was extraordinarily extensive. The following summary lists plants where this technology was transferred directly, i.e., with the help of General Electric engineers; it does not include those plants and industries benefiting from an indirect infusion of equipment made in plants with General Electric technical assistance.[41]

According to General Electric engineers then working in the Soviet Union, the Soviets had 'full rights to all patents and working drawings of the American

---

[38] *Ibid.*, 861.74 RADIO CORPORATION OF AMERICA/38, Letter, RCA to State Dept., April 30, 1941.

[39] *Ibid.*, Letter, RCA to Kalinin.

[40] Amtorg, *op. cit.*, IV, No. 11 (June 1, 1929). This contract was in addition to a previous contract concluded in 1928 which covered purchase of $26 million worth of General Electric equipment over a period of several years with credit terms of five years granted by General Electric. See Sutton, *Western Technology . . ., 1917 to 1930*, p. 198.

[41] This supply of equipment was considerable. For example, in the case of the Dniepr Dam, General Electric supplied enough oil circuit breakers to occupy 50 railroad cars. [Amtorg, *op. cit.*, VI, No. 20 (October 15, 1931), p. 465.]

concern.'[42] Although the equipment had been designed by Americans, most of it came from Siemens in Germany and some from British and French manufacturers. At the time, Amtorg noted that 'much of the American equipment purchased in past years is used by the Soviets as models for the construction of similar machinery in their own plants.'[43]

Table 10–1 PARTIAL LIST OF PLANTS AND ACTIVITIES
BENEFITING FROM DIRECT INTERNATIONAL
GENERAL ELECTRIC TECHNICAL ASSISTANCE*

Magnitogorsk Iron and Steel Combine	VEO
Kazakhstan Copper Combine	Elektrozavod (Moscow)
Leningrad Electro-Technical Institute	Izolit Insulation Plant
Glavenergo (Leningrad)	Electric Welding Equipment Plant
Stalin Automobile Plant (Moscow)	Elektroapparat Plant
Elektrosila Plant (Leningrad)	KHEMZ Turbine Works
Grozneft oil fields	Elektroprom
Ukraine coal mines	Kuznetsk Steel Combine
Lena gold mines	Azov Steel Mill
Balakhna Paper Combine	Tomsky Steel Mill
Zaporozhstal Works	Dzherzhinsky Steel Mill
Baku oil refineries and oil fields	Orsk Benzine Cracking Plant
Suram Pass section of Transcaucasian Railroad	Zaporozhe Aluminum Plant
	Elektrik
Dynamo Electric Locomotive Plant (Moscow)	Dniepr Dam

Source: The Monogram, November 1943.
* Excluding power stations.

Unfortunately the General Electric Company instructed its engineers not to discuss conditions in the U.S.S.R. with State Dept. officers, and corporate files covering work in the U.S.S.R. have been destroyed.[44] Thus the only record is from those engineers who, when interviewed by State Dept. officials, 'forgot' their instructions and gave details of their work. For these reasons our knowledge is fragmented.

[42] *Ibid.*
[43] *Ibid.*
[44] U.S. State Dept. Decimal File, 861.5017—Living Conditions/428. Unfortunately, General Electric engineers mostly abided by this corporate injunction. For example, H. H. Fisher contacted (for his 1934 Hoover Institution study) a number of General Electric engineers, but only two replied; O. B. Bemis said that he had worked for G.E. on the Dniepr Dam (see Folder 1) and C. Thomson, G. E. chief erector, in a 1934 letter indicated that he had worked on the Stalingrad stations and at Dnieprstroi, adding that he might have to return, so that 'tact plus the danger of involving my Company in an unpleasant situation bars me from making any statements.' A subsequent letter, January 9, 1936, added nothing new to the 1934 letter. (See correspondence folder.)

We do know that one group of seven engineers worked at VEO offices in in Moscow designing steel-mill equipment for location in the Urals and Siberia. The equipment itself was supplied by General Electric and Siemens Schukert.[45]

The General Electric adviser on transfer of electric welding technology, particularly important in shipbuilding and submarines, was E. J. O'Connell.[46] With the assistance of the company, a number of new welders were developed: multi-operator machines of 1,500-ampere capacity, automatic welders, spot welders, butt welders, and roller welders. Expanded in the early 1930s, the Elektrik Plant (Moscow) became the principal supplier of welding machines. Electric welding was then used extensively in shipbuilding, submarine construction, steel construction, machine-building, and boiler manufacturing.

One consulting General Electric power plant engineer, Solomon Trone, spent about six months of every year from 1927 to 1933 in the U.S.S.R. and claimed that in his work he visited 'nearly every important electrical project.'[47] The inference that General Electric equipment became the Soviet standard throughout the country is not unbelievable. It is supported by the fact that the writer has found no evidence of indigenous Soviet development in the electrical-equipment field.

It is also a reasonable inference that General Electric transferred the latest technology under its various assistance agreements. For example, in 1938–9 the General Electric Company was negotiating the sale of $500,000 worth of General Electric equipment 'including high power transmission lines of a higher voltage capacity than any in use in the United States except on the Boulder Dam project,'[48] and in 1944–5 the General Electric Company made a second set of generators for the Dniepr Dam, but more advanced and of greater capacity than generators supplied by the company more than a decade previously.[49]

THE BROWN INSTRUMENT COMPANY TECHNICAL-ASSISTANCE AGREEMENT

Problems in developing instrument-manufacturing technology noted by Mr. 'A' and others[50] led to a second agreement with an American manufacturer

[45] U.S. State Dept. Decimal File, 861.5017—Living Conditions/515.

[46] *Ibid.*, 861.5017—Living Conditions/421. In accordance with Company instruction O'Connell would not discuss technical aspects of his work with the State Dept. officer.

[47] *Ibid.*, 861.5017—Living Conditions/616.

[48] *Ibid.*, 861.6463/68.

[49] See p. 168. The interested reader should also see the November 1943 issue of *The Monogram* (published by the General Electric Company), which supports these arguments in great detail. The *General Electric Review* also published a few articles in the 1930s which give support.

[50] See p. 150.

of recording instruments, but only after the Soviets had tried unsuccessfully to copy the company's instruments.

The technical-assistance contract with the Brown Instrument Company was signed in January 1936 for three years and included 'furnishing measuring instruments and instruction to the Soviet heavy industries.'[51] Instruction was given to Soviet engineers in the U.S. plants of the company and in Soviet plants. In the words of M. Mark Watkins, Brown Export Division Sales Manager, instruction was for 'learning the intricacies of making recording instruments. . . .' The purchase of at least $500,000 worth of instruments was contingent upon provision of this instruction. Watkins noted that there was a considerable demand for such instruments in the steel and oil industries but that the Soviets were not yet technically equipped to make them. This observation was based on

> . . . the fact that during his travels in the Soviet Union for the last month he has seen many copies of the Brown instruments made in this country and they were so poorly constructed and were working so inefficiently that he was convinced that the Soviet authorities had signed the technical aid contract with his firm since they had been unable to copy their instruments satisfactorily. . . .[52]

Another contract, rather similar to the Brown contract, was made by J. J. Higgins, an engineer with patents in the field of electrical equipment. This contract with GET (State Electro-Technical Trust) and the Moscow lamp works required Higgins to provide technical assistance in the manufacture of incandescent lamps and radio tubes and to undertake the design work for these products. Higgins, having spent 20 years with the Westinghouse Company in the United States, was well qualified for such work.[53]

THE GREAT NORTHERN COMPANY TELEGRAPH CONCESSION[54]

Maintaining one of the very few foreign concession operations to survive the 1920s, Great Northern Telegraph operated its international telegraph concession from 1919 until the late 1930s. This Danish company was given the 'exclusive concession for an indefinite period to provide service from all points in the Union of Soviet Socialist Republics to all foreign countries except Finland.'[55] The agreement was revocable by either party on six months' notice. The company handled about eight million words a year in the 1930s, all in international messages.

[51] U.S. State Dept. Decimal File, 861.602/278.
[52] *Ibid.*
[53] *American Engineers in Russia*, Fisher material.
[54] See Sutton, *Western Technology . . ., 1917 to 1930*, pp. 249–50.
[55] U.S. State Dept. Decimal File, 861.72/13.

Great Northern had numerous offices in the Soviet Union, each under a Danish manager, with a total employment of about 200; the Moscow office employed 23, including 10 Danes. There was an even larger staff in Leningrad. In 1935 it was reported that there was no real friction between the Soviets and the company, although the Soviet Government did operate its own radio and land lines for most government messages, thus infringing on the agreed concession monopoly. However, the company's relative efficiency operated to its advantage; Great Northern handled messages from London to Moscow in five to six minutes, whereas the Government transmissions 'usually require hours'; Moscow-New York was handled by the company in one hour, but by the Soviet offices in two to ten hours.

Accordingly, the commercial, diplomatic, and even official Soviet traffic went Great Northern, and the Government was not seen as a serious competitor. It was 'an interesting fact that official government messages written in illegible longhand and those containing texts difficult to transmit, frequently are given to the Company although not intended for Company transmission by the sender.'[56]

AMERICAN, BRITISH, AND CANADIAN LEND-LEASE SHIPMENTS

Shipments under United States Lend-Lease were considerably greater than either British or Canadian shipments of electrical generating stations. George Jordan notes that 17 stationary steam stations and three hydroelectric power stations were sent with a value in excess of one-quarter billion dollars.[57]

According to the State Department, power plants were supplied both for the reconstruction of damaged plants in recaptured areas and for new plants behind the Urals. Up to September 1945, $135 million worth of equipment was shipped, with another $32 million worth following under the agreement of October 15, 1945. A more revealing way of looking at this is in terms of physical capacity; the total capacity supplied was 1,457,274 kilowatts, divided as follows:[58]

Stationary steam plants	631,939 kilowatts
Stationary diesel plants	327,498 kilowatts
Railroad power trains, steam	267,500 kilowatts

[56] *Ibid.*

[57] Jordan, *op. cit.*, p. 51. He gives the figures as $263,289,000; the State Department as $178,000,000. There were additional shipments under the October 15, 1945 'pipeline agreement' to be covered in Sutton, *Western Technology and Soviet Economic Development, 1945 to 1965.*

[58] U.S. State Dept. *Report on War Aid Furnished by the United States to the U.S.S.R.* (Washington: Office of Foreign Liquidation, 1945), p. 16.

Trailer-mounted diesel plants	72,945 kilowatts
Railroad power cars, diesel	103,000 kilowatts
Hydroelectric stations	54,392 kilowatts

In 1944 the General Electric Company received a contract to build another nine hydroelectric turbogenerators to fit the same foundations at the Dniepr Dam as the original General Electric installation in 1931; however, as designed, the generators produced 15 percent more energy and the systems were re-engineered by General Electric to incorporate the 15 years of technical advances since 1930.[59] There is no question that this assistance was vitally needed; the Moscow Embassy reported in 1943 that the 'extreme importance attached to delivery of equipment for Soviet hydro-electric stations was the subject of special request by Mikoyan.'[60]

Altogether about two million kilowatts of generating capacity was supplied before the end of 1945 under the U.S., Canadian, and British Lend-Lease programs to the Soviet Union. The capacity lost in German-occupied areas was fully replaced.

Although a large number of power stations were sent under U.S. and British Lend-Lease, there is no record of their final location in the Soviet Union. We can deduce some possible end-uses from a comment by the British Thomson-Houston Company of the United Kingdom:

> . . . normal peace-time products of the B.T.H. Company were urgently required for war production purposes. . . . Equipment for five complete power stations was sent to Russia, as well as a large number of 500 kW transportable turbo-generators, which were used for supplying electricity to damaged towns as they were re-taken from the enemy. . . .[61]

Altogether, 40 of these transportable turbogenerators, each suitable for supplying a complete town with electricity, were supplied.

Up to mid-1944, Canadian companies supplied equipment valued at $25 million for eight or nine hydroelectric power stations[62] under Lend-Lease. The United Kingdom also supplied equipment valued at about $30 million for about a dozen power stations.[63]

[59]   *Electrical World*, October 21, 1944, p. 6. The original General Electric turbines had been removed in 1941 and relocated east of the Urals.

[60]   U.S. State Dept., 861.24/1564, Telegram 809, Moscow to Washington D.C., July 6, 1943.

[61]   H. A. Price-Hughes, *B.T.H. Reminiscences: Sixty Years of Progress* (B.T.H. Ltd.: 1946), p. 111–2.

[62]   *Electrical Review*, June 23, 1944, p. 887. There is an unsubstantiated report that the U.S.S.R. established a purchasing agency in Canada in 1944 for H.E.P. equipment. See U.S. State Dept. Decimal File, 861.24/1775a, April 22, 1944.

[63]   *Electrical Review*, May 19, 1944, p. 690. This question will be taken up in Sutton, *Western Technology and Soviet Economic Development, 1945 to 1965*.

FOREIGN EQUIPMENT AND SUPERVISION FOR CONSTRUCTION OF LARGE POWER STATIONS

In 1933 the Soviet Union had 10 power stations operating with generating capacity in excess of 100,000 kilowatts; these were Kashira, Shterovka, Shatura, Krasnyi Oktiabr' in Leningrad, Moges in Moscow, Zuevka, Dniepr, Nivges at Gorki, Chelyabinsk, and Krasnya Zvesda at Baku. Table 10–2 illustrates the extensive, if not complete, utilization of Western equipment installed under foreign supervision.

Table 10–2   FOREIGN EQUIPMENT IN LARGE POWER
STATIONS OPERATING IN 1933*

Power Station	Capacity (Kilowatts)	Western Equipment
Kashira	186,000	Babcock & Wilcox boilers (enlargement of tsarist station)
Shatura	136,000	Metropolitan-Vickers,[6] Brown-Boveri turbo-generators[10]
Moscow (Moges)	107,000	Metropolitan-Vickers turbines[1]
Krasnyi Oktiabr' (Leningrad)	111,000	Metropolitan-Vickers turbines and boilers,[4] German and Swedish transformers and circuit breakers,[4] U.S. insulators on high tension lines[4]
Shterovka	157,000	Metropolitan-Vickers (2 turbo-generators), Brown-Boveri (2 turbo-generators), Siemens-Schukert (2 turbo-generators)[5]
Zuevka	150,000	Metropolitan-Vickers turbines[1]
Dniepr	310,000	Newport News turbines[3]
Gorki	158,000	Metropolitan-Vickers turbo-alternators,[7] AEG[8]
Chelyabinsk	110,000	Metropolitan-Vickers turbines[1]
Baku	109,000	Siemens-Schukert turbines,[2] Metropolitan-Vickers generators[9]

Sources: Stations in operation: *Pravda*, No. 13, January 13, 1933.

Western origins: [1] Great Britain, *Correspondence Relating to the arrest . . .*, Command Paper 4286 (London, 1933).
[2] *U.S.S.R. in Construction*, No. 3, March 1932.
[3] Sutton, *Western Technology . . ., 1917 to 1930*, p. 204.
[4] *The Electrician*, April 11, 1930, p. 464.
[5] Sergei Koptewski, *The Costs of Construction of New Metallurgical Plants in the U.S.S.R.* (New York: East European Fund, Inc., 1952).
[6] Allan Monkhouse, *Moscow 1911–1933* (Boston: Little, Brown & Co., 1934).
[7] Amtorg, *op. cit.*, V, No. 11 (June 1, 1930), p. 224.
[8] *Ibid.*, VII, No. 7 (April 1, 1932), p. 164.
[9] *Ibid.*, V, No. 20 (October 15, 1930), p. 400.
[10] *Ibid.*, No. 18–19 (October 1, 1930), p. 365; VI, No. 8 (April 15, 1931), p. 178.

* Includes all stations over 100,000 kW.

It is from Allan Monkhouse, Metropolitan-Vickers Chief Engineer in the U.S.S.R., that we derive information concerning skilled engineering and operating labor for power stations. Monkhouse suggested in 1935 that the prewar 'technical intelligentsia' in electrical power generation was not 'decimated' (as in other sectors) and that from 1923 onwards electrification plans were put into effect by those who had held similar responsible positions before the Revolution. In addition, by this time the Soviets had 'turned out many thousands of young men trained in the rudimentary theories of electrical engineering.' Monkhouse makes an interesting comment:

> With regard to skilled workmen, this has not been as serious a difficulty in the building and operation of power stations as might be generally thought because during the constructional periods the main responsibility for skilled workmanship fell upon the erectors sent to the U.S.S.R. by foreign contractors; and of course, once the stations are complete there is not a great deal of work about a power station which necessitates employing highly skilled workmen.[64]

If the reader combines the Monkhouse statement above with data in table 10–2 on the origin of power station equipment, he will readily envisage the primary role of Western contractors in Soviet power-station construction.

The Metropolitan-Vickers Company of the United Kingdom was probably the most important single foreign firm in the electrification of the Soviet Union.[65] Between 1921 and 1939 the company handled about $25 million worth of contracts in the U.S.S.R. involving installation of one million kilowatts of electrical generating capacity as well as other electrical equipment and the provision of technical assistance in the construction of steam turbines, generators, and other types of electrical equipment.[66] The company, according to its own history, trained 'large numbers of Russian engineers' at its works in the United Kingdom.[67] The importance of Metropolitan-Vickers may be gleaned from a series of articles in the London *Times* relating to the arrest of Metropolitan-Vickers engineers in Moscow in 1933 on charges of espionage:

> The Metropolitan-Vickers Company has been continuously engaged in Russia since 1923 and to a greater extent than any other British firm has worked on the electrification of that country. Over a period of ten years about 350 British subjects have from time to time been employed by the Company there, and the plant it has installed in Russia is said to be equivalent to one-sixth of the total generating plant of all kinds in Great Britain. . . .[68]

[64] Allan Monkhouse, 'Electrical Development in the U.S.S.R.,' *Proceedings of the Institute of Electrical Engineers* (London), LXXVI, No. 462 (June 1935), p. 641.
[65] See Sutton, *Western Technology* . . ., *1917 to 1930*, pp. 199–200.
[66] J. Dummelow, *1899–1949* (Manchester: Metropolitan-Vickers Electrical Co., Ltd., 1949).
[67] *Ibid.*, p. 121.
[68] 'The Moscow Trial, New Light on the Case of 1933,' reprinted from the *Times* (London) of May 22, 23, 24, 25, 1933.

The company certainly had its share of problems. After the company had worked for ten years on Soviet electrical projects, its engineers were arrested in 1933 in a raid reminiscent of the 1930 Lena Goldfields raids by the OGPU. The arrests were part of a widespread purge of 'wreckers' although the technical problems reported in the British press appear to have been similar to the usual 'teething problems' of all new plants, as the *Times* noted.

There is some confusion concerning the 1933 Metropolitan-Vickers case, unlikely to be solved until the British Foreign Office records are examined.[69] There is no question that Metropolitan-Vickers, like other foreign firms and engineers working in the Soviet Union, tried to protect Russian engineers, insofar as they could, from absurd charges of sabotage and wrecking. Russian engineers were taking the blame for the ineptitudes and failures of central planning. In this regard,

> the Metropolitan-Vickers Company habitually took the blame for such defects as occurred and made a practice of replacing parts long after the maintenance period had expired, irrespective of whether the defects were the fault of the Company or, as was more frequently the case, were due to the inefficiency of the customers operating staff. . . .[70]

It was the pressure from the Party to rush installation and operate equipment far beyond its safety limits that was leading to breakdown. The British installation engineer, Gregory, for example, regarding the outdoor switchgear and the 12 oil circuit breakers of 165 kilovolts each for Dnieprstroi, says, 'These switches are the largest switches that have ever been made by our Company. The largest switches erected in Russia. . . .'[71] Given all the known difficulties in installing such new and major equipment of this type, the Soviets still blamed Gregory for faulty installation, after themselves attempting to rush the job. Gregory pointed out in his defense that the oil filters were very difficult to obtain and that there was a lot of work to be done.

> So it really amounted to this, that in spite of the delays there were three switches completed in 48 days. These switches were 45 tons each. So now I will leave that to the technical experts to judge whether those switches were done in good time, and whether if done in a shorter time, they would be done properly. . . .[72]

[69] The British Government records became available after this book went to press. Extensive information is listed in *Index to the Correspondence of the Foreign Office for the Year 1933* (Kraus-Thomson, Nendeln/Liechtenstein, 1969) and *Index to "Green" or Secret Papers* (Kraus-Thomson, Nendeln/Liechtenstein, 1969), under both Metropolitan-Vickers, Ltd., and names of individual company engineers.

[70] 'The Moscow Final, New Light on the Case of 1933,' reprinted from the *Times* (London) of May 22, 23, 24, 25, 1933, p. 12.

[71] Dummelow, *op. cit.*, p. 150.

[72] State Law Publishing House, *Wrecking Activities at Power Stations in the Soviet Union*, II, p. 111.

Table 10–3 MAIN PLANTS MANUFACTURING ELECTRICAL
EQUIPMENT IN COMMISSARIAT OF HEAVY
INDUSTRY, 1933

Name of Plant	Product	Western Technical Assistance (1929–33)
Leningrad District		
Stalin Metal works	Steam boilers Steam turbines	Babcock & Wilcox Metropolitan-Vickers
Elektrosila works	Turbo-alternators Generators Rolling-mill motors Mercury-arc rectifiers Marine equipment	International General Electric
Elektrik	Electric welding equipment Induction furnaces	International General Electric
Elektroapparat	Heavy switchgear	International General Electric
Elektropribor	Switchboards Instruments (industrial) Sperry gyroscopes	Brown Instrument Co. Sperry Gyroscope Co.
Radio works	Radio equipment X-ray apparatus	Compagnie de TSF
Svetlana works	Rectifiers Radio receiving valves	AEG (Germany) Siemens-Schukert
Krasnyi Zoria telephone works	Telephone equipment	Ericsson (Sweden)
Moscow District		
ATE works	Electrical equipment for automobiles and tractors	AEG
Transformer works	Transformers	Siemens-Schukert Sperry Gyroscope
Lamp works	Lamps Neon-tube advertising signs Sodium lamps	International General Electric
Electric furnace shop	Electric arc furnaces	Vom Bauer
Dynamo works	Traction equipment Locomotives	International General Electric
Projector and domestic equipment works	Projectors	W. Coffman & Co.
Isolator works	Electrical porcelain Electrical insulating materials	Vakander International General Electric
Moscow Röntgen works	X-ray equipment	Compagnie de TSF
Elektrougli	Brushes Batteries	Ex-AGA concession
Electric lamp works	Electric lamps Valves	J. J. Higgins (U.S.)

Table 10–3 (Continued)

Name of Plant	Product	Western Technical Assistance (1929–33)
Other Districts		
Revtrud works	Train-lighting sets	
	Locomotive head lamps	Not known
KHEMZ	Large motor generators	General Electric
	Industrial motors	
	Industrial switchgear and	General Electric
	control gear	Metropolitan-Vickers
	Relays	
	Meters	
	Steam turbine	General Electric
Volta Works	Motors	
	Industrial equipment	Not known
Uralmash	Electrical equipment	See text

Sources: Plants and products: Monkhouse, *op. cit.*
Technical assistance: see text.

Metropolitan-Vickers was the major influence in almost all power projects besides the Dniepr Dam (a General Electric-Newport News project). However, there were also a few foreign engineers on individual contracts for design and supervision of dam construction. B. E. Torpen worked on hydro-electric design and construction in the Don Basin for about three years.[73] Major G. R. Olberg was requested to supervise construction of the Mingechaur Dam in Azerbaidjan, as large as the Coolidge Dam in the United States. This contract was apparently terminated during the valuta crisis.[74] Two governments supplied advice and aid: four Swedish experts from the Stockholm Hydraulic Bureau came to assist construction of the Svir Dam,[75] and the United States Government supplied 'drawings, photostats and specifications of machinery' used on the Fort Peck and Sardis Dams in the U.S.[76]

Space precludes a thorough examination of smaller power stations, but some examples will suggest the number of such stations receiving foreign equipment; figure 10–3 also illustrates the impact of foreign equipment for one grid area, Leningrad. The Kusnetsk Iron and Steel Plant had two 6,000-kilowatt Rateau turbines and four 24,000-kilowatt Wumag main turbines. The condenser equipment was German but the generators were Soviet-built, probably at Elektrosila.[77] The Krasnyi Oktiabr' metallurgical plant at Stalin-

73 *American Engineers in Russia*, Folder 3, Item 7.
74 *Ibid.*, Item 14: see also U.S. State Dept. Decimal File, 861.5017—Living Conditions/602.
75 U.S. State Dept. Decimal File, 861.6463/44.
76 *Ibid.*, 711.00111 Armament Control/1525.
77 *Far Eastern Review*, January 1933.

Figure 10–3 ORIGIN OF STEAM AND HYDRAULIC TURBINES IN THE LENINGRAD GRID SYSTEM, 1930-44

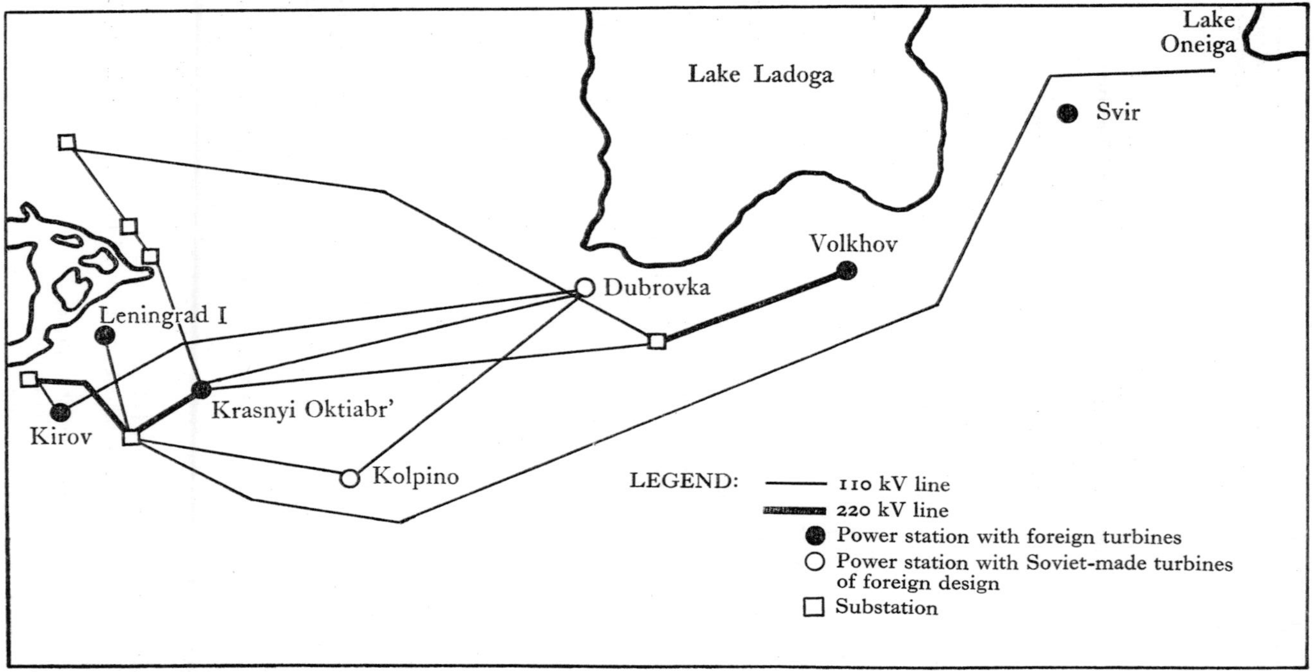

Lake
Oneiga

Svir

Lake Ladoga

Volkhov

Dubrovka

Kolpino

Krasnyi Oktiabr'

Leningrad I

Kirov

LEGEND:

— 110 kV line
═ 220 kV line
● Power station with foreign turbines
○ Power station with Soviet-made turbines of foreign design
□ Substation

Source: Oberkommando der Wehrmacht (OKW/Wi Rü Amt/Wi), *Schema des 220 und 110 kV Leitungsnetz von Leningrad: Karte II,* National Archives Microcopy T 84–122.

grad had three 2,230 MAN diesel engines coupled with AEG 1,610-kilowatt a.c. generators.[78] The Leningrad metal works had Metropolitan-Vickers turbines.[79] Plant 1 at Leningrad had five German 15,000-kilowatt turbines and one English turbine.[80] Plant 5 (Krasnyi Oktiabr') at Leningrad had Metropolitan-Vickers equipment.[81] The Svir hydroelectric station had four vertical Kaplan turbines: three from Sweden and one made by Lenmash.[82] The Volkhov plant had eight Swedish Francis vertical turbines coupled to four Swedish and four Soviet generators.[83] The Magnitogorsk Iron and Steel Plant power stations had two Bergman and one AEG turbine coupled with a Soviet-built turbine.[84] The Kalinin station had two Brown-Boveri turbines coupled with two from Elektrosila.[85] The Orechevo-Suchevo station near Moscow had Metropolitan-Vickers turbines.[86]

After about 1933, power stations began to receive Soviet-built standard turbines and generators based on foreign designs and built in the U.S.S.R., at first with foreign technical assistance and then completely as Soviet undertakings. These were of standardized sizes.[87]

Much of the Don Basin equipment was destroyed or evacuated in 1941 and the Germans were not completely successful in restoring the electric power generation industry in the occupied areas. According to one report, probably written in July and August of 1943, the Germans had restored about one-fifth of electric power capacity in the occupied territories, or about 500,000 kilowatts of operating capacity (against an original installation of 2.5 million kilowatts).[88]

---

[78] *Izvestia Vsesoyuznogo Teplotechnicheskogo Instituta*, No. 1, 1931, p. 10.

[79] Monkhouse, *op. cit.*, p. 185.

[80] Oberkommando der Wehrmacht (OKW/Wi Rü Amt/Wi), March 1941, Plant No. 21, National Archives Microcopy T 84-122-1421674/749.

[81] *Electrician*, April 11, 1930.

[82] Oberkommando der Wehrmacht (OKW/Wi Rü Amt/Wi), March 1941, Plant No. 44, National Archives Microcopy T 84-122-1421674/749.

[83] Monkhouse, *op. cit.*, pp. 138-41.

[84] Oberkommando der Wehrmacht (OKW/Wi Rü Amt/Wi), March 1941, Plant No. 313.

[85] *Ibid.*, Plant No. 50.

[86] State Law Publishing House, *op. cit.*, p. 62.

[87] See p. 154.

[88] Breakdown of the figures does not indicate any particular preference for restoration of industrial, mine, armament, or town electrical power supply systems. Restoration was accomplished as follows:

District power supply	21.8 percent of original installation
Local power supply	15.9 percent of original installation
Mines (original plant very small)	0 percent of original installation
Foundries	21.5 percent of original installation
Iron and steel works	23.3 percent of original installation
Industry	16.4 percent of original installation

Source: Oberkommando der Wehrmacht (OKW/Wi Rü Amt/Wi), March 1941, National Archives Microcopy T 84-122-1421745.

CONCLUSIONS

There was a considerable manufacturing of electrical equipment in tsarist Russia; the facilities were later re-equipped and expanded and then supplemented by several giant new manufacturing plants. This program was undertaken in close cooperation with internationally known companies, including International General Electric, Metropolitan-Vickers, and RCA. Two plants, the KHEMZ and the Urals Elektromash, were truly gigantic—much larger than the main home plants of General Electric and Metropolitan-Vickers. Agreements with RCA, Sperry Gyroscope, Brown Instrument Company, and others provided assistance in specialized areas.

The 10 largest power stations built by 1933, in addition to numerous smaller stations, had Western equipment; later stations received equipment that was Soviet-made to standardized Western designs.

It is not an exaggeration to say that by 1945 Soviet electrical equipment was completely based on Western (mainly General Electric) models. This is one sector where a truly remarkable pattern comprising thousands of transfers can be precisely identified.

CHAPTER ELEVEN

Technical Assistance to the Automobile and Tractor Industries

DEVELOPMENT OF AN AUTOMOBILE INDUSTRY

THE Soviet automobile industry before 1930 was limited to production of the prerevolutionary Fiat light truck, utilizing imported parts. After 1930 the industry relied completely on American technical assistance. One completely new plant, the Gorki, was built under Ford Motor Company supervision in the early 1930s[1] and two tsarist plants in Moscow and Yaroslavl were expanded and completely re-equipped with up-to-date American machine tools. These three plants, together with a smaller Moscow assembly plant which opened in 1940, constituted the Soviet automobile industry before World War II.

THE AMO PLANT IN MOSCOW

This tsarist plant, owned by Ryabushinski and Kuznetsov before the Revolution, was still producing a few 1912-model Fiats (the original model) in early 1929. In mid-1929 the A. J. Brandt Company of Detroit undertook an extensive two-year reorganization and expansion of Amo, which was then renamed Automobile Works No. 2 (Stalin), and is today known as the ZIL (plant im. I. A. Likhachev). This plant produced 50,000 medium-sized trucks per year, in addition to large automobiles and buses. The early Amo-Fiat models were hand-built. The reconstructed plant mass-produced the ZIS 5 and ZIS 6 trucks (i.e., the Autocar $2\frac{1}{2}$-ton truck) until 1944 and the heavy ZIS 101 and ZIS 102 automobiles until 1941. Both were based on U.S. designs and specifications.[2]

---

[1] The important Ford Motor Company agreement of 1929 to build the Gorki plant is described in Sutton, *Western Technology . . . 1917 to 1930*, pp. 243–9: the equally important Fiat agreement of 1966, which transfers mainly U.S. (not Italian) machine tools, will be covered in Sutton, *Western Technology . . . 1945 to 1965*.

[2] Alexander Barmine, *One Who Survived* (New York: G. P. Putnam, 1945), p. 237.

This Brandt-built plant was described by Carver, a skilled American observer, as 'by far the largest and best-equipped plant in the world devoted solely to the manufacture of trucks and buses. Basically, the equipment is the last word in American practice.'[3]

A similar comment was made by C. P. Weeks, Vice-President of Hercules Motor Corporation (Canton, Ohio). After a four-hour tour of the expanded Amo, Weeks commented that it was superior to both the Mack and White plants and was 'the best-equipped plant in the world.'[4] Amo was further described by Carver as follows:

> From the forge shop, which is equipped with batteries of steam and board drop hammers, forging machines and furnace equipment, and the foundry with its bull ring, continuous pouring floor, sand conditioners, etc., through to final assembly and finishing department, no detail has been missed. The press room is a dead ringer for some of ours. . . .'[5]

The production equipment was entirely American and German.[6] In late 1929 Amtorg placed an order on behalf of Amo with the Toledo Machine and Tool Company for $600,000 of cold-stamping presses.[7] In 1932 an order was placed with Greenless Company of Rockford, Illinois for multi-cylinder lathes.[8]

In 1936 a second technical-assistance agreement was concluded for Amo with the Budd Manufacturing Company of Philadelphia and the Hamilton Foundry and Machine Company of Ohio to produce 210,000 chassis and bodies per year for a new ZIS-model automobile.[9]

The Budd Company sent engineer R. L. Adams and two shop men to supervise installation of $1 million worth of dies made by the company for ZIS production. One feature of the contract which intrigued the Budd Company was a requirement that 100 finished sets of body stampings were to be made from the dies *in the United States* and shipped with the dies. These were to be used to build 100 ZIS automobiles under the supervision of Budd engineers in the Soviet Union to celebrate the 1936 anniversary of the October Revolution. The Hamilton Foundry supplied the presses required for follow-on fabrication of sheet metal for bodies and chassis in the Soviet Union.

In spite of this assistance, troubles were encountered in producing the Autocar model, although blueprints and technical advice had been freely

---

[3] W. L. Carver, 'AMO and Nizhni-Novogorod Plants Lead Soviet Plans,' *Automotive Industries*, LXVI (March 12, 1932), pp. 418–9.
[4] U.S. State Dept. Decimal File, 861.5017—Living Conditions/307.
[5] Carver, *op. cit.*, pp. 418–21.
[6] Amtorg, *op. cit.*, VI, No. 21 (November 1, 1931), p. 489.
[7] *Ibid.*, IV, No. 20 (October 15, 1929), p. 372.
[8] *Ibid.*, VII, No. 8 (April 15, 1932), p. 176.
[9] U.S. State Dept. Decimal File, 861.60/288.

given. For example, Weeks commented that 200 castings had been made of one part but that not one was usable, because of inaccuracies in dimensions and faulty materials.

In late 1937 neither the Ford-built Gorki (discussed below) nor the Brandt-built Amo plant was fulfilling production schedules, because of 'tremendous disorders.'[10] The truck conveyor at the Amo plant was idle 23 percent of the time, and the M-1 model conveyor at Gorki was idle 35 percent of the time. Serious technical difficulties were encountered in production of both the M-1 model and the ZIS. Parts were not supplied on schedule.[11] The U.S. Moscow Embassy concluded from various reports that the Soviet automobile industry was 'in sore need of further assistance.'[12]

These problems were overcome at least in part, and 1938 production, as reported by the Oberkommando der Wehrmacht intelligence, was not unsatisfactory, although raw output figures tell us nothing about quality. Production of the Amo plant in 1938 was given as follows:

ZIS Model 5 (2½ tons, Autocar)	59,724 units
ZIS Model 6 (4 tons, unknown model)	3,169 units
ZIS Models 101 and 102 (Budd design)	3,900 units
Buses (Autocar chassis)	1,335 units[13]

Some 40,000 workers were employed in this plant in 1940.

HERCULES MOTOR CORPORATION RECONSTRUCTION OF THE YAROSLAVL PLANT

In 1929 the Hercules Motor Corporation, of Canton, Ohio, received a contract similar to that of A. J. Brandt to expand and reconstruct on American lines the Yaroslavl Automobile Works No. 3, known previous to the Revolution as Akt Obs Vozdukhoplavanie. In 1915 the plant had been equipped to produce 1,500 Crossley and Wolsey automobiles per year. Although intact after the Revolution, the plant was used only as a repair shop from 1918 to 1931, producing a few trucks with imported engines.

The agreement with Hercules Motor Corporation was signed in August 1929, and Amtorg indicated that:

> The Hercules Company will supply the Soviet Automobile Trust with the necessary drawings and other technical data and will send engineers to the U.S.S.R. to assist in designing and manufacturing the engines. In addition, Soviet engineers will study the various phases of production of motors in the Hercules plant. . . .[14]

10 *Ibid.*
11 *Pravda*, No. 267, September 27, 1937.
12 U.S. State Dept. Decimal File, 861.60/289.
13 Oberkommando der Wehrmacht (OKW/Wi Rü Amt/Wi), March 1941, Miscellaneous German Records, National Archives Microcopy T 84–122.
14 Amtorg, *op. cit.*, IV, No. 18 (September 1929), p. 279.

Table 11–1　　WESTERN ORIGIN OF SOVIET AUTOMOBILES AND TRUCKS, 1930–45

Soviet Automobile or Truck Model	Description	Western Model of Origin	Western Technical Assistance
Amo-F-15	1.5-ton flatbed truck	Fiat 15 (1912 model)	Fiat S.p.a. engineering assistance, 1929.
GAZ A	Pickup truck	Ford Model A	Ford Motor Co. (new plant).
GAZ AA (also GAZ MM, and GAZ 63)	1.5-ton flatbed truck	Ford Model A (MM had Ford Model B engine)	Ford Motor Co. (new plant).
GAZ 410	1.5-ton dump truck	Ford Model A	Ford Motor Co. (new plant).
GAZ AA	Fire engine	Ford	Ford Motor Co. (new plant).
GAZ M-1 (and M-20)	Passenger automobile	Ford 1934 model	Ford Motor Co. (new plant).
ZIS 5	2½-ton flatbed truck	Autocar Model S.A.	Ryabushinski-Kuznetsov Co. plant (tsarist) re-equipped and expanded by A. J. Brandt.
ZIS 6	4-ton flatbed truck	Unknown; probably Autocar Model S.A.	Ryabushinski-Kuznetsov Co. plant (tsarist) re-equipped and expanded by A. J. Brandt.
ZIS 101	Heavy passenger automobile	Budd Co.*	Ryabushinski-Kuznetsov Co. plant (tsarist) re-equipped by A. J. Brandt (1929–30) and Budd Co. (1936).
ZIS 21, 21A	Gas generator truck	—	Ryabushinski-Kuznetsov Co. plant (tsarist) re-equipped and expanded by A. J. Brandt, Budd Co. and Hamilton Foundry.
YaZ 3	3-ton flatbed truck	Fiat S.p.a.	Fiat S.p.a. (pre-1929).
YaZ 6	5-ton flatbed truck, bus	Hercules Motor Co.	Akt. Obs. Vozdukhoplavanie plant (tsarist) re-equipped and expanded by Hercules Motor Co.
YaZ 10	8-ton dump truck	Hercules Motor Co.	Akt. Obs. Vozdukhoplavanie plant (tsarist) re-equipped and expanded by Hercules Motor Co.
L.K. 1	Trolleybus	Hercules Motor Co.	Akt. Obs. Vozdukhoplavanie plant (tsarist) re-equipped and expanded by Hercules Motor Co. (after 1933).

Sources: See text.

* Budd supplied body dies to Ford specifications.

The basic vehicle design used at Yaroslavl was American except that the engines were 'bored somewhat larger, the frames reinforced and special heavy axles . . . fitted.'[15] That is to say, a heavy truck specification was used.

In 1932 Yaroslavl was again expanded, in order to produce 4,000 heavy trucks per year, although even by 1938 production had only reached a total of 2,377 YaZ 5-ton trucks and buses.[16] This 1938 output, requiring about 15,000 workers, was distributed as follows:

YaZ 3 (3-ton truck)	826
YaG 6 (5-ton truck)	1,289
YaG 10 (8-ton truck)	27
L. K. 1 (trolleybus, chassis)	235[17]

As noted, this was also the Soviet bus-building plant, the chassis being made at Yaroslavl and the bodies in Leningrad and Moscow. The single-deck four-wheel trolleybus, known as the L.K. 1, had a Yaroslavl chassis and traction equipment made at the Dynamo plant in Moscow.[18]

THE CONSTRUCTION OF OTHER AUTOMOBILE PLANTS

Construction of a large new automobile plant (modeled after the River Rouge plant) at Gorki by the Ford Motor Company has been described in Volume I.[19] This plant started operation on January 1, 1932, but in 1936-7 it still had major operating problems. In 1937 S. S. Dybets, Director of the Gorki plant, former mechanic, and reputed active member of the I.W.W. in the United States, was removed from office. The charges included Menshevik associations and Bukharinist tendencies.

As built, the plant had a capacity to produce 140,000 vehicles per year. In 1938 it was reported operating at about 85 percent capacity, producing the following:

GAZ AA (light truck)	84,288
GAZ M (automobile)	23,256
Gas generator vehicle (M chassis)	1,738

---

[15] Carver, *op. cit.*, p. 419.
[16] Oberkommando der Wehrmacht (OKW/Wi Rü Amt/Wi), March 1941, Miscellaneous German Records, National Archives Microcopy T 84-122.
[17] *Ibid.*
[18] No technical-assistance agreement was traced for these buses. The specification given by W. Konovaloff ('The First Trolley Buses in Moscow,' *The Electric Railway, Bus and Tram Journal*, June 15, 1934, pp. 286-8), however, would have been too advanced for Soviet capabilities in the early 1930s—so presumably some agreement was made. The exterior is rather similar to some German models. See also U.S. State Dept. Decimal File, 861.5017—Living Conditions/688.
[19] Sutton, *Western Technology . . . 1917 to 1930*, pp. 246-9.

GAZ AAA (2-ton truck)   6,314

S, 193, M55 (buses)   1,796[20]

This represented some improvement over 1937, when the M-1 conveyor line had been reported idle 35 percent of the time.[21] Further improvements were registered after the invasion of the Soviet Union by the Nazis and after Lend-Lease equipment assistance.

Two assembly plants were supplied with parts for assembly manufactured at Gorki. One was the Gudok Oktiabr' (with an annual assembly capacity of 6,000 automobiles), which merged with the main Gorki plant in 1932. The other was Automobile Assembly Plant No. 2 (the KIM, in Moscow), with an assembly capacity of 24,000 automobiles. This plant had been erected with Ford technical assistance in 1930–1. Employment was reported at 10,000 in 1940, with a probable output of 50,000 vehicles in 1941.[22]

UNITED STATES AND SWISS ASSISTANCE IN THE MANUFACTURE OF AUTOMOBILE PARTS

Construction of truck and automobile production plants required the establishment of a series of smaller industries supplying parts. In the United States these are partly supplied to the major automobile producers on a subcontract basis; in the U.S.S.R. such parts had previously been imported.

For the manufacture of automobile springs, bumper bars, and similar components, VATO made an agreement with the Gogan Machine Company of Cleveland, who sold them the necessary equipment and sent an engineer and two mechanics to the Soviet Union to supervise equipment installation and initial production operations. Emil Lutzweiler, the Gogan engineer, and the two mechanics were sent first to the Moscow truck plant (Amo) and then to the Ford plant at Gorki.[23]

Amtorg reported in late 1930 that a former samovar factory—the Kirjanov—was being rebuilt with 'the assistance of German and American specialists' to produce Ford headlights: the 'first of its kind in the U.S.S.R.'[24]

Automobile glass was produced in a Moscow plant of Steklofarfor (Glass and Ceramics Trust), with C. E. Alder as supervisor of some 300 Russian workers. The plant used imported American machinery.[25]

[20] Oberkommando der Wehrmacht (OKW/Wi Rü Amt/Wi), March 1941, Miscellaneous German Records, Microcopy T 84–122.

[21] U.S. State Dept. Decimal File, 861.60/288.

[22] Oberkommando der Wehrmacht (OKW/Wi Rü Amt/Wi), March 1941. Miscellaneous German Records, National Archives Microcopy T 84–122.

[23] U.S. State Dept. Decimal File, 861.5017—Living Conditions/441, Report No. 615, Stuttgart, March 16, 1932.

[24] Amtorg, *op. cit.*, V, No. 24 (December 15, 1930), p. 494.

[25] U.S. State Dept. Decimal File, 861.5017—Living Conditions/287, Report No. 889, Stockholm, June 27, 1931.

Electrical equipment for automobiles, trucks, and tractors was the subject of an agreement between VEO and the Electric Auto-Lite Company of Toledo, Ohio. The company prepared 'a detailed layout and working project for a plant to manufacture complete electrical units for automobiles and tractors.'[26] This plant, the only one of its kind in the U.S.S.R., had the capacity to produce 450,000 complete electrical units per year for automobiles and 270,000 electrical units for tractors. The agreement called for furnishing manufacturing information, providing American engineers to work in the U.S.S.R.,[27] and training Soviet engineers in the United States.[28] The agreement was implemented in the Soviet Union by M. Buchenberd, Vice-President of the Electric Auto-Lite Company. Magnetos (Bosch design) and spark plugs (design unknown, but possibly Champion) were produced in a Moscow electric-apparatus factory where 'German and Swiss machinery is used almost exclusively and it is all new.'[29]

The Swiss company Scintilla A-G had a technical-assistance contract similar to those of Ford and Hercules Motors to erect and start up a plant for the manufacture of ignition equipment.[30]

The rapidity with which the Soviets were able to acquire even closely guarded Western processes is little short of amazing. The manufacture of carburetors provides a good example. In 1928 the Holley Permanent Mould Machine Company in the United States developed a mechanized metal-casting process for producing carburetors to replace the previous slow-earth-moulds technique. The new technique was much quicker and required much less labor. The secret was in the composition of the heat-resistent lining of the moulds. The Holley Company sold only two sets of equipment: one to Ford in the United States and one to Siemens-Schukert in Germany. Then the Soviets announced that they too had the 'Kholley' carburetor manufacturing process and were going to put it to use.[31] The Samara carburetor and motor plant was sub-

---

[26]   Amtorg, *op. cit.*, V, No. 6 (March 15, 1930), p. 106.

[27]   *Ibid.* See also U.S. State Dept. Decimal File, 861.6463/46. The Electric Auto-Lite employees raised the question of their status and rights if they became employees of the Soviet Government. Clearly they preferred to remain employees of Electric Auto-Lite.

[28]   U.S. Congress, *Investigation of Communist Propaganda* (71st Congress, 2nd session, Special Committee to Investigate Communist Activities in the United States), Part 3, Vol. 3 (Washington, D.C.: 1930).

[29]   U.S. State Dept. Decimal File, 861.5017—Living Conditions/417.

[30]   *Automotive Industries*, LXI, No. 17 (October 26, 1929).

[31]   *Pravda* (Leningrad), No. 24, October 15, 1932. The 'advantage of coming late,' even with the carburetor, may be suggested by the observation that, in Great Britain alone, some 28 different carburetor models were developed between 1889 and 1933. [See *Motor Cars: Handbook of the Collection*, Part II (London: H.M.S.O., 1959).]

sequently developed to supply the entire automobile, tractor, and airplane industries with carburetors.[32]

In early 1932 the 'first automobile repair station of a standard type' was opened in Moscow; it was 'equipped with American machinery.'[33]

At this time a large plant for the manufacture of rubber and asbestos parts for automobiles and tires for automobiles, bicycles, and motorcycles—'one of the largest in the world'—was erected at Yaroslavl. Designed to employ 22,000, the plant came into production at the end of 1932 and cost more than $100 million. Technical assistance for the rubber-tire plant was supplied by the Seiberling Rubber Company of Akron, Ohio, which supervised initial operations and trained Soviet engineers and foremen at Akron. Amtorg stated that the Seiberling Company 'will prepare all the designs, plans and specifications for the construction. . . .'[34] The automobile-tire-producing capacity was 3,100 per day, in addition to 9,000 bicycle and 480 motorcycle tires.[35] Some 35 different asbestos parts, including brake linings and clutch facings, were also made.[36] Technical assistance to the asbestos unit was supplied by the Multibestos Company of Walpole, Massachussetts, and a number of American engineers were hired on individual contract.[37]

Another rubber-tire plant was supplied by the United States under Lend-Lease: this was the Ford Motor Company tire plant, capable of producing one million automobile tires per year. It was dismantled and shipped complete to the U.S.S.R.[38] There were some problems in re-erection of this tire plant in Moscow, as the Soviet Union was not able to duplicate the basement and sublevel features 'which were part of the Detroit plan.'[39] By February 1944, 75 percent of the plant equipment was on site and another 15 percent en route. A request was then made for installation drawings for Goodrich-type tire-building machines from the National Rubber Company and for two American engineers to handle the erection of the Farrel-Birmingham calendars; given these, the Russians expected that production would start in June 1944.[40]

In the allied field of highway construction, the Seabrook Construction Company provided technical assistance for road construction in the Moscow

[32]   Amtorg, *op. cit.*, VI, No. 23 (December 1, 1931), p. 533.
[33]   *Ibid.*, VII, No. 2 (January 15, 1932), p. 43.
[34]   *Ibid.*, IV, No. 16–17 (September 1, 1929), p. 279.
[35]   *Automotive Industries*, LXI, No. 17 (October 26, 1929).
[36]   U.S. State Dept. Decimal File, 861.659—ASBESTOS, Report No. 623, Riga, August 11, 1932.
[37]   *Ibid.*
[38]   U.S. State Dept. Decimal File, 861.24/1567.
[39]   *Ibid.*, Telegram 810, Moscow to Washington, D.C., July 6, 1943.
[40]   U.S. State Dept. Decimal File, 861.654/19, Telegram 451, Moscow to Washington D.C., February 10, 1944.

area and had road-building contracts in Turkmenistan and possibly in the Caucasus.[41] Technical assistance for bridge construction was provided by a highly qualified consultant, Leon S. Moisseiff, Consulting Engineer to the Port of New York Authority.[42]

THE ORIGIN OF THE STALINGRAD TRACTOR PLANT

Site selection and staking out for the Stalingrad Tractor Plant were reported in 1926.[43] Little else was done for three years. In March 1929 a delegation of 13 Soviet engineers arrived in the United States and in co-operation with several American companies outlined a plan for a plant to produce 50,000 Caterpillar-type tractors (of 15 to 30 horsepower) per year.[44] The Stalingrad Tractor Plant, largest in Europe, was a packaged plant built in the United States, dismantled, shipped to the U.S.S.R., and re-erected at Stalingrad under supervision of American engineers. All equipment was manufactured in the United States by some 80 firms; the plant produced the International Harvester 15/30 model.

The original Gosplan request had been for a plant to manufacture only 10,000 tractors per year. The Russian planners estimated a construction time of four or five years even for a U.S. construction company.[45] Work on a 50,000-tractor-per-year plant actually started in June 1929. The framework was completed December 23, 1929[46] and the structure roofed and walled by February 15, 1930.[47] Three months later 20 percent of the equipment in the machine shops and assembly departments, 75 percent of the forge-shop equipment, and 40 percent of the casting-shop equipment had been installed.[48] In the following month the balance of the equipment was received and installation of the foundry completed.[49]

The Stalingrad Tractor Plant was the first of three massive plants for the production of tractors in peace and tanks in war. It was built in every sense

[41] Amtorg, *op. cit.*, IV, No. 12–13 (July 1, 1929), p. 232.
[42] *Ibid.*, No. 18 (September 15, 1929), p. 306.
[43] Report of the Ford Delegation to Russia and the U.S.S.R., April–August 1926 (Detroit, 1926), Ford Motor Company Archives Accession No. 49.
[44] 'While preliminary work on the site of the Stalingrad Tractor Plant had been conducted for some time, the actual work on the construction of the principal departments started only in June when the plans arrived from the United States.' [Amtorg, *op. cit.*, V, No. 7 (April 1, 1930), p. 135.] 'The entire designing of the Stalingrad . . . tractor plant, which is to produce annually 40,000 wheel tractors of 15–30 h.p. was carried out in the United States.' [Amtorg, *op. cit.*, IV, No. 19 (October 1, 1929), p. 336.]
[45] Amtorg, *op. cit.*, V, No. 7 (April 1, 1930), p. 135.
[46] *Ibid.* See photograph on p. 134.
[47] *Ibid.* See photograph on p. 135.
[48] Amtorg, *op. cit.*, V, No. 13 (July 1, 1930), p. 287.
[49] *Ibid.*

of the word in the United States and reassembled by 570 Americans and 50 Germans in Stalingrad. The plant was delivered in component parts, and installed in a building supplied by McClintock and Marshall and erected under John Calder of the Austin Company. *Za Industrializatsiiu* pointed out that 'it is very important to note that the work of the American specialists . . . was not that of consulting but of actually superintending the entire construction and the various operations involved.'[50]

Each item of construction and equipment was the responsibility of a major U.S. firm. This effort is summarized in table 11–2.

Table 11–2   DESIGN AND CONSTRUCTION OF THE
STALINGRAD TRACTOR PLANT

Operation or Supply	U.S. Firm
Design of plant	Albert Kahn, Inc.
Design of forge shop	R. Smith, Inc.
Design of foundry	Frank D. Chase, Inc.
Equipment for cold-stamping department	Niagara, Bliss
Equipment for heat-treating shops	Rockwell
Equipment for power station	Seper
Equipment for power-station equipment	Westinghouse
Equipment for chain-belting, conveyor system	Chain Belt Co.
Supply of buildings	McClintock & Marshall
Superintendent of construction	John Calder

Sources: *Za Industrializatsiiu*, July 5, 1930.
Amtorg, *op. cit.*, V, No. 7 (April 1, 1930), p. 135.
Norton T. Dodge, 'Trends in Labor Productivity in the Soviet Tractor Industry,' Ph.D. Dissertation, Harvard University, Economics Department (February 1960).

The American chief engineer had no administrative chores. These were handled by Russian and American assistants. All technical problems were settled by American engineers on the spot. The Stalingrad Tractor Plant, therefore, was American in concept, design, construction, equipment, and operation. It could just as easily have been located outside Chicago, except for the placards claiming 'socialist progress.'

It is worthwhile to recall that the contemporary Soviet press was reasonably open about this U.S. assistance. For example, an article in *Za Industrializatsiiu*[51]

---

[50] *Za Industrializatsiiu*, July 5, 1930. The original Gipromez plant was significantly changed by the American construction companies and equipment suppliers. The floor area of the forge shop was decreased from 12,600 to 7,200 square meters and the forge shop work force from 655 to 335 men.
[51] *Ibid.*

drew three conclusions: first, that the preparation of the plans for the Stalingrad plant by American engineers with 'participation' of Soviet engineers made completion of the plant possible within a 'very short time'; second, that work and training by Soviet engineers in the United States resulted in a 'considerable improvement in engineering processes' and the application of American standards; and third, that work in the United States gave the Soviets a first-hand opportunity to study American tractor plants and verify data on operation of American machine tools. Even though this article understated the amount of American assistance, it constituted altogether a quite remarkable admission.

THE KHARKOV TRACTOR PLANT

Kharkov was identical to the Stalingrad plant. By using the steel-work dimensions given in the Stalingrad blueprints, the Soviets anticipated saving 440,000 rubles in the purchase of fabricated structural steel in the United States. A *Pravda* article[52] noted this and questioned whether the assembly shop trusses, doors, and windows should be bought in 'knocked-down' form from the United States (as in the Stalingrad plant) or built and assembled by Soviet plants and engineers. Finally much of the structural steel was bought in Czechoslovakia.

Although the original intention was to build Kharkov as an all-Soviet undertaking, American engineers were called in at a very early point. Leon A. Swajian, for example, became Chief Construction Engineer and was subsequently awarded the Order of Lenin for his work at Kharkov.[53] A fairly large number of foreign specialists were invited in; a booklet of 80 pages (including 74 illustrations) is devoted to the activities of foreign workers at the Kharkov Tractor Plant.[54]

To Leon Swajian we owe the observation that these tractor plants were built very much more quickly in the U.S.S.R. than in the U.S.A. although the same supervising engineers and equipment were used. After commenting that no other construction job had required so much work in a single year, Swajian added that in the U.S. giant plants are not built all at once; we build a few departments, subcontract, and buy spares outside, so that:

> Ford's River Rouge plant was more than a dozen years in building. When I took charge it was already partly built; I worked there six or seven years and when I left construction was still in progress. But in the U.S.S.R. with government financing and no other plants from which to buy spare parts, with the plant dependent on itself—down to the smallest operation

[52] June 5, 1930.
[53] F. E. Beal, *Foreign Workers in a Soviet Tractor Plant* (Moscow: Co-operative Publishing Society of Foreign Workers in the U.S.S.R., 1933), p. 9.
[54] *Ibid.*

on the basic raw material—the whole plant must be built at once. And very swiftly too, if it is not to tie up capital too long. The Kharkov job was pushed to completion more swiftly than any job I have ever had to do with.[55]

Even in mid-1933, when the plant was in operation, there were still 25 Americans at Kharkov, including the Foundry Maintenance Superintendent, the Assistant Maintenance Superintendent, and the engineer in charge of pyrometer equipment.[56]

As at Stalingrad and Chelyabinsk, the equipment was almost all foreign—'either German or U.S.—if German then patterned after American makes';[57] in fact no equipment at the Kharkov plant has been identified precisely as Soviet. The forge shop had $403,000 worth of American forging machines and dies;[58] and the heat-treating equipment, automatic furnace-temperature controls, and similar equipment were supplied by Leeds and Northrup of Philadelphia.[59]

Kharkov produced the International Harvester 15/30 model until 1937, when it changed over to the Russian NATI model. After World War II the plant went back to production of the original International Harvester 15/30.

THE CHELYABINSK TRACTOR PLANT

The Chelyabinsk plant was started in 1930 without foreign technical assistance as another duplicate of the Stalingrad Tractor Plant. One year later, in March 1931, a letter to the Soviet press signed by 35 Chelyabinsk Tractor Plant engineers and economists charged that the plant was 'on the verge of total collapse.'[60] The letter explained that planning had begun early in 1930 and construction in April. Supposedly the building had been completed in September of that year. Although operation had begun on November 6, 1930, no usable tractors had been produced as of March 1931. The first 'tractors' were built of 'junk,' there were 'freaks' in the design of the metal stamps, there was no hoisting gear in the mechanical and assembly shops (the walls were not strong enough to bear the weight), the compressor shop

[55]   Amtorg, *op. cit.*, VI, No. 18 (September 15, 1931), pp. 413–5.
[56]   U.S. State Dept. Decimal File, 861.5017—Living Conditions/677, Report No. 155, Riga, June 14, 1933.
[57]   *Ibid.*
[58]   Amtorg, *op. cit.*, V, No. 22–23 (December 1, 1930), p. 462.
[59]   L. M. Herman, 'Revival of Russia's Tractor Industry,' *Foreign Commerce Weekly*, XXI, No. 2 (October 6, 1945), p. 12.
[60]   'The Chelyabinsk Experimental Tractor Plant on the Verge of Collapse,' *Za Industrializatsiiu*, No. 77, March 19, 1931, p. 3. Subsequent articles indicate further delays and problems. See *Izvestia*, March 22, 1931, and *Za Industrializatsiiu*, April 18, 1931.

was not working, and the boilers received from Germany had not been installed. So ran some of the complaints in the letter.

American engineers, including John Calder, the expert trouble-shooter, were then called in to take over reconstruction of the plant and operating responsibility. A pilot plant was established and operated by John Thane and an American assistant, both former employees of the Caterpillar Company.[61] The Chief Consulting Engineer from 1931 to 1933 was Edward J. Terry. An interview with Terry by a State Department official[62] provides information on the fate of the plant in the next two years. Even by early 1933 'very little had actually been completed'; the foundry and the forge were not finished, nor were the conveyors nor the sand-handling equipment for castings.

One puzzling point concerning Chelyabinsk is the extent of the assistance rendered by the Caterpillar Company, of Peoria, Illinois. In 1968 company officials did not have a technical-assistance agreement on file nor could any current official recall an agreement. However, the Stalinets S-60 tractor was an exact copy[63] of the Caterpillar 1925–31 model. Ex-Caterpillar engineers supervised operations, and one of these stated 'that he had seen at the works American specifications and drawings and also standard drawings belonging

Table 11–3 SUMMARY OF SOVIET TRACTOR PRODUCTION
AND WESTERN MODELS, 1930–45

Soviet Model	Years Produced	Soviet Plant	Western Origin
Wheeled Tractors			
FP 10/20	1928–33	Putilovets (Kirov)	Fordson
International 15/30	1930 after 1948	Kharkov, Stalingrad	International Harvester
Universal 10/20	1934–7, after 1945	Kirov, Vladimir	International Harvester Farmall
Track-Laying Tractors			
NATI	1937–41 1944–9	Kharkov Stalingrad	No data on origin of the NATI
Stalinets S-60	1931–7	Chelyabinsk	Caterpillar
Stalinets S-65	1937–41	Chelyabinsk	Diesel version of Caterpillar 60

Sources: See text.

[61] *Factory and Industrial Management*, LXXXII, 1931, p. 804.
[62] U.S. State Dept. Decimal File, 861.5017—Living Conditions/663, May 27, 1933.
[63] U.S. State Dept. Decimal File, 861.659/TRACTORS/5, October 26, 1933.

to the American company.'[64] Moscow *Pravda*[65] agreed that negotiations with Caterpillar were inconclusive. The Soviet representative at the Chelyabinsk Detroit office then reportedly purchased a Caterpillar tractor, took it to pieces in his Detroit office, and proceeded to design the plant.[66] This is rather an unlikely way to design a tractor plant and would certainly account for construction problems at Chelyabinsk.

In May 1933 'practically all the machine tools and production equipment in the plant was [sic] either American, English or German of the highest quality and the most modern for that time. . . .'[67]

German equipment installed at the Chelyabinsk Tractor Plant included oil breaker switches (700,000 marks' worth),[68] various drop hammers (about half a million marks' worth),[69] a wheel lathe (300,000 marks),[70] a compression unit (200,000 marks),[71] forging machines ($1\frac{3}{4}$ million marks' worth),[72] 15 gear-cutting machines (200,000 marks),[73] a mold for the iron foundry (400,000 marks),[74] a Universal milling machine (200,000 marks),[75] grinding machines (350,000 marks' worth),[76] and heavy presses (1 million marks' worth).[77]

By 1937 the plant employed about 25,000 workers. The only model produced between 1933 and 1937 was the Stalinets (Caterpillar) S-60; a 50-horsepower (drawbar) model of the crawler type. About 6,460 were produced in 1937:[78] a long way from the planned 50,000 per year. In 1937 the production model was changed to the Stalinets S-65, which was a Caterpillar 60 with slightly increased horsepower and a diesel engine. A total of just over 3,000 were produced, including another model with a gas generator.

[64]   *Ibid.*

[65]   No. 146, May 29, 1933. *Za Industrializatsiiu*, No. 125, June 1, 1933, says that the company rejected a technical-assistance contract.

[66]   *Za Industrializatsiiu*, No. 125, June 1, 1933.

[67]   Norton T. Dodge, 'Trends in Labor Productivity in the Soviet Tractor Industry,' Ph.D. Dissertation, Harvard University, Economics Department (February 1960).

[68]   *Sowjetwirtschaft und Aussenhandel*, Handelsvertretung der UdSSR in Deutschland, Berlin SW, X, No. 17 (1931), p. 30.

[69]   *Ibid.*, XI, No. 6 (1932), p. 15.

[70]   *Ibid.*, XI, No. 7 (1932), p. 18.

[71]   *Ibid.*, XI, No. 10 (1932), p. 21.

[72]   *Ibid.*, XI, No. 6 (1932), p. 14.

[73]   *Ibid.*, XI, No. 16 (1932), p. 23.

[74]   *Ibid.*, XI, No. 10 (1932), p. 21.

[75]   *Ibid.*, XI, No. 8 (1932), p. 31.

[76]   *Ibid.*, XI, No. 15 (1932), p. 22.

[77]   *Ibid.*, XI, No. 10 (1932), p. 21.

[78]   Oberkommando der Wehrmacht (OKW/Wi Rü Amt/Wi), March 1941, Miscellaneous German Records, National Archives Microcopy T 84–122.

THE PUTILOVETS (KIROV) TRACTOR PLANT IN LENINGRAD

The Putilovets, oldest engineering plant in Russia, attempted to produce copies of the Fordson tractor in the late 1920s.[79] This was unsuccessful and the plant was rebuilt and greatly expanded in 1929–31 under the supervision of Ford Motor Company engineers to produce the Fordson-Putilovets (FP) tractor.[80] Thus by 1931 the plant was organized along American lines with completely new American and German equipment. An American engineer, Bowers, was running the two foundry shops;[81] Karl Holgdund, an American citizen, was superintendent of the drop hammer shop;[82] and the modern forge shop was also under American management. According to one observer, the design, drawings, specifications, and equipment were all American.[83]

The first Soviet motor for combines, the Viskhom-2, was a modified Fordson tractor motor. Production started in March 1932.[84] In the spring of 1934 the tractor model was changed from the Fordson, found to be too light for Russian conditions, to the International Harvester Farmall tractor, known in the U.S.S.R. as the Universal. The changeover may in part have been brought about by what C. P. Weeks, Vice-President of Hercules Motor Corporation, calls the 'acknowledged failure' of the FP in workmanship and engineering detail.[85] The Farmall was the standard row-crop steel-wheeled tractor even after World War II, when it was produced at the Vladimir Tractor Plant, opened in 1944.

Another tractor plant added in World War II was the Altai (Robtovsk), opened in 1943 with equipment evacuated from the Kharkov Tractor Plant.

AGRICULTURAL COMBINE PLANTS

Of five agricultural combine plants, four produced copies of the Holt machine, although, according to the J. I. Case Company representative in the U.S.S.R. 'they do not stand even a modest comparison with our products....'[86]

The first 'Soviet Holt' combine harvesters were supplied with engines by the Hercules Corporation in the United States, although, according to Vice-President Weeks, these were not ordered until the machines were completed.[87]

[79] Sutton, *Western Technology . . ., 1917 to 1930*, p. 140–1.
[80] U.S. State Dept. Decimal File, 861.50—FIVE YEAR PLAN/60, p. 5 of attached report.
[81] U.S. State Dept. Decimal File, 861.5017—Living Conditions/689.
[82] *Ibid.*,
[83] *American Engineers in Russia*, Folder 4, Item 2, G. R. Cody.
[84] Amtorg, *op. cit.*, VII, No. 6 (March 15, 1932), p. 140.
[85] U.S. State Dept. Decimal File, 861.5017—Living Conditions/307.
[86] *Ibid.*, 861.5017—Living Conditions/517.
[87] *Ibid.*, 861.5017—Living Conditions/307.

The Selmash (All-Russian Syndicate of Agricultural Machines and Implements) Agricultural Equipment Plant, located at Rostov on Don, was a large new plant equipped with 2,802 new imported machine tools.[88] A short published list of these machines included a milling machine,[89] a steam turbine,[90] and a gas producer.[91] Twenty-eight American and German technicians instructed technical personnel and workers to operate the imported equipment; construction at Selmash was supervised by U.S. engineers. Production was planned at 100,000 each of wagons, plows, and hay mowers per year, in addition to 30,000 drills and 40,000 binders.[92] A separate combine harvester plant to produce 5,000 'Soviet Holt' combines per year was also erected.

Table 11–4   AGRICULTURAL COMBINE PLANTS, 1930–45

Name of Plant	Annual Capacity	Origin of Technology and Assistance
Selmash	15,000 combines	Holt combine
Kommunar (Zaporozhe)	10,000 combines	Holt combine
Saratov	25,000 combines 13,000 pickups 15,000 windrowers	Soviet motorless combine — —
Novosibirsk	25,000 combines	Holt combine
Krasny Aksai	Combines (number not known) Corn harvesters (number not known)	Holt combine New Idea corn harvester

Source: U.S. State Dept. Decimal File, 861.5017—Living Conditions/517, Gloeckler Report, p. 12.

Increases in the production of corn, beans, sugar beets, and sunflowers required special equipment such as the row-crop tractor, first introduced into the United States in 1925.[93] The first Soviet row-crop tractor, produced in 1935, and called the Universal, was a steel-wheeled reproduction of the International Harvester Farmall tractor. But this hardly worried the J. I. Case Company sales representative in the U.S.S.R., who commented:

> 'That insignificant plant Krasny Aksai . . . is an old plant not fit for mass production. They are copying . . . the New Idea Corn Picker. Our corn harvester showed better results in the test contracted last year in the Caucasus than the New Idea or any other of our competitors [*sic*] machines.'[94]

[88] Amtorg, *op. cit.*, V, No. 9 (May 1, 1930), p. 187. (The size of the plant is illustrated on pp. 180–1.)

[89] *Sowjetwirtschaft und Aussenhandel*, IX, No. 6 (1930), p. 18.

[90] *Ibid.*, IX, No. 20 (1930), p. 38.

[91] *Ibid.*, IX, No. 11 (1930), p. 44.

[92] Amtorg, *op. cit.*, V, No. 9 (May 1, 1930), p. 187.

[93] Naum Jasny, *The Socialized Agriculture of the U.S.S.R.* (Stanford: Stanford University Press, 1949), p. 462.

[94] U.S. State Dept. Decimal File, 861.5017—Living Conditions/517, Gloeckler Report, p. 12.

Similarly, the Novosibirsk combine plant, expanded from the old International Harvester plant, had 10,000 workers producing about 40 'Soviet Holt' combines per day. This plant had four Americans and one German technician to help start production.[95]

This close relationship between the United States and development of a modern Soviet agricultural equipment industry was recognized in the Soviet press. For example, the following comment was made in reference to the start of manufacture of the Holt combine at the Kommunar plant in Zaporozhe:

> It is quite obvious that carrying out this huge program within such a short time would be impossible without utilizing the technical experience of capitalist countries. America is the leading source of modern engineering practice. Some things can be learned from Germany, but in the agricultural machine building industry the United States must be taken as a model. . . .[96]

Izvestia pointed out[97] that the Krasny Aksai works was building combines according to a U.S. model.

In August of 1930, however, it was announced that the Saratov Combine Plant was to produce 15,000 combines per year; this combine was to be a type 'not popular in the United States,' i.e., a five-meter motorless combine with a power take-off from the tractor. Said *Pravda*, 'The preparation of these models was done without foreign technical assistance . . . because foreigners could not be helpful in designing a machine entirely unknown to them. . . .'[98] The article added that a group of American and European engineers skilled in conveyor methods of production was to be hired.[99] The plant utilized German press equipment.[100]

CONCLUSIONS

The building of the new Ford Gorki plant, the reconstruction of the Moscow and Yaroslavl auto plants, and the construction of three giant tractor plants were all undertaken between 1929 and 1934. The second half of the decade was generally occupied in bringing these enormous plants into operation, although several new automobile-assembly plants were also started. Both automobile and tractor capacities were the same in 1941 as in 1933; the reported increase in production came by utilizing the capacity built in the early 1930s to its fullest extent.

[95] U.S. State Dept. Decimal File, 861.5017—Living Conditions/537, Interview with A. D. Korn. Mr. Korn's contract is attached to the report.
[96] *Torgovo-Promyshlennaya Gazeta*, LXX, No. 1771 (December 10, 1929).
[97] *Izvestia*, April 18, 1930.
[98] *Pravda*, August 11, 1930.
[99] *Ibid.*
[100] Amtorg, *op. cit.*, VII, No. 13–14 (July 15, 1932), p. 295.

The automobile and tractor industries were completely dependent on foreign (primarily American) technology for design, construction, and equipment, as well as initial operation. There was a German contribution, but this mainly consisted of supplying equipment manufactured to U.S. designs.

The product of these gigantic plants were Fords, a specially designed Budd Company model with a Hercules engine, Caterpillar and International Harvester tractors, and Holt and Farmall agricultural machines. No indigenous Soviet technology has been traced, with the exception of the five-meter motorless combine produced at Saratov. Indeed, the Soviets had enormous problems just assimilating transferred U.S. technology; and this objective itself was not achieved until about 1941.

At the time of the German invasion in 1941, the Soviet Union had one completely new automobile plant (the Ford Gorki unit) and two greatly expanded and reconstructed units for trucks at Moscow (the Amo) and Yaroslavl. The Rostov plant was probably not in production in 1941; other units were assembly plants only. At the same time tractor production was concentrated in three new very large plants at Stalingrad, Kharkov, and Chelyabinsk, together with the expanded and rebuilt Putilovets at Leningrad. The Altai (Robtovsk) plant, added in 1943, and the Vladimir plant, added in 1944, both produced Western models.

CHAPTER TWELVE

Technical Assistance to the Railroad System

THE DEVELOPMENT OF A MODERN RAILROAD SYSTEM

In February 1930 a delegation of 34 Soviet railroad engineers arrived in the United States to make a study of Pennsylvania Railroad operations. As D. E. Sulimov, First Vice-Commissar of the Commissariat of Transportation, noted, 'This is the first Soviet railway delegation to make a comprehensive study of American railway systems, the technical achievements of which have aroused the greatest interest in the Soviet Union. . . .'[1]

The commission was interested, he added, in studying American rolling stock and hoped to accomplish much with 'the co-operation of American engineering and industry.'[2] The delegation traveled more than 16,000 miles examining United States railroads[3] and concluded that adoption of the American railroad system was essential for Soviet economic progress:

> . . . we realize well that we shall not be able to carry through this program in the most effective manner unless we avail ourselves of the great fund of experience accumulated by the most technically advanced countries, particularly the United States.[4]

This implied a comparison to the lightweight European rails then utilized in Russia which limited train loads, speed, and equipment utilization.

Sulimov added that the delegation was interested in making arrangements with American firms to further this technical transfer and that they would negotiate agreements for designing locomotives, freight cars, and gondolas, and were interested in technical assistance for production in the Soviet Union.

---

[1] Amtorg, *op. cit.*, V, No. 5 (March 1, 1930), p. 74.
[2] *Ibid.*
[3] Amtorg, *op. cit.*, V, No. 8 (April 15, 1930), p. 147.
[4] *Ibid.*

In conclusion, thanks was given to the Pennsylvania Railroad, Great Northern Railroad, American Locomotive Company, and the Baldwin Locomotive Company for their assistance.

An agreement was concluded immediately with Ralph Budd, President of Great Northern Railroad, to visit the U.S.S.R. and present a plan for reorganization of the industry along American lines.[5] Budd returned with Sulimov and the delegation to Russia.[6]

On returning to the United States at the end of 1930, Budd released public statements which glossed over the many problems of Soviet railroading,[7] but the official report which he submitted to the Soviet Government left no doubt as to the backwardness of their railroads.[8] The objective of his trip was reported as follows:

> [In 1930] they [the Russians] were undecided as to whether they should modernize to the so-called transcontinental railway plant or change to the American system and standards. It was for the purpose of reporting on this question that I spent the summer of 1930 in that country. . . .[9]

To achieve such modernization, it was suggested that grade reduction was one means to increase capacity; a reduction from the prevailing 0.6 to 0.8 percent to the United States standard of 0.3 to 0.4 percent would be an effective means of increasing capacity and avoiding double tracking. After listing grade practices that should be halted, such as level tracking across bridges and frequent changes of gradient, Budd recommended extensive grade reductions and studies toward that end. Practically all sidings were on level gradients, whereas in good railroad practice 'sidings are not allowed to determine gradient but the location of sidings is influenced by gradient. . . .' Budd noted that main line tracks varied from alignment, that clearances were insufficient, that ballast had been neglected, that ties were not satisfactory (Budd provided repair specifications), and that existant rails should be replaced with 110-pound rails (Budd gave U.S. rail specifications), among other technical considerations.

Budd's recommendations are an excellent indicator of the state of railroad conditions in 1930 and provide a standard with which to measure progress in the following decade. In order to acquire the best transportation system at the lowest cost, according to Budd, Soviet railroads would have to:

---

[5]   Amtorg, *op. cit.*, V, No. 9 (May 1, 1930), p. 188.

[6]   *Ibid.*, No. 12 (June 15, 1930), p. 257.

[7]   *Ibid.*, No. 22–23 (December 1, 1930), p. 464.

[8]   Ralph Budd, *Report on Railways of the U.S.S.R. 1930.* The Soviets, of course, did not publish the report, but a copy of Vol. I is in the National Archives and another copy is in the Hoover Institution.

[9]   *American Engineers in Russia*, Letter from Ralph Budd to H. Fisher, February 7, 1934.

(1) Adopt automatic couplings on all cars and locomotives

(2) Adopt air brakes throughout

(3) Strengthen the track, particularly with more and heavier ties and improved ballast

(4) Improve track standards, with better rail sections, bolts, and tie plates

(5) Carry out extensive track realignment

(6) Reduce main line gradients

(7) Adopt the train order system of handling

(8) Use larger modern cars

(9) Use larger modern locomotives

(10) Use heavier rail sections

(11) Use passing sidings and yard tracks for longer trains

(12) Build engine houses and terminals for larger locomotives

(13) Adopt automatic block signals

(14) Modernize repair shops

(15) Adopt a consolidation program to reduce number of lines

(16) Undertake a campaign for safety, cleanliness, and better care of material[10]

Budd further noted that climate and topography were quite similar to those in the United States and that, except for Moscow and Leningrad suburbs, electrification was not justified 'to any considerable extent.'

Brief extracts from the diary of W. Robert Wood,[11] who also made a long official inspection of the complete Soviet railroad system, illustrate the magnitude of the problem then facing Soviet railroad authorities and pointed out by Budd.

> June 11, 1930   Today we inspected round houses and shops, and I must say it looks rather hopeless as the workers seem to do about as they please. . . . Their day's output is eleven freight cars repaired and three or four passenger cars; with many less men at our St. Cloud shops we could turn out nearly that number *new* freight cars besides the repaired cars of twenty or thirty per day [*sic*]. . . .

---

[10]   The reader is directed to two excellent reports published by the Association of American Railroads which are indicators of the considerable progress made in Russia between 1930 and the 1960s: Association of American Railroads, *Railroads of the U.S.S.R.* (Washington, D.C., n.d.), and *A Report on Diesel Locomotive Design and Maintenance on Soviet Railways* (Chicago: AAR Research Center, 1966).

[11]   *American Engineers in Russia*, 'Trip to Russia,' Folder 7. Numerous comments similar to those of Budd were made. Wood noted, for example, that the Russians were using untreated pine ties with a life expectancy of only four to five years and said no larch was available in the U.S.S.R. However, larch is a common soft wood in the Soviet Union and was noted by American engineers as being found 'in abundance and not used.' (P. 14.)

July 18, 1930   [At Penza] . . . walked over the yard where they have made a problem by building four bridges right in the terminal.

August 5, 1930   Arrived at 8 a.m. at a tunnel that presents a problem. It is wet and ice forms in the winter. It also is caving in. Tunnel is about $1\frac{1}{2}$ kilometers long and at east end has a reverse curve due, they told us, to missing their alignment when constructing. This is probably the only tunnel in the world with three curves in it. The Engineer must have missed connecting by twelve feet. . . .

August 5, 1930   [At Sverdlovsk] The station layout and yard layout is the worst we have ever seen . . . the project was most fantastic.

August 6, 1930   . . . there are reverse curves at every station and between stations put in for no apparent reason. . . .

Thus in 1930 the problems observed by Budd and Wood were undeniably substantial. A decision was made to overcome them by adopting American railroad practice and specifications. American operating personnel were hired, including a large group from the Baltimore and Ohio Railroad. C. A. Gill, formerly with the Reading Railroad, was made Chief Consulting Engineer of the Soviet railroads.[12]

However, the track reforms instituted in the early 1930s were several years coming to fruition, and this particularly limited the use of American-sized engines, which were too heavy for the weak track. Five locomotive types were put on trial, including two of unusual design. Three types were standard: the FD, which was Soviet-made, embodying many U.S. features; the U.S. 2–10–2; and the U.S. 2–10–4. In addition an articulated Beyer-Garrett was bought from the United Kingdom and a Soviet-built 4–14–4 was also placed under test; these last two engines were the results of an attempt to overcome the weak-track problem by lowering the load per wheel: i.e., spreading the weight over a greater number of wheels. This effort was not, however, successful, and concentration was placed on standard tsarist and American locomotives.

Between 1935 and 1945 many American recommendations were implemented. The decade was marked by reconstruction, double-tracking of key routes, installation of automatic block signals, and new siding and loop construction. This, coupled with the extensive reorganization of railroad operations, led to major improvements: increased loads, greater average speeds and faster turn-around times.

World War II did not affect the railroad system as adversely as might be expected. Railroad mileage by 1943 had been reduced by one-third,[13] and most of this had to be rebuilt after recapture. Lend-Lease provided an ample supply of railroad materials for this purpose. The locomotive stock fared even better. Locomotives were moved back behind the lines in 1941. Only about 15

[12] *Ibid.*, Folder 1.

[13] J. N. Westwood, *Soviet Railways Today* (New York: Citadel Press, 1964), p. 17.

percent fell to the German armies,[14] and these were of the older types. Lend-Lease supply of 2,600 new locomotives (see table 12–1) placed the Soviets in a better position by 1943–4 than before the German invasion.

Table 12–1   ORIGIN OF SOVIET STEAM LOCOMOTIVES, 1930–45

Soviet Locomotive Class	Years Made	Wheel Arrangement	Number Produced or Purchased	Origin of Locomotive Class
B	1929	2–10–2 tank	6	Skodawerke Pilsen (Czechoslovakia)
K	1931	0–6–0	'Batch'	Henschel and Sohn (Germany)
Ta	1931	2–10–4	5	American Locomotive Co.(U.S.)
Tb	1931	2–10–2	5	Baldwin Locomotive Co. (U.S.)
FD	1931–41	2–10–2	3,220	Based on U.S. 2–10–2 (U.S.), manufactured at Voroshilovgrad (Lugansk)
Ja	1932	4–8–2 and 2–8–4	1	Beyer-Peacock (U.K.)
Is	1933–41	2–8–4	650	Based on U.S. 2–10–2 (U.S.), manufactured at Kolomna (passenger version of FD type)
C	1933	0–6–0 tank	'Batch'	Beyer-Peacock (U.K.)
B	1933	0–4–0 tank	'Batch'	Beyer-Peacock (U.K.)
So	1936–54	2–10–0	5,000	Bryansk (tsarist E 0–10–0)
AA	1936	4–14–4	1	Voroshilovgrad (Lugansk)
Su	1940 1926–51 (all classes)	2–6–2	2,830	Tsarist Class S (Kolomna, Sormovo)
Sh, a	1943	2–8–0	200	Standard U.S. Army type
E	1943	0–10–0	9,500	Prerevolutionary Class E (Kuibyshev and other works)
—	1943	2–10–0	2,400 (?)	Baldwin Locomotive, American Locomotive (U.S. Lend-Lease)

Sources: H. M. Le Fleming and J. H. Price, *Russian Steam Locomotives* (London: Marshbank, 1960).
Neue Zürcher Zeitung, July 26, 1944.

THE DESIGN OF RUSSIAN STEAM LOCOMOTIVES

The Vladikavkaz steam locomotive, first produced in 1910, became in its several versions the basic Soviet steam locomotive until the end of World War II. Westwood estimates that it was the most numerous class of steam locomotive in the world, accounting as late as 1960 for about one-third of the Soviet locomotive stock.[15] Another type—the FD—was placed in production

[14]   *Ibid.*
[15]   J. N. Westwood, *History of Russian Railways* (London: George Allen & Unwin, 1964), p. 87.

in 1933 at Voroshilovgrad (the old Lugansk works), and is described by Westwood as 'a Soviet 2–10–2 design embodying many American features.'[16] In 1935 series production started of a similar but smaller locomotive, the SO 2–10–0.

During World War II some 2,000 American 2–10–2 engines were received by the Soviets under Lend-Lease (forming the Ea class). Some features of this engine were incorporated into the L class which first appeared in 1945 from the Kolomna works. Other numerous classes of locomotives are the TE and TL series, formed from German locomotives captured in World War II. Table 12–1 summarizes by class the origin of Soviet steam locomotives (both prototype and production) between 1930 and 1945.

SOVIET ELECTRIC LOCOMOTIVES

The first Soviet electric locomotives were made by the General Electric Company and were to form the basis of Soviet-designed and built locomotives. General Electric supplied eight locomotives, of which two were complete and six provided with engines manufactured at the Dynamo works in Moscow with General Electric technical assistance. With a total weight of 124 tons, each had an axle weight of 22 tons. The traction motors had an hourly rating of 340 kilowatts and developed 2,760 horsepower.[17] These were called the Ss class and between 1932 and 1934 some 21 were built at the Kolomna locomotive works with electrical equipment from the Dynamo works.

The General Electric locomotive design was not produced between 1934 and 1938. Seven similar engines were bought from the Brown-Boveri Company of Italy.[18] These had dimensions similar to those of the General Electric but were not developed further.

In addition to these purchases of foreign electric locomotives, the Soviets developed the VL 19, the prototype of which was tested in late 1932. This locomotive had an axle weight of 19 tons with 340-kilowatt traction motors. Westwood notes that about 150 were built between 1932 and 1938. The VL 19 was a Soviet design, although it used a 340-kilovolt General Electric motor. It was made the production standard. However, mechanical and other weaknesses led to abandonment of the standard VL 19 and a return to the General Electric design. The first of these was produced in 1938 and designated VL 22; a more powerful 400-kilowatt unit replaced the earlier engine in 1941 and this model became the postwar standard.[19]

---

[16] *Ibid.*, p. 88.
[17] *General Electric Review*, XXXVIII.
[18] Westwood, *Soviet Railways Today*, p. 46.
[19] *Ibid.* Westwood notes on p. 47 of *Soviet Railways Today* that other prototypes (the SK and the PB) were built but not multiplied. An experimental high-voltage

Electrification of suburban services began at Baku in 1926 with German equipment, withdrawn in 1940. Moscow suburban electrification was based on the Sv class using Vickers electrical equipment and operated until replacement by the Sd class in 1939. The Sd equipment built in the Moscow Dynamo plant was similar to the Vickers with a 170-kilowatt motor.[20]

Attempts to develop diesel electric locomotives provide an example of the ineffective transfer of foreign technology, ending in abandonment of the dieselization program in 1937. A number of diesel electric locomotives were built for the Soviets before 1930 in Germany. The first was Lomonossoff's 1-Eo-1 model of 1924–5, with a MAN 1,200-brake-horsepower engine. This was followed in 1927 by another with a Krupp gear box and the same MAN engine. Several other oil-engine locomotives were built as prototypes between 1928 and 1933, all, except one, utilizing MAN engines with horsepower ranging up to 3,000 in twin units.

The exception was a prototype built by the Hohenzollern works of Krupp with two Sulzer engines and Brown-Boveri traction motors.[21] This Krupp prototype was copied by the Kolomna works near Moscow and after encouraging trials was put into series production and became the Soviet Class E el 12. A motor was built for the unit at Kolomna on the MAN diesel system.

The locomotives worked well enough around Moscow but when sent to the arid areas of Turkestan their performance deteriorated. Westwood comments on the problem as follows:

> . . . the work of the diesel locomotives was quite unsatisfactory, and did not match the results achieved on trials. . . . Not only design faults, but also poor quality manufacturing and assembly began to be revealed in day-to-day operation. Fuel pumps failed, cylinders developed cracks, bearings overheated, there were transmission failures, crews were sometimes driven from the cab by smoke and smouldering lubricants. These troubles were aggravated by lack of spare parts and the unavailability of skilled technicians. . . .[22]

Construction of diesel electric locomotives was halted in 1937 and effort was concentrated on steam locomotive production.[23] The significance of this failure in the light of expectations may be judged from the Second Five-Year

---

locomotive, based on the G.E. Ss class, was designed, and a prototype was built in 1938, tested for three years, and then abandoned (p. 54). Another, built at the Dynamo works was similar to the German Höllentalbahn locomotives, except for the cab structure. Technical details are in *Electric Railway Traction*, December 8, 1939, pp. 139–41.

[20] Westwood, *Soviet Railways Today*, p. 60.

[21] See 'Dieselelektrische Lokomotive für Russland,' *Zeitschrift des Vereines Deutscher Ingenieure*, September 16, 1933, for technical details.

[22] Westwood, *Soviet Railways Today*, p. 69.

[23] *Ibid.*, p. 70. Postwar diesels were based on General Electric/Alco Products technology. This will be covered in the concluding volume.

Plan estimates that by 1937 Kolomna would have an annual capacity of 100 diesel locomotives and Orsk a capacity of 540.[24]

CAR, WAGON, AND AXLE MANUFACTURE

Until 1933 axles for railroad wagons and cars were manufactured on a small scale in the old tsarist locomotive plants. In 1933 'an interesting plant for machining railway carriage and wagon axles on a vast scale' was bought from Craven Brothers (Manchester), Ltd., in the United Kingdom.[25] This enormous plant, comprised of numerous special machines (such as four-axle parting, ending, centering, and shouldering machines), was designed to produce 270,000 axles per year of a standard type—a capacity equal to total railroad axle requirements projected through 1945. The equipment was specially designed 'in order that the machines [could] be operated by semi-skilled or possibly by unskilled workpeople.'[26]

Considerable amounts of new railroad rolling stock were supplied under the Lend-Lease program. By 1945 the following had arrived in the U.S.S.R.: 1,900 steam locomotives, 66 diesel electric locomotives, 9,920 flat cars, 1,000 dump cars, 120 tank cars, and 35 heavy-machinery cars.[27]

Car repair work was developed along lines adopted from the Japanese flow repair system; for example, it was announced that the Dzerzhinsky locomotive repair plant at Voronezh had adopted a new method of locomotive repair 'which is a combination of American and Japanese methods.'[28]

THE BEGINNING OF RAILROAD ELECTRIFICATION

The Suram Pass section of the Transcaucasian Railroad was selected for the initial installation of a 3000-volt d.c. electrified railroad system. The initial project was a 40-mile stretch with a maximum grade of 3 percent—not only the most difficult on the Baku-Batum railroad but possibly in all of the Soviet Union. A little over one-half the mileage consists of curved track, with a $2\frac{1}{2}$ mile tunnel at the summit.

Both General Electric Company and Westinghouse drew up plans for electrification of this section.[29] General Electric obtained the contract. Three substations were installed and the 1500-kilowatt motor-generator sets were manufactured by Italian General Electric of Milan, which also built the high-

---

[24]   Gosplan, *op. cit.*, I, pp. 579–80.
[25]   *The Engineer*, CLVI, October 1933, pp. 331–4. This article describes the technical characteristics of the equipment supplied.
[26]   *Ibid.*
[27]   U.S. State Dept., *Report on War Aid Furnished by the United States to the U.S.S.R.*, p. 20.
[28]   Amtorg, *op. cit.*, VI, No. 7 (April 1, 1931), p. 165.
[29]   U.S. State Dept. Decimal File, 861.64/4.

speed circuit breakers and d.c. lightning arrester. Auxiliary apparatus and secondary distribution material was manufactured in the U.S.S.R.[30]

Figure 12–1 PROFILE OF THE TRANSCAUCASIAN RAILWAY,
GIVING ELEVATIONS AND GRADE OF
THE ELECTRIFIED ZONE, 1930

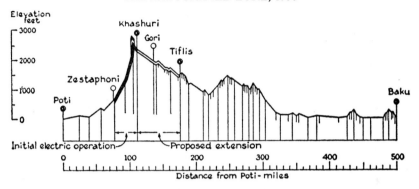

At about the same time, a Soviet commission visited most of the 3000-volt electrification systems in the U.S. and Mexico and selected the General Electric C-C locomotive weighing 133 tons for Suram Pass operations. Eight of these were supplied by the company.[31] Erection and placing in service were under supervision of two General Electric engineers, who also trained operative and maintenance personnel. For the next stage of Suram Pass electrification (the easy downward gradient towards Tiflis), the Soviets utilized their own resources.

THE MOSCOW SUBWAY

The lavish Moscow subway was originally intended as a foreign concession. In early 1929 the Rosoff Subway Construction Company of New York concluded an agreement for construction of a 12-mile belt subway and a 120-million-gallon waterworks in Moscow. It was suggested in the *Engineering News Record* that the agreement would not be ratified by the Soviets until 'the company [had] succeeded in negotiations to obtain the required capital from outside sources.'[32] This concessionary arrangement was not implemented.

Construction was begun, therefore, in 1932, with Soviet material resources and advisers from the London, New York, Paris, and Berlin subway systems and utilized layout plans originally drafted by the Russians in 1908.[33] John Morgan, an American, acted as consultant to Mosstroi (Moscow State

[30] *General Electric Review*, XXXVIII, May 1935, p. 220.
[31] *Ibid.*
[32] *Engineering News Record*, CII, June 13, 1929, p. 967–8.
[33] U.S. State Dept. Decimal File, 861.5017—Living Conditions/780.

Table 12-2   PRODUCTION AND ORIGIN OF LOCOMOTIVES IN THE U.S.S.R., 1938

Type (Model)	Diesel Locomotives	Electric Locomotives			Steam Locomotives		Armored Locomotives	All Types
		VL-22	SO	E	FD	SU		
Western Influence	Krupp Design Mann A-G Motor Lomonosoff	General Electric Design	U.S. 2-10-0 Design	German, Swedish Design	Soviet 2-10-2 Design Plus U.S. 2-10-2 Design Features	Tsarist Russian Design (1910)	None	
Plant								
Komintern works (Kharkov)	—	—	6	112	87	—	36	241
October Revolution (Voroshilovgrad, ex-Lugansk works)	—	57	—	—	215	128	77	477
Novocherkast works	—	—	—	4	—	—	14	18
Sormovo (Gorki)	—	—	32	—	86	96	—	214
Kolomna (Moscow)	Production abandoned 1937	80	—	200	86	105	52	523
Stalin (Orsk)	—	—	—	—	134	98	—	232
Ulan Ude works	—	—	16	84	—	—	—	100
Total	—	137	54	400	608	427	179	1,805

Source: Oberkommando der Wehrmacht (OKW/Wi Rü Amt/Wi), March 1941, Miscellaneous German Records, March 1941, National Archives Microcopy T 84-122.

Construction and Installation Trust).[34] A German engineer, M. Schmidt, who had been with the Berlin subway, worked on the plans of the Moscow system.[35] An extensive study of foreign systems was made in both the United States and Europe.[36] A Soviet subway commission visited Berlin, and Amtorg commented that:

> ... Berlin authorities have given the commission every facility for studying the trolleys and subways, street lighting, sewage systems, etc., of Berlin. The commission is authorized to order machinery and equipment for public utilities.[37]

Skilled workers were drawn from all over Europe. Skilled underground laborers came from Vienna.[38] Underground workers and technicians were hired in Great Britain, Germany, France, and the United States.[39] In addition, all known tunneling methods were tried before the British shield method was chosen. Amtorg noted that 'practically all known construction methods were tried out.' They included the British shield system, the French caisson system, the Belgian double passage, artificial freezing (a German method) and the American 'flying arch.'[40]

As finally built, the Moscow system was very much like that of the London Underground, and Westwood points out that 'Soviet engineers made a careful study of the Underground before embarking on their own project, which to some extent represents a significant improvement on the London system.'[41] The escalators, however, were probably of Otis design.[42]

The first section, Sokolniki-Gorki Park, 7½ miles in length, was opened in May 1935.[43]

THE INSTALLATION OF AUTOMATIC BLOCK SIGNALS[44]

The installation of automatic block signals is a good example of the Soviet approach to foreign technology: buying as little as necessary and then duplicating without regard to patent rights.

---

[34] *Izvestia*, January 14, 1935.
[35] Amtorg, *op. cit.*, VI, No. 24 (December 15, 1931), p. 575.
[36] *Ibid.*, IX, No. 4 (April 1934), p. 92.
[37] *Ibid.*, VII, No. 1 (January 1, 1932), p. 22.
[38] *Ibid.*, V, No. 20 (October 15, 1932), p. 417.
[39] *Ibid.*, X, No. 3 (March–April 1935), p. 92.
[40] *Ibid.*
[41] Westwood, *Soviet Railways Today*, p. 65.
[42] See chapter 16 for the adventures of an Otis Company engineer who attempted to take Otis company blueprints out of the U.S.S.R.
[43] *Izvestia*, January 14, 1935.
[44] Based on U.S. State Dept. Decimal File, 861.5017—Living Conditions/409, Report No. 8424, January 22, 1932, Riga Consulate.

In 1930 there was only one automatic-signal railroad section in the Soviet Union: it was on the Northern Railroad for 30 kilometers north and east of Moscow. This was installed by German engineers in the late 1920s and comprised all-German equipment.

In 1928 the Union Switch and Signal Company, a division of Westinghouse Electric, sold the Soviet Government about $500,000 worth of apparatus for automatic block signals. This order was on five-year-credit terms and at a 25-percent discount from Union Switch's previous lowest prices. This discount was apparently in anticipation of further large orders.

The equipment was shipped late in 1928 and intended for a section of the Moscow-Sebesh Railroad. Soviet engineers attempted to install the equipment, were unsuccessful, and requested assistance from Union Switch. The company sent an engineer—John M. Pelikan—who was placed in charge of the 17 Russian engineers and 450 workers making the installation. While supervising this installation, Pelikan was approached by the Soviet authorities, who, according to a contemporary Riga Consulate report,

> . . . offered him $100 per month more than he receives from his company if he will resign from it and enter into a personal contract with them for five years. His work would be the same—that of superintending the installation of signal equipment anywhere in the Soviet Union.[45]

This is in itself, of course, both usual and quite acceptable, but the report added that Pelikan 'had seen exact duplicates of the American apparatus which have been manufactured by hand in Soviet Russia. This apparatus, he believes, will operate as efficiently as the American originals.'[46] The apparatus was covered by patents which the Soviets ignored and infringed upon without compensation to Union Switch.

This *modus operandi* was also found, for example, in the field of excavating machinery. The Soviets duplicated without license agreement, company permission, or patent rights, and then approached company engineers in the Soviet Union installing *imported* equipment, offering them a higher rate of pay to supervise installation of the Soviet-duplicated equipment.[47]

Lend-Lease provided automatic signal-operating equipment, also supplied by Union Switch, for a further 3,000 kilometers of railroad track in 1944 and 1945 in a project valued at $10.9 million and designed to increase capacity of existing rail facilities without increasing the amount of rolling stock.[48]

[45] *Ibid.*
[46] *Ibid.*, p. 5.
[47] *Ibid.*
[48] U.S. State Dept., *Report on War Aid . . .*, p. 17.

CHAPTER THIRTEEN

Technical Assistance to the Shipbuilding Industry and the Red Fleet

THE TSARIST SHIPBUILDING LEGACY

ALMOST all of the Imperial Russian Navy, which included comparatively large warships, was built in Russian shipyards. Just before World War I four battleships of 23,000 tons' displacement were launched: the *Petropavlovsk*, *Sevastopol*, *Gangout*, and *Poltava*, built in the Baltic and the Admiralty yards in St. Petersburg.[1] In addition to construction of such large battleships, there was also a remarkable Russian submarine-development program before and during World War I.[2]

These same yards were utilized by the Soviets to build the Red Fleet; once again the concentration was on submarine construction. The Soviet merchant marine, on the other hand, was mainly built in foreign shipyards. As of 1941 only one Soviet destroyer—the *Tashkent*—had been built abroad, while three-quarters of the Soviet merchant marine had been built in foreign shipyards. In general, however, the Soviets had not reached even by 1940 a level of shipbuilding activity equal to that of the private Russian yards in the first decade of the twentieth century.

Analysis of the Red Fleet at the beginning of World War II indicates that one-quarter consisted of ex-tsarist warships and the other three-quarters had been built in modernized tsarist shipyards. By 1939 the largest warships completed under the Soviets were in the 8,000-ton *Kirov* class, very much smaller than the 23,000-ton battleships built in 1910–3 in the same shipyards under the tsar. Consequently the naval assistance forthcoming to the Soviet Union under the Nazi-Soviet pact of 1939 and from American and British

[1] H. P. Kennard, *Russian Year Book for 1912* (London: Macmillan, 1912), pp. 63–7.
[2] E. M. Penova, *Podvodnoe korablestroennie v Rossii (1900–1917)* (Leningrad: Sudostroennie, 1965).

Lend-Lease was very welcome and formed, from the Soviet viewpoint, the key component of each agreement.

In 1941 the Soviet merchant fleet, unlike the Red Fleet, had very few tsarist-era vessels. Only 11 ships, all below 5,000 gross tonnage, have been traced.[3] Most of these had been built at the Nevsky yards or at the long-established Sormovo works. One incidental feature is worth noting; the *Yalta*, a small 600-tonner built at Kolomensky, had an Italian hull coupled with a *Russian* engine, reflecting the early start in diesel-engine manufacture in tsarist Russia. Since 1917 it has been more common to import engines rather than hulls.

These tsarist-era yards then, their names suitably proletarianized, formed the basic structure of the Soviet shipbuilding industry.

Table 13–1 MAJOR RUSSIAN SHIPBUILDING YARDS, 1930–45

Tsarist Name	Soviet Name	Employment (1937–40)
Leningrad Yards		
Putilov	Severny yard, Zhdanov (part of Kirov Works)	1938: 40,000 in three shifts
Baltic	Ordzhonikidze	1940: 10,000 in one shift
Société Franco-Russe	Andre Marti	1938: 11,000 in three shifts
Admiralty	Sudomekh	1938: 7,000 in three shifts
Black Sea Yards		
Nikolaev Works Co.	Andre Marti, at Nikolaev	1938: 20,000
	Kolomna, at Kuibyshev	1938: 20,000
	Yard 61	1938: 7,000
	Andre Marti, at Odessa	1940: 1,200
Sommer	Sevastopol	1940: 12,000 in three shifts
Inland Yards		
Sormovo	Krasnoye Sormovo (Yard 92)	1937: 27,000 in three shifts
	Komsomolsk, at Khabarovsk	1938: 5,000
Far East		
—	Voroshilovsk, Vladivostok	1938: 5,000

Sources: Oberkommando der Wehrmacht (OKW/Wi Rü Amt/Wi) March 1941. Miscellaneous German Records, National Archives Microcopy T 84–122.
M. G. Saunders, ed., *The Soviet Navy* (London: Weidenfeld and Nicolson, 1958)

---

[3] Calculated from data in *Lloyd's Register of Shipping, 1941* (London, 1942). This chapter is based in the main on three sources: *Lloyd's Register of Shipping, Jane's Fighting Ships* (New York: Macmillan, 1942), and the Oberkommando der Wehrmacht archives. *Lloyd's Register* for 1941 reported a Soviet mercantile fleet of 716 ships (gross tonnage 1.3 million tons) in 1939 and include construction details of most ships built to this date.

SHIPBUILDING TECHNOLOGY

Shipbuilding consists of two distinct technologies: design and construction of the hull, and design and construction of the propulsive units. A third supporting category is shipbuilding yard equipment: gantries, welding facilities, and machine shops ancillary to construction slips.

There were several technical-assistance agreements and extensive transfers in each category of shipbuilding technology. Veritas Cie., a French company, supervised construction of tankers at the Odessa Marti yards and the Nikolaev yards in the early 1930s; M. Richard was the French engineer in charge of this work.[4]

Persistent efforts were made in 1937–9 to purchase a 45,000-ton battleship, two destroyers, submarines, and other naval equipment in the United States. These efforts, including the construction of a 45,000-ton battleship (which would have been above current international size and weight standards) had the support of President Roosevelt, the Department of State and Admiral Leahy. However, little came of the effort; it is surmised that officers in the Navy Department may have been at least partly responsible.[5] Assistance to the Leningrad yards was forthcoming from Germany under the Nazi-Soviet pact of 1939. Lend-Lease provided American and British skills and techniques, including vast amounts of shipbuilding equipment.[6]

THE SOVIET MERCANTILE FLEET IN 1941

About three-fourths of the Soviet mercantile fleet of the 1930–45 period was built in foreign yards.[7] The United Kingdom was by far the most important foreign supplier. More than 28 percent of Soviet hulls and almost 32 percent of Soviet merchant marine engines added between 1917 and 1941 were built in British shipyards. Germany was next, represented by almost 20 percent of the tonnage and 12 percent of the engine capacity. Holland was third, with almost 10 percent of the tonnage and more than 6 percent of the engine horsepower. The United States contributed 8 percent of both tonnage and engine capacity. In sum, between 1917 and 1941, 72 percent of Soviet merchant marine hulls and 77 percent of marine engine capacity were built in foreign shipyards and engine plants.

Construction of diesel marine engines inside the U.S.S.R. was concentrated on two systems (MAN and Sulzer) built in eight prerevolutionary plants. The

---

[4] Amtorg, *op. cit.*, V, No. 16–17 (September 1, 1930), p. 360.
[5] For further details, see U.S. State Dept. Decimal File, 711.00111, Armament Control.
[6] U.S. State Dept., *Report on War Aid Furnished by the United States to the U.S.S.R.*, p. 21.
[7] Calculated from *Lloyd's Register of Shipping, 1941*.

Russky diesel works, an expanded tsarist plant and the largest supplier of marine diesels, supplied the Severney yards with 13 four- and six-cylinder marine diesels of between 500 and 750 horsepower and supplied another dozen four- and twelve-cylinder marine engines to the Baltic and Andre Marti yards in Leningrad and the Nikolaev Yard 61 on the Black Sea.

The Kharkov locomotive works, a tsarist plant, built four types of marine diesel engines of between 350 and 475 horsepower in both six- and eight-cylinder versions for the Sevastopol yards. The Kolomensky engine works in Moscow concentrated on 12-cylinder diesels for the Black Sea yards (Sevastopol and Odessa). Six MAN-type 200-horsepower 12-cylinder marine diesels were built for Sevastopol, and five of the same type and two MAN-type 100-horsepower diesels for Odessa.

The Leningrad engine works supplied 237 standard 62-horsepower four-cylinder diesels for use in the Severney yard fishing-boat construction program. In addition to receiving marine engines from engine plants, the shipyards themselves produced a range of engines; for example, the Severney yard produced three standard 62-horsepower units for fishing boats.

SOVIET NAVAL CONSTRUCTION[8]

Soviet-built naval ships were heavily influenced by foreign design and technology.

Only one new battleship was built before World War II—the *Tretii International (Third International)*, laid down on July 15, 1939 in the Leningrad yards. This was a 35,000-ton battleship; the guns, turrets, armor, and boilers were purchased in the United States and Germany, but the ship was probably not completed by 1947.[9] The other Soviet battleships—the *Marat, Kommuna*, and *Oktyabrskaya Revolutsia*—were ex-tsarist vessels reconditioned and refitted. Attempts to build three battleships of the Italian *Vittorio Venuto* class came to nothing. One, the *Krasnaya Ukraina*, was 'captured half-completed by the Germans at Nicolaiev in 1941.' The machinery had been ordered in Switzerland, but was bought by the British Government as a pre-emptive purchase in case the Germans tried to complete the vessel 'and it remains in packing cases in Switzerland to this day,' according to a 1965 report.[10] The other two were not started.

Three aircraft carriers were undergoing construction by the end of the 1930s; the *Stalin* (formerly called the *Admiral Kornilov*) was a 9,000-ton ship built in 1914, redesigned in 1929 and completed in 1939 as an aircraft carrier.

---

[8] Based on *Jane's Fighting Ships, 1941*, and M. G. Saunders, *op. cit.*, pp. 57–8.
[9] Saunders, *op. cit.*, pp. 57–8.
[10] David Woodward, *The Russians at Sea* (London: William Kimber, 1965), p. 205.

Two other carriers of 12,000 tons each were built 'on the basis of American blueprints':[11] the *Krasnoye Znamye* and the *Voroshilov*, both laid down at Leningrad in 1939 and 1940.

Several cruisers were refitted tsarist-era vessels, including the *Krasni Kavkaz* (formerly the *Admiral Lazarov*, built in 1916 at Nikolaev), the *Profintern* (formerly the *Svetlana*, built in 1915 at Reval and refitted in 1937), and the *Chevonagy Ukraina* (formerly the *Admiral Nakhimov*, built in 1915). The first Soviet attempt at cruiser construction was the *Kirov* class of 8,800 tons. Three ships were laid down in 1934–5. These ships had engines made by Tosi in Italy and were built according to Italian drawings at Putilovets (the *Kirov* and *Maxim Gorki*) and at the Marti at Nikolaev (the *Kuibyshev*) under the technical direction of Ansaldo.[12]

There were three categories of destroyers. First, there were 14 tsarist vessels —four in the *Petrovski* class (built in 1917–8), nine in the *Uritski* class (built in 1914–5), and one ex-*Novik* (built in 1911). Secondly, new classes of destroyers were built under the Soviets, to French and Italian designs.[13] Between 1935 and 1939, 15 destroyers (based on French drawings) of 2,900 tons each were built in the *Leningrad* class: six in the Leningrad yards, eight on the Black Sea, and one at Vladivostok. The first units, supervised by French engineers, were quite similar to the French contretorpilleurs (motor torpedo boats).

The *Stemitelnie* was the largest class; 35 were built between 1936 and 1939. These were 1,800-ton ships mostly built in Leningrad and Black Sea yards to an Italian Odero-Terni-Orlando design, under Italian supervision with some British machinery; most engines were Tosi 50,000-shaft-horsepower geared turbines.[14] In addition, the *Tashkent*, another Odero-Terni-Orlando design, was built in Italy—the only Soviet naval surface vessel ordered abroad in the 1930s.[15]

In January 1939 the firm of Gibbs and Cox, naval architects, was approached with a request to design two destroyers in addition to the 45,000-ton battleship already under design for the Soviet Union.[16] In July of the same year General

---

[11] Saunders, *op. cit.*, pp. 57–8.

[12] However, according to Woodward, *op. cit.*, p. 205, some machinery was built in the United Kingdom, 'the manufacturers being supplied with blank plans of the ships, showing only the dimensions of the machinery spaces and a 'torpedo compartment.'

[13] Saunders, *op. cit.*, pp. 57–8.

[14] Woodward, *op. cit.*, p. 203.

[15] *Ibid.* Woodward comments: 'The fact that the Communist and Fascist regimes were working hand in hand on this project is, to this day, somewhat piquant, as is the fact that when the Italian-built Soviet destroyer 'Tashkent was launched at Livorno in 1938 she was blessed by a Catholic priest and flew the Italian flag.' (P. 205.)

[16] U.S. State Dept. Decimal File, 711.00111 Armament Control/1470, January 3, 1939.

Electric and Westinghouse signified their intention to quote on the propulsive units for these destroyers.[17] After a few months of correspondence, the Navy Department indicated to interested manufacturers that such construction would tax U.S. capability which might be required for domestic purposes,[18] and the proposal was not implemented.

Figure 13–1   ORIGIN OF SOVIET NAVAL VESSELS, 1941
(IN TONNAGE)

Total Tonnage 119,500

Submarines

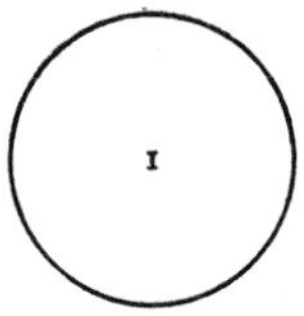

(1)   119,500 gross tons, mostly with German and British technical-assistance

Total Tonnage 115,650

Destroyers

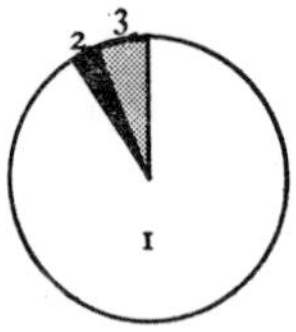

(1)   106,500 gross tons, Soviet-built to French and Italian designs
(2)   2,800 gross tons, built in Italy
(3)   6,350 gross tons, tsarist ships

Total Tonnage 104,000

Battleships

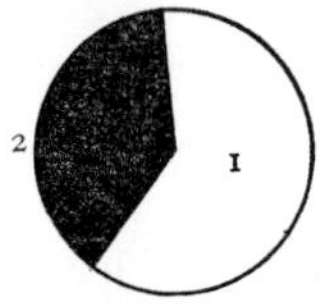

(1)   69,000 gross tons, tsarist ships
(2)   35,000 gross tons, Soviet-built with German and American technical-assistance

Total Tonnage 47,964

Cruisers

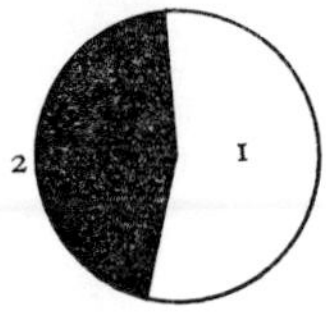

(1)   26,400 gross tons, Soviet-built to Italian design
(2)   21,564 gross tons, tsarist ships

Sources: See text.

---

[17]   *Ibid.*, 711.00111, Armament Control/2024, July 27, 1939.
[18]   *Ibid.*, 711.00111, Armament Control/2158, October 3, 1939.

A large number of small torpedo boats ranging in size from 6 to 35 tons were built in the 1930s to Italian design. These were the Italian MAS type, with Italian-designed machinery and built under license in the Soviet Union. Twelve were built at the Marti yards in Leningrad and the remainder in Black Sea yards. These were supplemented by 23 other unknown types and seven converted tsarist gunboats.

SUBMARINE CONSTRUCTION BEFORE WORLD WAR II

Submarines have always occupied a primary place in Russian naval policy. Extensive tsarist work[19] was adapted by the Soviets at the end of the 1920s, although few tsarist-model submarines survived to become part of the Red Fleet—only the Metallist class (Electric Boat design) and three Russian submarines of the Bolshevik class made by Nobel and Lessner in 1915–6 were still operating in 1940.

Soviet construction began in 1928 with the L and M classes. The L class was based on a British L 55 sunk off Kronstadt and raised by the Soviets; 23 of the L class and one L Special were built to this model by 1938.

The largest class in numbers was the M, a small 200-ton coastal submarine of limited performance, built inland at the Krasnoye Sormovo works in Gorki and transported in sections to the sea. Saunders[20] suggests that such pre-fabrication was possible only because of the introduction of electric welding, which had been achieved under the General Electric technical assistance contract. The Malodki class appears to have been a Soviet design; there is no trace of direct Western antecedents.

There is evidence, however, that all other Soviet submarine development was heavily influenced by German U-boat design. In 1926 a German naval mission under Admiral Spindler visited the U.S.S.R. and, according to Woodward,[21] the Germans were asked to provide plans of the most successful German submarines, details of operational experience, and the services of German submarine experts. At the same time the Russians requested assistance in the design and building of motor torpedo boats and aircraft launching catapults. Thus the Russians 'obtained various sets of U-boat plans, the most important of which were those of the B-III type, one of the most successful designs for a conventional submarine ever produced.'[22] The B-III was developed by the German Navy into the Type VII, the backbone of the German U-boat fleet in World War II (some 600 were built). Woodward adds: 'In the

19 E. M. Penova, *op. cit.*
20 Saunders, *op. cit.*
21 Woodward, *op. cit.*, p. 202.
22 *Ibid.*

Table 13–2　　　ORIGIN OF SOVIET SUBMARINES IN
WORLD WAR II

Class	Weight (Tons)	Number Built	Year Built	Western Design Source
Bolshevik	650	3	1915–16	Nobel and Lessner, Reval
Metallist	400	4	1916–24	Electric Boat
L 55	1100	1	1918	Ex-British made in Fairfield, Glasgow
L	896 and 1300	23	1929–35	Based on British L 55
L Special	1100	3	1933	Based on British L 55
Malodki	200	50	1928–30	Probably Soviet design
Garibaldietz	1200	8	1933–35	Italian Adriatico design
Pravda	1200 and 1800	17	1936	Italian Adriatico design
Chuka	650	46	1935–38	German B-III design
S (enlarged Chuka)	780	16	1937	German type VII U-boat
Kaler, Lembit	600 and 820	2	1936	Vickers-Armstrongs (Barrow)
V	—	—	1944	British Lend-Lease, Vickers-Armstrongs design

Sources: *Jane's Fighting Ships, 1941* (New York: MacMillan, 1941).
D. Woodward, *The Russians at Sea* (London: Kimber, 1965), p. 202.

meantime a variant of the design was built in Russia—first known as the N class, and nicknamed "Nemka" ("German girl") and later as the "S" class.'[23] The Chuka class was based on the German B-III plans, and the S class (an enlarged Chuka) approximated the German Type VII U-boat.

Italian influence came in two submarine classes. The eight vessels in the Garibaldi class were of Adriatico design and the 17 Pravda-class submarines were a development from the Garibaldi.[24]

In addition, two submarines were bought from Vickers-Armstrongs in the United Kingdom in 1936.[25] The Soviet V class comprised Vickers-Armstrongs submarines built in the United Kingdom in 1944 and transferred to the U.S.S.R. under Lend-Lease.[26]

German naval instructors were provided to the U.S.S.R. in the 1920s and also under the 1939 Nazi-Soviet pact. Later British officers were supplied under Lend-Lease to provide training in methods of submarine attack.[27]

Attitudes of the U.S. Executive Branch toward the sale of submarine equipment to the Soviet Union changed in the first five or six years of the 1930s. A proposal received by the Electric Boat Company of Groton, Connecticut

[23]　*Ibid.*
[24]　*Jane's Fighting Ships, 1946–47.*
[25]　*Ibid.*
[26]　*Ibid.*
[27]　Saunders, *op. cit.*, p. 78.

in January 1930 for the construction of submarines and submarine ordnance equipment for shipment to the U.S.S.R. was the subject of a company enquiry to the U.S. Navy. The latter, in a letter to the Secretary of State, argued that there was 'no objection' to the construction of submarines, etc., for such 'friendly foreign powers,' and further said that this was to the interest of the Navy as it kept domestic shipbuilders at work. The State Department, after noting the Navy position, pointed out that, although there was no legal restriction on shipments of munitions to the Soviet Union, the matter was 'viewed with disfavor by the Department. Consequently the Department views with disfavor the construction of periscopes, submarines and ordnance equipment for shipment to Russia.'[28]

Thus in 1930 the Navy Department was for shipment of munitions to the Soviet Union and the State Department against such shipment. By 1937 the Navy position was reversed. Another enquiry to the Electric Boat Company was referred to Washington. This time the Navy Department took detailed exception and the proposal remained dormant.[29]

There was a flow of American technology, however, under the Sperry Gyroscope technical-assistance contract for marine instruments, and a large number of Soviet engineers were trained by the company in the United States,[30] although attempts in 1937–8 to buy fire-control equipment were thwarted by Navy Department officers.[31]

ASSISTANCE UNDER THE NAZI-SOVIET PACT OF AUGUST 11, 1939

In exchange for raw materials, the Soviets received some German technical and military assistance. The Nazis handed over the partly finished cruiser Lützow, laid down at Bremen in 1937, and in May 1941 the latest available report was that the 'construction of the cruiser "L" in Leningrad is proceeding according to plan, with German supplies coming in as scheduled. Approximately seventy German engineers and fitters are working on the cruisers in Leningrad under the direction of Admiral Feige.'[32]

[28] U.S. Dept. of State Decimal File, EE861.34/66, Letter, Navy Department to Secretary of State, January 29, 1930; and letter, Department of State to Electric Boat Company, February 5, 1930.

[29] *Ibid.*, Letter, Secretary of Navy to Electric Boat Company, January 18, 1937. See also U.S. State Dept. Decimal File, 711.00111, Armament Control/547, March 26, 1937, in which Cordell Hull refers to an agreement by Electric Boat for construction of Soviet submarines.

[30] U.S. Congress, *Investigation of Communist Propaganda.*

[31] U.S. State Dept. Decimal File, 711.00111, Armament Control/1018, February 25, 1938.

[32] A. Rossi, *Russo-German Alliance 1939–41* (Boston: Beacon Press, 1951), p. 96, quoting a German report.

Table 13–3   ORIGINS OF THE RED FLEET IN 1945
(In units)

Type of Warship	Renamed Tsarist Vessels[1]	Foreign Purchases[1]	Supplied under Nazi-Soviet Agreement (1939)[2]	Supplied under U.S. Lend-Lease*[3]	Foreign Design, Foreign Machinery, Soviet Construction[1]	Soviet Design, Soviet Machinery, Soviet Construction[1]
Battleship	3	—	—	—	2	—
Aircraft carrier	1	—	—	—	2	—
Cruiser	3	1 (Tashkent)	1 (Lützow)	—	4	—
Destroyer	14	—	—	105	50	—
Torpedo boat	7	—	—	221	153	—
Other vessel	—	—	—	165	—	—
Total	28	1	1	491	211	0

Sources: [1] *Jane's Fighting Ships, 1941.*
[2] *Hauptarchiv*, Boxes 1137 and 1138, at Hoover Institution, Stanford University.
[3] U.S. State Dept., *Report on War Aid Furnished by the United States to the U.S.S.R.* (Washington: Office of Foreign Liquidation, 1945), p. 21.

* Excludes 137 merchant ships and 2,398 pneumatic floats.

In the Leningrad yards German technicians took over construction and repair of several big Soviet ships. This cooperation lasted about 18 months, from late 1939 until May 1941, and, although the Soviets made great efforts to obtain German advanced technical data, there is no evidence that they succeeded to any great extent.

The benefit of this cooperation in the naval field is in some doubt. Admiral Miles of the British Naval Mission in Moscow sums the position in 1942 as follows:

> Although they [the Russians] had been in close touch with the Germans for nearly two years of war, their technical ignorance was surprising . . . they had only inefficient hydrophone submarine detecting gear, no magnetic mines, no concept of degaussing, no radar, and . . . no idea how to sweep magnetic or acoustic mines.[33]

LEND-LEASE ASSISTANCE TO THE SOVIET FLEET, 1941-5

The Soviet Fleet in 1941 comprised three battleships, eight cruisers, 85 destroyers and torpedo boats, 24 minelayers, 75 minesweepers, 300 motor torpedo boats and gunboats, and 250 submarines.[34] Lend-Lease added 491 ships to this total, comprising 46 submarine chasers (110-foot) and 59 submarine chasers (65-foot), 221 torpedo boats (24 of them from the United Kingdom), 77 minesweepers, 28 frigates, 52 small landing craft, two large landing craft from the United Kingdom, and six cargo barges. These were combat vessels, and quite distinct from the Lend-Lease merchant vessels, marine engines, and other maritime material.[35]

In tonnage terms, Lend-Lease probably doubled the Soviet Navy. Only a small number of ships have been returned, although the Lend-Lease master agreement required return of all vessels.

A certain amount of British Lend-Lease went to Russia, and Admiral Miles has left a pertinent comment on Soviet use of this assistance:

> Through either an inferiority complex or a completely misplaced confidence in their own technical ability they felt that as long as they were supplied with blueprints or instruments they had no more to worry about. All our advice was ignored on details as for example, the best position for fitting the asdic transmitter into a ship, or the necessity for training operators to work the gear. They refused to give us drawings of their destroyers and submarines wherewith to calculate the best position. The result was that they fitted the asdic dome in the wrong place and then accused us of sending them faulty equipment.[36]

[33] Saunders, *op. cit.*, p. 76.
[34] *Ibid.*, p. 75.
[35] U.S. State Dept. *Report on War Aid Furnished by the United States to the U.S.S.R.*
[36] Saunders, *op. cit.*, p. 76. This is similar to comments made by American engineers throughout the 1930s.

Despite this flow of assistance, the Soviet Fleet, according to German, French, British, and American observers, was most ineffective during World War II. After initial operating problems, such as when submarines broke surface after firing torpedoes, the naval forces appeared to keep to home waters. British naval opinion suggested that the Soviet Fleet spent its sea time patrolling at high speed in order to use up fuel and return to port for 'welcome home' parties.[37]

[37] *Ibid.*

CHAPTER FOURTEEN

Technical Assistance in Aircraft and Aircraft Engine Production

TECHNICAL-ASSISTANCE AGREEMENTS IN THE AIRCRAFT INDUSTRY

AIRCRAFT development and manufacture in the 1920s rested heavily on foreign aircraft and engine imports[1] and Junkers design and manufacturing techniques, even after Junkers personnel left the Fili plant in 1925. (See table 14-1.) Although there was considerable Soviet design activity,[2] this was not converted into a usable aircraft technology. From about 1932 onward, and particularly after 1936, there was extensive acquisition of Western aeronautical advances. This, fortuitously for the Soviet Union, coincided with an increase in competition among Western aircraft manufacturers, enabling the U.S.S.R. to acquire without much difficulty the latest Western developments. In several cases military aircraft were designed on Soviet account. Thus the heavy, slow, underpowered designs of the early 1930s were replaced by efficient Western designs.

Further, as N. M. Kharlamov, Director of TsAGI (Central Aero-Hydrodynamic Institute im. Zhukovski) informed the U.S. Moscow Embassy in 1937:

> . . . the Soviet Government had become convinced that the American manner of building aircraft was best suited to Soviet conditions since the American system of construction could more easily be adapted to mass production than any of the European systems.[3]

The United States thus became the main source of Soviet aircraft technology; between 1932 and 1940 more than 20 companies supplied either aircraft

---

[1]   See Sutton, *Western Technology . . . , 1917 to 1930*, pp. 256–7, 259–62.
[2]   R. A. Kilmarx, *A History of Soviet Air Power* (New York: Praeger, 1962), p. 107.
[3]   U.S. State Dept. Decimal File, 711.00111 Armament Control/607, March 25, 1937.

or accessories. Technical-assistance agreements were made for Vultee attack bombers, the Consolidated Catalina, Martin Ocean flying boat and bombers, Republic and Sikorsky amphibians, Seversky amphibians and bombers, Douglas DC-2 and DC-3 transports, and the Douglas flying boat. Even smaller aircraft companies were not overlooked; for example, the entire Fairbanks Aviation Corporation and one of its managers—George Crandall—went to the U.S.S.R. to supervise their assembly and utilization.[4]

Italy was also an important supplier, with Savoia and Macchi technical assistance for flying boats and Isacco assistance for helicopters. French manufacturers supplied the Potez design. British manufacturers supplied the Fairey model and flying boats. Czech manufacturers supplied bombers. German assistance was forthcoming in the form of Heinkel and Dornier designs in the early 1930s and also under the Nazi-Soviet pact of 1939.

Finally, Lend-Lease provided an unprecedented technical bonanza, so that by 1945 the Soviets were on a par with the United States in aeronautical

Table 14-1   ORIGIN OF MILITARY AIRCRAFT IN THE
SOVIET UNION, 1932

Plant	Number Produced	Type of Aircraft Produced
Aircraft Plants		
Plant No. 1 (formerly Dux, Moscow)	260	160 de Havilland Type 9a 100 Heinkel H.D. 43 fighters
Moscow plant	80+	80 Avro 504k training biplanes Moraine-Saulnier monoplanes
Plant No. 22 (Fili)	414	52 R3 biplanes (TsAGI design) 20 R6 reconnaissance (TsAGI design) 242 I4 Jupiter engine planes 80 Ju30 and ANT 6 (Junkers and TsAGI design) 20 ANT 6 bomber seaplanes
Plant No. 23 (Leningrad)	58	18 Avro 504L seaplanes 40 Savoia S.62 Scouting flying boats
Plant No. 31	251	150 Heinkel H.D. 55 scouting flying boats 46 MR-5 (Savoia S62 license) flying boats 12 T.B. 1 (TsAGI design) 45 Ju 30 and ANT 6 naval bombers
Engine Plants		
Plant No. 24 (Moscow)	400	280 M5 (Liberty) 120 Mono-Gnome rotary engines
Plant No. 26 (Rybinsk)	600	600 B.M.W. VI type for Heinkel H.D. 45 fighters
Plant No. 29 (Zaporozhe)	330	260 Bristol Jupiters 70 Hispano-Suiza

Source: C. G. Grey and Leonard Bridgman, eds., *Jane's All the World's Aircraft*, (London: Sampson Low, Marston and Co., Ltd., 1933), pp. 243c–244c.

4   *Ibid.*, 861.5017—Living Conditions/538, Helsingfors, September 22, 1932.

design and probably in aircraft production techniques, with only a comparatively small deficiency in engine technology and electronic equipment.[5]

THE GLENN L. MARTIN COMPANY
TECHNICAL-ASSISTANCE AGREEMENT

In late 1937 the Soviets acquired the world's largest plane—the first commercial plane able to cross the Atlantic nonstop with a payload of 7,500 pounds: more than any other aircraft of the time. This was a definite improvement in design over any plane then built.

Known as the Martin Ocean Transport, Model 156, the plane was built by the Glenn L. Martin Company of Baltimore with four 1,000-horsepower Wright Cyclone engines.[6] It was reported to have cost the Soviet Union $1 million.[7] Although capable of being flown to the Soviet Union, it was flown only to New York, dismantled, and shipped to the U.S.S.R. by boat.[8]

Also in 1937 the Glenn L. Martin Company made an agreement for the design of a Soviet bomber. There is some conflict over the details of this contract, summarized by Loy Henderson, the U.S. Chargé in the Soviet Union, in a letter to the State Department. In reference to a conversation with Kharlamov, director of TsAGI, Henderson says:

> . . . he [Kharlamov] made no mention to the effect that the Glenn L. Martin Company would also send engineers to this country. In this connection it may be of interest to note that since January 1, 1937, the Embassy granted visas to fourteen Soviet engineers and specialists who are proceeding to Baltimore to the Glenn L. Martin factory. This information would appear to be significant in view of the statements made by Mr. Dormoy . . . relative to the difference between the contract signed by the Soviet authorities with the Consolidated Aircraft Corpora-

---

[5] Kilmarx, *op. cit.*, p. 163, has the following excellent summary of this assistance, which is consistent with the data presented in this study:

> The objectives of the Soviet Union were more straightforward than its methods. By monitoring aeronautical progress and taking advantage of commercial practices and lax security standards in the West, the Russians sought to acquire advanced equipment, designs, and processes on a selective basis. Emphasis was placed on the legitimate procurement of aircraft, engines (including superchargers), propellers, navigational equipment, and armament; specifications and performance data; design, production and test information and methods; machine tools; jigs and dies; semi-fabricates and critical raw materials. Licenses were obtained to manufacture certain modern military aircraft and engines in the U.S.S.R. At the same time, a number of Soviet scientists and engineers were educated at the best technical institutes in the West. Soviet techniques also included assigning purchasing missions abroad, placing inspectors and trainees in foreign factories, and contracting for the services of foreign engineers, technicians and consultants in Soviet plants.

[6] *New York Times*, October 18, 1936.

[7] *Time*, December 6, 1937.

[8] *Ibid.*

tion and the Glenn L. Martin Company, in which he points out that he understands that the Martin Company is to design and develop a new type of large plane for the Soviet air force instead of selling somewhat obsolete models which may have been released for export by the American military authorities. . . .[9]

Thus the Soviet DB-3, which many observers have noted as quite similar to the Martin 10 and 12 bombers, was probably designed in the Baltimore plant of the company by American engineers. The Soviet engineers were trained at the Martin Company in more advanced techniques, and took credit for its design.

SEVERSKY AIRCRAFT CORPORATION DESIGN CONTRACTS

The *New York Times* reported in May 1937[10] a $780,000 contract with Seversky Aircraft Corporation involving construction of, and manufacturing rights for, Seversky amphibians, which held the current amphibian world speed record of 230.4 m.p.h. The contract included an order for two complete aircraft with manufacturing rights for a total of $370,000. The balance of the order comprised a 60-day option for two additional aircraft and tooling for production of the aircraft. Under a technical-assistance clause, the company provided assistance for manufacture of these planes at the rate of 10 per day in the Soviet Union.

Late in the following year, Alexander P. de Seversky, President of the company, informed the State Department that the Soviets 'had contracted to purchase from the Company a large number of bombing planes of a new type to be designed by him. . . .'[11] A fee of $100,000 had been paid for design services, and de Seversky wanted to know whether any difficulty would be made in obtaining an export license. After being informed that a license would be granted if the planes involved no military secrets, de Seversky indicated that although the plane did not involve military secrets he 'feared that the War and Navy Departments might object to its exportation merely on the ground that it would be superior to any bombing plane now in existence.'[12] He quoted his recent difficulties in exporting internal bomb racks to the Soviet Union and cited a letter from the War Department stating that any license would have to come either from the Chief of the Air Corps or the Bureau of Aeronautics.[13] Finally, de Seversky indicated that he intended to address his request for an

---

[9]   U.S. State Dept. Decimal File, 711.00111 Lic. Consolidated Aircraft Corp./1.
[10]   *New York Times*, May 26, 1937, p. 27, col. 3.
[11]   U.S. State Dept. Decimal File, 711.00111 Armament Control/1384, November 4, 1938.
[12]   *Ibid.* From memorandum by Green, Chief Office of Arms and Munitions Control.
[13]   *Ibid.*

export license to the State Department, 'in hope that this Department might expedite action in this matter.'[14]

THE UTILIZATION OF BOEING AND VULTEE AIRCRAFT DESIGNS AND U.S. EQUIPMENT

The Soviet Chatos used in the Spanish Civil War was 'almost an exact duplicate' of the Boeing P-26.[15]

The Boeing Aircraft Company four-engine bomber design, far more advanced than the heavy, slow six- and eight-engine Soviet designs, also attracted the Soviets. In 1939 the Boeing Company was approached 'with a view to the purchase of four engine bombing planes and manufacturing rights for the same. . . .'[16] It is probable, however, that the Boeing Aircraft Company was informally dissuaded from pursuing the agreement in light of the November Soviet attack on Finland. On the other hand, there is evidence that the Soviets were producing copies of the Boeing four-engine bombers during World War II. This could have been done only with American knowledge and assistance.[17]

Finally, in March 1937 production engineers from the Vultee Aircraft Division of the Aviation Manufacturing Corporation of Downey, California began arriving in Moscow 'in order to assist the Soviet Government in building in Moscow a factory which [could] turn out light combat planes.'[18]

Efficient specialized tools were also developed by American aircraft manufacturers and their equipment suppliers for aircraft production and purchased by the Soviets. For example, in 1938 the Lake Erie Engineering Corporation received a Soviet order for six hydraulic presses for forming metal aircraft sections.[19] In the same year Birdsboro Steel Foundry and Machine Company of Birdsboro, Pennsylvania filled a half-million-dollar order for hydraulic presses for aircraft manufacture.[20] Similarly, in 1938 the Wallace Supplies Manufacturing Company of Chicago, Illinois sold seven bending machines 'specially designed to bend tubing for aircraft and parts of motors' for $34,000.[21]

[14] *Ibid.*
[15] *New York Times*, April 21, 1937, 4:1.
[16] U.S. State Dept. Decimal File, 711.00111 Armament Control/2424.
[17] Luftwaffe Files, B-17 Project, National Archives Microcopy T 77-642-1837712.
[18] U.S. State Dept. Decimal File, 711.00111 Armament Control/607, March 25, 1937. Six or seven production engineers remained about one year. The use of Vultee engineers was confirmed by N. M. Kharlamov, Director of TsAGI. (U.S. State Dept. Decimal File, 711.00111 Lic. Consolidated Aircraft Corporation/1.)
[19] *Aero Digest*, February 1938, p. 100.
[20] U.S. State Dept. Decimal File, 861.60/315, East European Division Memorandum, August 16, 1938.
[21] U.S. State Dept. Decimal File, 861.60/310, Report No. 1542, Moscow Embassy, August 9, 1938. The Soviets deducted $1,600 for late delivery.

Most, if not all, aircraft accessories were straight copies of foreign products. When biplanes were used, 'the streamline wires [were] of English pattern, landing wheels of Palmer type, bomb-releases . . . of their own design, and the duralumin machine-gun rings . . . of French pattern.'[22] Aircraft fuel pumps were the French A.M. type and mobile starters were the Hucks type.[23]

A number of government-financed aviation developments—and U.S. Government records on these developments—were released to the Soviet Union. In 1931 at the request of the State Department and the Buckeye Pattern Works of Dayton, Ohio, the Secretary of War granted 'release of Records of Tests made of certain aluminum exhaust stacks at the Aviation Depot at Wright Field, Dayton, Ohio, for benefit of the Russian Soviet Government.'[24] No military objections were made to production of Wright aeronautical engines in Russia,[25] or to the application by Sperry Gyroscope to sell bomb sights.[26] Neither was objection made to export of Type D-1 and D-2 oil bypass relief valves in 1935[27] by the Fulton Sylphon Company of Knoxville.

Such purchases were, however, subject to interruption. According to Guy Vaughn, President of Curtiss-Wright, he broke off negotiations for sale of the manufacturing license for one of the company's propellers. Although the sale involved only two or three sample propellers 'he was so enraged by the behavior of the Soviet Government in its attack on Finland that he was going to call off the whole deal.' This termination involved some $1.5 million.[28]

THE DERIVATION OF SOVIET AIRCRAFT DESIGN

Until about 1934 Soviet aircraft design was characterized by heavy, slow, ungainly aircraft whose only possible advantage was payload. Beginning in the mid-1930s we find a succession of cleanly designed, fast, and probably efficient aircraft.

The clue to the sudden transformation lies in the technical-assistance agreements and specialized purchases described in the preceding sections. From these came a flow of modern aircraft heavily dependent on Western ideas and particularly production methods. Space prohibits complete description of origin; the Douglas Aircraft Company is therefore taken as a case

22 C. G. Grey and Leonard Bridgman, eds., *Jane's All the World's Aircraft* (London: Sampson Low, Marston and Co., Ltd., 1933), p. 243c.

23 *Flight*, October 23, 1941, p. 274.

24 U.S. War Dept. File, 452.8 Aluminum Exhaust Stacks and 400.112.

25 *Ibid.*, 452.8 Wright engines.

26 *Ibid.*, 471.6 Sperry Bomb Sights.

27 *Ibid.*, 400.3295 Sales Abroad.

28 U.S. State Dept. Decimal File, 711.00111 Armament Control/2389, December 4, 1939.

study and presented, with the DC-3 as a model, in more detail. In addition, table 14–2 lists major Soviet aircraft by type at 1943 and refers to some brief statements in Western sources concerning their origin.

Table 14–2　WESTERN DESIGN INFLUENCE ON SELECTED
SOVIET FIGHTER AND BOMBER AIRCRAFT

Soviet Model	Normal Range (Miles)	High Speed (M.P.H.)	Suggested Western Design Influence	Reference to Citation
Fighters				
I-15			Boeing P-12	Kilmarx, p. 163
I-16	450	280	'Developed from old Boeing P-26'	*Aviation*, Feb. 1943, p. 16
I-17	600	300	'Patterned on the Submarine Spitfire'	*Engineer*, Nov. 7, 1941
I-18 (MIG-3)	—	375	Origin derived 'to a considerable extent from the British Hurricane'	*Engineer*, Nov. 7, 1941
I-26 (YAK-1)	—	400	'Resembles the Hurricane'	Stroud, p. 32
SU-2	—	275	Possibly developed from Brewster B2A Bermuda	*Aviation*, XLII, No. 2 (Feb. 1943), p. 221
Bombers				
SB-3	550	250	'Was developed to a considerable extent from Martin bombers (B-10 and B-12 series)'	Kilmarx, p. 227
CKB-26	2,500	240	'Many features of Douglas DC-2'	Kilmarx, p. 229
DB-3F	1,500	270		
ZKB-26	—	310	'A considerable resemblance to the American Martin 139'	*Engineer*, Nov. 1941, p. 134
PE-2	—	342	'Based on the French Potez 63'	Stroud, p. 36
YAK-4	—	315	'Appears . . . to have been based on the French Potez 63'	*Aviation*, Feb. 1943, p. 225: Stroud, p. 38
IL-2 Sormovik	—	250	'Similar . . . to . . . Fairey Battle'	Stroud, p. 36
Tu-4	—		Copy of Boeing B-29	Hooftman, p. 154

Sources: R. A. Kilmarx, *A History of Soviet Air Power* (New York: Praeger, 1962).
　　John Stroud, *The Red Air Force* (London: Pilot Press, 1943).
　　H. Hooftman, *Russian Aircraft* (Fallbrook: Aero Publishers, 1965).
　　Aviation, XLII, No. 2 (February 1943).
　　Engineer (November 7, 1941).

Although the Soviets produced more than 30 transport aircraft designs after 1934, their indigenous development work was severely limited. During the twenties the Russian designer Tupolov had produced, with Junkers technical assistance and in the Junkers concession plants,[29] the ANT-9 all-metal aircraft. This was followed in 1931 by the less successful ANT-14. With a top speed of 130 to 150 miles per hour, these were slow, gigantic aircraft and were abandoned after several crashes.[30] This left the Soviets without a modern transport aircraft, and in 1936, rather than pursue further development work, they made a technical-assistance agreement with the Douglas Aircraft Company of Santa Monica for production of the DC-3, renamed the PS-84 and then the LI-2.[31] This plane had more than double the range and more than twice the speed of the Soviet ANT series. However, it took until 1940 to get the first Soviet DC-3 off an assembly line, even with extensive assistance from Douglas Aircraft.[32]

The first flying boats built under the Soviets were constructed at Leningrad and Taganrog. In 1932 Plant No. 23 in Leningrad produced 18 Avro 504L seaplanes and 40 Savoia S-62 scouting flying boats, the latter under a license from the Società Idrovolanti Alta Italia of Milan—an outstanding designer of high-performance flying boats.[33] Also in 1932 the Taganrog Plant No. 31 on the Sea of Azov produced 251 planes, of which 196 were flying boats: 150 scouting H.D. 55s, built under the Heinkel license, and 46 MR-5s, built under the Savoia license.[34] The Soviets also acquired a license from the Macchi Company of Italy to produce the MBR series of flying boats, typical of Soviet flying boat design until 1945.[35] In 1937 an agreement was made with the Consolidated Aircraft Company of San Diego for technical assistance in the design and supervision (under Etienne Dormoy) of sea plane construction in the Soviet Union at Taganrog on the Sea of Azov.[36]

Meanwhile, tsarist work in the aviation field was being further developed. Several autogiro and helicopter designs were produced in the late 1920s and early 1930s: the KASKR-1, the TsAGI in various versions, and the Kamov A7 are examples of this early Russian design work. It is unlikely that these

[29] For material on Junkers, see Sutton, *Western Technology . . ., 1917 to 1930*, pp. 256–63; see also Auswartigen amts., *Akten zur Deutschen Auswärtigen politik, 1918–1945* (Göttingen: Vandenheock und Ruprecht, 1967).

[30] Kilmarx, *op. cit.*, p. 161.

[31] See p. 232.

[32] See p. 234.

[33] Grey, *op. cit.*, p. 244c.

[34] *Ibid.*, p. 246c.

[35] *Aviation*, September 1942, p. 286.

[36] U.S. State Dept. Decimal File, 711.00111 Armament Control/607, March 25, 1937. See also 711.00111 Lic. Consolidated Aircraft Corporation/1.

were successful,[37] although they had Western power plants; for example, the K-17 one-place coaxial rotor helicopter had a modified 17-horsepower Aubier-Dunne engine.

The Italian designer Vittorio Isacco worked in Russia in the early 1930s and developed a helicopter with blade tip power plants (the 120-horsepower de Havilland Gypsy 3) with a 300-horsepower Wright radial nose engine. *Aviation Week* commented that, 'In 1935 [Isacco] was given what in the U.S. would be known as the 'bum's rush' and he left the U.S.S.R. To this day the designer does not know the fate of his machine.'[38]

The first successful Soviet-designed helicopter, powered by two M-11 engines and produced at Tushino, was flown in 1941. In general, Soviet success with helicopters came after World War II; efforts between 1939 and 1945 were halting, dependent on Western engines, and could hardly be called successful.

In the field of airship design, the Italian general, Umberto Nobile, worked in the Soviet Union providing assistance in construction of Soviet airships.[39]

TECHNOLOGICAL ORIGINS OF SOVIET AIRCRAFT ENGINES, 1945

The bottleneck in tsarist aircraft production was engines; during World War I, owing to limited domestic capacity, three-quarters of Russian aircraft were equipped with imported engines; the only aircraft engine plants were the Tushino and the Russo-Baltic. The Soviets also imported aircraft engines during the 1920s. Then, by acquiring rights to manufacture foreign engines under license and with Western technical assistance, the Soviets were able to acquire rapidly a sizable engine-producing capacity.

Plants No. 24 and 25 were built in Moscow; No. 24 made Wright Cyclone engines under license and No. 25 made parts for Wright engines. Production was about 250 engines per month in 1938; some 12,000 workers were employed on three-shifts. Models produced were the M-25, M-34, M-63, and M-64, all based on Curtiss-Wright developments.

Although between 1939 and 1941 the Soviet Union had to depend on its own technical resources 'because so many foreign engineers at work in the U.S.S.R. were recalled to their own countries,'[40] after 1941 Lend-Lease played a role in providing a flow of designs and manufacturing equipment. The

---

[37] H. Hooftman, *Russian Aircraft* (Fallbrook: Aero Publishers, 1965), p. 79.

[38] March 5, 1956.

[39] See Zara Witkin papers, Hoover Institution Special Collection, p. 82. Nobile's book [Umberto Nobile, *My Polar Flights; An Account of the Voyages of the Airships Italia and Norge* (London: F. Muller, 1961)] contains no mention of this work.

[40] Kilmarx, *op. cit.*, p. 162.

Soviets standardized on a few successful types developed from Western designs and installed these into a large number of planes.

Prototypes of every Western aircraft engine were acquired. These were minutely examined, and composite 'Soviet' designs were built incorporating the best features of each. A report by Bruce Leighton describes one of these models at the Engine Research Institute in 1931:

> They've taken Packard, Conqueror, Rolls-Royce, Kestral, Hispano-Suiza, Fiat, Isetta-Franchini—tested them all, analyzed them down to the minutest details, including microphotographs of piston rings, flow lines in crank shafts, etc., taken good features of all, added some ideas of their own (particularly regards valve cooling) and built-up [*sic*] an engine which we're going to hear more of or I miss my guess.[41]

These early Soviet conglomerate designs were not successful; 'copying' is not always the outright gift it might at first sight appear to be. Neither is the process of taking the best features from several models always advantageous. There is a unity in good engineering design, and this unity can be sacrificed in the copying process without gaining compensating advantages.

In the entire world in 1944, about 130 basic types and 275 variations of aircraft engines, excluding German diesel engines, were either in production or had recently been in production. Of the 130 basic types, 48 were produced in the United States, 28 in Great Britain, 20 in Germany, 17 in Italy and 3 in the Soviet Union. Each of the three Soviet types was an adaptation of a foreign engine built under a licensing agreement. The M-38 liquid-cooled 12-cylinder V model was developed from the 1936 M-34, in turn developed from the Wright Cyclone. The M-88 was a 14-cylinder air-cooled radial engine based on the French Gnome-Rhône 14 N. The third engine type was the M-105, a 12-cylinder liquid-cooled V type based on the Hispano-Suiza 12Y engine.

PRODUCTION OF THE WRIGHT CYCLONE ENGINE
UNDER LICENSE

Bruce G. Leighton, of the Curtiss-Wright Corporation, was given a seven-day reception and tour of Soviet aircraft plants in 1931.[42] At this time the Curtiss-Wright liquid-cooled engine was the only liquid-cooled American engine still in production. The U.S. Army initially supported development but, dissatisfied with the basic design, cut off funds in 1932. Development support for two other liquid-cooled engines, one of them the Curtiss-Wright H-2120, was continued by the U.S. Navy. Testing and development continued

---

[41]   U.S. State Dept. Decimal File, 360.02, Bruce G. Leighton Report, December 10, 1931, p. 5.
[42]   *Ibid.*

from 1933 to 1936, when the Navy withdrew support and reverted to air-cooled engines. The company, convinced that the design was mechanically poor, did not press further development. The second Navy-supported Curtiss-Wright project was a 12-cylinder V engine known as the V-1800. This was intended to replace the Curtiss-Wright Conqueror, and successfully completed its testing in 1934:

> Shortly after this test was completed, however, the Navy was forced by lack of funds to abandon most of its high-speed program and to cease support of the V-1800. The Army refused any appreciable support and the company did not wish to do further development at its own expense.[43]

As a result of the Leighton visit, the V-1800 engine was licensed to the Soviet Union, which funded further research work to raise the engine rating to 900 horsepower from the Navy test rating of 800 horsepower. This work was centered at Aircraft Engine Plant No. 24 (the Frunze) in Moscow, with parts manufactured at Works No. 25. By 1938 these plants employed about 12,000, producing about 250 Wright Cyclones (Soviet M-25) per month.[44]

A plant for manufacturing Cyclone engines was also built at Perm. This was about twice the size of the Wright plant in the United States, and by 1937 this facility was producing Wright Cyclone engines in quantity, although quality left something to be desired.[45]

LICENSING OF THE GNOME-RHÔNE (JUPITER) ENGINE

At the start of World War I, French builders were the leaders in air-cooled engines. The British and United States Air Forces both used French engines built in France or under license in the United Kingdom and the United States. The Gnome rotary, manufactured by the Société des Moteurs Gnome et Rhône, was one of the best of these early engines. After the war the Gnome Company purchased the license of the British Bristol Jupiter II; during the decade of the 1920s the Gnome-Rhône engineering department was dominated by English engineers from the Bristol Aeroplane Company. The only major innovation of Gnome-Rhône at this time was the Farman reduction gear, licensed back to the Bristol Company in 1926. After producing the Bristol Jupiter engine for some years, the Gnome Company came up with an improved engine of its own design, using American lined cylinders.[46] This cross-fertiliza-

---

[43] R. Schlaifer and S. D. Heron, *Development of Aircraft Engines and Fuels* (Boston: Harvard University, 1950), p. 267.

[44] Oberkommando der Wehrmacht (OKW/Wi Rü Amt/Wi), March 1941, VIII 7b, National Archives Microcopy T 84–122.

[45] Arthur Nutt, 'European Aviation Engines,' *S.A.E. Journal*, XLI, No. 1 (July 1937), pp. 14–5.

[46] Schlaifer, *op. cit.*, pp. 138, 142, 146, 148.

tion of ideas led to the exceptional Gnome rotary engines of the 1930s; these were adopted by the Soviets.

The Jupiter, or Gnome-Rhône 114, was built at the Kharkov engine-building plant (Plant No. 29). Without question there were initial difficulties. Leighton reported:

> They are not happy about the Jupiter and have been having indifferent success with it. Too much skilled hand work I suspect. . . . In Paris a Gnome-Rhône man later told me they are now building 40 of their latest Jupiters for Russia. . . .[47]

Kharkov Plant No. 29 persisted and the Jupiter became Soviet Models M-85, M-87B, and M-88, of the last of which about 1,500 a year were produced by 1940.[48]

In the same manner the Hispano-Suiza engine was produced in Moscow at an enormous plant twice the size of either the Pratt & Whitney or the Wright factories in the United States. This engine became the Soviet M-105. A western observer noted that although the engine was 'somewhat heavy,' they were doing a good job and quality had noticeably improved between 1934 and 1937.[49]

THE PRATT & WHITNEY AIRCRAFT ENGINE LICENSING AGREEMENT

In July 1939, in a discussion between State Department and three repre-sentatives of the United Aircraft Corporation, the corporation attempted to ascertain the view of the U.S. Government toward a licensing agreement with the Soviet Union for the Pratt & Whitney Twin Wasp 1830 and the Twin Hornet 2180 aircraft engines. The State Department official did not reply directly but suggested that the sale of naval vessels should offer a guideline. United Aircraft then stated that in this case they would probably 'seriously consider' entering into a contract. To avoid the perennial problem of overly inquisitive Soviet inspectors in their plant, they proposed to insert a number of restrictive clauses.[50] No further data has been traced concerning this agreement.

---

[47] U.S. State Dept. Decimal File, 360.02, Bruce G. Leighton Report, December 10, 1931, p. 7.

[48] Oberkommando der Wehrmacht (OKW/Wi Rü Amt/Wi), March 1941, National Archives T 84–122.

[49] Nutt, *op. cit.*, pp. 14–5.

[50] U.S. State Dept. Decimal File, 711.00111 Armament Control/1982, July 20, 1939. There was probably an earlier agreement, as the Soviet M-26 was based on the Pratt & Whitney Hornet. See Kilmarx, *op. cit.*, p. 112.

EARLY DOUGLAS DC-2 SALES TO THE SOVIET UNION[51]

The Douglas Company files on sales to the Soviet Union open in December 1933 with a letter from G. A. Gertmenian, a Los Angeles oriental-rug dealer, proposing a three-way deal under which Douglas would take payment for its aircraft 'in a credit with the Amtorg in rugs,' to be sold by Gertmenian. The latter suggested that Amtorg had a surplus of oriental Russian and Persian rugs accumulated in barter deals and was anxious to dispose of this stock. Indeed, added Gertmenian, they were more interested in 'arrangements for paying than . . . with the prices which they pay.'[52] Douglas Aircraft was understandably cool about tying aircraft sales to the rug market.

This initial approach was followed in early 1934 by a letter from Amtorg asking for details of the Douglas plant and its products, and whether a delegation of Soviet engineers could be received. Simultaneously, letters came from the International Seed Service (Internatsionalinii semenoi trest) suggesting 'publicity' for Douglas in the Soviet Union.

A Russian mission was sent to Santa Monica. This mission subsequently requested a quotation on the civilian DC-2 and data on the U.S. Army method of heating air-cooled engines on the ground in sub-zero weather. Then followed a request for detailed specifications of the new Northrop Gamma long-range bomber. The next day caviar and vodka were delivered to the home of G. W. Stratton, Vice-President of Douglas.

In June 1935 Amtorg ordered one DC-2 and one Northrop Gamma bomber and requested that Soviet engineers be allowed to enter both the Douglas and the Northrop plants for observation. Amtorg was promptly informed that the U.S. Government would not permit any representatives into the Northrop plant although permission might be granted for temporary entry to the Douglas plant. Then came an Amtorg request for four engineers of the Tupolov Commission, currently touring the United States, to visit the plant. This was followed by another wire two days later: 'TWO OUR ENGINEERS LEAVING FOR DOUGLAS FACTORY . . . AWAITING YOUR WIRE REGARDING THEIR WORK AT THE NORTHROP FACTORY.'

Douglas promptly reminded Amtorg that the U.S. Army had tagged the Northrop plant as 'absolutely closed,' but on July 5, 1935 Sokoloff, President of Amtorg, sent a telegram to Stratton: 'PLEASE AIR MAIL IMMEDIATELY COPIES YOUR COMMUNICATIONS TO AUTHORITIES REQUESTING PERMISSION OUR ENGINEER TO BE AT NORTHROP FACTORY FOR OUR GUIDANCE ENDEAVORING ASSIST IN THIS STOP.'[53]

---

[51] Based on Douglas Aircraft Co. files. The cooperation of the Douglas Aircraft Co. is gratefully acknowledged.

[52] Douglas Aircraft Co. files, *Russia—1934.*

[53] *Ibid.*

This was followed by a letter from Sokoloff expressing regret that negotiations 'had not been developing as smoothly and pleasantly as I hope,' and stating that the Douglas Company had agreed 'to obtain permission for our inspection on the parts and the complete airplanes. . . .'[54] A request for copies of the Douglas-War Department correspondence was repeated with the reasoning that unless Amtorg knew whom Douglas has contacted in the U.S. Army they would be unable to enlist the assistance of the Soviet Embassy.

On July 12, 1935 Donald Douglas ended the exchange by pointing out that application for permission had been made to the U.S. Army immediately upon receipt of the order, and that he personally had instructed his assistant not to furnish copies of the letters, as the U.S. Government would 'resent our turning over correspondence to you that they might regard as confidential.' Douglas concluded:

> Really Mr. Sokoloff, from Mr. Wetzel's talk of several hours with your two engineers, it is apparent that they are not so much interested in inspecting the parts of your airplane as they are in getting information on our building methods and equipment. . . . I must beg to point out to you that you have bought an airplane but not the right to our shop processes. . . .[55]

A CASE STUDY: THE DOUGLAS AIRCRAFT TECHNICAL-ASSISTANCE AGREEMENT FOR THE DC-3 TRANSPORT

Donald Douglas produced his first DC-3 in March 1935; within one year the Soviets decided this was to be the basic transport plane for the U.S.S.R. and concluded a technical-assistance agreement with the Douglas Aircraft Company, signed on July 15, 1936, for three years.

Within 30 days of contract signature, Douglas delivered the blueprint materials required to fulfill the assistance contract. The following were provided: three sets of manufacturing drawings and descriptions and specifications of materials; four sets of photographs (250 to a set); four copies of the *DC-3 Maintenance and Instructions Manual* and the *Pilots Operations Manual;* four sets of specifications 'in accordance with which Douglas purchases finished products, such as extrusions and forgings from third parties, including . . . source of supply and one set of sample pieces of extrusions'; three sets of static tests and laboratory reports; three sets of strength calculations; three reports of wind tunnel tests and the aerodynamic and stability calculations; three copies of the specifications for 'purchasing devices and other equipment'; three copies of descriptions of machines used in manufacturing (mainly bending machines, power brakes, and cutting tools), including names and

---

[54]   *Ibid.*
[55]   *Ibid.*

addresses of manufacturers; three copies of *Machinery and Equipment Used by the Douglas Company in Production of DC-3 Transports;* data pertaining to the technical conditions for producing important parts (such as process specifications; welding-flux, welding-rod, welding-torch tips; and tube-bending methods); three copies of methods of testing parts and special accessories; descriptions and/or drawings of necessary jigs, fixtures, and instruments for servicing; and a list of recommended spare parts.[56]

There are numerous detailed internal company memoranda still in the files which leave no question that instructions were to fulfill the agreement in a detailed and precise manner. The Soviet Union had no cause for complaint concerning the manner in which the company fulfilled its requirements under the agreement; the assistance was prompt, accurate, and such that any competent engineering organization could move into production of DC-3 transports in short order, as did other countries, such as Japan, with similar agreements.

In October 1937 the Soviet aircraft industry placed a $1.15 million order with Douglas for additional parts, tools, assemblies, and materials. The order included one complete DC-3 in subassembly and another in 'first-stage' production; both were minus engines, propellers, and automatic pilots. In addition, aluminum extrusions were ordered for another 50 aircraft, together with two complete sets of raw materials and 25 sets of finishing materials ranging from ash trays to zippers. Construction facilities, ordered at the same time, included one complete set of 6,485 templates, a set of 350 lead and zinc drop hammer dies, three sets of hydraulic mechanisms, all the necessary wood and plaster patterns, drill and assembly fixtures, a complete set of drop-hammer stamps, hydraulic-press parts, two crowning machines, and a set of 125 special tools. These were supplemented by information on the hydraulic-press process and the training of engineers in its operation.

Almost half of this second order consisted of 50 complete sets of raw materials, including aluminum castings, aluminum-alloy castings, forgings, extrusions, sheets and plates, bearings, stainless steel sheets, C.M. sheets, and Alclad sheet and strip.[57] It was rather like supplying 50 toy construction sets; the Russian plant engineers needed only to follow the drawings and put the pieces together.

In February 1938, however, another order was placed for nine more Douglas-made DC-3s, and in November 1938 (a year after the parts order)

---

[56] Copies of these items are in the Douglas Aircraft Co. files. The writer attests to their completeness; it took a day just to scan the material.

[57] The Douglas Co. threw in a set of special loft tools at no charge. The gift was criticized by the GUAP Commission because a straightedge and a spare part were missing.

yet another six complete transports were purchased.[58] It was not until 1940, four years after the agreement, that the Soviets got any domestic DC-3s, renamed the PS-84 or the LI-2, off a Soviet assembly line.

By early 1938, then, the Soviet DC-3 program was behind schedule. Even with 50 sets of 'first-stage' material, tools, specifications, materials lists, and other assistance, they were unable to get into production. One source of trouble may have been welding sections; the October 1937 materials and parts order contained a very large quantity of welding materials: too much, thought Douglas, for only fifty DC-3s. Yet on January 17, 1938 Amtorg came back to Douglas for still more welding rods and other welding materials (more than $7,000 worth, in all). These (Purox 1, Alcoa No. 1 and No. 2, etc.) were not made by Douglas, and as Alcoa was exchanging aluminum for Soviet oil, the use of Douglas as a purchasing agent is, in this instance, a mystery.[59] Another source of trouble was the hydraulic press for shearing and forming panels; events in early 1938 indicated pressure upon Amtorg in New York to obtain equipment and information. Douglas, however, did not make the hydraulic press, and only the provision of operating methods was included in the agreement.

The Amtorg order of October 1937 called for the supply of technical information on the Douglas method of hydraulic-press forming of sheet metal. The Soviets obviously recognized the central importance of this process and, it appears, were unable to get either a press or the requisite technical knowledge from the American manufacturer. The order to Douglas called not only for technical information and calculations relevant to the Douglas use of the press, but also for information obtainable only from Hydraulic Press Manufacturing Company, as the Douglas files reveal ('all erection and assembly drawings . . . drawings for spare parts . . . drawings of the dies'). Obviously Douglas did not agree to supply these, but on the Amtorg 'confirmation of order' these items are listed and then crossed out by someone at Douglas. This rather crude attempt to get the Hydraulic Press data was followed in March 1938 by an exclusive license granted by Douglas to Narkomvneshtorg (People's Commissariat for Foreign Trade) for the Guerin process (Douglas Patent No. 2,055,077 and others) 'whereby sheet metal may be mechanically cut to form a blank which may thereafter be formed into a part of objects and unique methods and apparatus of forming metal blanks. . . .'[60]

The Soviets then withheld payment for the manual and the list of parts for the Birdsboro press (required and supplied by Douglas under the agreement).

[58]   Douglas Aircraft Co. files. Data taken from letter of V. K. Bogdan to Stratton, October 1, 1937.
[59]   Douglas Aircraft Company files, 'Amtorg—Misc. Orders,' January 18, 1938.
[60]   *Ibid*

In turn, Douglas withheld permission for Soviet engineers to visit the press until Amtorg paid. On March 28 Amtorg wired Douglas Aircraft that the check in settlement of the manual and parts had been mailed. The check did not arrive. On April 15 Amtorg wired that the check had been withheld because of Item 10, Paragraph K of 25–80/70143. The Douglas Company reply was very much to the point:

> The only part of this item upon which you have received no information is that, desired by you, from the Hydraulic Press Manufacturing Company. . . . It seems very strange to us, Mr. Bogdan, that you would withhold payment to us of some $30,000 in an effort to force us to get from the Hydraulic Press Manufacturing Company what they don't want to give us. If you have purchased Birdsboro Presses . . . and if you are so entitled to get the information you desire, it would seem much more reasonable to get it from Birdsboro who can get it from Hydraulic Press Manufacturing Company. We have made it very clear to you from the first that we are not selling you the design of the press, but that we would *endeavor* to get such information as the Hydraulic Manufacturing Company was willing to give you. . . .[61]

On April 19, the Soviet engineers came back once again about the Birdsboro press. A rubber change on the hydraulic mechanism had taken place without a Soviet engineer being present (the foreman who normally informed the Soviet engineers was absent and the shop men decided to go ahead with the change on their own), so that the change was made without Soviet knowledge. The Soviets immediately protested and Stratton took this opportunity to remind the GUAP (Main Administration of the Aircraft Industry) Commission of the terms of the agreement: 'I can assure you that we have no objection to your men observing our overhaul operations on the press. The only restrictions we have placed on your men is that they do not make sketches of anything in the plant.'[62]

Like other American companies and individual engineers, the Douglas management developed pragmatic rules for dealing with the peculiar Soviet outlook. Threats and bluff were met by firmness, and objection by counter objection.

---

[61] *Ibid.*
[62] *Ibid.*

CHAPTER FIFTEEN

Technical Assistance to Military Industries: Tanks, Guns, and Explosives[1]

ALTHOUGH this study is concerned with economic development, a section on military development is included for completeness. The Soviet Union has concentrated significant resources in this field and this, of course, has diverted resources both from capital expenditure and the standard of living. Further, although it appears unlikely that Western governments supporting free-enterprise systems could also rationally have supported the long-run military endeavours of the Soviet Union in the years before the Nazi invasion, such support, indeed, seems to have been the case.

In the 1920s it had been the U.S. State Department that had objected to shipments of armaments to the U.S.S.R.; the War and Navy Departments, however, found such shipments acceptable on the grounds that they maintained military suppliers in business. These positions were later reversed, and after the early 1930s we find the State Department encouraging shipment of military assistance[2] and the War Department expressing greater reluctance. This executive schizophrenia was carried to a point suggesting that Navy officers were unofficially sabotaging military sales already approved by Admiral Leahy, President Roosevelt, and the State Department.[3] A quotation from a State Department memorandum recommending approval to A. W. Hahn, a consulting engineer, to design and operate an aluminum-powder plant in the U.S.S.R. suggests, however, that the Department itself was somewhat self-conscious about its position. On January 3, 1931 Senator Smoot had inquired about the Hahn plant, and the Department handled the Senator's inquiry as follows:

---

[1] For information on searchlights see chap. 10, for aviation see chap. 14, and for shipbuilding see chap. 13.
[2] U.S. State Dept. Decimal File, 711.00111, Armament Control/583.
[3] *Ibid.*, 711.00111, Armament Control/1127 and /1841.

No reply was made to Senator Smoot by the Department, as the Secretary did not desire to indicate that the Department had no objection to the rendering by Mr. Hahn of technical-assistance to the Soviet authorities in the production of aluminum powder, in view of the possibility of its use as war material, and preferred to take no position at the time in regard to the matter.[4]

The same memorandum reviews the State Department position on sale of armaments to the Soviet Union. Previously, according to the memorandum, the Department had refused permission for export to the Soviet Union of guns, rifles, ammunition, periscopes, submarines, naval planes, and machinery for the manufacture of smokeless powder. On the other hand, the Department had made no objection to the sale of blasting caps and fuses, commercial airplanes and engines, and helium gas. On the question of technical services for military end-use, the Department had viewed with disfavor the sale of a method 'for causing mustard gas to be indefinitely persistent' but had not objected to the sale, construction, or operation of a system of aerial survey, and assistance for production of nitrocellulose and purification of cotton linters.[5]

This distinction made between civilian and military products is hardly clear. The State Department had disapproved the sale of naval bombers by the Glenn L. Martin Company but had approved the sale of aircraft engines and technical assistance for the production of aircraft engines by Curtiss-Wright on the grounds these were for civilian use. The Curtiss-Wright engines had both civilian and military uses and certainly were used for military planes and tanks by the Soviets. Disapproval was voiced over the sale of submarine periscopes on the grounds that this was war material, but approval was given to the Hercules Powder Company to offer technical assistance for a large plant 'in the production of nitrocellulose,'[6] in the face of a letter from the War Department specifically stating that the assistance would be 'a very material military asset.'[7]

By 1938 the State Department had approved ammunition and battleships. In reply to a letter from the E. W. Bliss Company concerning a proposal to supply the U.S.S.R. with 'a complete plant for the manufacture of small arms ammunition, including the necessary machinery and full information concerning the operation thereof,' it was asserted on April 27, 1938 that this would not

[4] U.S. State Dept. Decimal File, 861.659—DUPONT DE NEMOURS & CO./5. Aluminum powder is used, as an additive, to raise the explosive force of ammunition.

[5] *Ibid.*

[6] U.S. State Dept. Decimal File, 861.659—Nitrocellulose/5: ' . . . this Department does not desire to interpose objection to your Company rendering technical-assistance to the Soviet authorities in the production of nitrocellulose and the purification of cotton linters, along the lines outlined in your communication.'

[7] *Ibid.*, 861.659—Nitrocellulose/1 through/5.

contravene any existing treaty provided there were no military secrets involved.[8] President Roosevelt personally instructed the State Department to 'give all help' to the Soviet Union to have a 45,000-ton battleship built in the U.S.[9]

In brief, the grant of permission to export or not to the Soviet Union was obviously not always based on the question of the military end-use of the products.

European governments were even more active than the United States in approving the supply of armaments and providing technical assistance for their production. Germany supplied organizational assistance and later extensive military supplies under the Nazi-Soviet pact.[10] France supplied military assistance after the detente of 1933. Italy built the destroyer Tashkent, and the Fiat and Ansaldo companies were major suppliers of weapons.[11] Another major supplier was Vickers, which had a close relationship with the British Government and which supplied tank designs and models which became the basis for the standard Soviet tanks of World War II.

NEW TRACTOR PLANTS AND TANK PRODUCTION

A plant for the erection of tractors is well suited to the production of tanks and self-propelled guns. The tractor plants at Stalingrad, Kharkov, and Chelyabinsk, erected with Western assistance and equipment, were used from the start to produce tanks, armored cars, and self-propelled guns. The enthusiasm with which this tank program was pursued and the diversion of the best Russian engineers and material priorities to this end were responsible for at least part of the problem of lagging tractor production.

As early as 1931 the Chain Belt Company representative at Stalingrad reported that the newly opened tractor plant was making 'small tanks.'[12] In 1932 A. A. Wishnewsky, an American whose specialty—production methods—took him into many Soviet plants, reported that the principal emphasis in these plants was on production of munitions and military supplies. In all factories, he stated, at least one department was closed, and he would from time to time run across 'parts, materials, shells and acids' having no relation to normal production.

He stated that it was particularly true of Tractorostroy [*sic*] where emphasis is being placed on the production of tanks rather than tractors.

[8] U.S. State Dept. Decimal File, 711.00111 Armament Control/1076.
[9] *Ibid.*, 711.0011 Armament Control/1154. See marginal notations by the President.
[10] See *Hauptarchiv*, Hoover Institution.
[11] A. Barmine, *op. cit.*, p. 189.
[12] U.S. State Dept. Decimal File, 861.5017—Living Conditions/248, Report No. 608, Interview with E. T. Riesing, May 8, 1931.

In his opinion, a least for the time being, the development of tractor production there has been designed to lead up to the production of tanks for military purposes.[13]

Such reports were confirmed a few years later by German intelligence, which concluded that in 1937–8 the Stalingrad Tractor Plant was producing a small three-ton armored car and a self-propelled gun at a rate of one per week, and the T-37 tank, patterned on the British A 4 E11, at the rate of one every four days. The 1937 Soviet War Mobilization Plan, of which the German Wehrmacht apparently had a copy, planned to double this output in case of war.[14]

A similar report was made in late 1932 from the Kharkov Tractor Plant by Ingram D. Calhoun, an engineer for the Oilgear Company of Milwaukee who was servicing hydraulic presses and boring machines for cylinder blocks. The Kharkov Tractor Plant, Calhoun stated, was turning out 8 to 10 tanks a day which had a maximum speed of 30 kilometers per hour. Tank production took precedence over tractor production and operators for these were being trained 'night and day.'[15] Calhoun added that 'they can fool the tourists but not the foreign engineers.'[16]

According to the Wehrmacht, the Kharkov tractor plant (the Ordzhonikidze) was producing in 1938 a self-propelled gun at a rate of slightly less than one a week and an armored car at a rate of one every four days. Kharkov also produced the T-26 tank, patterned after the British Vickers-Armstrongs six-tonner. The Soviet War Mobilization Plan envisaged a wartime output tripling the self-propelled gun rate and doubling that of armored cars, but maintaining the same tank production rate.[17]

In 1937 the Chelyabinsk Tractor Plant, known as the Stalin, was producing tanks of the BT series, patterned after the American Christie. Output in 1938 consisted of 32 of the 12-tonners and 100 of the BT-38, a 16-tonner. Mobilization Plan output was double these figures.[18]

Thus not only were all three of the new tractor plants producing tanks throughout the 1930s from the date of opening but they were by far the most important industrial units producing this type of weapon. As the projected War Mobilization output was only double the existant output, it can be

---

[13]   U.S. State Dept. Decimal File, 861.5017—Living Conditions/420, February 8, 1932.

[14]   Oberkommando der Wehrmacht (OKW/Wi Rü Amt/Wi), *Kampf-und Panzerkraftwagen-Werke*, List VII6, March 1941, p. 3, National Archives Microcopy T 84–122.

[15]   U.S. State Dept. Decimal File, 861.5017—Living Conditions/576, December 28, 1932.

[16]   *Ibid.*

[17]   OKW *op. cit.*, p. 2.

[18]   *Ibid.*, p. 5.

reasonably inferred that about one-half the productive capacity of these 'tractor' plants was being used for tank and armored car production from 1931 onwards. Thus the armaments program obviously reduced tractor production and adversely affected the agricultural program.

There are also, in the State Department files and elsewhere, numerous reports confirming the adaptability of Soviet general-equipment plants for war use. For example: 'The heavy industry plants are fitted with special attachments and equipment held in reserve which in a few hours will convert the plants into munitions factories. . . .'[19]

THE DEVELOPMENT OF SOVIET TANK DESIGN PRIOR TO WORLD WAR II

Soviet tanks before World War II owed much to American, British, and, to a lesser extent, French and Italian design work. Little German design influence can be traced in the period before 1939, except through the German tank center at Kazan, although there were other Soviet-German military links.

During the 1920s and 1930s the Soviets acquired prototype tanks from all producing countries and based their own development upon the most suitable of these foreign models. The 1932 Soviet tank stock is summarized in table 15–1.

Table 15–1 SOVIET TANK STOCK AND ITS ORIGINS, 1932

Tanks Available	*Origin*
20 Carden-Lloyd Mark VI	Made in United Kingdom by Vickers-Armstrongs, Ltd.
1 Fiat Type 3000	Made in Italy
20 Renault	Made in France, captured in Civil War
16 'Russian-Renaults'	Made in France, modified in U.S.S.R.
70 light tanks	Vickers 6-ton, Alternate A
40 Vickers Mark II	Made in United Kingdom by Vickers-Armstrongs, Ltd.
2 Christie M 1931	Made in United States by U.S. Wheel Track Layer Corp.
8 Medium Mark A	Probably Vickers-Armstrongs
25 Mark V	Captured from White armies in Civil War
8 eighty-ton	Not known; possibly Soviet manufacture based on Vickers designs, Mark V, (i.e., U.K. Flying Elephant of 1916)

Sources: R. E. Jones *et al. The Fighting Tanks Since 1916* (Washington: National Service Publishing Co., 1933), p. 173.
R. M. Ogorkiewicz, 'Soviet Tanks,' in B. H. Liddell Hart, ed., *The Red Army* (New York: Harcourt, Brace and Co., 1956).

[19] Horace N. Gilbert, *The Russian Industrialization Program* (unpublished manuscript in the Hoover Institution at Stanford University), p. 3.

From this early stock of Western models, together with technical-assistance agreements and the continuing purchase of foreign prototypes, we can trace the origins of Soviet tank models of the 1940s.

The Carden-Lloyd was a 1.69-ton machine-gun carrier (predecessor of the British Bren gun carrier of World War II) first produced by Vickers-Armstrongs, Ltd., in 1929. The Mark VI model sold to the Soviets had a Ford Model T 4-cylinder 22.5-horsepower water-cooled engine and a Ford planetary transmission.[20] This became the Soviet T-27 light reconnaissance tank produced at the Bolshevik plant in Leningrad.[21]

The Ordzhonikidze Tractor Plant at Kharkov started work on the T-26, based on the British Vickers-Armstrongs six-tonner (probably Alternative A), at about the same time. There were three versions—A, B, and C—of which B and C became the Soviet standard models produced until 1941.[22] Similarly the Soviet T-37 and T-38 amphibious vehicles were based on the Carden-Lloyd Amphibian, known as the Model A4 E 11 in the British Army.[23]

Walter Christie, well-known American inventor with numerous automotive and tank inventions to his credit, developed the Christie tank—the basis of World War II American tanks. Numerous versions of Christie tanks and armored vehicles were produced in the late 1920s and 1930s. Two chassis of the Christie M 1931 model medium tank (MB) were purchased by the Soviet Union in 1932 from the U.S. Wheel Track Layer Corporation.[24] After further development work this became not only the Soviet T-32 (the basic Soviet tank of World War II) but also several other development models in the U.S.S.R.: first the BT (12 tons), followed by the BT5 and the BT28, of which 100 were produced at the Chelyabinsk tractor 'school'[25] in 1938. They were standard equipment until 1941.

The Soviet T-34 and the American M3, both based on the Christie, had the same 12-cylinder aero engine: a V-type Liberty of 338 horsepower. Ogorkiewicz comments on the Christie model series as follows:

[20] R. E. Jones *et al.*, *The Fighting Tanks since 1916* (Washington, D.C., National Service Publishing Company, 1933), p. 122. See also Sutton, *Western Technology . . ., 1917 to 1930*, p. 245–8, for Ford Motor Company technical-assistance agreement for the production of Ford engines; and R. M. Ogorkiewicz, 'Soviet Tanks,' in *The Red Army*, ed. B. H. Liddell Hart (New York: Harcourt, Brace and Company, 1956), p. 297.

[21] *Genie Civil*, CXVI, No. 9 (March 2, 1940), pp. 154–5.

[22] *Ibid.*

[23] R. E. Jones, *op. cit.*, p. 304. Ogorkiewicz points out that Vickers-Armstrongs was the 'undisputed leader in tank design' in the 1920s. The Vickers six-tonner influenced the development of the American M3 and M5 Stuarts and was also adopted in the U.S.S.R. as the prototype of the T-26.

[24] *Ibid.*, pp. 168–9.

[25] Oberkommando der Wehrmacht (OKW/Wi Rü Amt/Wi), March 1941, Miscellaneous German Records, National Archives Microcopy T 84–122.

The power-weight ratio was actually higher than could be efficiently used, but the Russians copied it all and confined their development largely to armament, which increased from a 37-mm gun on the original models of 1931–32, to 45-mm guns on BT5 of 1935 and eventually to short 76.2-mm guns on some of the final models of the series.[26]

Both the Soviet T-28 medium 29-ton tank and the T-35 heavy 45-ton tank resembled British models—the A6 medium tank and the A-1 Vickers Independent, respectively. However, Ogorkiewicz suggests that, although the layout 'closely resembles' the British models, these tanks were actually a sign of 'growing Soviet independence in the design field.'[27]

Imported French Renault designs were not developed, although they no doubt contributed to Russian tank knowledge. During the 1933 entente between France and the Soviet Union, the Renault Company delivered $11 million worth of 'small fast tanks and artillery tractors'[28] to the Soviet Union and supplied experts from the Schneider works and Panhard Levasseur, both skilled in the armored-car and tank field. Renault FTs or T-18s were not, however, produced in Russia.

SOVIET MACHINE GUNS AND AIRCRAFT WEAPONS[29]

Machine-gun development in tsarist Russia was limited to small-lot production of the Maxim machine gun at the Tula armory. The Soviet regime placed great emphasis on the development and production of this type of weapon, particularly for aircraft use. In 1944, for example, they produced:

Maxim machine gun	270,000
Degtyarev infantry machine gun	120,000
Degtyarev tank machine gun	40,000
Degtyarev Shpagin heavy machine gun	50,000 (for anti-aircraft use)
Goryunov machine gun	10,000
Shkas aircraft gun	40,000
Beresin aircraft gun	60,000
Total	590,000

[26]   Ogorkiewicz, *op. cit.*, p. 298.

[27]   *Ibid.*, p. 299. The reader is referred to Ogorkiewicz's excellent short paper (see fn. 20), which contains more detail on these Soviet tanks and a balanced assessment of their capabilities.

[28]   Philip Noel-Baker, *The Private Manufacture of Armaments* (London: Gollancz, 1937), p. 188.

[29]   Based on G. M. Chinn, *The Machine Gun* (Washington, D.C., U.S. Department of the Navy, Bureau of Ordnance, 1952), Vol. II, Part VII. This is an excellent declassified description of Soviet weapons in this class.

Table 15-2 SOVIET TANKS AND THEIR WESTERN ORIGINS, 1930–45

Soviet Tank Model Number	Based on:	1938 Production	Produced at:	Employment (1937–8)
T-18	Renault (F.T.)		Not produced	
T-26 (8-ton) A, B, C versions	Vickers-Armstrongs 6-ton A, B	Not known	Bolshevik works (Leningrad) Ordzhonikidze (Kharkov)	25,000 (1938) About 20,000 (1937)
T-27 (1.7-ton)	Vickers-Armstrongs (Carden-Lloyd) Mark VI	Not known	Bolshevik works (Leningrad)	25,000 (1938)
T-37 (3-ton)	British Army Model A 4 E 11 (Carden-Lloyd Amphibian)	At least 90	Lenin machine works (Omsk) Stalingrad tractor works Chelyabinsk tractor technical school	About 5,000 (1937) About 20,000 (1938) About 25,000 (1938)
T-32 (34-ton)	U.S. Christie, which became the B.T.; then T-29 experimental	14 19 15 (1937)	Kirov works (Leningrad) Stalin works (Kramatorsky) Uralmash	40,000 (1938) in 3 shifts 32,000 (1937) 60,000 (1937)
BT (12-ton)		8 (motors only) (1937) 32	Polytechnic Institute (Kiev) Chelyabinsk tractor technical school	About 1,500 (1937)
BT-28 (16-ton)	U.S. Christie	100	Chelyabinsk tractor technical school	About 25,000 (1938)
T-35 (45-ton)	Vickers A 1 of mid-1920s	About 5 (1939)	Probably Uralmash	60,000 (1937)

Source: Oberkommando der Wehrmacht, *Kampf and Panzerkraftwagen-Werke,* List VII6, March 1941, National Archives Microcopy T 84–122.

These weapons were characterized by extreme simplicity of design and rough exterior finish. They were, however, quite effective, and some Soviet weapons were probably the best in their class in World War II. Chinn commented in 1952 that because of the lack of skilled labor, 'weapons are designed to require a minimum of moving parts and fine finishes.'[30]

The Soviets borrowed heavily, but not completely, from the West in machine-gun technology. The Maxim, a famous Western gun, underwent various modifications by Soviet designers: i.e., the Maxim-Tokarev, the Maxim-Koleshnikov, and the Maxim-Esivnin. Thus the Maxim model 1910 became the basis of almost one-half of Soviet 1944 machine-gun production.

The Soviets, however, did introduce some innovations. The first of these innovations was the Goryunov (SG-43) machine gun, hailed as an entirely new weapon; as Chinn points out, some of its features were indeed new to Russian weapons, although 'they remind gun connoisseurs of principles and patents orginated earlier by designers in other countries.'[31] For example, the operating principle of the Goryunov gun was patented by John M. Browning 'but he never saw fit to put it into use.'[32] Certain other U.S. features were found in the weapon. It had, for example, a Mauser-type extractor and ejector. On the other hand, Chinn comments:

> Doing away with all unnecessary springs is one of the greatest accomplishments of Gurynev; in fact, the driving spring and its telescoping guide which is also spring loaded, are about all the springs employed for the gun's operation.[33]

During the 1920s the Soviets conducted an aircraft machine-gun development program 'with utmost secrecy.'[34] The result was the Shkas class of aircraft machine guns. The first production model appeared in 1933, followed by the standard version (KM-35), in steady production after 1935. The gun was capable of 1,800 rounds per minute and believed by the Soviets to be the best in existence. Chinn points out that:

> The Russians demonstrated great skill in adapting at low cost the best of time-proved principles to their particular needs. Construction was in two phases: a quick, coarse machining operation on all parts followed by final fitting and assembly on the work bench. Maximum use was made of semi-skilled labor with a minimum of fine gauged machine tool work. . . .[35]

Once again, however, we find some dependence on foreign ideas. Chinn describes the Shkas class: 'Thus the Shkas is an innovation based on the

[30] *Ibid.*, p. 20. It has been argued that extreme simplicity impaired their field use.
[31] *Ibid.*, p. 57.
[32] U.S. Patent No. 544657 of August 20, 1895.
[33] Chinn, *op. cit.*, p. 63.
[34] *Ibid.*, p. 72.
[35] *Ibid.*, p. 74–5.

Table 15–3   SOVIET MACHINE GUNS AND WESTERN
DESIGN INFLUENCE, 1930–45

Soviet Model	Year First Produced	Western Influence
Maxim-Tokarev Maxim-Koleshnikov Maxim-Esivnin }	1928	Maxim model 1910
SG-43 (Goryunov)	1928	Browning Patent No. 544657 Mauser-type extractor, ejector
Degtyarev	1926	Mauser locking; Vickers feed
Shkas aircraft gun	1932	Maxim ejection and buffer, Szakats (rotating feed), Berthier (piston actuated, propped breech, locking)
Shvak aircraft cannon	About 1944	Berthier action
Beresin aircraft gun	1940	Finnish Lahti 20 mm
V Ya aircraft cannon	1941	Scaled-up version of the Lahti

Source: G. M. Chinn, *The Machine Gun* (Washington D.C.: U.S. Dept. of the Navy, Bureau of Ordnance, 1951), Vol. II, Part VII.

features of the Maxim (ejection and buffer), the Szakats (rotating feed) and the Berthier (piston actuated, propped breech, locking).'[36]

By the same token the Shvak, a very light and extremely compact automatic aircraft gun with a range comparable to that of the U.S. M 3 cannon, was based on Berthier operating principles.[37] During the 1933 French-Soviet entente, the French sent experts on machine guns to the Soviet Union and their work can be recognized in the Shvak weapons and in the Shkas class.[38] The Shkas was replaced in 1940 with the 12.7-millimeter Beresin, deliberately constructed to be thrown away after a short period of use. Beresin design was 'greatly influenced' by a captured Finnish Lahti 20-millimeter machine cannon. The V Ya 23-millimeter aircraft cannon was a scaled-up version of the Beresin.[39]

In general, machine-gun development was reasonably successful and might be described as a blend of skilled adaptation of foreign ideas with indigenous innovation. Soviet small arms were plagued with faults; 85 percent of the malfunctions were reported, however, to be due to bad cartridges rather than mechanical failures.[40]

[36] *Ibid.*, p. 79.
[37] *Ibid.*, p. 82.
[38] Noel-Baker, *op. cit.*, p. 188.
[39] Chinn, *op. cit.*, p. 94.
[40] *Ibid.*, p. 96. Ammunition also shows Western influence. The 12.7-mm cartridge was 'influenced' by the German T.u.F. 13-mm of World War I. The 20-mm had

THE HERCULES POWDER COMPANY AGREEMENT FOR MANUFACTURE OF COTTON LINTERS AND NITROCELLULOSE

In mid-1930 an agreement was concluded between Vsekhimprom and the Hercules Powder Company of Wilmington, Delaware for technical assistance in the production of nitrocellulose and cotton linters for explosives manufacture. Under the agreement the Hercules firm was to 'communicate the secrets of production and indicate all the production methods of bleaching common as well as oily linter, first and second cut of any viscosity. . . .'[41] for a number of grades—MVL 5, 10, 30, 50, 150, 250, and 500—with specified viscosity ranges and according to a stated specification. This had to be done in existing Soviet plants using existing equipment, and for this purpose Hercules sent an engineer to the U.S.S.R. and received three Soviet engineers annually into its U.S. plants for periods ranging from three to six months.

For nitrocellulose, more extensive assistance was agreed upon. The Hercules Powder Company was to

> . . . prepare a complete design of a nitrocellulose plant for the production of 5,000 tons yearly, arranged so as to enable the Vsekhimprom to double production in the future. The design shall be according to the method used in the plants of the Hercules Powder Co. and shall include all the mechanical appliances of production and all the technical improvements of the present time.[42]

The complete detailed design had to include cost estimates, description of the technological process involved, description of equipment, and dimensions of the building, in addition to 'working drawings of the apparatus and dimensions of the buildings, foundations for the apparatus, [and] calculations of the loads on the walls' which would enable Vsekhimprom to design the buildings. Also required were diagrammatical designs for the heating, ventilation, and refuse removal systems (with indications for steam pipes, water pipes and airconductors) and designs for raw material storage facilities, finished and semi-finished products, and mechanical appliances used in connection with loading and unloading.

The agreement also required disclosing processes for production of artificial leather, airplanes, medical colloids, cement for leather and Herculoid nitrocellulose for plastics (celluloid). Hercules guaranteed that quality would not be below its own production; supervised installation of equipment, construction

---

a very strong physical resemblance to the nineteenth-century Gatling cartridge. The 23-mm, however, was distinctly different and according to Chinn had 'features of refinement' (p. 180). The reader is referred to Chinn's excellent study for further details.

[41] U.S. State Dept. Decimal File, 861.659 Nitrocellulose/1.

[42] *Ibid.*

and start-up; and sent its engineers to the U.S.S.R. for this purpose. Further, 10 Soviet engineers were admitted to Hercules plants in the United States for periods of three to six months to study nitrocellulose production methods.[43]

THE DRIVE TO PURCHASE ARMAMENTS IN THE UNITED STATES AND GERMANY AFTER 1936

Foreign purchases of armaments and technical-assistance agreements were expanded after 1936 and a determined effort was made to purchase new, advanced armaments systems and plants to manufacture these systems.

The United States was a prime focus of this drive. For this purpose the Carp Export and Import Corporation was established on Fifth Avenue in New York as a Soviet-front company. The President was Sam Carp, whose sister was married to V. M. Molotov, President of Council of People's Commissars of the U.S.S.R. The staff was American, including some retired officers of the U.S. Army and Navy.[44] This corporation had considerable influence in the United States.

In November 1936 the Soviet Embassy requested the State Department to intercede with the Navy Department for permission necessary to purchase heavy armor for battleships and cruisers from several steel companies.[45] This request was followed by a visit to the State Department by a group of Carp officials, who were assured by the Department that the proposed purchase of unassembled battleships would not be illegal or contrary to U.S. policy.[46] In a subsequent letter the State Department indicated it would not be possible, however, to supply 'designs, plans, working drawings and specifications of such vessels as the U.S.S. *Lexington, Colorado*, and *Mississippi*,' although there was nothing to prevent U.S. naval architects from preparing such designs on behalf of the Soviet Union.[47]

Purchases of war materials were, therefore, made directly from American manufacturers. Thus in 1938 the William Sellers Company of Philadelphia was reported negotiating a contract for the sale of heavy machinery for the manufacture of 12-inch steel plate known as 'stacked plate' for multiples for

---

[43] *Ibid.* This transfer had a favorable impact on the Soviet rocket program. Zaihringer points out that Soviet World War II rockets used 'Russian Cordite' with a composition of 56·5 percent nitrocellulose, similar to British and American propellants. 'Thus United States and U.S.S.R. propellant compositions were close by experimental coincidence and similar technology.' [A. J. Zaehringer, *Soviet Space Technology* (New York: Harper and Row, 1961), pp. 11–2.]

[44] U.S. State Dept. Decimal File, 711.00111 Armament Control/431.

[45] *Ibid.*, 861.6511/39, April 16, 1938.

[46] *Ibid.*, 711.00111 Armament Control/1153a.

[47] *Ibid.*, 711.00111 Armament Control/455, January 13, 1937.

armor-plate manufacture.[48] In March 1939 the State Department approved a proposal (already approved in the Navy Department) under which the Electric Boat Company of Groton, Connecticut would furnish plans, specifications, and construction services in the Soviet Union for a submarine.[49]

Both the Russians and the Germans initially expected benefits from the Soviet-Nazi military alliance of 1939, but the evidence is that the Soviet Union, at least, did not receive anything near its expectations. Rossi concludes from his study of the Fuehrer Conferences on Naval Affairs:

> From all the available evidence . . . the military collaboration between Germany and Russia does not seem to have gone very far in the technical field. Stalin asked for a great deal and was ready to give the necessary quid pro quo, but notwithstanding his eagerness to get hold of prototypes and the secret manufacturing processes of certain German weapons, he was to some extent restrained by the need not to endanger the profits he hoped to make out of his policy of neutrality. Over and above all this there was Hitler's deep distrust of Soviet Russia, once he had sobered down after his early successes. . . .[50]

This weapons-acquisition process culminated in the Lend-Lease program, under which large quantities of war materials were transferred to the Soviet Union.[51] However, about one-third of early shipments, and almost all shipments after 1944, were of industrial equipment, and not military end-use goods.

CONCLUSIONS

Although Soviet tanks and some guns were directly descended from Western models, a much greater degree of innovative effort was utilized on military products than in other sectors, so that the Soviets, in effect, had an indigenous military technology by 1941. Further, weapons were produced in large quantities over a full decade by using productive equipment and facilities built in 1930–2. This prudent, far-sighted policy accounts for Soviet ability to turn back the Nazi invasion before Lend-Lease goods flowed in in any great quantity.

In appears, although all the evidence is not yet available, that most Western governments (particularly the United States, Britain, France, and Italy) were willing to supply armaments and design assistance to produce armaments in the period before 1941, and that Germany also provided military assistance up until the eve of her 1941 'drang nach osten.'

[48]   *Ibid.*, 861.6511/39.

[49]   *Ibid.*, 711.00111 Armament Control/540, March 9, 1937.

[50]   A. Rossi, *The Russo-German Alliance 1939–1941* (Boston: Beacon, 1951), p. 97. For details of 1930–40 Krupp shipments, see *NIK 11625, Krupp—Report of the Department for War Material 1939–1940*, at Hoover Institution.

[51]   See U.S. State Dept., *Report on War Aid Furnished by the United States to the U.S.S.R.*

CHAPTER SIXTEEN

Technical Assistance to Planning and Construction Projects

THE DESIGN OF INDUSTRIAL PLANTS BY ALBERT KAHN, INC., OF DETROIT

ONE of the truly great surprises in researching this study was the discovery that the architectural design and supervision of construction of industrial units as well as the supply of equipment and similar assistance was very much an American responsibility. In the words of the Albert Kahn Co., Inc., the foremost industrial architects in the United States:

> It was in 1928 . . . that the most extraordinary commission ever given an architect came in the door unannounced. In that year a group of engineers from the U.S.S.R. came to the Kahn office with an order for a $40,000,000 tractor plant, and an outline of a program for an additional two billion dollars' worth of buildings. About a dozen of these factories were done in Detroit; the rest were handled in a special office with 1,500 draftsmen in Moscow.[1]

The 'outline of a program' presented to the Kahn organization in 1928 was nothing less than the First and Second Five-Year Plans of 'socialist construction.' Gosplan had decided upon those sectors it wanted developed and their approximate capacities.[2] No foreign influence has been found at the Gosplan level. These plans were then turned over to the Albert Kahn Company for conversion into production units.

Albert Kahn, Inc., probably unknown to even well-informed readers, is the most famous of U.S. industrial architects. In 1938 the company handled 19 percent of all architect-designed industrial building in the United States,

[1] G. Nelson, *Industrial Architecture of Albert Kahn Co., Inc.* (New York: Architectural Book Publishing Company, Inc., 1939), pp. 18–9.

[2] Planned capacities of some units, notably the automobile and tractor plants, were increased after consultation with U.S. firms.

in addition to projects in most major countries elsewhere in the world. Prior to 1939 the company designed and supervised construction of about $800,000,000 worth of industrial buildings in the United States alone.[3] This included the famous River Rouge plant of Henry Ford, plants for the Chevrolet, Packard, Hudson, General Motors, Oldsmobile, Cadillac, Chrysler, and De Soto automobile companies, Kelvinator, United Air Lines, Burroughs Adding Machine, Pratt & Whitney Aircraft, the Glenn L. Martin Company, and dozens of similar firms. For one customer alone, General Motors, the Kahn Company designed 127 major structures prior to 1939.

The $2-billion Soviet design project was two and a half times greater than all the U.S. business handled by the company between its foundation date, 1903, and 1939. As Kahn described the contract:

> Probably no organization has ever had a more severe test of its flexibility, speed, and competence. Not only did the plants have to be designed, but machinery had to be selected and ordered, process layouts had to be prepared and the very tools needed to build the plants had to be ordered here and shipped over.[4]

The formal agreement between Albert Kahn, Inc., and Vesenkha, under which the Kahn Company became consulting architects to the Soviet Union, was concluded in early 1930; upon signing the agreement Moritz Kahn (one of the three Kahn brothers) commented:

> In a short time I shall proceed to Moscow with a staff of twenty-five specialist assistants. We shall then help the Soviet Government to organize a designing bureau which will comprise about forty-five hundred architectural and engineering designers, selected principally from Soviet Russia, but also from America and other foreign countries. The bureau will be directed by the head of the Building Commission of the Supreme Economic Council.[5]

This bureau became Gosproektstroi (State Project Construction Trust) the major Soviet design and construction organization. Chief of Gosproektstroi and Chairman of the Vesenkha Building Commission was G. K. Scrymgeour, a Kahn engineer and the only American on the National Technical Soviet.[6] Scrymgeour outlined the Kahn unit functions as follows:

> The Albert Kahn unit was engaged to control, teach and design all light and heavy industry. . . . By the end of the second year we controlled in Moscow, and from Moscow branches in Leningrad, Kharkov, Kiev,

---

[3] Nelson, *op. cit.*, p. 18.
[4] *Ibid.*
[5] Amtorg, *op. cit.*, No. 3–4 (February 15, 1930), p. 55.
[6] *American Engineers in Russia*, Folder 3, Letter from Scrymgeour; and Folder 4, letter from G. Growcott, Kahn engineer in Gosproektstroi.

Dniepretrovsk, Odessa, Sverdlovsk and Novo-Sibirsk 3,000 designers, and completed the design of buildings costing (these are Soviet figures) 417 million rubles.[7]

The 3,000 designers in Gosproektstroi can be compared to the small size of the Kahn Company in the U.S. The company handled the immense volume of work outlined above, and then absorbed the Soviet design contract, with the following staff:

> In normal times the firm . . . employs about 400 men and women; among them some 40 secretaries, stenographers, typists and file clerks; about 15 accountants; 80–90 mechanical and electrical engineers; 40–50 field superintendents; some 30 specification writers, estimators, expeditors etc., 175 architectural designers and draftsmen.[8]

The problem, according to Kahn, was that 'a large percentage of Soviet draftsmen . . . had apparently never seen a pencil before and Kahn representatives not only had to run it by day, but hold classes at night.'[9]

Albert Kahn attributed further major advantages to the Soviet Union in its relationship with the Kahn Company. For example, said Kahn, there was only one client: 'this permits standardization of building construction; all factory buildings for any one type of construction can be built on standardized principles. The result will be a great saving in time and in cost in the preparation of plans and the cost of buildings.'[10] Moreover, added Kahn, this would enable revision of the Soviet building code with a 'saving of millions of dollars per annum because of the ultra-conservative character of that code.'[11]

There is in the State Department files an interesting report of an interview with nine engineers from the Albert Kahn unit who called at the U.S. Riga consulate in late 1930 for renewal of entry permits.[12] The report confirms that Kahn was undertaking supply of 'engineering and architectural talent' and that 27 American structural engineers, architects, sanitary engineers, and draftsmen were working in one large building in Moscow with 300 Russian engineers.[13] They reported that the Soviet planners indicated the nature of the plant required and the Kahn unit made the designs and drawings. Albert Kahn also maintained its own representatives at larger projects under construc-

---

7   *Ibid.*, letter from Scrymgoeur.
8   Nelson, *op. cit.*, p. 19.
9   *Ibid.*, p. 18.
10 Amtorg, *op. cit.*, February 15, 1930, p. 55.
11 *Ibid.* For a detailed description of Kahn-designed industrial buildings in the U.S.S.R. see 'Sowjetrussische Notkonstruktionen' Ing. Schauder, in *Beton und Eisen*, July 20, 1933, pp. 213–6.
12 U.S. State Dept. Decimal File, 861.641/9.
13 *Ibid.* However, the consensus was that only four or five of the Russians were engineers; the rest, with the exception of 20 girl tracers, were 'worse than useless.'

tion; for example a Mr. Drabkin was the Kahn representative at the Stalingrad Tractor Plant.[14]

MANAGEMENT ASSISTANCE AT THE PLANT LEVEL

Vesenkha had responsibility for implementation of the Five-Year Plans; this it passed onto designated construction trusts, although the responsibility for policy remained with Vesenkha. The decision was to utilize U.S. methods not only in construction but also in production planning.

A technical-assistance agreement was therefore concluded with W. N. Polakov, a management-consultant firm based in New York. Polakov became Chief Consulting Engineer to Vesenkha for the period December 1929 to May 1931. In a plant selected for the purpose, the firm demonstrated and tested the possibilities of scientific management applied to Sovietized plants. The plant selected manufactured machine tools, cutters, taps, dies, and a full line of standard metal-cutting tools; employed about 5,000; and was well equipped with modern American and German machine tools. Polakov estimated that the number of parts entering main production was about 200 and the number of consecutive operations varied from 10 to 70. Planning, scheduling, and dispatching of these operations and products were his most valuable contributions.

Polakov reorganized all departments, starting with the grinding and polishing shop. His basic innovation was the introduction of a layout chart representing jobs for each machine and progress made on each job.[15] The plant director issued an order requiring conformity to the Polakov proposals, and it was estimated that the annual cost saving by using Gantt Charts was in excess of one million rubles for this one plant, while production increased by 400 percent.

The Gantt Chart had been translated into Russian as early as 1924[16] and by 1934 was in its twenty-first Russian edition, with 100,000 copies in circulation. The problem tackled by the Polakov firm was translation of paper diagrams to shop-floor practice, a problem pointed out by many foreign delegations to the U.S.S.R. Soviet industry was swamped with paper calculations and diagrams unrelated to practice. Polakov's contribution was to translate Gantt methods into action in one model plant.

14 *American Engineers in Russia*, Fisher material, Folder 1.
15 W. N. Polakov, 'The Gantt Chart in Russia,' *American Machinist*, LXXV, No. 7, August 13, 1931, pp. 261–4.
16 W. Clark, *Grafiki Ganta* (Moscow: 1931). Permission was granted by Wallace Clark & Co. to translate and publish in the U.S.S.R. without royalties. Another publication, *Shops and Office Forms*, had been translated and published in the Soviet Union without permission. Clark said he had never received a copy. *American Engineers in Russia*, Letter from Wallace Clark & Co., March 9, 1934.

Vesenkha also negotiated with Wallace Clark & Company, American distributor of Gantt methods in 1934; but the company 'came to the conclusion that they [the Russians] were not yet ready to accept our advice and follow it out in a way which would ensure successful results.'[17]

Other bureaus for design and construction received similar assistance, many under contracts with individual consultants. C. Butterworth, for example, was a consultant metallurgical engineer to Orgametal[18] (Institute for Organization of Production in Machinery and Metalworking Industries).

Butterworth specialized in organization of the heat-treating and working of steel and was made responsible for training graduate Soviet engineers in these processes. Butterworth's program included eight months organizing production in the Putilovets plant in Leningrad, two months in Moscow to select equipment and to design the plant layout for a forge shop, followed by five months in Rostov at Selmashstroi to establish process organization and control. Two months were then spent at Dnieprstroi designing plant layouts and finally eight months at the Nizhni-Novgorod plant planning and erecting forge equipment. Butterworth's last job was as consulting engineer on a project for building heavy railroad equipment.[19] It may readily be seen therefore that a single highly skilled and resourceful engineer could have an impact in a short space of time on a number of different projects.

F. A. Hannah was a similar specialist in reorganization for the NKRKI (People's Commissariat of Workers' and Peasants' Inspection).[20] B. E. Torpen was attached to Vsekomvodgosplan (All-Union Committee for Planning of Water Projects)[21] to provide technical assistance to Steklostroi (Glass and Ceramic Trust).[22] Many such individual consultants were attached to project-design and inspection organizations. For example, in a single Amtorg announcement in August 1930, the following 39 U.S. consulting engineers were listed as having been hired:

27 for the Commissariat of Transportation

3 for Grozneft (Georgian Oil Field Administration)

2 for Dnieprstroi

2 for Stalingrad Tractor Plant (33 had already left)

2 for the United Machine Building Trust

1 for Burtsvetmet (Non-Ferrous Drilling Trust)

[17] *Ibid.*
[18] Amtorg, *op. cit.*, February 15, 1930, p. 57.
[19] *American Engineers in Russia*, File 1, Letter of Charles Butterworth.
[20] Amtorg, *op. cit.*, February 15, 1930, p. 57.
[21] *Ibid.*
[22] *Ibid.*

1 for Dalles (Far East Lumber Trust)

1 for NKRKI (People's Commissariat for Workers' and Peasants' Inspection)[23]

The valuta crisis brought an end to this assistance and such contracts were not renewed after 1932. The First Five-Year Plan was hastily telescoped into a four-year plan to prepare the way for another propaganda assault: the Second Five-Year Plan. Vesenkha, the control for the Kahn unit, was dissolved and replaced by the ministries structure in January 1932.

SOYUZSTROI (ALL-UNION CONSTRUCTION TRUST) AND OTHER CONSTRUCTION UNITS

Soyuzstroi had responsibility for about one-quarter of new construction until 1933 when it was broken into smaller units attached to individual combinats. The Director of Soyuzstroi was Sergei Nemets, formerly an engineer with the Philadelphia construction company of Stone and Webster, Inc. The Chief Engineer of Soyuzstroi was Zara Witkin, whose early projects included the Hollywood Bowl and several large Los Angeles hotels. Initially

Table 16–1   SELECTED EXAMPLES OF TECHNICAL ASSISTANCE AT THE PLANNING AND DESIGN LEVEL

Function	Soviet Organization	Foreign Assistance
Long-term planning (to Jan. 5, 1932)	Gosplan Vesenkha	None identified W. Polakov and Co.
Design and planning	Vesenkha Gosproektstroi	Albert Kahn, Inc. Faudewag A-G Individual consultants
'Stroi' units	Magnitostroi Soyuzstroi Chemstroi Vsekhimstroi Gosstroi	McKee Corp. Zara Witkin Alcan Hirsh Nitrogen Engineering Corp. Longacre Construction Co.
Control and inspection Military construction	OGPU NKRKI	Individual engineers,usually members of Western Communist parties.
Design units	Gipromez (State Institute for Design of Metallurgical Works)	Freyn Engineering Corp.
	Giproshakht (State Institute for Design of Coal Mines)	Allen and Garcia, Inc.

[23]   *Ibid.*, August 1, 1930, p. 328.

Figure 16–1 LAYOUT OF KUZNETSK IRON AND STEEL PLANT PREPARED BY FREYN ENGINEERING COMPANY UNDER TECHNICAL-ASSISTANCE CONTRACT OF 1930

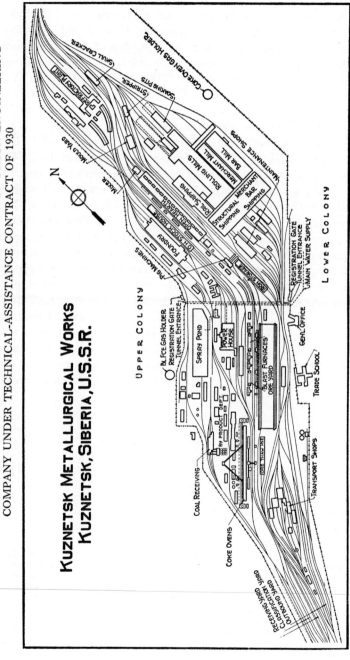

KUZNETSK METALLURGICAL WORKS
KUZNETSK, SIBERIA, U.S.S.R.

Source: Freyn Design, No. 10, October 1932, p. 2.

offered a position as Consulting Engineer in construction of the Palace of Soviets, Witkin supervised construction, in Moscow and elsewhere, of apartment houses, industrial units, and a number of the 'secret industry' units; these Witkin defined as 'having to do with the production or storage of war material or military equipment.'[24] There was no question in Witkin's mind when he was interviewed by the U.S. Consul in Poland at the end of 1933 that every tractor plant 'is of course a tank factory and an automobile plant a factory which may at any time produce mobile artillery.'[25] According to Witkin the best construction work was that done under the supervision of the OGPU, which handled all military work, confirming the evidence that the OGPU has built itself up into a major construction force in the Soviet economy.

Zara Witkin was also employed by Soyuzstroi to undertake a program of organization for the Second Five-Year Plan. According to Nemets, Director of Soyuzstroi, there had been no co-ordination in the First Five-Year Plan between new plants and older established plants. In order to avoid a repetition of this problem, Witkin was instructed to formulate a 'rationalization program' —in effect a program to integrate new construction projects for 1933–7 with existing plants. In order to do this, Witkin requested, and received, material to calculate the actual volume of construction achieved between 1928 and 1932.

Witkin's analytical summary includes his methodology and conclusions, including a series of charts relating actual accomplishments to plan variants between 1928 and 1932 and projections for 1932 to 1937. The most meaningful indicator of Soviet progress is Witkin's comparison of actual construction volumes in the United States and the Soviet Union, in which he concludes:

> In the decade 1923–1932 the average annual total volume of construction in the United States was slightly less than nine billion dollars. The entire five-year plan in construction . . . generally understood to compress 30 to 50 years of industrial development into 5 years, actually amounts to two-thirds of the average annual American construction in the last decade (1923–1932) including three years of unparalleled depression. That the far-famed Soviet Union five year plan was equivalent to less than one average year of American construction has a profound economic significance for both countries.[26]

[24] U.S. State Dept. Decimal File, 861.50–Five Year Plan/276, December 27, 1933.
[25] August 9, 16, and 30, 1934. See also unpublished manuscript in the Special Collections of the Hoover Institution at Stanford University. Unfortunately other papers and reports were destroyed after Witkin's death in 1948. Reports containing military information from Witkin and made to State Department officials were stamped 'No distribution' and filed. Eugene Lyons calls Witkin's task 'the most important assignment given to any single foreign specialist.' [*Assignment in Utopia* (New York: Harcourt, Brace and Co., 1937), p. 529.]
[26] *Engineering News Record*, August 16, 1934, p. 211. This conclusion is preceded by four pages of small print—a carefully structured analysis of construction volume.

In his final article Witkin related this fact to construction possibilities in the period 1932–7 and concluded: 'It furnishes the quantitative proof that the second five year plan is slightly smaller than the first.'[27]

The reader will recall the increasing censorship of information in the Soviet Union throughout the 1930s, culminating in the purge trials of 1937 and recurrent accusations of wrecking. Soviet trade journals abroad ceased publication after 1933 or so. The usual explanation has been Stalinist paranoia. A more likely factor may have been a dawning awareness of the inherent weakness of the socialist form of construction.

Although the exact construction volume achieved is not an integral part of the argument of this study, it is important to note that the actual volume of construction between 1928 and 1941 was probably less than has been generally accepted, and that this was achieved with extensive absorption of Western technology. By integrating these two key observations, we begin to get close to the reality of Soviet industrial development.

Thus the growth-rate figures originating in Soviet sources are maximal. Further, they include an unknown proportion of defective, low-quality output and probably double-counting. These qualifications do not, however, alter our conclusions concerning the relationship between rates of growth in specific sectors and assimilation of foreign technology.

The Fourth Gosstroi (State Construction) Trust in Leningrad provides another example of the extensive penetration of Americans and foreigners into actual construction work even at the lower levels. In 1930 the trust, handling construction in Leningrad, employed about 30 Americans and an unknown number of foreigners; in 1932 there were 141 aliens working for the trust, including 60 to 70 Americans.[28] Their purpose was to introduce the use of reinforced concrete in industrial buildings.[29]

The number of foreign workers in various construction trusts varied greatly. At the one extreme the Stalmost (Steel Bridge Construction) Trust in Moscow had, so far as we know, only one foreigner, Kaare Salberg,[30] a draftsman employed on checking specifications for bridges, plants, and buildings. At the other extreme there is a report that 200 new buildings were under construction at Petrozavodsk—all by American-Finns, of whom there were about 4,000 in an 'American village.'[31] This last example is unusual, although it was common for Finns and American-Finns to seek work in that part of Russia.

[27] *Ibid.*, August 30, 1934, p. 275.
[28] U.S. State Dept. Decimal File, 861.5017—Living Conditions/501 and /508.
[29] *Ibid.*, 861.5017—Living Conditions/508. There may be an element of exaggeration in this report; the interviewee says that an American bricklayer will lay 2,500 bricks per day versus 350 for a Russian.
[30] *Ibid.*, 861.5017—Living Conditions/696.
[31] *Ibid.*, 861.5017—Living Conditions/689.

It can be argued that in some cases American construction assistance, particularly in the housing sector, was not useful; i.e., the transfer was ineffective. The Longacre Construction Company had a contract to supply technical services and supervision on about $10 million worth of apartment buildings in Moscow and other large cities. The company also assisted in financing, so that there was a minimal valuta problem for the Soviets. In the first year all the $2-million construction was Soviet-financed, but in the second year $3-million worth of construction financing was shared 50–50, and in the third year the $5-million worth of construction work was 100 percent Longacre-financed. Longacre supplied an architect, an engineer, and 14 construction superintendents under the contract. A company member commented:

> We soon found that they did not want American apartments at all as the living conditions were such that three or four families had to occupy each apartment and they stated that this overcrowding was likely to obtain for some years to come in spite of the new apartments contemplated and under construction. They objected to providing a bathroom with each apartment; they did not want any hot water supply; they did not like the joist floor construction; they wanted brick walls 30 in. thick; they had no kiln-dried lumber; they wanted to use a cement mortar of 1–9 mixture instead of 1–3 in order to economize in cement; they had no check valves, no thermostatic traps, no automatic air valves so that hot water was the only method of heating that could be installed. When we got all through instead of having an apartment built in the American style we had plain Russian apartments the same as they were building themselves.[32]

Soviet architects during the 1930s had the responsibility of reflecting both Marxist ideology and modern technology (preferably American), and consequently had to strain after dual objectives.[33] Thus the principle of collectivization has influenced architectural development in housing, so that housing and cultural facilities reflect communal life rather than the individual. The large blocks of apartments constructed by Longacre achieved this objective. Factory kitchens, public bathing facilities, and communal clinics reflect the same objectives, and were also included in assistance agreements. Design had to reflect the dynamic features of a revolutionary society; therefore the advantages of standardization and simplification were consistent with this ideological objective. Some of the work of Le Corbusier, Wright, and modern European architects was consequently acceptable and referred to as the Soviet style, not because it was Russian but because it conformed to ideological prerequisites.

---

[32] *American Engineers in Russia*, Fisher material, anonymity of writer requested.
[33] See Arthur Voyce, *Russian Architecture* (New York: 1948), for an excellent summary of the philosophy of prerevolutionary and Soviet architecture.

Figure 16-2 LAYOUT OF NIZHNI-NOVGOROD (GORKI) CITY AND AUTOMOBILE PLANT, PREPARED BY THE AUSTIN COMPANY UNDER TECHNICAL-ASSISTANCE CONTRACT OF AUGUST 1929

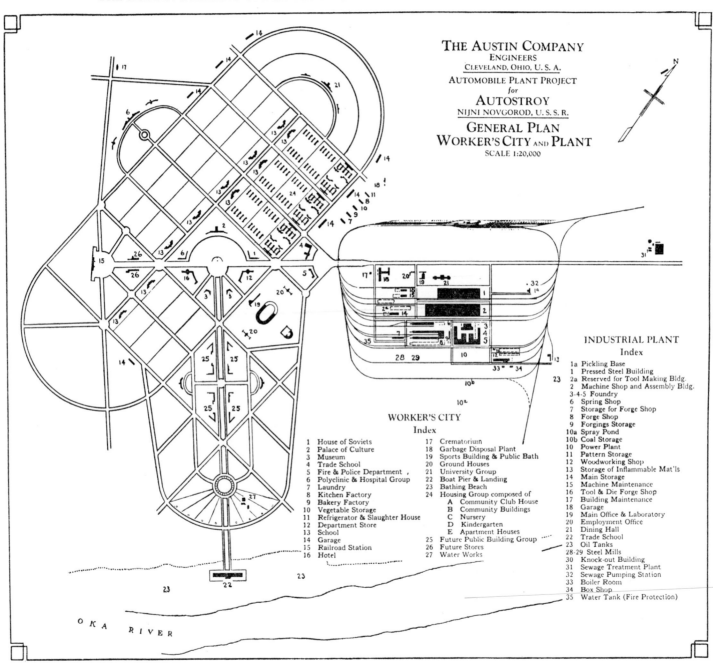

THE AUSTIN COMPANY
ENGINEERS
CLEVELAND, OHIO, U. S. A.
AUTOMOBILE PLANT PROJECT
for
AUTOSTROY
NIJNI NOVGOROD, U.S.S.R.
GENERAL PLAN
WORKER'S CITY AND PLANT
SCALE 1:20,000

WORKER'S CITY
Index

1 House of Soviets
2 Palace of Culture
3 Museum
4 Trade School
5 Fire & Police Department
6 Polyclinic & Hospital Group
7 Laundry
8 Kitchen Factory
9 Bakery Factory
10 Vegetable Storage
11 Refrigerator & Slaughter House
12 Department Store
13 School
14 Garage
15 Railroad Station
16 Hotel
17 Crematoriun
18 Garbage Disposal Plant
19 Sports Building & Public Bath
20 Ground Houses
21 University Group
22 Boat Pier & Landing
23 Bathing Beach
24 Housing Group composed of
      A   Community Club House
      B   Community Buildings
      C   Nursery
      D   Kindergarten
      E   Apartment Houses
25 Future Public Building Group
26 Future Stores
27 Water Works

INDUSTRIAL PLANT
Index

1a Pickling Base
1 Pressed Steel Building
2a Reserved for Tool Making Bldg.
2 Machine Shop and Assembly Bldg.
3-4-5 Foundry
6 Spring Shop
7 Storage for Forge Shop
8 Forge Shop
9 Forgings Storage
10a Spray Pond
10b Coal Storage
10 Power Plant
11 Pattern Storage
12 Woodworking Shop
13 Storage of Inflammable Mat'ls
14 Main Storage
15 Machine Maintenance
16 Tool & Die Forge Shop
17 Building Maintenance
18 Garage
19 Main Office & Laboratory
20 Employment Office
21 Dining Hall
22 Trade School
23 Oil Tanks
28-29 Steel Mills
30 Knock-out Building
31 Sewage Treatment Plant
32 Sewage Pumping Station
33 Boiler Room
34 Box Shop
35 Water Tank (Fire Protection)

OKA RIVER

Source: The Austin Co.

This argument does not conflict with the Longacre experience; the commentator felt he had been hired to build 'American style.' In fact, Longacre was hired to build the standard Soviet multistory communal apartment buildings but with American methods. These did not 'take' because the specialized materials and equipment required were not available, so that the Longacre Company and other foreign construction firms were forced to 'make do.'

DUPLICATION OF AMERICAN EXCAVATION EQUIPMENT

In return for equipment orders, American manufacturers often supplied the Russians with construction superintendents. When the Western equipment was later duplicated by the Russians, the superintendents were often asked to stay on and break in the Soviet-made duplicates.

One of these American superintendents was John E. Cook of the Ohio Locomotive Crane Company, sent to the U.S.S.R. by his company to erect, operate, and service cranes at the Dniepr Dam, Nizhni-Novgorod, and Kuznetsk.[34] Another was Gustav S. Bell, an engineer employed by Sauerman Brothers, Inc., of Chicago, who was in the Soviet Union for 20 months supervising the operation of equipment bought from Sauerman for construction of the canal and locks at Svirstroi.[35] Another superintendent at Svirstroi was Gustav A. Johnson, an engineer for Bucyrus Erie Company, employed to erect and start operation of Bucyrus steam shovels and grading machinery. Johnson also worked at the Magnitogorsk Iron and Steel Plant supervising excavation of the foundations and on a drainage project in Krasnodar.[36] The Thew Shovel Company of Lorain, Ohio supplied W. R. Parker to supervise excavation with its shovels at the Bobriki chemical combine.[37] Parker made the interesting comment that the work he supervised was continued day and night and that it was 'common knowledge' that the work was rushed so that the plant could produce poison gas.

The extensive use of foreign companies and their equipment in excavation work is exemplified in the Magnitogorsk iron and steel project—probably the largest single project undertaken in the U.S.S.R. in the period 1930–45. Table 16–2 gives a full list of excavating equipment used at Magnitogorsk; all

[34] U.S. State Dept. Decimal File, 861.5017—Living Conditions/240, Report No. 7623, Riga, April 10, 1931.

[35] *Ibid.*, 861.5017—Living Conditions/314, Report No. 7939, Riga, August 11, 1931. See chap. 19 for copying of Sauerman equipment.

[36] *Ibid.*, 861.5017—Living Conditions/200, Report No. 214, Riga, November 28, 1930. For other engineers and conditions at Svirstroi see /283, Report No. 7830, Riga, June 30, 1931.

[37] *Ibid.*, 861.5017—Living Conditions/349, Riga, October 16, 1931.

units are of either American or German manufacture. It was not until 1933 that early Soviet copies of this equipment began to appear in excavation work, and Lend-Lease import figures suggest that there was still a strong demand for excavation equipment in the 1940s.[38]

The extensive field tests of foreign equipment under Russian working conditions generated accurate data for evaluation and choice of models for duplication. American engineers themselves played a role in the selection process. Gorton, Chief Engineer for the Vaksh project in Central Asia, was assigned the task of preparing a mechanization plan for Glavklopkom. His main recommendation was that single units of American agricultural and construction equipment be 'purchased for study,'[39] as these had been thoroughly tested under 'practical conditions' in the United States and found to be successful.[40]

Table 16–2   ORIGIN OF ALL EXCAVATION EQUIPMENT
USED IN MAGNITOGORSK CONSTRUCTION

Name of Firm and Type of Excavator	Bucket capacity (Cubic Meters)	Number of Units
Electric		
Bucyrus 50-B	1.5	2
Oren-Koppel multi-bucket	—	1
Steam		
Bucyrus 3-B	0.5	1
Bucyrus 41-B	0.95	2
Marion 450	0.75	5
Marion 32	1.00	1
Oren-Koppel	1.00	1
Oren-Koppel (with grab bucket)	—	2
Meck and Gambrok-C	1.5	1
Meck and Gambrok M-U	1.5	1
Meck and Gambrok	0.75	1
With Internal Combustion Engine		
Oren-Koppel Type 6	0.75	1
Parson	—	1
Lubeck	—	1

Source: Magnitostroi, *Informatsionnyi Biulleten'* (Magnitogorsk: 1930) p. 64.

[38]   U.S. State Dept. *Report on War Aid Furnished by the United States to the U.S.S.R.*, p. 23.
[39]   W. L. Gorton, *The Mechanization of Excavation Work on Irrigation Canals and Drainage* (Tashkent, July 2, 1931), p. 36.
[40]   *Ibid.*

Gorton also investigated possible manufacturing facilities and for this purpose visited Rostov on the Don. He estimated that the new Selmashstroi plant could, after installation of the new equipment expected, manufacture Fresnos, wheel scrapers, Miami-type scrapers, Chattin-V-type diggers, and plows. Investigation of two smaller plants in Rostov, on Ilych and Pushkin streets, led to the conclusion these plants were not in a position to make even the simplest equipment. The Trust construction department shop was also not in a position to manufacture new equipment, although it could undertake repairs.[41]

So we find that American engineers were not only responsible for implementation of the First Five-Year Plan in such positions as Chairman of the Building Committee of Vesenkha, but that they also superintended such jobs as the operation of excavation equipment on site and the selection of construction equipment models for duplication in the new Soviet plants.

[41] *Ibid.*, p. 36.

CHAPTER SEVENTEEN

The Process of Technical Transfer: Firms, Engineers, and Institutions

FOREIGN FIRMS IN THE SOVIET UNION [1]

Most leading American corporations and many smaller firms have had trade or technical-assistance agreements with the Soviet Union, although these have generally not been made public. Documentation has survived in the State Department files, and it appears that many corporations either informed the Department of their intentions or worked very closely with the Department. No case has been found in the files, after about 1919, in which a U.S. company acted contrary to the expressed wishes of the Department. There is some evidence, not conclusive, that some companies, rather hesitant about negotiating a contract with the Soviet Union, were tacitly encouraged to do so by the Department.[2]

Insofar as Germany is concerned there was until 1941 a unified approach to Soviet trade, with the German Foreign Office playing a dominant role over individual German firms. It is surmised, but without archival evidence, that links between British firms and the British Government were also close; there is no question, for example, that compensation for the Lena Goldfields expropriation was achieved only by the refusal of the British Government to conclude a new trade agreement until the Lena question had been settled with some semblance of equity.

One generalization can be made: throughout the 1917–45 period, transfers of technology to the Soviet Union were made not only with the acquiescence of Western governments but with their approval and often encouragement. There is no question about the fact that the slightest sign of disapproval by

---

[1] This section is based primarily on the recorded experience of American firms. Experience of foreign firms (for example, Metropolitan-Vickers of the United Kingdom) was not significantly different.

[2] See Sutton, *Western Technology . . . , 1917 to 1930*, p. 347.

any Western government would have choked off such an agreement. Any credit or blame for these transfers must in the final analysis be placed with Western political circles and government administrators and not with private corporations.

BREACHES OF CONTRACT WITH FOREIGN FIRMS BY THE SOVIET UNION

The widely held assumption that the Soviet Government has not defaulted on commercial agreements with individual firms is inconsistent with evidence in the Decimal File and elsewhere. Almost all known concessions provide examples of gross breach of contract on the part of the Soviet Government;[3] there is a strong probability that other concessions did not publish their experiences for fear of ridicule. Expropriation utilized economic pressure; physical violence has been identified in very few cases. The Soviets were careful to cover expropriation with a façade of legality, and to this end numerous newspaper articles, a few books, comments by sympathetic businessmen, and court 'trials' were developed to weave a fabric of legality. Concession expropriations were, however, not the only examples of Soviet commercial default. Nonpayment of salaries, consultant's fees, and debts to private Western firms —and expropriation of patents, designs, drawings, prototypes, and equipment without payment—are also recorded in the Decimal File.[4]

One of the largest contracts concluded with an American firm was the McKee Corporation contract for construction of seven blast furnaces, some steel mills, and a town at Magnitogorsk. McKee maintained 80 American engineers on the project for one year and then cut the contract back to 'one unit':

> This happened because the Soviet Government was too inaccurate in the payments provided for in the contract. The McKee Company was compelled to draw up supplementary provisions according to which the Soviet Government was to make payments three months in advance. However, when the Government failed to comply with this provision, the firm of McKee stated that it would take advantage of its right to annul the contract and would recall all its personnel from Magnitogorsk within one month.[5]

The J. G. White Engineering Corporation of New York suffered monetary losses in two separate contracts with the U.S.S.R. The first breach involved

[3] See chap. 2.
[4] The writer has had access to *complete* corporate papers or documents based on corporate resources in only two instances. In both cases there was clear evidence of Soviet default.
[5] U.S. State Dept. Decimal File, 861.5017—Living Conditions/452, March 19, 1932, quoting *Zarya* (Harbin, China).

the comparatively small amount of $7,000 in nonpayment of expenses for railroad men whom the White Company had sent to the Soviet Union. This was similar to numerous other cases of nonpayment of expenses.[6] The second case was a more significant breach of contract. The Soviets requested the White Corporation to make a proposal for supervision of construction at Svirstroi Dam. The proposal submitted required a total payment of $975,000 with an advance retainer of $100,000 to protect White against contracts made with U.S. engineers hired for the project. The proposal was accepted by cable from Moscow and orally by Amtorg in New York, and, said White, 'Amtorg pressed us very hard to start designing work and get our men off before the retainer was received, which [delay] they explained on the basis of red tape. . . .'[7]

The White Corporation therefore, at Amtorg insistence, hired the engineers and started design work. As the White Corporation reported it, sometime later the Soviets 'advised us they had changed their plans and had decided not to engage us. . . .'[8] The Company claimed $400,000, comprising White's costs for 'the designing and organization work we had been prevailed upon by Amtorg to start here, notwithstanding we had not received our $100,000 retainer.'[9]

Amtorg offered $10,000; this was refused. Amtorg then raised its offer to $20,000; this was accepted by White Engineering 'because of our belief that Russian credit was insecure. . . .' The amount was promptly paid.

Thus on a claim of $400,000, of which $50,000 was out-of-pocket costs, White Engineering suffered a loss of $30,000 out-of-pocket expenses due to breach of contract by the Soviet Union, in addition to loss of the contracted work.

Treatment of foreign firms was clearly unethical in yet another way. Firms were played off one against another in an attempt to get free technical data and drawings in a manner usually amounting to fraud. The case of E. B. Badger & Sons and Alco Products is a good example. Both firms were negotiating with Mashinoimport for construction of a large oil refinery and had submitted bids in 1934 on construction and equipment.[10] Amtorg in New York invited both firms to send representatives to the Soviet Union for further negotiations with the declared intent of letting a construction contract. E. B. Badger said that Amtorg indicated that another firm would also be sending representatives, but Alexander M. Hamilton, Export Sales Manager of Alco Products, said he was told by Amtorg that Alco Products alone would be

---

[6]　U.S. State Dept. Decimal File, 861.602/252, December 31, 1930. See also chap. 3.
[7]　*Ibid.*
[8]　*Ibid.*
[9]　*Ibid.*
[10]　U.S. State Dept. Decimal File, 861.602/263.

sending representatives. Both principals brought two engineers to the U.S.S.R. and started separate negotiations with Mashinoimport in Moscow. The State Department report claims that:

> Mashinoimport took advantage of the competitive spirit between the two firms in order to obtain unusually detailed information regarding their manner of arriving at estimates and regarding the various processes and types of machinery which they proposed to employ.[11]

As neither firm wanted to prejudice its negotiating position, the information was freely provided by both companies. The Badger bid was $1.8 million, 25 percent to be paid in cash and the balance over four years; the Alco bid is not known. After some three weeks of negotiations in Moscow, each party was informed *independently, without knowledge of the other*, that if its bid was reduced by approximately 40 percent Mashinoimport would consider giving it the contract, paying for both the equipment and the work in cash. Both firms refused the offer and went to the U.S. Embassy on account of the attempted 40-percent reduction—not because they were then aware of unethical practices.

The U.S. Embassy reported both firms as indicating the lower prices would have meant a loss. Badger, for example, said 'his firm had prepared the estimates in the same manner as it would have prepared them for an American firm.'[12] Both Badger and Hamilton, reads the Embassy report, expressed indignation that when Amtorg had invited their respective firms to send representatives to Moscow it had not intimated that there was such a wide difference between the bid and the price the Soviet Government was prepared to pay. Hamilton said that the cost of the trip alone to Alco Products was $50,000 and that if Alco had known the Soviets could only pay such a small amount they would have dropped the matter.

As in other cases, the Soviets then demanded all drawings, documents, blueprints, technical descriptions, and similar material brought into the Soviet Union and viewed as confidential by both firms. Mr. Badger was informed that 'before departing from the Soviet Union he should leave these documents with Mashinoimport which would see that they were inspected by the customs authorities and sealed.'[13] Badger did not hand over his blueprints, no doubt having been forewarned of past Soviet appropriations. Some he burned and some handed over to the Embassy with a request that they be sent out in the diplomatic pouch or burned. Hamilton, on the other hand, handed over his documents to Charles H. Smith in Moscow.[14] The Soviet authorities

---

[11] *Ibid.*

[12] *Ibid.*

[13] *Ibid.*

[14] For the background of Charles H. Smith, of the American-Russian Chamber of Commerce, see Sutton, *Western Technology. . . , 1917 to 1930*, pp. 119, 284–5, and 289–90.

refused to allow Badger's assistant to be present during the 'customs' examination of the other documents, which lasted one and one half hours, 'during which period,' according to Badger, '. . . it would have been possible for most of the important documents to have been photographed.'[15]

.The Embassy report concludes:

> The Embassy is of the opinion that when Mashinoimport issued through Amtorg invitations to the two firms to send representatives to Moscow it believed that by offering to pay cash and by playing one bidder against the other it could obtain the plant at costs greatly below those set forth in the original estimates.[16]

The Embassy further comments that:

> . . . the type of questions put to Mr. Badger and [one of the engineers] by various Soviet engineers with regard to the machinery and processes which his firm proposed to employ led him to believe that the Soviet Government was considering, in case it could not obtain the desired reduction in price, the possibility of using Soviet engineers to build the plant and of purchasing abroad only those machines which could not possibly be manufactured in the Soviet Union.[17]

This question of Soviet expropriation of drawings and technical data occurred many times; indeed, one has the impression there was an almost compulsive intent to collect such material, although drawings by themselves, without material specifications and extensive backup data, would have had only limited usefulness.

The Radio Corporation of America had similar problems with drawings, even after the State Department obtained a promise from the Soviets to desist. In 1937 RCA engineers in Moscow were being searched and their documents and drawings retained for examination.[18] This was coupled with a refusal to let the engineers be present while the drawings were being examined.[19] A 1938 memorandum by George F. Kennan summarized Soviet intent; after pointing out that some Soviet practices aroused resentment, Kennan added:

> An example of these practices is provided by the efforts which are frequently made by Soviet officials to utilize business connections in order to get possession of foreign plans, charts and diagrams, by the use of which Soviet factories can themselves undertake production of commodities previously purchased abroad.[20]

---

15 U.S. State Dept. Decimal File, 861.602/263.
16 *Ibid.*
17 *Ibid.*
18 U.S. State Dept. Decimal File, 861.602/267 and 361.11—Employees/349.
19 U.S. State Dept. Decimal File, 36.11—Employees/349.
20 U.S. State Dept. Decimal File, 124.61/119.

Kennan pointed out that written assurances were given in 1937 that American nationals would be permitted to remain during examination of their possessions. He continued:

> Nevertheless in the current year [1938] we have witnessed the violation of these assurances in the case of engineers of the Radio Corporation of America working in the Soviet Union and the retention by Soviet authorities of drawings, plans, et cetera for periods long enough to permit copies to be made. There is good reason to believe that papers taken by Soviet authorities from American citizens have led to infringement of important American patents.[21]

The State Department did not protest in the RCA case, as the company did not want to alienate further orders from the Soviet Union.[22]

Another case of expropriation of drawings and patents was that of Joe Lavelle, a case which occupied the U.S. Embassy in Moscow from 1936 to 1939. Joe Lavelle, an inventor living in Montana, patented a railroad frog[23] in April 1931. Drawings and technical data were given to a Soviet representative, Ulanov, to consider use of the patent in the Soviet Union. That was the last Lavelle heard of his drawings and patent. Successive inquiries by the State Department over three years, through the Moscow Embassy, yielded only the response that the drawings could not be found.[24]

The common thread in these cases—White Engineering, E. B. Badger, Alco Products, RCA, and Joe Lavelle—and many others not here described is that the Soviets obtained technical information (particularly drawings) unethically and at the expense of the originator.[25]

DEFAULTS ON SALARY PAYMENTS TO FOREIGN ENGINEERS

There is considerable evidence that the Soviets defaulted extensively on payments to foreign engineers. This assertion, however, is modified by a clause in many individual contracts granting the Soviets a right to cancel the

---

[21] *Ibid.*

[22] U.S. State Dept. Decimal File, 124.61/134.

[23] U.S. Patent No. 1,802,057.

[24] U.S. State Dept. Decimal File, 861.542 Lavelle, Joe. *Subject: Protection in U.S.S.R. of Patent Right of Joe Lavelle, American Citizen, in a Railroad Frog.*

[25] For a few of numerous similar cases see U.S. State Dept. Decimal File, 861.541/1 (seizure of papers on manufacture of aluminum foil); 861.542/62 (copying Central Railway Signal Co. devices); 861.602/264 (Otis Elevator); 861.42761/65 (IBM); 861.42761/71 (National Cash Register); 861.544/5 (Universal Picture Corp. accuses Soviets of stealing story of *Once in a Lifetime*); and 124.61/134 (U.S. Embassy protest re engineer Wood in which Soviets retained his drawings and plans. Also see 361.11—Employees/349 and 124.61/118 and 119.

Such behavior is, of course, ethical under Communist philosophy as it advances world revolution; indeed, it would be grossly unethical for a Communist *not* to undertake such acquisitions if there were any chance they would advance the cause of Communism.

contract freely.[26] Those contracts examined by the writer are worthless from the viewpoint of protection of the foreign engineer; it is presumed that potential employees were so anxious to obtain business that insufficient care was taken to have contracts examined by competent lawyers in the United States or Germany before signature.[27]

During July and August 1931 a large number of such contracts were cancelled outright due to the valuta shortage. The exact number is not known 'but it is thought that it affected a very large number of persons employed in Russia, particularly Germans.'[28] Many contracts were broken unjustly but, so far as German workers were concerned, little was made public, as the German Government had a policy of not making trouble for the Soviets 'on behalf of these little people, [and] little was done in their behalf.'[29]

Many similar American cases were reported to the State Department; they include August Tross (a drilling superintendent in the Baku oil fields),[30] Mitchell N. Jordan,[31] George F. Hardy,[32] Balog,[33] Willard Gorton,[34] E. G. Puttmann,[35] Olson,[36] and others.

Also in the Departmental file are letters from legal firms in the United States on behalf of clients. For example, the New York lawyers Murphy and Fultz made inquiry in 1937 on behalf of a client engineer who was paid no

[26] See U.S. State Dept. Decimal File, 861.602/248.

[27] See Appendix A. See also U.S. State Department Decimal File, 861.5017—Living Conditions/537 and /771 for an example of an individual work contract. The Gorton contract (Appendix A) is one of the better contracts, yet Clause 13 give the Soviets the right to cancel 'at any time.'

[28] U.S. State Dept. Decimal File, 861.5017—Living Conditions/248.

[29] *Ibid.*

[30] U.S. State Dept. Decimal File, 861.5017—Living Conditions/771. Soviets 'did not keep conditions on payment.'

[31] *Ibid.*, 861.5017—Living Conditions/518. Jordan deposited $3,800 in Soviet bank but was not allowed to withdraw it.

[32] *Ibid.*, 861.5017—Living Conditions/458. 'After he had been working for five months the Soviet official in charge of employing foreign specialists sent for him and told him that his contract was broken and that they would no longer pay him in American dollars. He was offered a new contract in rubles. . . ." He had no funds to return to the U.S. and therefore had to accept.

[33] *Ibid.*, 361.11—Employees/291. The Soviets broke his contract. 'It is apparent from the statements made and the evidence submitted by Mr. Balog that the contracts offered by the Russian representatives in New York to American engineers etc. are tricky instruments which are not worth the paper upon which they are written, and that Americans who venture to Russia having faith in such contracts are bound to be very much disillusioned and to be put to great inconveniences and expense. . . .'

[34] See p. 34.

[35] *Ibid.*, 861.602/254. Ten engineers were dismissed on 'trumped-up charges.' One month later the remaining engineers had their dollar allowances cut.

[36] *Ibid.*, 861.5017—Living Conditions/423. 'Like so many others Mr. Olson complained that the Russians failed to live up to their contract with him and sought to evade it from the outset through technicalities.'

salary at all for the second year of his service with the Soviets.[37] The widespread nature of Soviet default on individual work contracts is indicated by the inquiry of a single Detroit attorney handling no fewer than 10 claims from former employees of the Stalingrad Tractor Plant. John L. Sullivan wrote the State Department, saying: 'I have about ten claims of former employees . . . and it appears to the writer that their contracts have been violated by the above named concern [Stalingrad Tractor Plant].'[38] The State Department referred attorney Sullivan to Congressman Fish for information on Amtorg and made no further comment.

Details of a single case will illustrate the personal hardship often caused by such Soviet defaults. In 1930 Homer Trecartin was hired by Sharikopodship-nikstroi (Ball-Bearing Construction Trust) as a consultant on the construction of a gigantic ball-bearing plant.[39] The one-year contract, dated March 17, 1930, was made with Amtorg, with the right of renewal at $20,000 per year to supervise construction of the Kaganovitch plant. Although it was agreed that his salary would begin in the U.S., with 60 percent of it to be deposited in dollars at the Chase Bank in New York and the balance payable in local currencies, Trecartin received no funds before sailing from New York to England on August 16, 1930. The Soviet Embassy in London then sent him to Italy to discuss equipment for the plant. At this point, September 1, he had received neither travel nor salary funds and so cabled Amtorg. Having received no reply by September 10, Trecartin then cabled Amtorg: 'FOUR TELEGRAMS TO WISHNEVESTSKY SINCE AUGUST 30 UNANSWERED ABSOLUTELY WITHOUT FUNDS SITUATION DISGRACEFUL CABLE TWO HUNDRED DOLLARS IMMEDIATELY.'

On September 22 he sent a further cable: 'NO MONEY RECEIVED SALARY LONG OVERDUE THREATENED ARREST EVICTION YOUR TREATMENT SCANDALOUS CABLE ME DIRECT IMMEDIATELY PALACE HOTEL MONEY AND FUTURE INTENTIONS.' Amtorg's answer to this cable was 'REMITTING FUNDS TOMORROW.'

Trecartin finally received $200; he was then owed $666, plus $1,000 which should have been deposited in New York, plus travel expenses. The point to be emphasized is that Trecartin was one of a small group of top consultants, a man of wide experience and first-rank qualifications. The treatment accorded lesser-ranking engineers, without even considering the fate of specialists and skilled workers, can be readily envisaged.[40]

[37]   *Ibid.*, 861.5034/59. See f.n. 40 (below) for State Department action.

[38]   *Ibid.*, 861.60/231.

[39]   *Ibid.*, 861.6511 Officine Villar-Perosa.

[40]   Trecartin asked the State Dept. to bring this matter to the attention of other engineers and several companies. There is no indication in the files that this was done. It could have been done informally but, if so, it had no impact, as this was one of the early agreements. One copy of the material was sent to the Dept. of Commerce marked 'Strictly Confidential,' but the State file was not declassified until the writer's application on May 19, 1967.

One rather small group of engineers tried to ingratiate themselves with the Soviet regime. It is suggested (there is no evidence either way) that this group may have been trying to substitute political ardor for their own technical deficiencies. One group of 16 engineers wrote articles favorable to the Soviet regime.[41] Sixty Germans, Americans, and others—mainly technicians—supplied letters favorable to Soviet propaganda image for publication.[42] A bond issue was promoted inside the Soviet Union by a group of U.S. specialists including Guy C. Riddell, Miles W. Sherover, William C. Aitkenhead, Atherton Hastings, and others.[43]

On the whole, however, American engineers were strictly nonpolitical and hardworking, tried to do their jobs and, as their writings show, were shocked at the privations of the Russian people. It is the misery and privation, rather than criticism of the Soviet system, which is reflected in the interviews and writing.[44] Some engineers, it is true, received Soviet rewards; the Order of the Toilers of the Red Banner was received by six U.S. engineers at the Dniepr Dam, but there was nothing political about this award so far as the recipients were concerned.[45] Several received the Order of Lenin and one—F. B. Haney—did become a Soviet citizen.

In general, there was little ideological sympathy attached by individual Americans to their contribution to Soviet development. There were ideological connections in the early 1920s (the 'arm's length hypothesis' is discussed in the first volume) and certain ideological links between American firms and the Soviet Union will be traced in *Western Technology and Soviet Economic Development, 1945 to 1965*, but these are relatively minor. The years 1929–32 witnessed the Great Depression in the United States; engineers went to the Soviet Union because they could not find work in the United States. Only a fraction could even be termed sympathizers. Most were disgusted by the brutality and coercion.

George Burrell, working for Grozneft (Georgian Oil Field Administration) is typical: 'I myself am no Communist, for if the Soviet dictatorship should be

---

[41] U.S. State Dept. Decimal File, 861.5017—Living Conditions/584 contains a translation of these articles sent to Washington, D.C.

[42] *60 Letters: Foreign Workers write of their Life and Work in the U.S.S.R.* (Moscow: 1936).

[43] Gorton Special Collection at Hoover Institution, Stanford University, Envelope 12.

[44] The interviews filed by the State Dept. under 861.5017—Living Conditions support this point at considerable length and in great detail. This is a superlative primary source for a study of living conditions in Soviet Russia during the time of the First Five-Year Plan.

[45] U.S. State Dept. Decimal File, 861.6463/62. The Order was awarded to Col. Cooper, Frank Pfeiffer, Murphy, Miles, Winter, and James Thompson. Banner recipients received a pension, free transport, rent reduction, and exemption from Soviet income tax if their income was not over 6,000 rubles per year; not a great advantage.

established here I would probably be chased down a back alley along with more affluent and wealthy people.'[46]

In the final analysis these American engineers could see what had happened to their professional confrères in Russia; they worked with 'prisoner engineers' and appreciated and even tried to lighten their burden.

Several engineers sent by firms were offered individual contracts to stay and work directly for Soviet organizations in order to copy foreign equipment. J. Urbanik, at the Stalin Auto Plant, reported that after copying several of the older Gleason machines the Soviets tried to enlist his assistance in copying a new Gleason gearmaking machine.[47] Emil Lutzweiler, employed by the Gogan Machine Company of Cleveland to install machinery for making automobile bumpers, was offered 650 rubles per month to sever his connections with Gogan and stay in the U.S.S.R.[48] In the field of automatic railroad signals, the Soviets were having trouble installing equipment copied from signal units covered by U.S. patents and offered John M. Pelikan '$100 per month more than he receives from his company if he will resign from it and enter into a personal contract with them for five years.'[49] There is nothing unethical about such offers, but they do illustrate the point that the Soviets probably had difficulties copying foreign equipment in a satisfactory manner.

There is a problem concerning reports by returning workers on Soviet conditions. One can find detailed reports from workers in the same industry—even in the same plant—at the same time, reporting quite opposite events and conditions. There is no question that this has led to confusion concerning the nature of Soviet technological development. For example, a toolmaker, Walter Wells, wrote an article for *American Machinist* in 1931 concerning his professional experiences in Moscow. All in all he produces three pages of favorable impressions, with hardly a single criticism of the Soviet way of life. His impressions are sufficiently detailed to indicate that, unless he were a complete liar, he was not at all unhappy and left for reason beyond his control.[50] On the other hand, most foreign engineers' reports in the State Department

---

[46]　G. A. Burrell, 'Life in a Soviet Town' (unpublished manuscript in the Hoover Institution, Stanford University). It is worthy of note that it was the smaller companies and individual engineers that contributed to the Fisher data *(American Engineers in Russia)*. No large company made a contribution.

[47]　U.S. State Dept. Decimal File, 861.797/37.

[48]　*Ibid.*, 861.5017—Living Conditions/441.

[49]　U.S. State Dept. Decimal File, 861.5017—Living Conditions/233.

[50]　Walter Wells, 'An American Toolmaker in Russia,' *American Machinist*, LXXV, November 26, 1931, pp. 816–18. A careful reading of this article leads to the conclusion that it may not have been written by a tool and die maker. Although some tool and die makers are well read I find it difficult to accept such phrases as 'delicate viands' and 'stipulation is precie in the contract.' No one except Mr. Wells has ever praised Russian sanitary facilities.

files describe bad conditions and give wholly unfavorable impressions of the Soviet system and standard of living at the same time as Wells.

These conflicting reports can, however, be reconciled. For example, in the Wells article, as in numerous books written in the 1930s favorable to the 'Soviet experiment,' attention is focused *only* on the favorable or that which can be interpreted favorably. This is the essence of Soviet censorship: only the favorable is reported. Objectivity reflects both good and bad aspects, and these must be blended for an accurate picture.

There is evidence that the Soviets tried to ensure that only favorable aspects would be reported by returning workers. However, in talking with State Department officials most—but not all—such workers felt they were safe enough to tell the truth as they saw it, so that the State Department files are understandably much closer to the truth than published material. There *was* an incentive, however, to present the Soviet line after return to the U.S.—the possibility of further employment: not a small consideration in the 1930's. A number of engineers, however, said they had been threatened by the OGPU, and there is evidence of OGPU activities inside the United States against American engineers who spoke too freely.[51]

In sum, there were several incentives to continue the Soviet line and very few incentives to tell the whole story concerning Soviet conditions. This interpretation is supported by the requests in both the State Department files and the Fisher material at the Hoover Institution for confidence and anonymity.[52]

SUITS BY GERMAN ENGINEERS AGAINST THE SOVIET UNION FOR BREACH OF CONTRACT

German as well as American engineers endured breach of employment contracts by the Soviet Union. The State Department contains an excellent report on applicable suits filed in the Prussian Labor Courts (Preussische Arbeits-Gerichte). This report was the result of an interview by the Berlin Consul General with Judge Tuchler, head of the press department of the court system, at the end of 1932.[53] Judge Tuchler estimated that there had been about 150 such suits filed between 1930 and 1932 in the Prussian Labor Courts,

---

[51] See V. A. Kravchenko, *I Chose Freedom* (New York: Scribner's Sons, 1946), p. 185. Information is given on how the NKVD controlled American engineers after their return to the U.S.

[52] The writer has honored these requests where made in the Fisher investigation at the Hoover Institution. These were private requests in a private investigation. The State Department material is public property and has been officially declassified; therefore similar requests made to State Department officials in the 1930s have not been recognized (with one exception in which the Department made adverse comments on an individual), and names are incorporated into this text.

[53] U.S. State Dept. Decimal File, 861.602/249, Report No. 1075, Berlin, December 19, 1932.

and that if all German engineers with grievances had filed, the number of suits would have amounted to several thousands.

According to Judge Tuchler the contracts varied greatly in content (this was also the case with American contracts), but 'the general impression which the judges in the German courts got from the suits was that there was a general tendency upon the part of the Russians not to observe their contracts.'[54]

German suits for breach of contract were directed at the Soviet Trade Delegation in Berlin; this organization, however, claimed that it was not responsible, as the contracts were in the names of various internal Soviet organizations. The German courts held that the Delegation had power of attorney, as the contracts had been signed in Berlin. Unfortunately, most Germans overlooked a clause which said that the Trade Delegation signature alone did not put the contract into effect. Thus the Soviets were able to insert further clauses in Moscow—and did so; the German engineers had no choice but to submit to the arbitrary new terms.

The chief basis for claims in the Prussian courts was nonsupport of German families remaining behind in Germany while the breadwinners worked in the Soviet Union. The contracts agreed that part of the salary, averaging about 150 marks per month, should be paid in Germany. Because of the valuta shortage, this arrangement was not welcome in Moscow, and ways were found to circumvent part-payment in foreign currencies. A common circumvention was to submit the contract to Vesenkha, where it was cancelled and an all-ruble contract arbitrarily substituted. These unilateral contracts placed German workers in an impossible position; they could not support their families, had no way of converting ruble salaries into marks in order to transfer funds back to Germany, and when they tried to return home the Soviets refused to pay return fares on the ground that the *Germans* were breaking the contract.

There was another less-common type of suit, in which German workers sued for the return of funds deducted from wage payments as 'voluntary' subscriptions to Soviet loans. When the German courts found evidence of pressure or breach of contract, they decided in favor of the German workers. The report concludes that 'most of these cases were settled amicably, the Russians agreeing to pay.' However, it is estimated that only about 10 percent of such breaches came to court; the greater number did not, therefore, receive compensation.[55]

INSTITUTIONAL INFLUENCES ON THE TRANSFERS

The influence of political forces and Western foreign offices on the transfer, and particularly its major vehicle—trade—is an important topic which can only be touched upon here.

[54] *Ibid.*
[55] *Ibid.*

No evidence exists in State Department or the German Foreign Office files to show an awareness of the links between trade, the transfer of technology, and ultimate Soviet objectives. Politicians and foreign office officials were apparently unaware of such links. Certainly German Foreign Office and U.S. State Department policy statements support the argument that the links were not recognized. The only evidence of such recognition is in the subsequent reluctance of Goering and Hitler to send weapons under development to the U.S.S.R. U.S. Navy officers also actively opposed Roosevelt's approval of battleships and destroyers for the Soviet Union; and the State Department did act in 1940 to stop transmission of technical data and aviation gasoline equipment after the Soviet invasion of Finland. These objections, however, were in reference to outright military goods. Nowhere, with two minor exceptions, does the evidence show recognition of the connection between ultimate Soviet objectives and the necessity for an industrial structure to fulfill these objectives.[56]

This has possibly been the result of a superficial definition of a strategic good: i.e., in terms of immediate military use rather than in terms of economic principle. A State Department memorandum argued that the Hercules Powder contract to supply nitrocellulose technology should be approved on the grounds that 'no munitions are involved but merely services.'[57] In 1934 Henry Morgenthau removed restrictions on trade with Russia (which had been imposed as a result of the dumping of goods in the United States) although the U.S. Government had evidence concerning forced-labor camps in the Soviet Union. If forced labor was used, then production costs would be artificially lowered. The general objective of all Western governments up to 1945, including Nazi Germany, was to encourage or at least not to hinder trade and its embodied technical transfers. The writer does not accept the argument that 'times were different' and that criticism of this view is hindsight. Soviet objectives were as plain in 1917 as they are today. The Communist Party has never been coy or reluctant to expand on its intentions regarding the capitalist world. Immediate operational or tactical aspects may be obscure, but never the long-term objectives. Neither have foreign Communist parties nor the Soviet Union denied the link between trade and military-strategic objectives; they are intimately linked in the dogma. On the other hand, we have seen since 1918 in major Western countries a pervasive mythology that the Soviets do not really mean what they say, or if they do, their objectives have no relationship to economic or industrial factors—particularly trade.

[56] Military Intelligence in the U.S. War Department hinted at such a link, as did a German Foreign Office memorandum in 1928. See Sutton, *Western Technology . . . 1917 to 1930, p. 11.*

[57] U.S. State Dept. Decimal File, 861.659 Nitrocellulose/4, reply from W. R. Castle.

In brief, the policies of all Western governments in regard to technological transfers between 1917 and 1945 were inconsistent with declared Soviet intentions regarding the Western world.

THE ROLE OF SOVIET NATIONALS IN THE UNITED STATES

While American engineers designed and supervised projects in the Soviet Union and American and European firms manufactured equipment for Russian plants, there was a counterpart flow of Soviet nationals to the United States and, to a lesser extent, to European countries. There were legal and illegal elements in this flow; only the legal elements are considered here.[58] Soviet nationals were sent abroad in large numbers to be trained; to acquire information, drawings and designs as part of study commissions; and to conduct negotiations for purchase of complete plants, equipment, and technical assistance.

The flow of Soviet nationals to the United States between 1929 and 1945 falls into three time periods. Between 1929 and 1931 there was heavy traffic to fulfill numerous technical-assistance agreements in force and to negotiate the purchase of equipment. This flow tapered off as Soviet supplies of hard currency declined. The second stage extends from 1934 to the Nazi-Soviet pact of 1939; Soviet engineers visited the U.S. for lengthy training but in more specialized activities: oil-refining, aviation, and military industries. The third stage came under the Lend-Lease program and included the training of Soviet personnel and the grant of engineering and technical information. An illegal acquisition known as Super-Lend-Lease may have been as important but is not here considered.[59]

In the 18 months between January 1, 1929 and June 15, 1930, just over 1,000 Soviet nationals arrived in the United States (see table 17–1); only four (Soviet wives joining their husbands) came for personal reasons. Eighty-one percent (or 842) came for training courses under technical-assistance contracts with American firms or for purposes related to such contracts. Just over 13

---

[58] The illegal flow of information has been extraordinarily large. See David J. Dallin, *Soviet Espionage* (New Haven: Yale University Press, 1956), pp. 103–2. The history of this aspect remains largely unwritten. It may be inferred from an official F.B.I. statement, 'The facts are that Soviet agents for three decades have engaged in extensive espionage against this country, and through the years have procured a volume of information which would stagger the imagination' and '[a] large group of Soviet-bloc officials stationed in the United States has systematically over the years developed a most important part of the modern intelligence machine which was referred to by one Soviet official as the best industrial spying system in the world. Volumes could be written as to the techniques used. . . .' [U.S. Senate Judiciary Committee, *Exposé of Soviet Espionage*, 86th Congress, 2nd session, May 1960 (Washington, D.C.: 1960), pp. 1 and 5.]

[59] See Jordan, *op. cit.*, p. 265.

percent had business in relation to the purchase of U.S. equipment, and only an insignificant 1.2 percent (or 12 individuals) came in connection with sale of Soviet products in the United States. It is clear that about 99 percent of the Soviet nationals came in relation to some phase of the transfer of U.S. technology to the Soviet Union.

This group has been further examined in regard to declared interests: i.e., the industrial sector they visited while in the United States. It was found that more than 46 percent were interested in automobiles, tractors, and aviation equipment, about 13 percent were in the machinery sector, 7 percent were in mining, and the remainder were scattered over the whole range of U.S. industry. It is interesting to note that some Soviet entrants gave rather unimaginative false reasons for their visits; this suggests that the percentages may not be wholly accurate. For example, Petr Kushnarev declared to immigration officials that he came to study agricultural equipment, although his destination was Pratt & Whitney, manufacturers of aircraft engines.[60] Anatoli Bariantinsky similarly gave study of agricultural machinery as his reason for a visit to the Ex-Cell-O Aircraft Corporation.[61]

On the whole, Soviet visits to American plants in 1929–30 did not occasion too much concern. Large groups of Soviet workers and foremen came for training—particularly to Ford Motor Company in Detroit and General Electric in Schenectedy. Smaller groups of Soviet engineers went to other companies for specialized training. Of these, 24 Soviets went to Sperry Gyroscope Company for training in searchlight manufacture; 10 went to the A. J. Brandt Company in connection with reconstruction of the Yaroslavl truck plant; another 10 went to Roberts and Schaefer, the coal-mine consultants; and smaller groups went to the Seabrook Company for training in road construction, the Du Pont Company in connection with nitric acid manufacture, American Locomotive and Car Works for locomotive construction, Newport News for turbine construction, and the Powers Company concerning office equipment. The largest group in the 1929–30 period was probably at Ford Motor Company; 81 Soviet engineers and technicians have so far been identified as resident at the Ford Detroit plant.

Concern grew after 1936–7, when Soviet emphasis in technical acquisitions shifted more overtly to military-related industries: oil refineries, aviation engines, aircraft, and radio communications equipment. At the same time, pressure grew to acquire far more data in these fields than had been agreed upon; indeed, sometimes such data could not be supplied at all. From about

---

[60] U.S. Congress, *Investigation of Communist Propaganda*, 71st Congress, 2nd session, Special Committee to Investigate Communist Activities in the United States. Part 3, Vol. 3 (Washington, D.C.: 1930), p. 194.

[61] *Ibid.*, p. 184.

1936 to 1941 there was a continuing battle between individual American firms, the Navy and War Departments, and Soviet engineers attempting to gain access to off-limits areas of plants, to send more engineers and observers than agreed, or to obtain information beyond that contractually stipulated.

Table 17–1   DECLARED PURPOSE OF SOVIET NATIONALS
ARRIVING IN U.S., JANUARY 1, 1929 TO JUNE 15, 1930

Purpose	Jan. 1 to Dec. 31, 1929 (12 Months)	Jan. 1 to June 15, 1930 (6 Months)	Total Number	Percent of Total Number Arriving
Visiting U.S. firms under technical-assistance contracts	157	268	425	40.9
Taking training courses in U.S. plants or studying U.S. industries	302	115	417	40.1
Purchasing equipment in U.S.	65	74	139	13.4
Other (including Amtorg personnel)*	19	27	46	4.4
Selling Soviet products in U.S.	8	4	12	1.2
Totals	551	488	1,039	100.0

Source: Based on data submitted by P. Bogdanoff (President of Amtorg Trading Company) to the Special Committee to Investigate Communist Activities in the United States. U.S. Congress, *Investigation of Communist Propaganda,* Part 3, Vol. 3 (Washington, D.C.: 1930).
* No personal travel, except four Soviet wives joining their husbands in the U.S.; balance are Amtorg and Vesenkha personnel.

The Douglas Aircraft Company provides a good example of these disputes. Its experience was typical and repeated wherever the writer has been able to discover information concerning activities of Soviet engineers. The Douglas 1936 technical-assistance and sales agreement allowed five (later eight) Soviet engineers to observe in the Douglas plant. These engineers were defined as production men, but it was understood that a group of Soviet inspectors would also be sent to check out DC-3s under construction on Soviet account. Five production men were indeed sent—but also 13 unannounced Soviet design engineers. This latter group contained some interesting names. One was M. Gurevich: probably the mathematician and designer of the MIG fighter (the 'G' in MIG). Another was Miasishchev: a seaplane designer. Lisunov, another design engineer, later gave his name to the Douglas DC-3 in the U.S.S.R.—first called the PS-84 and later the LI-2 and LI-24. Later in 1937, a group of three visitors at Douglas included a P. I. Baranov, introduced to Douglas as a chief engineer; a P. I. Baranov was also director of the aviation industry in the U.S.S.R.

In sum, although the five inspectors remained one year, numerous other permit applications by Amtorg were granted, so that there were no fewer than 77 Soviet engineers (excluding interpreters) in the Douglas plant: at least 20 at one time.

Douglas also had major problems with the Soviet inspectors. In March 1938 Stratton complained to Rosoff, President of Amtorg, that no parts were getting through inspection and that unusually rigid requirements were holding up shipment; in fact the inspectors demanded something for which they had not contracted. Stratton pointed out that Douglas had been led to believe that the parts were to be used in the Soviet Union in the manufacture of airplanes; but the inspectors argued that they were for instruction purposes in those Soviet plants where the DC-3 was to be built, and therefore had to be of a higher standard, and were in fact special parts.[62]

In February, Conant, Douglas's Production Chief, wrote an ironic letter to the GUAP Commission protesting such arbitrary inspection and pointing out that scratches occurred on aluminum panels because 'airplane parts are made by man on machinery and not laid like eggs by an Easter Rabbit.'[63] Added Conant, 'I still believe that somebody must have been in earnest when you bought these planes. . . . That wasn't stage money you gave us . . . we don't make these parts for our amusement, we actually use these contemptible pieces of metal to build damned good airplanes that actually fly. . . .'[64]

Conant's letter had little effect. In August, Douglas routinely informed Amtorg that two DC's had scratches in the aluminum center section corrugation but that these, according to standard practice, had been 'doubled' and passed inspection. Promptly, and predictably, Amtorg came back demanding a 'substantial discount.' The affair was settled only when Douglas gave a lifetime guarantee for the planes.[65]

There was a major problem with the attempt to gain unauthorized access to other U.S. plants.[66] The Soviets tried to gain access to the Consolidated Aircraft plant at San Diego under their technical-assistance agreement, although this was not, and could not be, included in the contract. Ambassador Troyanovsky wrote to Kelley, Chief of the East European Division of the State Department, asking him to expedite such permission and suggesting that it would do no harm, 'particularly since we can build similar airplanes only in the distant future.'[67] Troyanovsky also asked for the blueprints to be

62　Douglas Company Files, *Amtorg Outgoing Prior to 1939*, March 7, 1938.
63　*Ibid.*, February 1938.
64　*Ibid.*
65　*Ibid.*, Telegram, August 9, 1938.
66　As Kilmarx summarized this problem, 'Wherever controls existed the Soviet Government attempted to circumvent them. . . .' [R. A. Kilmarx, *op. cit.*, p. 86.]
67　U.S. State Dept. Decimal File, 711.00111, Armament Control/584, March 23, 1937.

delivered *with* the PBY-1 under construction and not later. Access was denied to the plant on grounds that 'particular equipment cannot be effectively isolated' and that a group of seven Soviet engineers had recently been conducted through the plant.[68]

In 1940 RCA queried the State Department concerning termination of that part of its agreement allowing training of Soviet engineers at the RCA Camden (New Jersey) plant, 'in view of the rise of anti-Soviet feeling.'[69] This suggestion was supported by Mr. Fly, Chairman of the Federal Communications Commission, who expressed doubts concerning the wisdom of allowing Soviet engineers to continue at the Camden plant.[70] A memorandum in the State Department European Affairs Division concluded, however, that it would be 'unfortunate' to request RCA to cancel.[71]

Another aspect of the Fish Committee data on Soviet nationals visiting the United States in 1930 is worth special mention. In a number of cases visits were made to U.S. firms where there was no other record of a technical-assistance agreement or large sale of equipment. For example, in the first six months of 1930, Soviet nationals are reported to have visited Richard Brothers in Detroit; the Accounting and Tabulating Machine Company; Oliver Farm Equipment; Kalitt Products, Inc.; Arthur Nickel Company of Cleveland; Yukon Fur Farms, Inc., of Petersburg, Alaska; Burd Piston Ring Company of Rockford, Illinois; Pontiac Engineering Company; John Deere Company; Bethlehem Shipbuilding; American Can Company, and the Pennsylvania Railroad. No source states that these companies had any form of technical-assistance agreement with the Soviet Union. It is obvious that the visits in question were important as they were cited by the Soviet nationals as the reason for entering the United States. In some cases, a group of Soviets were received; five went to the Pennsylvania Railroad, four to John Deere, three to Burd Piston Ring, five to the Arthur Nickel Company, and so on.[72] As this data covers only a six-month period, the proposition is suggested that many technical-assistance agreements are still to be revealed and that this three-volume study may well only scratch the surface.[73]

---

[68] *Ibid.*

[69] U.S. State Dept. Decimal File, 861.74 RCA/33, December 4, 1940.

[70] *Ibid.* Also see 861.74 RCA/30–39 concerning entry of Soviet nationals into the Camden plant and the problems created. (Item /30½ is missing; item /31 is still classified). This was similar to attempts to gain entry to the Douglas plant at Santa Monica.

[71] U.S. State Dept. Decimal File, 861.74 RCA/30.

[72] U.S. Congress, *Investigation of Communist Propaganda*, p. 183.

[73] *Ibid.* Another aspect worth noting is the existence of a Chelyabinsk Tractor Plant office in the Union Trust Building in Detroit. In the first six months of 1930 alone, no less than 33 Soviet nationals stated this office was the objective of their visit.

The length of stay in the United States generally varied between three and twelve months. Few cases were found in which the stay extended beyond one year. A 10-percent sample was taken (by the writer) of all arrivals in 1929, and six to twelve months was found to be the average duration in the United States. Short stays of one to three months' duration involved sales of Soviet products and purchase of equipment.

HIGH-LEVEL TECHNICAL ACQUISITION VIA DIPLOMATIC CHANNELS

One avenue of technical acquisition, obviously reserved for processes difficult to obtain by other means, was to appeal directly to the U.S. Department of State. For example, in February 1939, Umansky, Chargé d'Affaires in the U.S., indicated a desire to have

> . . . blueprints, specifications and photographs of certain machinery employed by the United States Army Corps of Engineers in the construction of Fort Peck and Sardis dams, and . . . the manufacture by the General Electric Company of exhaust driven turbo superchargers. . . .[74]

In response Secretary of State Hull forwarded drawings, photographs, and specifications used in construction of the dams but indicated that both the Navy and War Departments objected

> on the grounds of military secrecy . . . to the acceptance by the General Electric Company of any order from a foreign source involving the development and manufacture of an exhaust driven turbo supercharger for use on an internal combustion engine.[75]

Another example of a high-level approach to technical-data collection resulted from the successful use of new rescue equipment by the U.S. Navy to save 33 members of the U.S. Submarine *Squalus*, sunk on May 23, 1939 off Portsmouth, N. H. Within two months Chargé d'Affaires Chuvakhin informed the Secretary of State that the U.S.S.R. was 'impressed by the effectiveness of the rescue equipment developed by the United States Navy . . . which may be looked upon as a humanitarian rather than a military development,' was desirous of obtaining 'as much information as is available' conerning the use and construction of the Rescue Bell and Momsen Lung and training of personnel in use of the equipment,[76] and was prepared to purchase these items. On October 26, 1939, the Secretary of State forwarded a pamphlet

---

[74]   U.S. State Dept. Decimal File, 711.00111, Armament Control/1525. The writer conjectures that the Soviets really wanted only the G. E. supercharger design, were unable to get it, and included it in a 'package request' to the State Department, hoping that this would receive more favorable attention.

[75]   *Ibid.*

[76]   U.S. State Dept. Decimal File, 711.00111, Armament Control/2053, August 24, 1939.

entitled *Submarine Safety-Respiration and Rescue Devices*, which the U.S. Navy said contained the required information.[77]

RUSSIAN SCIENCE AND WESTERN TECHNOLOGY

After the Revolution, numerous Russian engineers found their way to the United States and started life anew, finally becoming American citizens. Although one would expect these Russians to have little sympathy for the Soviet regime it appears that considerable assistance was given to the Soviets by some of the more successful of these exiles.

It was argued in the previous volume[78] that Russia had a group of highly talented aircraft designers before the Revolution; most of them later came to the U.S. Igor Sikorsky became a leading designer of flying boats in the United States: his chief engineer was Michael Gluhareff, and Serge Gluhareff was his structural designer. The Sikorsky amphibian was sold to the Soviet Union.[79] Alexander de Seversky headed another group of prominent Russian aircraft designers, including M. Gregor, A. Kartvelli, A. Toochokoff, A. Pishvanov, S. Tchemesoff, and P. A. Samoilo. In 1937 Seversky received from the Russians a $370,000 contract for manufacturing rights and two model Seversky amphibians.[80]

Vladimir N. Ipatieff was equally prominent as a chemist. His personal history suggests that although the Soviet system is certainly well-designed to absorb Western technology it has weaknesses in the application of Russian scientific research to practical production.

Ipatieff was a great chemist by any standard. His work in catalysis and promoters and particularly in their application to petroleum technology ranks among the very finest of scientific achievements. Ipatieff was also a general in tsarist Russia. During World War I, while in charge of the Russian chemical industry, he built it up to the point of independence from Germany. Under the Soviet Government he continued his work toward the development of a chemical industry and, as laboratory facilities were lacking, he was allowed the extraordinary privilege of working several months of each year in Germany. Ipatieff had more than 300 publications to his credit, in addition to dozens of prizes, and was the only individual ever to hold membership in both the Russian National Academy of Sciences and the National Academy of Sciences in the United States.[81]

---

[77] *Ibid.*
[78] Sutton, *Western Technology . . . 1917 to 1930*, p. 259.
[79] *Time*, June 14, 1937.
[80] *Ibid.*
[81] American Institute of Chemists, *Vladimir N. Ipatieff, Testimonial in Honor of Three Milestones in His Career*, November, 1942. See also V. N. Ipatieff, *op. cit.*

In 1930 Ipatieff left the Soviet Union and came to the United States, where he worked first for Universal Oil Products, which built parts of the Ufa refinery, and then at Northwestern University. When he refused to return to the U.S.S.R. the Soviet Government withdrew his Russian citizenship, expelled him from the Academy of Sciences, and had him publicly denounced as 'an enemy of the people.'[82]

The history of Ipatieff and others such as Sikorsky, Ostrimilenski, and de Seversky must be kept in mind in any study of Western technology in relation to Russia. It is *not* that Russian talent is lacking;[83] indeed there appears to be an affinity between Russian scientists and certain theoretical and research areas in mathematics and physics. The heart of the problem is the great weakness of totalitarian systems in the application of scientific advance to the industrial structure in any rational manner. No chemist, nor indeed any scientist, of Ipatieff's stature has emerged during the 50 years after the Bolshevik Revolution, despite the enormous funds poured into science and the comparatively comfortable conditions in which scientists live and work.

The experience of Ipatieff and his fellow emigrés in the United States then suggests that the weakness is not in Russian scientific talent, but in a coercive system which stifles scientific achievement and provides no means for the rational application of technical progress.

[82]   It is a tribute to the courage of Russian scientists that only 62 of the 100 members of the Russian Academy came to vote and six dared even to vote against Ipatieff's dismissal.

[83]   As suggested by Werner Keller, *Ost minus west = null* (Munich: Droemersche Verlagsanstalt, 1960).

CHAPTER EIGHTEEN

The Process of Technical Transfer: Propaganda, Standardization and Duplication

THE 'INABILITY HYPOTHESIS' AND THE REQUIREMENT FOR PROPAGANDA

ABSENCE of detailed Soviet or foreign writing concerning *implementation* of construction work, except generalities on 'socialist construction,' leads to an examination of motives for this gap and a survey of the available evidence on the implementation process.

There are numerous Soviet publications with construction photographs published before 1934. Some 17 books in Western languages originated within the Soviet Union, together with various illustrated descriptions of construction during the First Five-Year Plan. A large multi-volume series[1] published between 1930 and 1934 has numerous pictures of construction, although few details are given. It is interesting to note, and explainable in terms of our study, that such publications were not issued after 1934.

When these publicized projects are identified and compared with data contained in this study, two ideas become evident: first, that each major project described in the Soviet publications utilized foreign assistance, equipment, and technology; and second, that actual construction generally took place between 1929 and 1934. Although the plan started in 1928 and was announced in mid-1929, contracts for construction were not let until 1929–30. Foreign engineers arrived on site a few months later. They noted only a small amount of ineffective preliminary work. For example, even Amtorg comments on the Stalingrad Tractor Plant:

> While preliminary work on the site of the Stalingrad Tractor Plant had been conducted for some time, the actual work on the construction of the principal departments started only in June when the plans arrived from the United States. . . .[2]

[1] *U.S.S.R. in Construction.*
[2] Amtorg, *op. cit.*, V, No. 7 (April 1, 1930), pp. 134–5.

This was three years after work at Stalingrad had started.

The backward nature of early Soviet efforts may be illustrated by several examples. These support an 'inability hypothesis': the Soviets were unable to implement construction of the First Five-Year Plan until foreign engineers arrived.

The Svir Dam was started in 1922—the first large Soviet power project. Although it was designed and intended to be built by Russian engineers, work was continually delayed from 1922 until the early 1930s due to the inexperience of Soviet designers. It was ultimately patterned on the Keokok Dam on the Upper Mississippi River in Iowa and was built with extensive Western technical assistance. As such, it is an excellent example of the 'inability hypothesis.'[3] There is no question that the Soviets reduced Western assistance on the Svir project as much as possible, that it took 10 years to get Svir into operation, and that the project ultimately required Western help.

Again at the Baku hydroelectric project we find a similar situation. The problem was well summarized by a Badger Company engineer working at Baku:

After working four years, spending in the neighborhood of four million dollars building the concrete flume to by-pass the river, all the auxiliary pump houses, the main pump house and installing all the machinery it was found they had no rock bottom on which to build the dam. . . .[4]

The 1926 Ford Delegation visited a proposed factory near Rostov and suggested it was nearer realization than Stalingrad, as 'a field office had been built and the buildings had been staked out.'[5] Several groups of engineers were working out details of various departments. These men all worked with American technical magazines and books as guides. The pressed-steel work specialist whose drawings were examined had not much practical experience, judging from the design of a blanking and perforating die which was faulty in several respects.[6]

A Stalingrad tractor plant to produce 10,000 tractors a year was also begun in 1926. The Ford Delegation said it was offered to them as a concession, but the Soviets were very vague about details. The Delegation was shown a picture of the plant, but when questions were raised about a number of tall chimneys the Soviets backed off and dropped the question.[7]

[3] U.S. State Dept. Decimal File, 861.5017—Living Conditions/283. See also Sutton, *Western Technology . . . , 1917 to 1930*, p. 201–2.

[4] *American Engineers in Russia*, Folder 3, Item 27.

[5] *Report of the Ford Delegation to Russia and the U.S.S.R.*, p. 53.

[6] *Ibid.*

[7] *Ibid.*, p. 52. A tractor plant in popular imagination might be thought of as having tall chimneys. In practice such chimneys are associated with smelting operations, which are not usually associated with tractor assembly. The reception of the Ford Delegation is reminiscent of the legendary Potemkin villages in the time of Catherine the Great.

Similar evidence of technical inability may be found in reports in the Soviet press. It was reported in 1929,[8] some 12 years after the Revolution, that 10 sugar plants in the Ukraine were still in a state of 'technical preservation,' i.e., capable of being operated but without the necessary managerial and engineering talent. Other examples will be found throughout this volume; an excellent instance is the Chelyabinsk Tractor Plant, which was started as a copy of the packaged Stalingrad plant but ran into such extraordinary problems that American engineers were called in to provide solutions.[9]

Moreover, the official review of the first year of construction, before Western companies entered the U.S.S.R., indicates a miserable picture. Gosplan, in reviewing the first year, 1928–9, entered the vague conclusion that '1928–9 was a year of increased creative revolutionary activity of the masses in town and country, the most important manifestation of which was socialist emulation.'[10]

Table 18–1 summarizes selected evidence concerning construction start dates and the introduction of Western skills.

Table 18–1   PREMATURE CONSTRUCTION STARTS ON SELECTED PROJECTS

Project	Construction Start	Source of Information
Turkmenistan irrigation	Davis arrived September 1929; work had earlier been started at four locations and stopped at three.	Gorton Special Collection, Hoover Institution, letter from Davis.
Selmashstroi (Agricultural Equipment Plant) Stalingrad Tractor Plant AMO Truck Plant	Ford Delegation of 1926 noted attempts to start each of these projects. Ground was marked out for the first two, and new equipment was idle for AMO truck plant.	*Ford Delegation Report (1926)*, pp. 49, 52–53.
Krivoi Rog Iron and Steel Plants	Project established about 1927 by Gipromez; described as 'inadequate' by U.S. consultants (Perin and Marshall).	Farquhar Papers, Box 4, Folder 3.
Dniepr Dam	Work started on site in 1926.	
Uralmash	Announced start February 1, 1927; actual start 1930.	*U.S.S.R. in Construction*, No. 9, p. 18.
Kuznetstroi	Plans ready 1928. Site still covered with grass in mid-June 1930.	Frankfurt, *op. cit.*, p. 26.

[8] *Pravda*, No. 98, April 28, 1929.
[9] See p. 188.
[10] *Izvestia*, No. 195, August 25, 1929.

It is therefore concluded that the Soviet Union actually started to work on projects of the First Five-Year Plan as early as 1926, but cautiously, doubting its own ability, and very wisely without publicity. The utter lack of internal technical resources for such a gigantic move forward became apparent about early 1929 and is well-described by Rykov:

> Money alone is insufficient for new construction work . . . we now have to make great efforts to assimilate West European and American technique . . . the utilization of foreign scientific technical experience in the course of the five year period is bound to attain immeasurable larger dimensions. It is not very often realized to what extent the utilization of foreign technique is needed . . . when our own new cadres have matured . . . the need for foreign specialists will decrease. But now . . . such measures as engaging only a few hundred foreign specialists will not solve the problem.'[11]

Rykov presents the example of artificial silk:

> . . . for instance . . . the production of artificial silk. . . . Here we are struggling no end with the thing, but are still unable to design and draw up a proper plan or form a sensible idea of a plan. Whereas abroad this branch of industry, notwithstanding all the obstacles resulting from the private ownership, is developing very rapidly. With us this branch might develop with immeasurably greater rapidity, but nevertheless we have shown ourselves as weak as children.[12]

This problem, a fundamental one, as suggested by Rykov, is therefore dubbed the 'inability hypothesis'; i.e., without assistance from capitalist countries the Soviet Union would not have had the technical resources to make any economic progress during the 1930s and 1940s.[13]

Realization of inability coincided with economic censorship. Increasingly tight censorship and increasing propaganda from 1927 onwards are directly related to this fundamental problem. In other words, the raison d'être for Soviet propaganda and censorship in the economic field was to conceal the prime role of capitalist technology in Soviet economic progress.[14]

[11] *Pravda*, No. 94, April 24, 1929.
[12] *Ibid*.
[13] Similar arguments were made by contemporary engineers; for example, John R. Westgarth, a British engineer employed by the Soviets as an inspector on the work of other foreign engineers, said: 'The ultimate objective of the Five Year Plan was to compass by economic warfare the destruction of the capitalist world. This became clear to anyone taking part in the working of the plan, but one of the things man had to learn was that the Communists simply had not the brains to carry out the gigantic task to which they had set their hands.' [John R. Westgarth, *Russian Engineer* (London: Denis Archer, 1934).] A careful reading of Westgarth's book suggests that the Soviets skillfully utilized his luke-warm attitude towards things non-British as a means to check on the work of other foreign engineers.
[14] For a fascinating explanation of other factors involved see Leon Herman, *Varieties of Economic Secrecy in the Soviet Union* (Santa Monica: The RAND Corporation, December 1963) (Report No. P-2840).

The problem of inability was compounded by the lack of technically trained men who were at the same time members of the Communist Party. To retain Party control it was essential that at least the directors of combinats should be Party members. To overcome the problem of technical inadequacy, the Party was forced to appoint to responsible technical positions Party members with no technical training whatsoever, irrespective of the consequences for efficiency and production. As noted in the previous volume, when there was a conflict between economic efficiency and Communist Party control, the Party always, without exception, took precedence.

Thus, most directors of combinats and large construction projects in the early 1930s were nontechnical party men, replaced only gradually with hastily-trained Party members. The director of the Karsak Pai copper mines had been a schoolteacher immediately prior to his appointment.[15] The director of the Stalingrad Construction Trust had been a barber immediately prior to his appointment to Stalingrad.[16] The backgrounds of the construction chiefs at Magnitostroi and Kuznetstroi, both top-priority projects, suggest the technical limitations facing the Soviets. Frankfurt, appointed Chief of Construction for Kuznetstroi on May 30, 1930, was a textile man, and by his own admission he 'had only a most perfunctory notion of metallurgy and particularly of Kuznetstroi. . . .'[17] At the same time J. P. Schmidt, also from the textile industry, was appointed Chief of Construction at Magnitogorsk. Both were Party members. These men could not make any contribution whatsoever to construction[18] but had impeccable Party credentials.

The cost of these nontechnical Communist Party functionaries to Soviet economic development was great. Time after time technical decisions were made on the basis of dogma; economic and engineering rationality were abandoned. Ideological solutions to technical problems sometimes had disastrous consequences. Geologist Ussov, in charge of exploration of Siberian iron ores in the late 1920s and early 1930s, was insistent that the projected Kuznetsk iron and steel complex could not be maintained on existing ore deposits. This conclusion was ridiculed by the Party. Frankfurt, the ex-textile-mill operator and Director of Kuznetstroi, stated:

> He [Ussov] was requested to come to Kuznetsk. Swamping us with geological terminology, references to world practice and science, Professor

---

[15] U.S. State Dept. Decimal File, 861.5017—Living Conditions/323.
[16] Lyons, *op. cit.*, p. 353.
[17] Frankfurt, *op. cit.*
[18] The author has had the opportunity to spend some six months in and around iron and steel plants combined with some metallurgical training, but would consider himself totally unable to contribute anything to the planning of such a plant; it would be problem enough to read the blueprints. Obviously an ex-textile operator would have less capability.

Ussov persistently tried to persuade Bardin and me that the deposits at Telbiss and Temir-Tau were not and could not be greater than the twelve to fifteen million tons that were already known. In his opinion prospecting for more ore in that region was a stupid waste of time and money.[19]

Poor Ussov was probably accused of being a 'wrecker' and a 'counter-revolutionary,' but in 1939 nature and Professor Ussov had the final word: Telbiss ran out of ore. The Temir-Tau deposits were more trouble than they were worth; they had .03 percent zinc content—treacherous to furnace linings.

It is therefore understandable that Party propagandists responsible for publicizing socialist progress were not always technically very sophisticated. One photograph, with the caption 'Testing an Airplane Motor,' shows a worker about to swing the propeller of an aircraft engine, obviously with the intention of starting the engine.[20] Unfortunately, the engine is mounted on a steel trolley, with four wheels; if the engine *had* started—worker, propeller, engine, and four-wheeled trolley would have gone on an eventful trip. Again, it was claimed that the turbo-generators of the Shatura generating plant were 'made in the U.S.S.R';[21] a picture of the generator casing showed prominently displayed the well-known symbol § of the Siemens-Schukert firm in Germany. Similarly the Berezniki chemical combine claimed that its 'girders were manufactured on the spot in a special factory . . . the tempo of the shock brigades allowed the building operations to proceed at a dizzy rate of speed.'[22] Examination of the photograph, however, reveals in large letters along the length of the girders the inscription, 'POWER-GAS CORP. LTD. STOCKTON-ON-TEES ENGLAND.'

The impatient propagandists could hardly wait for the motors to start and the paint to dry on the walls of newly built plants before claiming a victory for socialism. The previous volume of this study indicated how the development of the Soviet oil industry up to 1930 (and indeed after this date as well) was completely a product of Western technology skills and equipment. This remarkable construction program was, on completion, immediately claimed by T. Gonta in a little booklet, *The Heroes of Grozny, How the Soviet Oil Industry Fulfilled the Five Year Plan in Two and a Half Years*, published in Moscow in 1932.

In the pulp and paper industry, experiments were carried on to manufacture paper from peat to help solve the problems caused by the acute shortage of wood pulp. These were reportedly carried on at the Barkhat peat factory by Remmer, an engineer who produced a paper comprising 10 percent rag stock,

[19]   Frankfurt, *op. cit.*, p. 28.
[20]   Amtorg, *op. cit.*, VI, No. 12 (June 15, 1931), p. 275.
[21]   *La Vie Economique*, No. 115 (May 5, 1930), p. 4.
[22]   *U.S.S.R. in Construction*, No. 5, 1932.

20 percent waste paper, and 70 percent peat moss. This was publicized in the Moscow *Pravda* of April 20, 1932 together with the claim that the newspaper itself had been printed on the new peat paper. Samples of *Pravda* were forwarded to the U.S. Department of Commerce in Washington, D.C., for analysis, with this result: 'It is actually similar to the ordinary newsprint paper, being composed entirely of wood fiber in the proportion of sixty percent ground wood and forty percent sulphite wood fiber.'[23]

In brief, although the Communist Party accurately recognized technology and specifically Western technology as the engine of Marxist progress, its initial views of this technology were almost childlike. This should not obscure the fact that the Party was willing to learn from mistakes and that by 1940 and certainly after the Nazi invasion of 1941 the most extreme forms of ideological control of engineering functions had been dropped. As the reality of economic development dawned, propaganda became the means to hide the weaknesses of 'socialist construction' from the West, and probably from rank-and-file members of the Russian Communist Party itself.

Thus censorship and propaganda have played an essential role in the transfer process by obscuring technical backwardness and ineptitude from the outside world.

AMERICAN BUSINESSMEN AND SOVIET PROPAGANDA OBJECTIVES

There is no question that American businessmen, and to a lesser extent engineers, were utilized to further Soviet propaganda objectives and disguise Soviet technical inabilities. One must be careful to distinguish between the motivations of different groups of businessmen and engineers. There was one group, quite small, that knowingly promoted Soviet objectives and were sympathetic to the Communist cause. A second group denied the existence of such Soviet practices as forced labor but did so out of honest conviction and belief. A third group at first denied or excused Soviet brutality and then, as the facts came to light, revised its opinions. A fourth group, including most, but not all, of the engineers on site, was clear-sighted from the first.

The issue of forced labor is a good example to demonstrate the point. There was ample evidence in the early 1930s of forced labor in the Soviet Union. The State Department had a great deal of accurate information. Further, nine out of ten engineers interviewed by the Department mentioned this practice and provided evidence of it.

---

[23] U.S. State Dept. Decimal File, 861.656/4, Department of Commerce, letter dated July 7, 1932.

On the other hand, the American-Russian Chamber of Commerce was used as a forum for Soviet denials of the use of forced labor. A speech by Colonel Cooper, Chief Consultant to the Dniepr Dam, to the American-Russian Chamber of Commerce at the Bankers Club in New York on January 28, 1932[24] illustrates the point. After referring to the serious interference since 1922 with the flow of trade with the Soviet Union, Colonel Cooper said:

> . . . a hue and cry was raised against these limited Russian exports by politicians and propagandists and, I regret to say, some businessmen who because of their selfish interests are ready to injure the interests of our country as a whole. Last year they tried to convince the country that all Russian products that came into this country were manufactured by convict labor. . . . The Chamber has made a real study of these charges. It has obtained signed statements from many leading American businessmen, who have actually been to Russia and have personally observed labor conditions there, and I am glad to say that not one of these men think that labor in Russia is forced.

Colonel Cooper then points to the great turnover of labor on Russian construction sites as 'undeniable proof' of absence of forced labor. The interesting point is the reason why Colonel Cooper was so strongly convinced that forced labor did not exist, when hundreds of reports in the State Department files from returning engineers or those renewing passports indicated that it did exist. The explanation is roughly as follows: the Soviets valued Colonel Cooper highly as a businessman and as an engineer, and made great efforts to conceal conditions from him. We know this because of a detailed report by one of his assistants, Emegass, on this precise point: the devices utilized by the Soviets to keep Colonel Cooper in relative ignorance of conditions.[25]

Secondly, there are logical fallacies in Cooper's statement. One cannot argue that because forced labor is absent in one location it does not exist elsewhere. Nor can one infer from high turnover that forced labor does not exist. Nor can one prove a negative, as Colonel Cooper was attempting to do. There is ample evidence of forced labor on all major construction sites, and this is indeed admitted in the 1941 plan, which includes NKVD plan objectives and mentions the existence for example, of NKVD-Koppers coke-oven designs.

A few engineers knowingly made erroneous pro-Soviet statements to ingratiate themselves with the Soviets. For example:

> One of the American engineers who had been to the States brought back with him clippings of a speech he had made before an Engineering Society in the U.S. about Russia and conditions there. We congratulated him on

24 Amtorg, *op. cit.*, VII/VIII (1932–3) bound in rear (Hoover Institution, Stanford University).
25 U.S. State Dept. Decimal File, 861.50/FIVE YEAR PLAN.

being such a liar and he replied that was what the Russians wanted and what he was being payed [*sic*] for. . . .[26]

Others were apparently paid or threatened not to complain.[27]

Thus propaganda and the use of foreign firms and individuals to develop Soviet propaganda objectives are intimately related to the inability hypothesis and subsequent Western assistance. In the face of technical inability, propaganda became necessary. One of the most useful outlets was the vehicle of assistance itself—the Western firm and individual businessmen and engineers.[28]

THE STANDARDIZATION AND DUPLICATION OF WESTERN TECHNOLOGY

The operational key to the development and utilization of technology within the U.S.S.R. is contained in the two words 'standardization' and 'duplication.' Strategic objectives, such as world revolution, are disguised by evasion while technical inability is disguised by propaganda, technical extravaganzas, and censorship. The actual process of technical acquisition, apart from the semantic disguise, involves several phases: consideration of all Western processes, selection of a single standard process, and then multiplication of the single selected process.

The first stage required widespread acquisition of knowledge concerning technical processes, economic structures, and organizational techniques throughout the Western world. This technical dragnet was unbelievably thorough and complete. It is doubtful if any technical or economic development of consequence has escaped examination by the Soviets. When information could not be acquired overtly, it was acquired covertly, by espionage, from governments, companies, and individuals. Such information was translated, summarized, and distributed to planning, design, research, engineering, and economic bodies.

Prototypes of promising processes were acquired. These prototypes were examined, dissected, cataloged, and analyzed in the most minute detail. The process most suitable for Soviet conditions was then selected and became the standard. If the process was a leading or key activity, foreign engineers were

[26] *American Engineers in Russia*, Dickinson papers, Folder 4.

[27] Kravchenko, *op. cit.*, p. 185.

[28] After 1958 the Soviets developed a much more effective means of disguising their objectives. The Sputnik dramatically demonstrated Soviet rocket and space achievements, and made their missile capability credible. From this it was deduced, erroneously, that the Soviets had made technical progress along a broad front. From this erroneous assumption came decline of export control laws at precisely that time when Western technology was needed by the Soviets and when technology along a broad front was slipping well behind the West. This is the fallacy of composition in assessing Soviet technology—a predilection to assume broad Soviet technical progress where in fact it does not exist.

hired to carry out or assist in the selection process. When the standard had been identified, it was prepared for duplication and standard drawings were prepared.[29] *This process of identification of standards and subsequent duplication is found in all major Soviet industries for the period under examination.* In aircraft engines, the standard designs were the Gnome rotary air-cooled and the Hispano-Suiza liquid-cooled models. In aircraft the standard designs were by de Havilland, Junkers, Heinkel, Savoia, Douglas, Potez, Martin, Vultee, Sikorsky, Seversky, Consolidated, and Isacco. Tractors were standardized on the Caterpillar 15/30 and the International Harvester and the Farmall row-crop tractor. Combines used the Holt model, light trucks and automobiles were standardized on the Ford Model A, trucks were based on Fiat models and the Hercules, sintering plants were based on Dwight Lloyd designs, and ore crushers on Simons. Standard lathes were the German DIN and the Warner & Swasey turret lathe, and diesel engines were Sulzer, Deutz and MAN.

One question presents itself: why were the Soviet engineers and planners so successful in choosing the best foreign technologies? Given 25 or so competing Western transport planes, by what process did Soviet engineers choose the Douglas DC-3, the most prolific transport model in the history of aviation, within two years of its initial production? Why the Ford Model A, and not General Motors, Dodge, Studebaker, Fiat, Renault, or any one of a hundred other possible automobile model choices? Why Curtiss-Wright aircraft engines, RCA radio stations, General Electric electrical equipment, and Koppers coke ovens? In almost every case the Soviets made an excellent choice. They invariably chose a more successful, lowcost process. In the light of the history of technical transfers, the Soviet choice of Western techniques has been superb.

One explanation might be the highly detailed comparative technical studies conducted in the Soviet Union on Western technological processes. A recent example is N. N. Kalmykov, *Burovaya Tekhnika i Tekhnologiya za Rubezhom* (Moscow: Nedra, 1968). This study compares precise technical details of different makes of rock drills and other equipment; it includes diagrams and charts obviously not supplied by the Western manufacturer. It is clear then that the Soviet system has institutional procedures enabling the rapid, usually successful transfer of Western technology at low cost and in a relatively efficient manner.[30]

---

[29] *Vestnik Standardizatsii* (Komiteta po standartizatsii: Moscow) for 1928–32 has details for part of this standardization process.

[30] Transfer is not always successful. See pp. 312–4 on the single-tower sulfuric-acid process; an argument will be made in the next volume that the Soviets moved too quickly on cotton-pickers; they made the right choice (the Rust spindle principle, subsequently used by four American manufacturers), but underestimated the technical problems. Hence they had 800 cotton pickers in 1940 (the U.S. had none), and only 100 left in 1945. John Rust subsequently ironed out the design problems and production got under way in both the U.S. and Soviet Union on the Rust machine in the late 1940s.

First, since about 1920 the Soviets have conducted a thorough and continuing world-wide dragnet of technical advances. They have probably acquired or tried to acquire one of every article made in the West.

Second, specialized institutes, such as VINITI (All-Union Institute of Scientific Information), have been established with overseas branches to institutionalize this acquisition process.

Third, this dragnet has been aided by local Communist parties and sympathizers, particularly where industries have maintained secrecy over methods or where Western governments have maintained industrial security precautions. The relaxed nature of Western security precautions has been a major asset enabling Western Communists to acquire this technology.[31]

Fourth, co-operative Western manufacturers have provided data and samples in anticipation of large orders. The monopolistic nature of Soviet trade organizations has been utilized to extract more data than would usually be made available to a potential Western customer.

Fifth, the market system has already pointed the way to the most successful among competing Western methods, although the information may be obscured to Western buyers by advertising and sales pressures. Choice can be more objective and more knowledgeable under the Soviet system, which can derive the advantages of the market system without succumbing to its emotional pressures.

Finally, Western engineers have been hired as independent consultants to prepare reports and advise on the most suitable process or equipment.

These constitute a formidable package of advantages which the Soviet Union has used with great skill. In addition Soviet buyers have insisted without fail on the most advanced processes that can be supplied by Western companies. On numerous occasions special development work has been undertaken to advance the frontier of the technology to be transferred. For example, in the electrical equipment industry, Metropolitan-Vickers Company has commented:

> The Russians . . . have always been eager to have the very latest plant and a turbine now building for Moscow will have the highest combined pressure and temperature of any turbine in the world, this having been made possible by the metallurgical researches of the Metropolitan-Vickers Company. . . .[32]

---

[31] Whittaker Chambers comments on the role of the American Communist Party: ' . . . one of the periodic rituals at Gay Street was known as "filling the box." Every so often, Charlie, Maria and I would fill it with hundreds of thin leaflets in white paper covers. These were patents which anybody could then buy for a small fee from the United States Patent Office. . . .' [*Witness* (New York, Random House, 1952), p. 305.]

[32] *The Times* (London), May 22, 1933.

The British Thomson Houston Company made a similar observation in regard to a large Soviet order for special transformers in 1945:

> . . . [These are] the first transformers to be built in Great Britain for use on a 3-phase, 50 cycle system transmitting power at 242,000 volts between lines. The input voltage rating is 15,750. The transformers comprise three single phase units forming a 120,000 kvA bank. This was the largest bank rating for power supply yet made in Great Britain. . . .[33]

In Switzerland, the Brown-Boveri Company, also manufacturers of electrical equipment for industrial purposes, made a similar observation:

> In this field a whole series of exceedingly interesting new designs is to be reported,which we had an opportunity of developing in connection with the order we received for equipping the large aluminum works at Zwetmetsoloto in Russia with a large number of electric annealing and hardening furnaces.The large output required from this plant, the exceedingly large dimensions of the pieces to be treated and the resulting high power requirements made necessary designs which considerably exceeded in dimensions and type of construction the scope of our furnace design as used up to date. . . .[34]

With reference to aluminum plants, the International General Electric Company commented on the Stupino Aluminum Plant:

> For this plant, General Electric designed and furnished special electric furnaces, unusual in size, for aluminum ingot heating, aluminum coil annealing etc. as well as special heating elements and accessories for hardening large-size finished aluminum sheets in salt baths.[35]

In brief, the Soviets have demanded and been supplied with the frontier work of capitalist systems, *often before it is utilized in the country of origin* and sometimes to special order with the recipient firm working out the technical problems. This policy requires extensive information, assimilation of foreign techniques, and a great deal of skill to avoid mistaken choices. Such choices were the work of numerous specialized research institutes established by the Soviet Union in the 1920s and 1930s.

The years 1932–4 were critical for Soviet engineering and development. This was the period of change from all-imported equipment to absorption of the output of the new imported giant plants and the expanded and re-equipped tsarist plants.

Fortunately, we have a copy of the Glavkhlopkom plan, *Mechanization in 1932*, prepared by Willard Gorton, an American engineer, which illustrates the change in one sector.

---

[33]   H. A. Price-Hughes, *B.T.H. Reminiscences: Sixty Years of Progress* (B.T.H., Ltd., 1946), p. 112.

[34]   *Brown-Boveri Review*, January 1932, p. 24.

[35]   *The Monogram*, November 1943, p. 17.

The report describes new equipment for 1932 by origin and suggests how this change to standardized equipment based on Western models took place. This material is summarized in table 18-2.

In brief, the relatively simple equipment—horsedrawn dumpers, scrapers, ditchers, and plows—making up about one-quarter of the total capital expenditure for Glavkhlopkom—was to be produced by old tsarist plants. All the tractors were scheduled to be supplied by the new plants at Stalingrad and Kharkov, built with U.S. and German equipment and with technical assistance as outlined in the text.[36] This comprised about 40 percent of total expenditure. One-third of the expenditure was to be used for imported equipment, including 24 draglines, 10 elevator graders, and 20 Ruth machines. Thus it was the more complex, specialized equipment that had to be imported. From this and similar data from other sources, we can deduce the principle that

Table 18-2   1932 GORTON MECHANIZATION PLAN SUMMARY

	Imported from U.S.		Produced by New Plants		Produced by expanded Tsarist Plants	
	Units	*Million Rubles*	*Units*	*Million Rubles*	*Units*	*Million Rubles*
Group I:						
Heavy Equipment						
Draglines	24	2.40				
Dumpers					48	.14
Tractors (60 hp.)			48	.43		
Group II:						
Light Equipment						
Horse scrapers					—	—
Tractor scrapers					180	.36
Ditchers					140	.42
Elevator graders	10	.10				
Plows					239	.05
Tractors (30 hp.)			559	2.80		
Tractors (60 hp.)			10	.09		
Group III:						
Operating Equipment						
Ruth machines	20	.60				
Plows					60	.60
Dredges					20	.80
Tractors (60 hp.)			60	.54		
Total	54	3.10	677	3.86	687	2.37

Percentage imported from U.S.	33.2
Percentage from U.S.-built tractor plants	41.4
Percentage from rebuilt tsarist plants	25.4
	100.0

[36] P. 185-8.

substitution of domestic for foreign equipment started with that which was simple and easy to produce, and extended to that which was more complex and difficult to manufacture only as experience was gained.

This was a step-by-step procedure, but with its own problems. Louis Ernst suggests one, and his description is worth quoting in detail:

> The Russian usually has machines and equipment from the most widely separated sources, and no spare parts at all. In Voroshilovsk, for example, in the by-products department, we had pumps from Skoda, run by motors from Germany's A.E.G., some on Italian ball bearings and some on Swedish S.K.F. bearings. The steam pumps came from Worthington, in the U.S., while some small turbine pumps came from Britain's Metro-Vickers. Some relays came from G.E., and the motor controllers from Cutler-Hammer. No catalogues were available and, even if we had been able to select the necessary replacement or spare parts, currency was obtainable only under the most extreme circumstances. Therefore, the engineer in Voroshilovsk had to begin from the very beginning, by having drawings made of all parts. Then he had to plan changes to accommodate his machines to Russian parts if this should become necessary. In other cases he had to cast around for Soviet organizations capable of fabricating those parts that he knew might wear out or break. He had to be farsighted indeed, under these conditions, to avoid shutdowns because of machine failures.[37]

DUPLICATION OF THE SELECTED STANDARD DESIGN

Standardization was the prelude to production. The distinguishing feature of Soviet production has been gigantic runs of a standard model. Whereas the usual practice in Western systems is to have models appealing to different demand segments and relatively short production runs followed by a model change, the Soviet practice has been to utilize its giant plants to produce simplified models with no changes for long periods. This gives not only large quantities, but provides an excellent training ground for unskilled workers. Numerous model changes in the early stages of developing a modern technique may inhibit efficiency or at least the development of a 'learning curve.'

The tractor industry provides an excellent example of standardization practices. Three large plants were built by 1933; these comprised the Soviet tractor industry until 1943. Each of these plants turned out, apart from its military quota, a standardized tractor model based on a Western example. Large capacity, with only one model change in 1937, enabled gigantic production runs. Table 18–3 illustrates the capacity and production of these key Soviet tractor plants, as calculated by Dodge, compared to Western plants making the same model tractor.

---

[37] Louis Ernst, 'Inside a Soviet Industry,' *Fortune*, October 1949, p. 172.

Table 18-3   PRODUCTION CAPACITY IN SOVIET UNION
AND UNITED STATES FOR SELECTED TRACTOR MODELS

	United States	Soviet Union
	(In Drawbar Horsepower)	
Caterpillar 60 crawler	550,000 (Peoria)	1,500,000 (Chelyabinsk)
Fordson 10/20 wheel	1,000,000 (Dearborn)	200,000 (Krasnyi Putilovets)
International 15/30 wheel	600,000 (Milwaukee)	1,200,000 (Stalingrad and Kharkov)

Source: Adapted from Norton T. Dodge, 'Trends in Labor Productivity in the Soviet Tractor Industry' (Harvard University, Economics Department, Ph.D. Dissertation, February 1960).

In 1935 Soviet turbo-generators were standardized on 12,000 kilowatt and 24,000 to 25,000 kilowatt model sizes, produced with G.E. technical assistance at KHEMZ.[38] This standardization is reflected in the 1935 annual plan for the People's Commissariat of Heavy Industry.[39] All power-station turbo-generators scheduled for production in 1935 were multiples of these standard sizes and none were scheduled for import.

In sum, 12,000 kilowatt units were scheduled for Kuibyshev GRES No. 3 and Krimskaya GRES No. 1; 24,000–25,000 kilowatt units were scheduled for All Union Heat Institute No. 3, Stalinsky No. 1 and No. 2, Kisel GRES No. 3, Sverdlovsk No. 1, Chelyabinsk GRES II No. 5, Novosibirsk GRES, and Kiev II No. 1, and 50,000 kilowatt units were scheduled for Stalinogorsk No. 2 and No. 3, Sredne-Uralsk GRES No. 1, and Zuevka II No. 4.

This comprises the complete annual plan for 1935. The plan used no imported turbo-generators and only three models of domestic standard KHEMZ turbo-generators.

The same principle may be seen in coke ovens. At first they were imported in Koppers, Disticoque, and Otto variants. Soviet oven production was based on the Koppers design. These were produced in quantity at Kramatorsk[40] and became the standard coke oven; by 1940 even the NKVD was able to build Soviet-Koppers coke-oven batteries in distant areas using forced unskilled labor. (See table 18–4.) As Soviet organizations succeeded in adopting the Koppers design, imports were cut off entirely.

---

[38]   For G. E. technical assistance, see chap. X. For data on standards see John P. Hardt, *Dispersal of the Soviet Electric Power Industry* (Alabama: Maxwell Air Force Base, 1957), p. 39. The standard size for steam-condensing stations was changed in 1939 to either 6,000, 8,000, or 12,000 kilowatts.

[39]   Smolensk Archives, WKP 444 1935, National Archives Microcopy T 87-49.

[40]   See p. 131.

Table 18–4 THE DUPLICATION PROCESS IN COKE OVEN CONSTRUCTION, 1930 TO 1945

Plant Location	1928	1929	1930	1931	1932	1933	1934	1935	1936	1937	1938	1939	1940	1941	1942	1943	1944	1945
ALCHEVSK			KOPPERS A. G. (Germany)															
GORLOVKA I			DISTICOQUE S.A. (France)															
KERCH				KOPPERS COMPANY Inc (United States)														
MAGNITOGORSK I				KOPPERS COMPANY Inc (United States)														
RUCHENKOVO					'SOVIET' KOPPERS													
GORLOVKA II					'SOVIET' KOPPERS													
MAKEEVKA					'SOVIET' KOPPERS													
STALINO					'SOVIET' KOPPERS													
ZAPOROZHE						'SOVIET' KOPPERS												
KAMENSKOE							'SOVIET' KOPPERS											
KUZNETSK							'SOVIET' KOPPERS											
MAGNITOGORSK II							'SOVIET' KOPPERS											
MARIUPOL							'SOVIET' KOPPERS											
KRIVOI ROG							'SOVIET' KOPPERS											
GUBAKHA							DISTICOQUE S.A. (France)											
TAGIL											'SOVIET' KOPPERS							
CHELYABINSK											'SOVIET' KOPPERS							
KOMSOMOLSK											'SOVIET' KOPPERS							
MAGNITOGORSK III												'SOVIET' KOPPERS						
ORSK												'NKVD' KOPPERS						
IGARKA																'NKVD' KOPPERS		
PECHORA																'NKVD' KOPPERS		
MAGNITOGORSK IV																		'SOVIET' KOPPERS

CONCLUSIONS

The Soviets attempted to industrialize about the mid-1920s; this was not successful, and the evidence suggests an 'inability hypothesis.' This problem was overcome by contracting with foreign firms in the period from late 1929 to 1931 to fulfill the First Five-Year Plan.

It was most important, for political reasons, to disguise both local inability and the sources of industrial progress. This disguise was only partially successful; some information had to be publicized to allay apprehensions of Western companies. Some data were therefore made available by Soviet trade delegations. This information, coupled with reports from returning engineers, provides a means of penetrating the propaganda shield.

Western assistance was focused by the Soviets upon simple, clearcut objectives; to build new, gigantic, mass-production units to manufacture large quantities of simplified standard models based on proven Western designs without design changes over a long period. Thus after the transfer of Western technology, simplification, standardization, and duplication became the operational aspects of Soviet industrial strategy.

CHAPTER NINETEEN

Copying as a Development Mechanism

THERE has been a great deal of discussion, but without detailed empirical support, of 'copying' by Soviet engineers: i.e., the reproduction of processes and equipment already in use abroad without the permission or even knowledge of the foreign owner. This is, of course, both ethical and legal under a Communist system. It is ethical because no absolute industrial property rights can exist for individuals under Communism; it is legal because Soviet patent law, in reflecting this philosophical base, offers no meaningful protection. Protection is given to individual Soviet citizens only to protect the interests of the Soviet state, and not because the Soviet citizen has any economic rights.

In research for this study, an extraordinary amount of what is generally known as copying, was unearthed.[1] There is no question that the large number of single-sample items ordered or requested by Soviet trade organizations from the 1920s until the present day have been used as prototypes. From the Soviet viewpoint the foreign capitalist, inventor, or artist has no inherent property rights, and so this practice has extended from hand-tools and scientific books (for unauthorized translation) to industrial equipment.

Western economists suggest that socialist or planned systems have major innovative problems. Hirschman, for example, argues astutely that 'a planned economy is likely to behave much like the guild system; the process of 'creative destruction' is constitutionally alien to it because destruction here means self-destruction rather than destruction of somebody else.'[2]

---

[1] To a Communist copying is a moral act as it promotes Communism. Under Western law and ethics the same practice may be, if protected by patents, industrial theft. Copying and theft may therefore be synonymous in Western but not in Soviet ideology.

[2] A. O. Hirschman, *The Strategy of Economic Development* (Yale University Press: 1958), p. 59.

It follows, therefore, that, as innovation is the means to technical progress, a socialist system, if it cannot generate rational innovation internally, must assimilate innovation from outside: from capitalist systems. This transfer is precisely what the Soviet Union has achieved.

A preliminary stage and a common practice is to request literature, drawings, and samples from individual foreign companies. When attempts to copy on the basis of such freely-supplied data are inadequate or faulty, the next move is to acquire technical assistance or minor products without payment as part of another major contract. A case involving both technical assistance for a non-contracted product and acquisition of minor prototype items was the Amtorg technical-assistance contract with the Douglas Aircraft Company of Santa Monica for production of the DC-3 transport plane. As the author worked through files of orders placed by Amtorg with the Douglas Company, it became obvious that Amtorg had used Douglas facilities to purchase items (always one of each) made by other companies. For example, the Special Tool List in the October 1937 order[3] contains the following items chosen by the author at random:

Item	*Quantity*
Boyer air hammer UUB-63033	1
Utica pump nut pliers No. 517	1
Kennedy steel tool kit	1
Chromalox electrical welding pot, Model P-50, 230-volt, 1138 W, Serial No. P-39	1
Weston electric welding pot, 664 capacity model	1
Purox cutting torch	1
Buck bar, TB 1171	1

Examination of lists of special tools bought by Douglas Aircraft on behalf of Amtorg reveals that these were small tools manufactured by many different concerns and that the quantity ordered was *always one* only. This, unknown to Douglas, was part of the massive technical acquisition program carried out by the Soviets. A sample of every Western product and copies of patents, journals and other publications of possible technical value were shipped to the Soviet Union for analysis and reproduction, if possible.[4] Use of innocent 'front companies' was necessary to obscure the nature of this vast acquisition program. The manufacturer of the Boyer air hammer, for example, would be reluctant to fill an Amtorg order for one hammer, but would fill a Douglas

---

[3] Douglas Aircraft Company Files.
[4] Foreign Communist parties were enlisted in this dragnet. See p. 293.

Aircraft order without question. Only when outright copying on the basis of this type of indirect acquisition was impracticable was an agreement made to purchase technical assistance. Thus the many agreements which make up the bulk of this study tell only a part of the story; it may be presumed that far more technology was acquired without benefit of formal agreement.

By 1936 Soviet commentators began to claim indigenous Soviet designs, while admitting earlier copying. For example, E. Satel wrote:

> If during the first years of work our plants did copy foreign models, they are now successfully solving even more complicated problems of technique and design. Examples of these may be seen in aviation construction, as demonstrated by the flight of the ANT-25, the heavy diesel tractor, and the all-purpose caterpillar tractor. . . . Such complicated machines as slabbing and intermediate sheet-rolling mills for the sheet-rolling department of Zaprozhstal are our own Soviet design, the former created by the designers of the Krammatorsk Machine-Building Plant and the latter by those of the Urals Machine-Building Plant.[5]

None of these claims of Soviet design stand up to rigorous examination. Each of Satel's examples of Soviet design has been traced in this study to foreign origin, except the ANT-25, which was replaced by foreign designs.[6] Further, in the period under examination (1930–45), we have found no major Soviet industrial design to have been retained in preference to a foreign design.

THE EMPIRICAL EVIDENCE FOR SOVIET INDUSTRIAL COPYING

The evidence for extremely widespread copying of foreign equipment is overwhelming. Nearly every engineer interviewed by the State Department made some comment on the question, and many gave precise details concerning the uninhibited copying of Western equipment. Examples from some widely varying fields will suggest the extent of this practice.

In October 1931 the U.S. Warsaw Embassy reported an interview with an American engineer, C. E. Wildman, returning from a sales trip in the U.S.S.R., where he represented the Buckeye Incubator Company of Springfield, Ohio.[7] Wildman commented, 'The incubators used on the poultry farms are copies of American makes with steam and hot water systems of heating. . . .' Wildman

---

[5] *Za Industrializatsiiu*, No. 199, August 27, 1936.

[6] The ANT-25 was replaced by foreign aircraft designs between 1937 and 1941; the heavy diesel tractor was the Stalinetz 65, based on the Caterpillar 60; the 'all-purpose caterpillar tractor' was the Farmall; the slabbing mills were based on a Demag mill; and the sheet mills were developed under the United Engineering and Foundry contract.

[7] U.S. State Dept. Decimal File, 861.5017—Living Conditions/359.

offered his products to the Soviet organization, and when the Soviets had obtained from him the lowest wholesale prices, they offered to purchase a few units for exhibition and trial. The informant stated that this was a well-known Soviet method of obtaining American models for later duplication.[8]

The Embassy report continues:

> [Wildman] saw much evidence . . . that the Soviets have no respect whatsoever for patent rights. They consider patent rights as a part of organized capitalism and an institution from which laboring classes obtain no benefits. If the Soviets cannot buy models directly from modern countries they purchase them in the open market for shipment to Soviet Russia where they are later copied. . . .[9]

The Geary feeder[10] and Geary-Jennings sampler,[11] used in ore-treatment plants, are well-documented examples of Soviet copying. The Geary feeder was placed on the market in the United States in June 1927 and the Geary-Jennings sampler in December 1928. They came quickly into use throughout the world. J. F. Geary requested the State Department to obtain some protection in the Soviet Union.[12]

Numerous inquiries had been received by Geary from organizations and individuals in the U.S.S.R.; these Russian inquirers had been furnished catalogs, drawings, photographs, and other information on the same basis as inquirers from all other countries. As J. F. Geary himself said, ' . . . in spite of all the sales material sent into Russia, and in spite of the fact that similar material sent into other countries brought results in the form of orders, no orders whatever have ever been received from anyone in the Soviet Union.'[13]

At first Geary and his associates ascribed this to adverse business conditions. Then 'a succession of friends' brought back the same information: that Geary feeders were in use in the Soviet Union. This was emphatically confirmed when a group of Soviet engineers from Mekhanobr (State Institute for Planning Ore-Treatment Plants), touring local mines and mining plants in the Utah area, visited Geary:

> These men together with a Mr. Rundquist, came to this country to study American methods. They showed interest in the construction of the Geary feeders, but when solicited for an order remarked: 'Oh no, we built them over there ourselves!'[14]

[8] *Ibid.*
[9] *Ibid.*
[10] U.S. Patent No. 1,766,625, June 24, 1930.
[11] U.S. Patent No. 1,937,473, November 28, 1933.
[12] U.S. State Dept. Decimal File, 861.542—GEARY, J. F./2.
[13] *Ibid.*, 861.542—GEARY, J. F./3–6.
[14] *Ibid.*

The extent of copying within a single industrial sector—oil-well drilling—may be illustrated from the statements of August Tross, an American drilling superintendent in the Baku oil fields in the early and middle 1930s. According to Tross, who assisted in making up lists of equipment to be purchased in the United States, only a small part of the equipment was actually imported; the Soviets tried to make the rest domestically. 'In copying foreign equipment,' he said, 'there is a total disregard of patent rights.'[15] Tross added that German firms were at first utilized to produce American patented equipment, and cited the example of the Schaffer blowout preventer. In the same report, Tross provided a list of 'some types' in process of reproduction at the end of 1934 in the oil-drilling industry:

Equipment Copied	U.S. Firms Holding Patents
Rock bits	Hughes Rock Bit Co. (Texas)
Roller bits	Reed Roller Bit Co. (Texas)
Drilling bits	Zublin Drilling Bits Co. (Los Angeles)
Dunn tongs and elevators	Bryan Jacobson Co.
Blowout preventers	Schaffer Co. (Los Angeles)
Rotary rigs	Emsco Rotary Draw Works (Los Angeles)
Rotary rigs	National Oil Well Supply Co. (Los Angeles)
Butler elevators	Oil Well Supply Co. (Pittsburgh)

Insofar as copying of oil-field equipment is concerned, it was Tross's opinion that the Soviet copies, although almost identical to their prototypes in appearance, were poorer in quality.[16]

This flow of technical information was, of course, all in one direction. The Tross agreement[17] included the following clause: '11. The Employee [i.e., Tross] shall not disclose any business secrets which shall have become

---

[15] U.S. State Dept. Decimal File, 861.5017—Living Conditions/771, Moscow Legation Report No. 240, November 3, 1934. Tross was a drilling superintendent and had daily contact with the equipment listed over a period of some years, so that his evidence is more compelling than that of a sales engineer's, for instance, who visits the U.S.S.R. on a business trip and gets only a quick look at 'Soviet-made' equipment.

[16] For a later example of Soviet practice, N. N. Kalmykov, *op. cit.*, provides a detailed comparison of current (1968) American oil tool products (i.e., roller bits, spiders, rotary rigs, etc.) on a company-by-company basis. This type of comparative study has only one use: to enable Soviet engineers to reproduce foreign technology. Such detailed company-by-company comparisons of competitive products would hardly find a market in the United States. Examination of drawings in the book suggests that the focus is on reproduction of U.S. equipment. See, for example, the drawings on pp. 58 and 70, the temperature gradients diagram on p. 216, and the illustrations on pp. 230 and 234.

[17] U.S. State Dept. Decimal File, 861.5017—Living Conditions/771.

known to him during his employment. . . .'[18] On the other hand the Soviets made every effort to acquire business secrets from the United States and other countries. For example, Tross comments, 'Officials of Azneft . . . have to my knowledge requested American firms to send them free of cost samples of certain lighter types of machinery and have used the samples as models.'[19] The one-way nature of the flow is further illustrated by the quite different definitions of 'industrial secrets' used in the U.S. and the U.S.S.R. In the Soviet Union *any* information of an economic or technical nature is classified as secret.

There are several well-documented cases of the copying of excavation equipment. Kostiszak, resident construction superintendent in the Soviet Union for the Thew Shovel Company, was asked the circumstances under which duplication of Thew shovels took place. The interviewer's report is as follows:

> . . . without previous notice . . . two drag-line buckets of $2\frac{1}{2}$ cubic yards capacity, exact duplicates of the American equipment but manufactured in the mechanical shops of SVIRSTROY, were delivered to him on the job. Requesting an explanation he was informed by the Soviet engineer in charge of the excavating machinery that buckets and other repair and replacement parts would in the future be manufactured in Soviet shops. . . .[20]

Kostiszak later visited the Svirstroi shops and found other buckets similar to Thew equipment in process of manufacture: 'They were exact duplicates of the American buckets; American replacement teeth were fitted to the Soviet buckets but the rest of the material was Russian.'[21] The 'Soviet Thews' proved equal on the job to the American equipment.[22]

Kostiszak recounted a similar episode with drag-line cables. Each imported American machine came supplied with two replacement cables. Two feet was cut from several replacement cables and shipped to the Svirstroi laboratories in Leningrad. A few months later four cables of Soviet manufacture were supplied—of inferior wire—but Kostiszak believed that with the right grade of wire the Russians could supply a high-quality cable. In general he noted that 'Soviet mechanics are continually dismantling, measuring and reassembling machinery on the job'—possibly to acquaint themselves with it, but Kostiszak

[18] *Ibid.*
[19] *Ibid.*
[20] U.S. State Dept Decimal File, 861.5017—Living Conditions/283, pp. 13-4 of attached report.
[21] *Ibid.* Bucket teeth on drag lines wear out more quickly than any other part.
[22] U.S. State Dept. Decimal File, 861.5017—Living Conditions/283, pp. 13-4 of attached report.

believed that these activities had some connection with copying.[23]

The Rust cotton-picking machine offers an example of an assistance agreement which, although superficially beneficial to the Western company, was impossible to enforce and provided the same end result to the Soviets as copying. J. D. Rust, co-inventor, with his brother, of the Rust cotton-picking machine, came to the Soviet Union in 1936 at the invitation of the Soviet Government to demonstrate his machine. Two machines were bought by Amtorg, and Rust stayed with a mechanic for one month to demonstrate their operation.[24]

While in the Soviet Union, Rust negotiated a contract granting manufacturing rights for the machine under which the Rust brothers supplied detailed drawings. The circumstances making this move desirable were described as follows:

> Mr. Rust and his associates felt that it was advisable to reach an agreement with the Soviet Government by which they would obtain some compensation for the manufacturing rights of the machine, since they felt that if they refused to cooperate the Soviet Government could easily purchase one of the machines from an individual in the United States or elsewhere once they are in general use, and with this model they could manufacture their own units, without the necessity of compensating the Rust brothers for the rights. . . .[25]

The report continues:

> The Rust brothers made careful studies of the Soviet patent laws and realized that it would be extremely difficult for them to protect their interests in this country unless they reached an amicable agreement with the Soviet authorities. . . .[26]

The contract provided for a single lump-sum payment of $20,000 to Rust and his associates in the event that the machine was adopted and at least 10 units per year were manufactured, but there was to be no payment if fewer than 10 units were manufactured in any one year. Rust suggested to the U.S. Moscow Embassy that if Soviet engineers were unable to copy they would have to buy machines in the United States and in that case Rust would receive more than $20,000. In any event the Rust brothers felt that nothing had been lost.

---

[23] *Ibid.* Gustav S. Bell, a superintendent for Sauerman Brothers, Inc., in the Soviet Union, similarly reported that Sauerman excavators were copied and that he was offered a position to supervise erection and installation of 'Soviet Sauermans.' (See U.S. State Dept. Decimal File, 861.5017—Living Conditions/314.)

[24] U.S. State Dept. Decimal File, 861.61321/68, Report No. 1879, Moscow Embassy, September 14, 1936.

[25] *Ibid.*

[26] *Ibid.*

There is, of course, an obvious and major loophole. Rust was not to receive payment until 10 machines per year had been manufactured to his drawings. How was he to know whether 10, 20, 50, or *no* machines had been manufactured? Soviet plants are, with the exception of a few show plants, closed to outsiders. In brief, his protection was completely illusory.[27]

Another indication of the wide range of copying activities may be noted quite simply by examining domestic Soviet price lists of industrial equipment. The whole range of such equipment was based on Western models. For example, blast-furnace equipment produced by Uralmash and described in its 1934 price list included:

> Otis winch (with drum, no spares)
>
> Brosius tap gun (with attachments)
>
> McKee throat system
>
> Freyn burners (with dampers)
>
> Orr locks (stoppers)
>
> Theisen stack gas cleaner
>
> Demag stripping crane
>
> Simplex butterfly valve

All these, and numerous other items of foreign derivation, were priced in rubles in Decree No. 277, of May 10, 1934, issued by the People's Commissarist of Heavy Industry.

The U.S. Embassy in 1934 produced a short list of Soviet imitations of American products and reported that it was a 'well-known fact' that samples were purchased in the United States and copied. Among these copies, were,

> Morgenthaler linotype machines[28]
>
> Pressed Steel Company dumping cars
>
> Black & Decker electric power tools, including drills, bench grinders, drill stands, rock drills of the jack-hammer type and bronze stokers

---

[27] The subsequent history of this case is not known; the State Dept. files close at this point. Soviet cotton-picking machines are very similar to American models, as will be shown in the next volume. Given the history of Soviet-American economic relations, it is unlikely that any payment was ever made to the Rust brothers. They probably lost their investment in travel expenses to Moscow and the drawings supplied under the contract.

[28] This was copied at the Max Holz works in Leningrad, an ex-tsarist plant considerably expanded with imported equipment in 1932–3. The manufacture of Morgenthaler linotypes was started in 1932 'on the model of a typesetter imported from Germany.' Only two had been built by fall of 1932 and they could not be used 'owing to great errors of construction and to poor quality of the metal employed.' Approximately 6 to 7 percent of the 1,000 workers were German. (U.S. State Dept. Decimal File, 861.60/267.)

Hamilton Press Company presses

Cincinnati Milling Machine milling machines

American Tool Company lathes

Sullivan Machinery underground coal cutters

Buick automobile (copied at the Amo plant)[29]

Many similar examples could be quoted and, indeed, are found throughout the whole range of Soviet industry.

A number of cases in the State Department files demonstrate outright fraud on the part of the Soviets. The Cardox case shows the inability of Western companies to do anything in the face of such fraudulent practices. In 1925 the Safety Mining Company of Chicago developed a method and apparatus known as Cardox for use in lieu of explosives for blasting or breaking down coal underground. The great advantage of Cardox lay in its safety feature: it could be used in gassy mines. The company took out fundamental patents in the United States and major foreign countries. By 1930 the method was used with success in the United States and the United Kingdom and was being developed in France.

In 1935 the Safety Mining Company wrote the State Department: 'Several years ago our entire knowledge of the method was placed before responsible representatives of the Soviet Government with a view to laying the groundwork for future negotiations.'[30] The company learned that the information provided in confidence had been utilized, tested, and in 1934 published in a Soviet trade journal.[31] 'The trade journal admits that they have duplicated the best features of CARDOX as developed in the United States and Great Britain and that for 1934 the Government allocated about 350,000 rubles for this work.'[32]

The letter concluded by asking for State Department assistance and commented, 'We understand that the Soviet Government has been involved in a great many instances of this kind, to the immeasurable detriment of the creative and industrial interests of this country.'[33]

Although one could infer from the Safety Mining Company letter that knowledge of such appropriation was widespread, there is mixed evidence on this score. There is no evidence that the State Department warned business-men of this practice (this could, however, have been done verbally). By the 1930s all larger corporations were probably aware of the problem; for example,

[29]   U.S. State Dept. Decimal File, 861.797/35, Report No. 165, Moscow Embassy, September 7, 1934.
[30]   *Ibid.*, 861.542—CARDOX/1.
[31]   *Ugol'*, No. 105, June 1934.
[32]   *Ibid.*
[33]   U.S. State Dept. Decimal File, 861.542—CARDOX/1.

Du Pont de Nemours was approached by a Mr. Boston, who desired to make purchases on behalf of Carp Export and Import Corporation, the Soviet munitions-purchasing front in the United States. After company officers had been requested to accept orders for 'small sample quantities of very recent development,'[34] it was reported to the State Department that 'since it was clear that the object of the Corporation was merely to attempt to copy the trade secrets of du Pont [*sic*], Major Casey said that Mr. Boston's proposals had not been accepted.'[35]

On the other hand, in a case similar to that of the Safety Mining Company, we find a comparatively small company at the beginning of the 1930s under the impression that diplomatic recognition of the U.S.S.R. would overcome lack of patent protection and copying. The Sharples Specialty Company, centrifugal engineers of Philadelphia, were owners of a process used in the petroleum-refining industry. They made a single installation in the U.S.S.R. and were well aware that this was only 25 percent of the needed capacity. The Soviets had no other way of getting the first installation, which they could then copy. Sharples had no protection,[36] and suggested recognition of the U.S.S.R. would overcome the problem.

PATENT PROTECTION IN THE SOVIET UNION[37]

There was agreement in the United States that Soviet patents were worthless.[38] The Safety Mining Company, in writing about Cardox, stated:

> Every effort was made to obtain effective patents in Russia but this eventually proved to be impossible. The single patent which we did obtain was, in the opinion of competent counsel, utterly worthless and on advice of counsel, further efforts in this direction were abandoned.[39]

It is difficult, but not completely impossible, to present evidence concerning Soviet expropriation of foreign patents filed in the Soviet Union. It is difficult because mere collection of evidence of infringement in Soviet Russia would constitute espionage and lead to prompt arrest. For this reason there are no court cases involving infringement of foreign patents in the Soviet Union. However, the concessions provide evidence of patent expropriation because

---

[34] *Ibid.*, 711.00111/Lic. Carp Export and Import Corp/6, June 10, 1937.

[35] *Ibid.*

[36] U.S. State Dept. Decimal File, 861.6363/278, January 31, 1930.

[37] See Sutton, *Western Technology . . . , 1917 to 1930*, pp. 299–303.

[38] There were a few exceptions. (See U.S. State Dept. Decimal File, 861.542/31 and /32.) In the light of Whittaker Chambers's comments, one presumes the advice given by Lee Pressman to the Rust brothers (above, p. 306) was favorable to the U.S.S.R.

[39] U.S. State Dept. Decimal File, 861.542—CARDOX/1, May 22, 1935.

some concessionaires filed patents inside the U.S.S.R. on processes introduced under the concession agreement. The Richard Kablitz concession, one of the largest and most important, supplies a prime example.

Kablitz was the only U.S.S.R. manufacturer of economizers, stoking devices, and furnaces. Operating six plants in the U.S.S.R., Kablitz equipped more than 400 Soviet plants in the 1920s.[40] An advertisement in *Izvestia Teplotekhnicheskogo Instituta*[41] was used by the Kablitz concession to stress patenting of its devices in the U.S.S.R.,[42] and indeed the company habitually referred to its economizer as 'Pat. Kablitz' rather than just 'Kablitz.' The company obviously strove to publicize the claim of patent protection to inhibit Soviet organizations anxious to produce similar devices.[43]

When the Kablitz concession was expropriated,[44] the patented devices were also expropriated and taken over by the Soviets, notwithstanding Soviet patent protection. Kablitz finally limited its suit in the German courts to compensation for these expropriated patents and dropped the concession property claim.[45] The only reason, therefore, that evidence is available in this case is that Kablitz operated a concession inside the U.S.S.R. and had evidence in company files. Such evidence of infringement could not be collected by other foreign patentees suspecting patent infringement; indeed the thought of attempting to gain entry to the files of a Soviet organization is somewhat amusing.[46]

The practical difficulty of collecting such information, even officially, is illustrated in the Geary case discussed above. The Moscow Embassy was instructed by the State Department to investigate the case, and after so doing, reported 'that after careful investigation by the Embassy, no information can be secured in regard to the reported reproduction and use in the Soviet Union of machines developed and patented by Mr. J. F. Geary in the United States. . . .'[47] The report then added that such copying was a 'well-known fact.'

---

[40]   Sutton, *Western Technology . . .* , *1917 to 1930*, pp. 180, 302, 329, 333, 346.

[41]   No. 7 (9) 1925.

[42]   See *Vestnik Komiteta po Delam Izobretenii*, No. 4–5, April 8, 1925.

[43]   See p. 21. The advertisement mentions the fact of a 'patent' in no less than 16 places.

[44]   See pp. 21–2.

[45]   *Ibid.* There is no evidence of compensation for either the patents or the concession.

[46]   Consequently, the prevalent impression (even in 1968, by the U.S. Patent Office) that Soviet patents may offer some protection is wholly erroneous. There can be no meaningful protection of private industrial property under a socialist system of the Russian type.

[47]   U.S. State Dept. Decimal File, 861.797/35, Report No. 165, Moscow Embassy, September 7, 1934, p. 2 of attachment.

However, as noted above, the Geary machines *had* been reproduced (although the Embassy had not been able to so determine). Soviet visitors to the United States in search of further information admitted as much to Geary, quite apart from the reports brought back by associates and friends of Geary and by Soviet visitors.[48]

Some firms, without any clear notion of the disadvantages, have been anxious to patent their devices in the Soviet Union. For example, the Globe Steel Tubes Company of Milwaukee filed applications in the United States and 15 foreign countries on an entirely new method of manufacturing steel tubing and wrote to the State Department, 'Although we have spent more money in the prosecution of our patent application in Russia than in any other country, very little headway had been made. . . .'[49] The Soviets rejected the initial Globe application on the grounds of 'prior art' and quoted an old textbook article. This, according to Globe, 'really has no bearing whatsoever on the new invention.'[50] Globe appealed through Senator Follette to the State Department, which in turn instructed the Moscow Embassy to investigate. The Soviets quickly obliged by granting a patent. The Commissariat of Foreign Affairs is quoted by Ambassador Bullitt:

> On September 21, 1931 an application for the granting of a patent for a method and appliance for the production of seamless tubes was received from the foreign firm Globe Steel Tubes Company. On May 7, 1932 the Section refused to grant a patent. On October 9, 1932 the firm appealed to the Council for the Consideration of Complaints. By the decision of the Council of May 20, 1934 the decision of the Section was set aside and patent was granted.[51]

The basic problem facing these foreign equipment manufacturers and accounting for their anxiety was that no meaningful protection could be acquired against Soviet expropriation of industrial property. Russian law offered no protection, and the expensive exercise of filing a foreign patent in the Soviet Union was a waste of time.[52] On the other hand, Western manufacturers needed protection, as equipment was being openly copied with no regard at all for property rights.

Larger companies, such as General Electric and Westinghouse, have made agreements concerning patented devices and probably the Soviets have lived by such agreements, not because they thought such agreements were legal, ethical, or ultimately desirable, but because they temporarily needed G.E.

---

[48] See p. 303.
[49] U.S. State Dept. Decimal File, 861.542—GLOBE STEEL TUBES CO. /1–9.
[50] *Ibid.*
[51] *Ibid.*
[52] The Dorr Company had taken out a number of Soviet patents and found payment of the annual patent fee 'a considerable burden,' but continued to pay it as long as there were prospects of doing business there. (See U.S. State Dept. Decimal File, 861.542/31.)

more than G.E. and comparable firms needed the Soviet Union. It was the medium-sized manufacturers (like Richard Kablitz), the individual consulting engineers, and the individual foreign inventors who suffered—they had no bargaining power, and this weakness was ruthlessly exploited by the Soviets. Neither did these firms carry much weight in the State Department or in Western political circles: officials did take up such matters on request, and extensive reports were developed, but in all cases the end result was inaction.

Thus foreign manufacturers, except those companies with technological bargaining power, were faced with the problem that on the one hand a Soviet patent was worthless and on the other hand that their innovations were being expropriated without consideration for property rights. The only possible recourse, and a weak one, was to attempt to negotiate a formal agreement for use of patents, even in the face of monopolistic trade organizations and known expropriation. Colonel Pope of Nitrogen Engineering tried to do this in his second agreement[53] by formalizing the copying process. Similarly a smaller company, Dewey and Almy Chemical Company of Cambridge, Massachussetts found that Soviet canned crab meat sold in the United States was packaged in containers which made unauthorized utilization of the company's patents. To formalize this infringement, Dewey and Almy attempted to negotiate a technical-assistance agreement and obtain some compensation.[54]

The writer has found no evidence to suggest that these attempts were successful, and indeed has found no evidence that payment has been made for such use except when patents were transferred by agreement with large corporations whose technology was unique or desirable. Briefly, the Soviet Union has taken care not to disturb certain corporations—General Electric, RCA, Food Machinery Corporation, and IBM—for a pragmatic reason: these firms provide laboratories for Soviet technical advance, and have done so for some 50 years. On the other hand, size is by itself no protection. Ford Motor Company, Du Pont, and Sullivan Machinery, have all been faced with breaches of contract.

The next task is to examine technical transfers in more detail, and for this purpose three examples are considered: one unsuccessful transfer and two highly successful transfers.

AN UNSUCCESSFUL TRANSFER: THE SOVIET DESIGN FOR A ONE-TOWER CHAMBER SYSTEM FOR SULFURIC ACID

Interest was aroused in the United States in 1934 when two Soviet scientists announced in *Zhurnal Industrialnoi Khimii* (November 1933) a new process for

[53] See p. 98.
[54] U.S. State Dept. Decimal File, 861.602/293, East European Division memorandum, January 27, 1938.

Figure 19–1   SINGLE-TOWER METHOD OF PRODUCING
SULFURIC ACID: ORIGINAL U.S. DESIGN

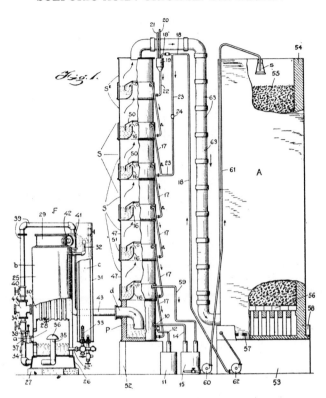

Source: U.S. Patent No. 1,513,903 of November 4, 1924.

manufacturing sulfuric acid, claimed to be of considerable significance. Sulfuric
acid is normally made in a series of six towers; P. V. Samarski and E. K.
Ziberlich proposed to substitute a one-tower design with a capacity about 18
times that of the standard Peterson six-tower process.

The article was translated and a summary appeared in the December 1934
issue of *Chemical and Metallurgical Engineering.* The editor of the American
journal appeared somewhat skeptical over the proposal and commented that
the theoretical aspects were not clear and that there were gaps 'in the details
of applying the process.'[55] An editorial note in the January 1935 issue made
yet another point: 'Furthermore, the one-tower type bears considerable

[55]   *Chemical and Metallurgical Engineering,* December 1934.

Figure 19–2   SINGLE-TOWER METHOD OF PRODUCING
SULFURIC ACID: SOVIET VERSION

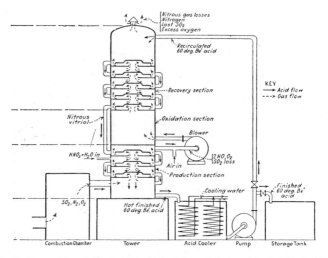

Source: P. V. Samarski and E. K. Ziberlich, *Zhurnal Industrialnoi Khimii,* November 1933, reproduced in *Chemical and Metallurgical Engineering,* XLI, No. 12 (December 1934), p. 643.

resemblance to a one-tower chamber system disclosed in U.S. Patent 1,513,903 of 1924, which, as has been pointed out by its owners, has never been successful.'[56]

The Soviet article avoided discussion of how to dissipate the enormous heat reaction inherent in the single-tower design. It is notable (see figure 19–2) that the Soviet design repeats the basic fault in the American patent and ignores the heat problem entirely.

Examination of the flows and mechanical arrangements in the tower in both the original 1924 U.S. patent and the Soviet version shows that these fall in the same positions and perform the same functions, particularly in the cases of the combustion chamber, the pumps, the acid cooler, and the storage tank. The only difference between the two versions is in the greater detail of the original design. There is no improvement nor distinguishing feature at all in the Soviet version; it is a much-simplified and rather crude copy of the U.S. patent. Nothing more has been heard of the single-tower design and Soviet manufacture of sulfuric acid continues to be based on multi-tower Western processes.

[56]   *Ibid.,* January 1935.

Figure 19–3   THE WARNER & SWASEY COMPANY NO. 2-A
UNIVERSAL HOLLOW HEXAGON TURRET LATHE (1929)

Source: Warner & Swasey Co. Cleveland, Ohio.

Figure 19–4   MODEL 1 K 36 TURRET LATHE PRODUCED BY THE IM.
ORDZHONIKIDZE TURRET LATHE PLANT, MOSCOW (1932–50)

Source: Warner & Swasey Co., Cleveland, Ohio.

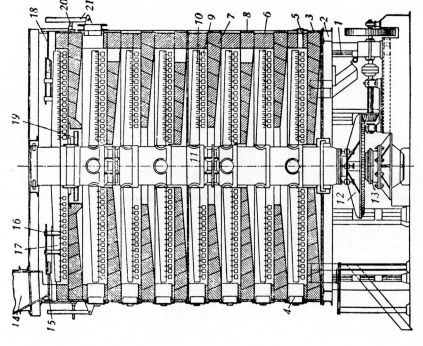

Figure 19–6 TYPE VKhZ 8-HEARTH ROASTER FOR PYRITE FINES

Legend:

1. Column
2. Ring
3. Jacket
4. Inspection door
5. Discharge
6. Insulation
7. Brick base of roof
8. Concrete (red brick normally used)
9. Rabble blade
10. Rabble arm
11. Shaft
12. Gear drive mechanism
13. Bearing
14. Hopper
15. Feed plate and apron
16. Feed arm
17. Feed scraper
18. Feed raceway
19. Iron plate
20. Lever
21. Outlet

Source: Bolshaya Sovetskaya Entsiklopediya, 1945 ed., LI, col. 14.

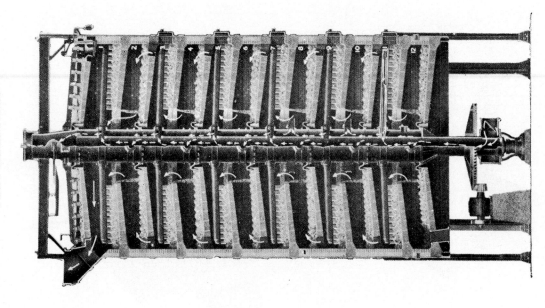

Figure 19–5 NICHOLS-HERRESHOFF 12-HEARTH ROASTER FOR PYRITE FINES

Source: A. M. Fairlie, *Sulfuric Acid Manufacture* (New York: Reinhold, 1936), p. 103.

A SUCCESSFUL TRANSFER: THE WARNER & SWASEY TURRET LATHE[57]

In 1932 the Ordzhonikidze, or Works No. 28, was opened in Moscow for production of machine tools. By 1940 the plant employed 5,000 people working in three shifts.[58] Some 35 million rubles were invested in the plant, which was planned to produce 3,400 machines annually, specializing in turret lathes.

Production started in 1932 with a 65-millimeter bar capacity turret lathe: a direct copy of the Warner & Swasey 65-millimeter turret lathe model No. 2-A of 1929. The degree of similarity between the two machines is remarkable; it appears the Soviet engineers did not try to 'improve' the American model (as they did in other cases) but faithfully reproduced the complete machine.

A SUCCESSFUL TRANSFER: MECHANICAL FURNACES FOR ROASTING PYRITES

The Nichols-Herreshoff pyrites-roasting furnace was developed by the Nichols Copper Company of New York (later called the Nichols Engineering and Research Corporation) and over the years modified and improved, until by the mid-1930s it had the form indicated in figure 19–5. The furnace was a cylindrical structure with from four to twelve hearths containing detachable rabble arms allowing replacement while the furnace was in operation.[59]

This design was adopted in the Soviet Union. It is widely used under the name 'VKhZ mechanical furnace,' after the Voskressensk Chemical Plant, where it was first utilized. The model shown in figure 19–6 is an eight-hearth VKhZ model.[60] Further, the summary article on sulfuric acid manufacture in *Bolshaya Sovietskaya Entsiklopediya* is little more than a discussion of foreign equipment types: Lurgi and Wedge furnaces, Cottrell-type electro-filters (called the XK-30) and the standard Gay Lussacs and Glover towers, among others.

CONCLUSIONS:
THE ADVANTAGES AND DISADVANTAGES OF COPYING

To a developing latecomer such as the Soviet Union, the obvious advantage of copying is that investment in research and development for a desired process can be avoided. There is, in addition, a less obvious and more important

---

[57] The assistance of the Warner & Swasey Co., Cleveland, Ohio is gratefully acknowledged.

[58] Oberkommando der Wehrmacht (OKW/Wi Rü Amt/Wi), March 1941, Miscellaneous German Records, National Archives Microcopy T 84–122.

[59] A. M. Fairlie, *Sulfuric Acid Manufacture* (New York: Reinhold, 1936), p. 103.

[60] *Bolshaya Sovietskaya Entsiklopediya* (Moscow, 1945) LI, Col. 14.

advantage; there is no necessity to invest in processes and experimentation that may prove fruitless. To achieve a single successful process, dozens (sometimes hundreds) of somewhat similar processes may have to be researched and partially developed. Most of these never pass beyond the research stage. Avoidance of the cost of unsuccessful but necessary product development, often called 'waste' by socialist ideologues, or the 'wastes of competition' in some textbooks, is the greatest gain for the latecomer. The latecomer also gains time as well as avoiding monetary investment. The gain in time by the Soviets has been extraordinary. The wide-strip mill—a fundamental development in iron and steel rolling—was installed in the Soviet Union within a few years of its development in the United States and before installation in Europe. The Warner & Swasey turret lathe copied in 1932 was the company's 1929 model. In chemical engineering, the processes acquired were ahead of those installed elsewhere in the world: a 1,000-ton-per-day nitric acid plant is large even today. The Douglas DC-3 contract was concluded within one year of the first flight. Although the tractor models (International Harvester and Caterpillar) were soon discontinued by their makers, any tractor is an advance over a yoke of oxen. It is not an exaggeration to say that the Soviets acquired 30 years of foreign technical development in three years, although it took 10 to 15 years to absorb the acquisition. Scarce resources may therefore be spread further by copying, either for the benefit of the consumer or—as in the Soviet example—to build a massive military complex and provide assistance for world revolution.

There are, however, disadvantages. The original expensive winnowing-out process of invention and the selection of desirable innovations were undertaken under circumstances differing from those in Russia. A process suitable for Pittsburg, Pennsylvania or Dortmund, Germany may not be suitable for Omsk, Siberia. Climate, natural resources, labor skills, and even topography may have an adverse influence. The Soviets are well aware of this problem, and plants have been specially designed or adapted by foreign firms for Soviet conditions. The onus of performance has often been placed upon the Western contractor by the insertion of penalty clauses in the contract.[61]

[61] For example, the 1937 E. B. Badger contract for supply and installation of three continuous alcohol and distillation and refining units. Pages 17–9 of the contract set forth the penalties payable by Badger in the event that the equipment does not meet guarantees. One formula among half a dozen provides for liquidating damages in the event the concentration of alcohol produced falls below guarantee and reads: 'Formula: Guaranteed strength (99.8 by Volume) minus the actual strength (percentage by Volume) × 1/3 contract price ($123,333.33) × .3 = Liquidated damage for one unit. The maximum liability of the COMPANY under this guarantee for liquidating damages shall be $7,333.32 per unit.'
This type of precise guarantee was typical.

A more subtle, very important, and long-range disadvantage is the loss of technical experience and initiative. It is unlikely that an imported technology can be efficiently operated, particularly when foreign advice and influence are shut off immediately after installation, as in the Soviet Union. Soviet claims demand cautious examination. For example, the Soviets claim that they have operated U.S.-installed steel mills at a rate far in excess of 100 percent capacity. This, however, is no great feat. Steel mills can be operated temporarily in excess of 100 percent capacity; the point missed by the Soviets is that continual operation in this high capacity range will lead to breakdowns and rapid obsolescence. This kind of operating experience, and the exchange of advice necessary between equipment manufacturer and user, is lost to a closed society.

Another definite disadvantage is that the Soviets have no way of being certain whether any specific foreign process is indeed the most advanced. How does one judge technical advance or the state of an art without oneself developing the frontiers of technology? This comes out clearly in the single-tower sulfuric acid example above. Superficially an attractive proposition, it is technically impracticable. Thus the Soviet engineer and planner, by virtue of lack of development experience, is led into technological traps—gigantomania, over-design, and the inability to distinguish between theoretical and practical solutions.

Above all, the basic flaws of centrally planned systems are obscured. Such systems are static. They do not have innate ability for rational self-generated technical advance. As Hirschman points out, in socialist societies the process of 'creative destruction' means 'self-destruction' rather than 'destruction of somebody else.' Centrally planned systems are permanently doomed—without capitalist help—to the era of gaslight and buggies, or Model Ts and crystal radios, or IBM 7090s and Fiat 124s, depending on the date of the final overthrow of capitalism. This is the Achilles' heel of socialism. Without capitalism, or some variant of a market system, centrally planned systems are doomed to technical stagnation. This is why copying is pervasive and has persisted for 50 years. It explains the perennial trumpeting of 'Soviet technical advance,' the ever-continuing flow of propaganda, and the abject fear of foreign political ideas.

CHAPTER TWENTY

Problems of Technical Assimilation

THE Soviet economy in the last half of the 1930s suffered from massive technical indigestion; it had absorbed at one gulp the most advanced of Western techniques. On the other hand—and this cannot be lightly dismissed —the Soviets did achieve their political goals; and this, from the Communist viewpoint, justified any sacrifices and problems. Some of the major problems, as they relate to the technical transfer, are briefly summarized below.

THE PROBLEM OF BACKWARDNESS

It is true that Russia in 1930 was backward, but not quite in the sense generally accepted. Tsarist Russia had a relatively advanced industrial structure with definite signs of indigenous Russian development.[1] Growth rates in the late nineteenth century were at least equal to, if not better than, anything achieved under the Soviets, and without the terrible cost incurred by the Soviet 'experiment.' However, Soviet Russia was backward in the sense that the Revolution had stripped Russia of technical, managerial, and certainly innovative skills; at the end of the 1920s the regime was in no condition even to maintain current operations without foreign help, and certainly in no position to consider the gigantic technical steps contemplated. The loss of skills had resulted from Revolution-induced emigration and from the backward nature of the Russian peasant, now more or less forcibly moved into new factories. There is no question that this ignorance in the working force led to massive spoilage of new equipment and gross inefficiency; *Za Industrializatsiiu*, for example, asked the rhetorical question, 'How is it possible that a factory built according to the last word in American technique and equipped with

---

[1] Sutton, *Western Technology . . . , 1917 to 1930*, pp. 183–4.

first-class foreign lathes and automatic machines cannot for 10 months emerge from its disorganized state?'[2]

There are numerous reports from foreign engineers supporting this charge of the improper use of equipment. For example, a State Department report of an interview with Paul Lauer, an electrical engineer formerly with Brown-Boveri and at the time of interview with I. G. Farbenindustrie, noted that 'although a great deal of the industrial equipment with which he came into contact was first class, machines would be operated day and night in an attempt to force production and . . . when they finally broke down no one was able to repair them.'[3]

Such reports of gross inefficiency, related to the low level of worker skills, are commonplace; what is noteworthy is the wide variety of sources generating such comments. An open letter to *Za Industrializatsiiu*[4] from 35 Russian engineers at Chelyabinsk said that the plant was on the verge of total collapse. An American engineer at Stalingrad, Ellwood T. Riesing, pointed out massive spoilage of new equipment and laid it to ignorance and perhaps 'a little sabotage.'[5] A German tool designer at Stalingrad said he had never worked under such inefficient conditions.[6] *Ekonomicheskaya Zhizn*[7] had numerous articles on 'technical illiteracy.'

By 1945 the factory worker had become somewhat more efficient, but a different form of backwardness remained. This might be called innovative backwardness. When compared to Japan, another country exemplifying development via foreign borrowing, the extent of this backwardness is surprising. The Russians have emphatically shown ability to absorb and adapt foreign methods and equipment; what is obviously missing—propaganda to the contrary—is clear-cut indigenous self-generated innovation. There is none that can compare in any way to outside development. If we compare Soviet Russia to Japan in 1945, ignoring tsarist development for a moment, we find that the Japanese were beginning to make successful self-generated efforts (in machine tools and optical equipment, for example), whereas similar efforts in the U.S.S.R. (synthetic rubber is an excellent example) were not successful. The Soviets *did* make advances in military production, which is amenable to central, bureaucratic direction.

---

[2] *Za Industrializatsiiu*, No. 123, May 6, 1931.
[3] U.S. State Dept. Decimal File, 861.50—FIVE YEAR PLAN/246.
[4] March 19, 1931.
[5] U.S. State Dept. Decimal File, 861.659—TRACTORS/2.
[6] *Ibid.*, 869.659—TRACTORS/3.
[7] For example, in the issue of April 3, 1931.

THE THEORETICAL VIEWPOINT OF SOVIET ENGINEERS

An argument can be made that the Soviet technological transfer was ineffective, or at least grossly wasteful, on the basis of charges by American engineers that the Soviet engineers were 'too theoretical' and that practice and theory differed.[8] While willing to teach the practical aspect as developed by years of experience, Americans found Soviet engineers distrustful and too willing to revert to theoretical discussion of why a specific American practice would not work. There is no question that this led to wasted time and effort and was partly responsible for ineffective transfers.

The Soviet attitude stemmed to some extent from a European and pre-revolutionary view of the place of an engineer; in this view an engineer wore white gloves and only gave instructions. The American engineer (and this accounts in some measure for the success of American practice) rolls up his sleeves and gets his hands dirty. The prerevolutionary attitude was encouraged in the Soviet era because there was safety in being able to point to theory if something went wrong and the OGPU made unwelcome inquiries. Possibly (and the importance of this should not be underestimated) the Russian engineer was thinking ahead to the time when he might have to 'prove' the correctness of personal actions before a commission of inquiry. The basic point is that the American engineer was well aware that theory applies to certain idealized conditions and that in practice events are not always covered by theory. For example, in the 1930s there was nothing in Western literature, and certainly not in Soviet literature, about the cause of local deformation of steels without wear or abrasion, although new gages had been reported as worn out within the first day of use. Theory, as known at that time, did not explain such a phenomenon; but experience provided a rudimentary safeguard against unwelcome results.

On the other hand, Russian engineers displayed great resourcefulness in keeping plants operating without spare parts, usually denied by the planners, and with widely varying types of equipment. In other words, the Russian engineer had technical adaptability when he needed it. Placing this observation alongside the 'too much theory' argument leads to the conclusion that the problem may stem mainly from ideological factors. Although capitalist

---

[8]   In almost every case in which the State Dept. interviewing officer touched on this problem, the American engineer made a comment to this effect. The criticism also appeared in official reports by American companies to the Soviet Union; for an example, see the report on the coal industry made by Stuart, James & Cooke, Inc., reported in the *Moscow Daily News*, June 3, 1931, p. 1.

It is interesting to note a current Soviet preoccupation with theory. At a time when the great need of Soviet industry is practical efficiency, we find, for example, an article on technical progress in the economy cast to a very great extent in terms of theoretical, not practical achievements. (See 'V avangarde tekhnicheskogo progressa,' by Academician M. Keldysh, in *Pravda*, No. 314, November 9, 1968.)

technology is held up as a model to be copied, the individual Western engineer has been, it is explained by the Party ideologue, held back by his capitalist masters and therefore does not appreciate new concepts and new methods; these can be achieved by Russian engineers under the guidance of the Party. In general, therefore, the writer is not willing to condemn individual Russian engineers. Part of the explanation for their theoretical attitude lies in the need for self-protection, part in ideologically tinted engineering decisions made by the Party, and part in training. In other words, if a Russian engineer is placed in a non-Soviet operating environment, he will probably act like a Western practitioner of the art.

The reason underlying the Soviet need for extensive Western assistance relates to the 'inability hypothesis'; Soviet engineers were unable to master the art of designing modern equipment within the Soviet environment. This statement is exemplified by the half-dozen Soviet attempts in the 1920s to produce a tractor.[9] The Karlick and similar designs were quickly abandoned as heavy, underpowered, and unworkable, and were replaced with the Fordson, Caterpillar, and International Harvester. In aircraft the slow, heavy ANT designs were replaced with cleanly designed, fast, and more powerful Western designs.[10]

It was recognized that these problems could be overcome. For example T. W. Jenkins, Chief Engineer for United Engineering at Zaporozhe, commented:

> Despite the many difficulties I have experienced in Zaporozhe and in other plants I feel that the enthusiasm displayed by the engineers and workers will eventually permit them to achieve a considerable amount of success in the operations of their plants. This undoubtedly will take a number of years, but in the end I feel that they will master the technique and eliminate most of the bureaucratic hindrances that prevent them from carrying out their work at the present time in a logical, orderly and efficient manner.[11]

In practice the problem was not overcome by 1945. Many of the copies in the early and mid-1930s suffered as a result of Soviet attempts to incorporate 'improvements' into the original Western designs. This was followed by a Party instruction not to incorporate changes; the result is that by 1940 or so we find *exact* copies of Western models in metric measurements. This is in itself quite an achievement; the Stalinets 80 tractor, for example, is a metric-system copy—very precise—of the Caterpillar D-7.[12]

---

[9] See Sutton, *Western Technology . . . , 1917 to 1930*, pp. 133–5: 'Attempts to Develop a Soviet Tractor, 1922 to 1926.' Also see V. A. Korobov, *Traktory avtomobili i sel'skokhozyaistvennye dvigateli* (Moscow: 1950). Compare pp. 6–7, the Mamin designs, with pp. 8–15, Western designs.

[10] See chap. 11.

[11] U.S. State Dept. Decimal File, 861.6511/34.

[12] The methods of copying the Caterpillar D-7 will be covered in Volume III.

THE PROBLEM OF IDEOLOGY VS. TECHNOLOGY

A major problem was created by the conflict between engineering logic and ideological objectives. At the outset it must be clearly stated that the Communist Party correctly recognized technology as the heart of economic development and since the beginning has placed continued emphasis on technology and technical progress; the power and discipline of the Party has remained solidly behind absorption and infusion of foreign technology. The analysis made by the Party is correct.

However, Party ideology is also responsible for the idea that the machine is in some way more productive under socialism than under capitalism. A machine is completely impervious to ideology; it must be operated within limits, it must be maintained, and it must have skilled operators; neglecting any one of these is perilous: the teachings of Lenin are no substitute for oil, maintenance, and skill. In the 1930s the Party injected itself into day-to-day operating procedures, and the efficiency of the machine suffered.

Ideology conflicted with efficient technical development in another way. Soviet purchasing and technical missions had a quota of Party members, whose contribution was repressive. In 1928, for example, a Soviet purchasing commission visited the Arthur G. McKee Company in Cleveland, Ohio; the chairman of the commission was a party member with no knowledge of metallurgy, but 'his father had been a worker in the South Urals steel plants and a great revolutionist and that made his son eligible.'[13] Three Russian engineers on the commission provided the technical experience necessary.

SABOTAGE OR INEFFICIENCY?

We are here concerned only with the possibility of sabotage insofar as it may have affected the transfer of technology. Possibly 20 percent of the interview reports in the State Department files refer to alleged incidents of sabotage in industrial plants. There is a distinction between overt sabotage and neglect, and certainly a difference between sabotage and inefficiency, although the end results may appear to be the same.

There was clearly sabotage before 1930 but probably less between 1930 and 1945. The question of how much cannot be answered. Whether the *real* sabotage was instigated by those on trial for *alleged* sabotage cannot be determined either. However, it is reasonably certain that there was some expression of opposition to the Soviet regime.

One report from the State Department files has been selected and summarized as an example. In 1932 the Riga Legation interviewed Edward Boyle, who had been in Russia from 1922 until 1932. Before 1921 he had been

[13]　*American Engineers in Russia*, Stuck MS, p. 21.

superintendent of the foundry in the Panama Canal Zone and was then utilized by the Soviets as a trouble-shooter on foundry problems.[14] The 14-page report suggests that Mr. Boyle was a stable individual (this was also the impression of the interviewing officer) who had had a lengthy uninterrupted stay in the U.S.S.R. Further, although he was a valuable employee he did not receive valuta payments and did not request payment in dollars. The report also suggests that he had adapted well to Russian life, had very few complaints, and in general was a well-balanced individual who asked only for work and enough to support himself. In brief, there is no evidence that Boyle was biasing his answers. Where his information can be checked, it checks out well with other reports.

Boyle stated he had encountered 'innumerable' acts of sabotage in the foundry industry, particularly in the years 1922–9:

> It was a simple matter for him to distinguish between lack of technical knowledge and a deliberate policy of sabotage. . . . Ignorant and inexperienced men whom force of circumstances had placed in charge of foundries were willing, and even anxious, to obtain the benefit of his knowledge and cooperation, while master mechanics and engineers of the former regime usually made it impossible for him to accomplish anything constructive in their plants.[15]

Boyle cited his first assignment at Mariupol, where two cupolas had not worked well since installation two years previously; he was told the assignment might be dangerous. The cupolas were perfectly designed. These were the first cupolas designed under the Soviets but 'minor obstructions and failures, obviously deliberately installed or caused, had prevented the cupolas from producing for two years.'

On the other hand, Boyle cited the case of blowholes in cylinder castings for locomotives being produced in Leningrad; these he quickly deduced as the result of poor pouring methods due to lack of experience.[16] This last example points up an abysmal lack of technical experience. Many problems blamed on sabotage may have been the result of sheer ignorance.

Although the evidence is fragmentary, there unquestionably was sabotage; how much will never be known. This, as Boyle stated, tapered off about 1930 for the simple reason that the penalties were too harsh. Sabotage or 'wrecking' became the excuse adopted by the Party after 1930 for the inefficiencies of a socialist system. It is suggested, again with fragmentary evidence, that after 1930 the sabotage claimed was not sabotage at all, but merely the result of inefficiency.

[14]   U.S. State Dept. Decimal File, 861.5017—Living Conditions/486.
[15]   *Ibid.*, p. 7.
[16]   *Ibid.*, p. 9.

THE PURGE TRIALS OF 1936–7

Reports of the American Embassy in Moscow also supported the view that the purge trials were not the primary cause of existing industrial problems.[17] The problems were due to more basic factors: 'the inability of Soviet engineers and workers to master fully the intricacies of modern industrial technique'; the refusal of workers to increase productivity without further compensation; and the periodic breakdown of production machinery and lack of proper repair and maintenance. The Stakhanovite (shock worker) movement was singled out for special mention as a factor in causing machinery breakdown.

A 1937 report[18] established four basic reasons for the current industrial setback. First was the inexperience and carelessness of Soviet engineers and workers 'and their present inability to fully appreciate and master the more complicated technique of modern industry.' This deficiency was explained on the ground that Russian workers were technologically backward, and that many if not most Russian workers with skills had been either driven out of Russia or liquidated at the time of the Revolution. Thus the 1937 labor force did not have the 'feel of the machine' and retained 'too much of the proverbial Russian spirit of "Nitchevo" . . . to have a real understanding of the care and accuracy needed to master fully modern industrial technique.'

The report pointed out (and this is supported by the findings of this study) that:

> . . . one of the principal complaints of foreign engineers who have worked for any time in the Soviet Union is the failure of Soviet workers and engineers to appreciate the necessity for doing painstaking and precise work. The foreign technician soon learns that generally speaking the Soviet worker is apparently incapable of, or at least does not understand the necessity for, observing the limited tolerances called for under modern engineering technique.

Another common complaint by foreign engineers with regard to Soviet engineers was that they very often endeavored to improve upon the design of foreign equipment without realizing that such efforts might throw the entire machine out of balance or cause other complications. These shortcomings caused the percentage of rejects to be very high. The model changeover in the Gorki Automobile Plant in 1935 is an example; the new model was essentially a copy of the 1934 Ford but Soviet engineers attempted to introduce changes

> which apparently led them eventually into difficulties. In any event, over a year and a half after production was started on the new car they have failed to attain the daily production figures for the old model, which

---

[17] These conclusions are based on interviews with U.S. businessmen and engineers and on Soviet sources.

[18] U.S. State Dept. Decimal File, 861.60/288.

was an exact copy of the 1930 American FORD and which they learned to build with the full assistance of a large number of American engineers and specialists.[19]

Second, was the failure of the Stakhanovite movement to increase productivity, under this plan, workers were sometimes encouraged to increase the capacity of their machines beyond that which they were built to stand. Boastful articles appeared in the Soviet press stating that machines were producing more under socialism than under capitalism; repair work was neglected and the wear and tear led to breakdowns. Third, the Soviet copies of foreign machines were the first to break down 'and it was not so very long before many foreign machines followed suit.'[20] The arrest or dismissal of members of commissariats and plant directors removed many of the more capable members of Russian industry. The report concluded that Russian youth were beginning to appreciate the intricacies of modern machinery and that although there was a 'definite crisis' in Soviet industry this did not presage a complete breakdown in industrial development.

There is also other evidence to suggest that inadequate technical knowledge was much more to blame than wrecking or carelessness. One example is the erection of three continuous alcohol distillation and refining units by E. B. Badger. These were linked up to fermentation tanks constructed by Soviet organizations to drawings supplied by the Badger Company. The first of three such units was brought into production in 1936, but by 1937 the Soviets were requesting Badger to return two American engineers to solve problems which had arisen in operation and 'alleging that the Company's equipment did not produce satisfactory results.'[21]

Two Badger engineers made the trip from the United States, briefly investigated, and found that the difficulty caused only by the lack, in the Soviet-constructed tanks, of an agitator from which the raw product was supposed to be taken before treatment by the American-installed equipment. Lack of an agitator gave the raw liquid a nonuniform consistency which affected the quality of the final product. An agitator had been included in the original design, but 'the Soviet engineers had for some reason failed to install this device.'[22] An agitator was then installed by the Badger engineers and the unit worked satisfactorily. Two rather obvious points may be made: first, to understand the necessity for uniform raw materials requires only elementary knowledge of chemical engineering—indeed little more than common sense, and second (this is common to other cases), the original American drawings and designs were not followed by the Soviet engineers.

[19] *Ibid.*
[20] *Ibid.*
[21] U.S. State Dept. Decimal File, 861.602/284. See also Chap. 8, p. 116.
[22] *Ibid.*

THE PROBLEM OF CENTRAL PLANNING

From the Western viewpoint, certain major elements in the Soviet economy are not quite what they seem. Above all the concept of central planning devolves into little more than a means of political control. In the period examined there was no case in which central planning achieved an end which could not have been achieved in some more efficient manner; given this observation, it is suggested that the objective of central planning is political, not economic.

The traditional objective of central control is reputed to be a balanced move forward on an integrated industrial front. The theory is that such a giant step forward achieves more than piecemeal efforts brought about by operation of the market system. The first observation is that over the last 50 years the Soviets have more or less utilized a system of central control and the United States has not. In terms of addition to the Gross National Product, general living standards, and overall technical progress, the United States is far ahead today, suggesting that over the long haul the enterprise system, or an approximation of it, is far more effective. Such a system also has certain human advantages.

Second, if we examine a lesser time period of Soviet development, such as the years 1930 to 1945, in more detail, the advantage of central planning is at best not clear. It took several years of statistical work to get ready for the First Five-Year Plan, and then the figures were revised (upwards) at the last minute as American companies indicated they could build units much larger than those requested. Construction starts did not coincide as they should have, the First Five-Year Plan was not integrated with the existing industrial structure, and construction finishes were even less well integrated.

The term 'Five-Year Plan' had no empirical significance whatsoever. A little thought will indicate why this is so. Even under conditions of perfect supply, abundant labor and technical skills, and a flexible transportation system, it would be difficult to start a large number of major projects at one time; it would be patently absurd to hope, or want, to finish them at the same point, because of the widely differing gestation periods of sophisticated industrial systems.

An attempt to match the actual start and finish dates with those indicated by the Plan reveals no correlation whatsoever. What actually happened is summarized in the following paragraphs.

Specific units were begun as soon as foreign contractors could supply the skills and the equipment. There were varying delays in installation because of unskilled labor, theoretically trained or entirely untrained Soviet engineers, and a basic apathy, whipped into action only periodically by udarnik campaigns. When the engineering time horizon more nearly matched the 'political planning' time objective, the engineering factors were disgracefully sacrificed to meet a propaganda deadline. In an efficient system, the start-up of blooming mills and blowing-in of blast furnaces should follow a precise timetable determined ONLY by engineering factors. When construction schedules were rearranged to build the most conspicuous plant features (i.e., smoke stacks) first, or mills were started up before all installations were complete and not in accordance with manufacturers instructions, then in truth the lunatics were running the asylum. This was well stated by the Chief Engineer of United Engineering:

> One of the principal weaknesses I have noted during my stay is that the directors of the plants and the engineers invariably send in optimistic reports to Moscow regarding performance and invariably make promises which they realize cannot be fulfilled. For example, the directors of the plants promised Moscow that the Soviet-made rolling mill would be in operation in October 1936. The mill was not completed as scheduled and the Soviet engineers sent a full explanation to the authorities, blaming the delay on the lack of materials and giving other excuses. Finally during the month of November and the first part of December strenuous efforts were made to complete the rolling mill before the end of the year. The Soviet engineers explained to me that it was absolutely necessary for them to operate the rolling mill before the end of the year in order to be in a position to request additional funds for the construction of the mill in 1937. They explained that larger credits were granted to Soviet mills which were in a position to show that they had more or less lived up to schedule. During the above-mentioned period I estimate that approximately 2,000 working hours were wasted in the effort to operate the mill before the end of the year. The equipment was installed in a temporary manner and finally on December 24 the rolling mill was operated for five hours and then shut down. The directors of the factory, however, were able to send telegram to Moscow on that date announcing that the rolling mill was in operation.[23]

Although much equipment was especially made to fit Soviet factor proportions and labor skills, problems arose with used equipment—for example, with the Ford automobile tire plant transferred to the U.S.S.R. in 1944. This was a two-story operation in the United States and the opinion of U.S. engineers was that 'it could not function properly unless it was housed in precisely the same type of building in which it had been housed in Michigan. . . .'[24] The

---

[23] U.S. State Dept. Decimal File, 861.6511/34. T. W. Jenkins, United Engineering Chief Engineer at Zaporozhe. For an excellent summary of start-up problems in the tractor plants see Dodge, *op. cit.*, pp. 281–7. A certain proportion of problems was created, of course, by general engineering factors normally connected with the establishment and start-up of new plants.

[24] U.S. State Dept. 861.645/17, Memorandum of Conversation, April 1, 1943.

Soviets could not provide such a building and the Ford plant was eventually housed in a one-story operation with consequent loss of efficiency.

Thus it may be concluded that the Soviets had numerous problems in technical assimilation. Many of these were problems associated with unskilled labor and normal technical assimilation procedures. Two factors, however, complicated the transition: the intervention of ideology into the technical sphere, and rigid central planning. Thus the transfer was far more difficult than that of Japan, for example, which absorbed Western technology and by 1945 was starting to forge ahead on her own.

CHAPTER TWENTY-ONE

Western Technology and Sectoral Rates of Growth, 1930-45

DURING the period from 1930 to 1945, Soviet technology was almost completely a transfer from Western countries; only two major Soviet innovations have been identified: SKB synthetic rubber and the Ramzin once-through boiler; both were supplemented with Western methods by 1945.[1] One significant Soviet achievement was the conversion of U.S. and British equipment to the metric system, with subsequent duplication of a metric copy rather than the imported original. Such conversion should not by any means be underestimated; it requires a great deal of technical ingenuity and engineering skill.

Thus the conclusion is that for the period from 1930 to 1945 Soviet technology was in effect Western technology converted to the metric system.

It was suggested earlier that the modus operandi during this period required Gosplan to estimate the desired capacity for each industrial sector while leaving the initial implementation process to Albert Kahn Company and the supply of initial engineering talent and equipment to other Western companies. At the same time, arrangements were made to duplicate this equipment in newly built plants. Gosplan objectives should logically have been related to the amount of Western assistance procured. This proposition may now be

---

[1] The almost complete absence of Soviet innovation was, so far as the writer is concerned, a surprise. Time after time a particular process or piece of equipment was assumed to be of Soviet origin (in accord with the bias noted on page 8), but in all cases except those few mentioned in the text a Western precursor was found. The explanation is simply that it was cheaper to borrow rather than develop internally; however, this explanation is limited to the period 1917 to 1945.

If any reader has specific examples of Soviet innovation for 1917 to 1945, information on them would indeed be welcome and certainly included in later work. It should be stressed that generalities are of little use—and indeed vague generalities account for much of the present confusion about Soviet achievements. The suggestion must be *specific*: for example, 'the Model Kh AZ-241 meat grinder is a Soviet innovation.' We are, of course, interested in innovation rather than invention or discovery.

profitably explored. There follows an examination of actual rates of growth by sector in relation to technical assistance. In sum, we first look at planning objectives and then at the fulfillment of these objectives in relation to Western assistance.

The initial problem is to measure effectively and accurately the degree of technical assistance in a quantitative manner. One method would be to compare that capacity built with the percentage of Western technical assistance received. For example, 100 percent of the Soviet automobile-manufacturing capacity was of Western origin and utilized Western equipment. However, such a measure cannot be calculated for those industries (such as flour milling and vodka manufacture) in which very little *qualitative* data exists. Neither can it be calculated in industries such as mining, in which individual Western mining engineers carried the initial burden of establishing the method by which a mine was to be developed, bringing the mine into operation, supervising initial operations while gradually introducing imported equipment (followed by Soviet equipment made to Western designs) and finally handing over operations to Soviet mining engineers. Neither does such a measure include situations in which a single piece of imported equipment (which might comprise less than one percent of the total capital expenditure) allows a new plant to operate, whereas without it production is zero. Thus while 'percent of capacity built to Western technique' is an initially attractive quantitative measure, it is not useful.

The measure used is a scale of 1 through 10, each value on the scale being determined by an assessment of the importance of technical transfers from the West. The scale takes into account not only the supply of Western designs, equipment manuals, and engineers, but operator training, quality and production guarantees, patents, and training of Soviet engineers in Western plants: in brief, the whole complex of transfers which make up technical assistance. In this system a large number of factors related to technical assistance enters into individual scale values. Where no foreign assistance at all can be identified and an indigenous process is used, then the scale value is zero: i.e., no technical assistance. At the other end of the scale, a value of 10 is assigned where, as in tire manufacture, a technical-assistance agreement provided the process, plant design, follow-up assistance, equipment, and operator training, and also provided more than 90 percent of the output in the period 1930–45.

One could argue that a value of 10 should require complete Western operation of the plant as a pure concession for the whole period 1930 to 1945 as well as other assistance factors. Under this definition there would indeed be no sectors with a value of 10, and only one or two with 9. The important point to be made is that the scale utilized does not define a value of 10 as indicating 100-percent operation by Western companies throughout the period 1930–45.

The scale ignores operation by Soviet personnel after installation. By the same token an operator of an automobile or a washing machine in the United States cannot claim or be held responsible for the design and manufacture of the product he uses.

In other words a maximum scale value of 10 includes operation by Soviet workers for the period after start-up to 1945, maintenance performed by Soviet engineers, and duplication of the equipment for use at other locations. Such duplication, of course, as in two categories of machine tools (lathes and vertical drilling machines), could account for most of Soviet productive capacity by 1945. The scale focuses then on *transfers and origin of technology* rather than composition of aggregate capacity in a sector at the end of the period.

PLANNING OBJECTIVES AND WESTERN TECHNICAL ASSISTANCE

It has been suggested in the light of preliminary evidence[2] that Gosplan decided upon those sectors it wanted developed under the plan and then contracted with foreign organizations to build large-scale units in those sectors. Capacity was then expanded by duplication of the transferred Western technology. The Gosplan estimates were, however, qualified by Western engineering advice. Cases are found in which Gosplan suggestions regarding capacity were considerably expanded when foreign companies indicated they could build much larger units than those requested. No cases were found where a company offered to build a smaller unit or refused to build that capacity established by Gosplan; modifications appear always to have been in the direction of increase.

If this assessment of Western participation is correct, there should be a relationship between planning objectives formulated in various plans and the degree of technical assistance introduced: the greater the increment in output planned then the greater (other things being equal) the foreign technical assistance. Unfortunately other things are not equal. There is a considerable difference between technological complexity and capital-output ratios, and consequently between the amount of foreign assistance required by different sectors. In blast-furnace construction, a straightforward and easily assimilated process, technical assistance was limited to the Western provision of designs. By 1937–8 Gipromez had its own design; in automobile assembly, far more complex, the Soviets had not mastered Western technology even by 1970.

With this qualification in mind, data were derived for a number of sectors in which it is possible to estimate both technical assistance and planning objectives. World War II cut short the Third Five-Year Plan; consequently

---

[2]   See pp. 249–52.

data was derived for 1937 objectives in relation to 1932 output. This is presented for a dozen sectors in table 21–1.

Table 21–1   SOVIET PLANNING OBJECTIVES
AND WESTERN TECHNICAL ASSISTANCE

Sector	Planning Objective of 1937 in Relation to 1932 Output (Percent)	Technical Assistance Scale
Zinc	608.0	9
Motor vehicle tires	543.0	10
Bicycles	447.8	10
Sulfuric acid	420.2	9
Steam locomotives	338.0	3
Sugar	302.0	4
Electric power	283.8	8
Canned food	279.3	7
Machine tools	266.7	9
Woolen fabrics	240.9	4
Boots and shoes	219.5	2
Cotton fabrics	187.5	4
Flour	142.8	2

Sources: Planning objectives: Gosplan, *The Second Five-Year Plan* (London: Lawrence
and Wishart, n.d.), pp. 545–55.
Technical-assistance scale: see text.

Examination of the data presented in table 21–1 and figure 21–1 suggests,
although the scatter is pronounced, that planning objectives were broadly
associated with technical assistance. Certainly this becomes clear if we examine
both ends of the range presented. Zinc, with the most ambitious planning
objective (a sixfold increase of output between 1932 and 1937), had a high
technical assistance scaling of 9. Similarly bicycles and motor vehicles, the
only sectors listed with scalings of 10, had very high planning objectives:
increase by a factor of five. On the other hand, if we examine the other end of
the range we find the flour sector had the lowest planning objective and the
lowest scale of technical assistance: 2.[3]

Thus in broad terms the extent of planning objectives may be, as we would
expect, related to the extent of foreign technical assistance.

[3]   The listing in table 21–1, plotted in figure 21–1, comprises all sectors (except one)
in which data for both planning objectives and technical assistance could be found
and related. One sector not listed—linen fabrics—had a high planning objective
and a rating of zero on the technical-assistance scale. This was rejected, as the lack
of evidence of technical assistance for this particular sector was not convincing;
the negative case is always difficult to prove.

Fig. 21–1   RELATIONSHIP OF PLANNING OBJECTIVES
TO TECHNICAL ASSISTANCE, 1932–7

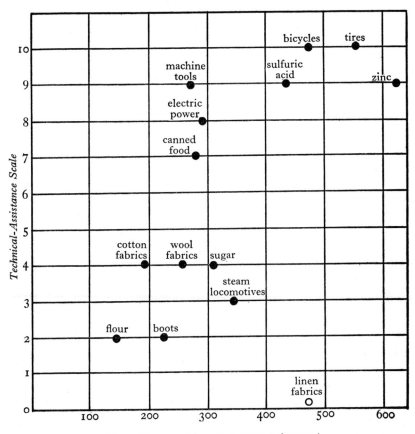

Planned increment in output, 1932–7 (percent)

Sources: Planning objectives: Gosplan, *The Second Five-Year Plan* (London: Lawrence and Wishart, n.d.), pp. 545–55.
Technical assistance: see text.

SECTORAL GROWTH RATES AND WESTERN TECHNICAL ASSISTANCE

If the hypothesis of this study is to be supported, those sectors of the Soviet economy with the highest growth rates should prove to be the recipients of consistent and significant foreign technical assistance. Conversely those sectors with low growth rates should *not* be recipients of foreign technical assistance.

These propositions can be examined in a reasonably precise manner by comparing rates of growth by industrial sector[4] with the amount of foreign technical aid in that sector. Tables 21–2 and 21–3 and figure 21–2 illustrate this relationship.

All sectors with rates of growth in excess of an annual average 11 percent and below 4 percent are listed in the tables and plotted in figure 21–2 and compared to technical assistance for that sector when it can be estimated.

SECTORS WITH HIGH GROWTH RATES

The sector with the highest annual average rate of growth between 1928 and 1955 was bicycle manufacture: 23 percent. This sector received the benefits of a technical-assistance agreement with the Birmingham Small Arms Company of England, manufacturers of the popular BSA bicycle. Steel tubes, a major input in bicycle manufacture, were manufactured on Western equipment using Mannesman, Pilger, Stiefel, and other German processes, possibly at the Nikopol plant installed by the Tube Reducing Company. Rubber tires for bicycles were manufactured at Yaroslavl, which received technical assistance from the Seiberling Rubber Company. Ball bearings for bicycles were manufactured at the plant erected under the Italian Villar-Perosa agreement. Thus the bicycle-manufacturing process was obtained from the West, operators were trained by Western companies, and input materials were wholly developed with Western technical-assistance agreements and equipment. This sector is therefore given a ranking of 10; it is difficult to envisage means of further assistance unless Western engineers had remained throughout the period 1930–45 to operate the Velo bicycle plant.

In lead and zinc mining and smelting (20 and 19 percent growth, respectively) development and operation of mines and construction of smelters and refineries was almost wholly American in the early 1930s. It was estimated that at the mining engineer level of skills, 90 percent of the underground engineers were American and only 10 percent Russian.[5] Americans handed over responsibility to hastily trained Soviet engineers in 1932–3; almost all Americans left by 1936. The underground equipment was initially American and German, replaced partly after 1934 with Soviet copies. Smelters and refineries were completely American-designed, equipped with British, German, American

---

[4]   G. Warren Nutter, *The Growth of Industrial Production in the Soviet Union* (Princeton: Princeton University Press, 1962), pp. 96–7. Nutter's data cover annual average rates of growth from 1928 to 1955; this volume is limited to 1928–45. This is not, however, a major qualifying factor, as the benefits of technical assistance persist after installation, and installations from the early 1930s were still operating in the 1950s and the 1960s. Further, the transfer continued in the 1950s and 1960s, as will be demonstrated in the next volume.

[5]   P. 44.

equipment, and initially operated by American superintendents. A scaling of 9 is therefore applied to both lead and zinc production.

Motor vehicle tires were made only in Western-supplied plants—the Yaroslavl plant built under the Seiberling contract of 1929 and re-equipped with British machinery in the 1950s; the Ford Motor Company truck-tire plant, with a one-million-tire-per-year capacity, supplied under Lend-Lease in 1942–5; the Toyo Tire Company, Ltd., plant at Mukden and Manchu Rubber Company, Ltd., tire plant at Liaoyank, both removed from Manchuria to the U.S.S.R. in late 1945.[6] This sector is scaled at 10.

Table 21–2   INDUSTRIAL SECTORS IN U.S.S.R. WITH ANNUAL AVERAGE GROWTH RATES GREATER THAN 11 PERCENT, 1928–55

Number on Figure 21–2	Industrial Sector	Annual Average Growth Rate, 1928–55[1] (Percent)	Position on Technical-Assistance Scale[2]
1	Bicycles	23.0	10
2	Lead	20.1	9
3	Motor vehicle tires	19.4	10
4	Steam turbines	19.2	8
5	Zinc	19.0	9
6	Diesel engines	18.7	8
—	Mineral fertilizer	17.1	Not estimated
7	Machine tools	16.3	9
8	Power transformers	15.5	9
9	Rayon and mixed fabrics	14.7	9
10	Asbestos shingles	14.5	9
11	Electric power	13.9	8
12	Natural gas	13.4	5
—	Roll roofing	12.9	Not estimated
13	Canned food	12.8	7
14	Clocks and watches	11.9	10
—	Macaroni	11.8	Not estimated
15	Sulfuric acid	11.2	9
16	Silk fabrics	11.3	10

Sources: 1 G. Warren Nutter, *Growth of Production in the Soviet Union* (Princeton: Princeton University Press, 1962), p. 96.
    2 Text.

[6] Edwin W. Pauley, *Report on Japanese Assets in Manchuria to the President of the United States, July 1946* (Washington: 1946), p. 204. Reparations will be covered in Volume III.

Fig. 21–2   RELATIONSHIP OF TECHNICAL ASSISTANCE
TO ANNUAL AVERAGE RATE OF GROWTH, 1928–55

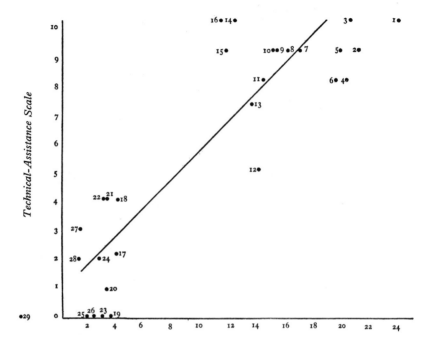

Annual average rate of growth (percent)

The only plant making steam turbines was the Stalin at Leningrad, producing Metropolitan-Vickers models to company drawings and initially with British technical assistance.[7] The British engineers left in 1933, and from that time on the Soviet engineers were on their own; this sector is scaled at 8 as there is evidence that by World War II turbine technology had been mastered and some independent work started.

Diesel engines are scaled at 8. Three systems (Sulzer, MAN and Deutz) were used—all from Germany. The technical-assistance agreements expired in the early 1930s, and from that time on eight plants manufactured diesels to these systems. Attempts to produce locomotive diesel engines with General Electric assistance failed, and production was abandoned in 1937 and not resumed until the 1950s.

---

[7]   P. 160.

SECTORS WITH LOW GROWTH RATES

Examination of those sectors with the lowest growth rates also provides support for our hypothesis. Table 21–3 lists those sectors for which Nutter estimates less than 4 percent average annual growth between 1928 and 1955.

Five sectors have a zero rate of growth. Of these, three are hardly candidates for technological improvement and indeed are traditional Russian peasant industries: low-grade tobacco (makhorka), vodka, and felt footwear all had growth rates of only 1 or 2 percent and utilized no foreign technology. Salt (3.4 percent) and linen fabrics (2.1 percent) similarly had low rates of growth and used no identifiable foreign technology.

The case of flour is interesting in the light of the hypothesis. The sector had a growth rate of only 1.1 percent and a low incidence of identifiable foreign technology. On the other hand, a resolution passed by the Collegium of the People's Commissariat of Foreign and Domestic Trade on November 27, 1929 decreed that contracts should be concluded with American firms for the planing of new flour mills, for the employment of six U.S. engineers to provide technical assistance for machinery construction, and for the employment of 10 U.S. engineers to establish a standard flour mill and assist in its construction.[8] In brief there was clear formal intent to supply technical assistance to this sector. There is, however, a report from one of the Americans later employed in design of flour mills which confirms, in the final analysis, the lack of technical transfers from abroad:

> Mr. Hess was employed in Kazakstan where he was designing and building flour mills, under the supervision of American engineers. These flour mills were built entirely with Russian material, except part of the machinery. Work on the flour mills has ceased on account of the lack of local material. It was agreed that the Russians would buy milling machinery and construction machinery in the United States. For this undertaking thus far no machinery has been purchased. Part of it is Russian made machinery which is very low in grade and of which there is only a meager supply.[9]

Thus the flour sector in the final analysis had *incomplete* technical assistance. Steam locomotives had an annual average growth rate of 1.2 percent. Out of approximately 25,000 locomotives built or acquired between 1928 and 1945, about 6,500 were imported (almost all U.S. Army types or German and British prototypes). The remaining 18,500 were based on successful tsarist models and built in the expanded tsarist-era plants. The basic Russian steam locomotive (indeed, the most numerous class of locomotive in the world) was the Vladikavkaz, first built in 1910 and then adopted by the Soviet. The Su and SO classes built by the Soviets were also tsarist models. Thus only about one-

---

[8] U.S. State Dept. Decimal File, 861.6584/3.
[9] *Ibid.*, 861.5017—Living Conditions/239.

quarter of the 1945 locomotive stock was imported, the balance being Soviet-made to tsarist design. The scale of technical impact is given as 3 (by virtue of the import of General Electric, Brown-Boveri, U.K., and German prototypes and the use of individual consultants for wheel-making, etc.). The annual average growth rate of 1.2 percent is also low.

A group of sectors with low growth rates includes boots and shoes, raw sugar, starch and syrup, matches, cotton fabrics, woolen and worsted fabrics, and vegetable oil. The common link between these sectors is that they all relate to the consumer—consistently the lowest priority in the Soviet Union. Although these sectors used some foreign equipment and the textile industries used early technical assistance, the growth rates reflect both the low priorities given to consumer sector imports and the low percentage of foreign assistance.

Table 21–3 INDUSTRIAL SECTORS IN THE U.S.S.R. WITH
ANNUAL AVERAGE GROWTH RATES LESS
THAN 4 PERCENT, 1928–55

Number on Figure 21–2	Industrial Sector	Annual Average Growth Rate 1928–55[1] (Percent)	Position on Technical-Assistance Scale[2]
17	Boots and shoes	3.7	2
18	Raw sugar	3.7	4
19	Salt	3.4	0
—	Starch and syrup	3.3	Not estimated
20	Matches	3.3	1[*]
21	Cotton fabrics	3.0	4[**]
22	Woolen and worsted fabrics	2.9	4[**]
23	Vodka	2.8	0
24	Vegetable oil	2.4	2
25	Linen fabrics	2.1	0
26	Felt footwear	1.7	0
27	Steam locomotives	1.2	3
28	Flour	1.1	2
29	Low-grade tobacco	1.7	0

Sources: 1. G. Warren Nutter, *Growth of Production in the Soviet Union* (Princeton: Princeton University Press, 1962), p. 96.
   2. Text.

* Matchmaking equipment was imported and negotiations were reported for a concession with the Swedish match-maker, Kreuger. This small sector not covered in the text.

** There was considerable assistance to the textiles industries (all sectors) in the early to middle 1920s. In the period 1930–45 assistance took the form of equipment imports only; thus the sector is scaled at 4.

In conclusion, if we examine the findings of this study concerning technical assistance in relation to annual average rates of growth we can make two points. First, those sectors with high rates of growth had high levels of technical assistance. Second, those sectors with low rates of growth had low levels of technical assistance. It is interesting to note that this relationship is only broadly in accord with planned objectives, as was pointed out at the beginning of the chapter. For example, the high growth rate of bicycles and the low growth rate of steam locomotives were certainly not in accord with planned objectives.

Consideration of the factors making for economic growth given in the text suggests that Western technical assistance was the major causal factor in Soviet economic growth for the period 1928–45.[10]

The imposition of 'domestic savings' on the Russian people is not an alternate explanation for Soviet development, but, in the Soviet scheme of things, it is a necessary prerequisite to the basic method used: transfer of Western technology.

What is 'domestic savings' in the Soviet scheme? It is the planned direction of resources into industrialization at the expense of personal consumption. This the Soviets have done ruthlessly. Agricultural products—eggs, butter, grain, flax, etc., were exported to pay for imports of Western technology. Capital construction in the consumer sector—housing, roads, hospitals, etc.,—was curtailed and resources diverted into industrial and military construction.

Forced saving of this type, however, will not by itself bring about rapid development, although it may be a necessary prerequisite for the release of resources. This road to development also requires either an outside source of technology or the diversion of resources into research and development to achieve technology internally. In the West, technology developed over a period of several hundred years during the gradual industrialization of Europe and the United States; it was this enormous pool of technology which was successfully tapped by the Soviets. They tapped it by imposing forcible saving on the Russian consumer and exchanging released resources for Western processes, plants, and equipment. Consequently, although such saving is a necessary prerequisite, it is not an alternate explanation for Soviet growth.

Therefore, the Soviet road to development will not work without cooperative capitalist neighbors with advanced technology which can be introduced into the socialist system.

---

[10]   It is, of course, possible to make more precise statistical determinations; however, calculation of the technical-assistance scale is to some extent arbitrary and does not justify more than preliminary statistical treatment. It is the direction of the argument that is important, not precise calculation of correlations.

CHAPTER TWENTY-TWO

Conclusions

THIS study provides empirical support for the traditional argument in economic development theory that borrowed technology from advanced countries is a primary explanation for economic growth among latecomers. Although the study is based on the economic history of one country—the Soviet Union—that country is among the largest in population and resources and the most important in strategic terms.

Conclusions are acceptable only to the extent that data sources are acceptable. The official Decimal File (the central file of the U.S. State Department) and the Oberkommando der Wehrmacht Archives provided extensive and accurate detail, some of which has been previously unavailable to nonofficial researchers. The technical detail extracted from these sources constitutes the main empirical base for this volume; the abundance is fortuitous, as it coincides with significant industrial growth in the Soviet economy. It should be pointed out, however, that the conclusions presented here are quite different from—in fact, almost completely opposite to—those arrived at by State Department report writers and researchers presumably using the same source material.[1] Obviously, these differences require explanation.

The Decimal File records include texts of technical-assistance agreements between Western firms and the U.S.S.R. and reports made by departmental field officers after interviewing returning American engineers. These interview reports, although often filed under 'Living Conditions,' are an excellent source of technical detail. The Wehrmacht Archives establish the structure of Soviet

---

[1] See pp. 4–6. There are statements, from 1918 (Minutes of the War Trade Board) to 1968 by State Department officials from the Secretary of State downwards, to the effect that trade and the transfer mechanisms described in this and the previous volume have had no major effect on Soviet economic development. On the other hand there is a report in the State Department files that names Kuhn, Loeb & Co. (the long-established and important financial house in New York) as the financier of the First Five Year Plan. See U.S. State Dept. Decimal File, 811.51/3711 and 861.50 FIVE YEAR PLAN/236.

industry: i.e., the numbers, types, and locations of individual plants. In general, the Decimal File contains information on the nature of the technology or processes used and the Wehrmacht data provide the output, capacity, and location of each plant. Integration of both the State Department and Wehrmacht data provides a reasonably complete picture of technical transfers and their focus and effect within the Soviet Union. Soviet source material provides supplementary information.

The initial and obvious conclusion is one of significant growth in the Soviet economy between 1930 and 1945, although this growth was irregular over the course of time and between sectors. The widespread impression of smooth, regular, balanced growth, with major production increases and fulfillment or near-fulfillment of plans from year to year is not valid. If central planning is intended to provide balanced industrial development it has been, in the Soviet experience, a miserable failure. Some recent Soviet books, in fact, now characterize the period 1936 to 1940 as one of fluctuation and even decline in output—a pattern confirmed by this study.[2] During the period as a whole, there was major but fluctuating growth in the output of a wide range of products; the fluctuations provide additional support for the argument.

The increase in output came from two types of productive units: new gigantic plants, such as KHEMZ and Uralmash, with modern, sophisticated technology; and ex-tsarist plants, such as Putilovets and Dynamo, greatly expanded and re-equipped. Some new giants, such as Kramatorsk and Berezniki, were located at or near small ex-tsarist plants, no doubt to make use of existing transportation and raw materials facilities. A general observation is that in both groups of plants the technology was always the most advanced known and very commonly on a scale far beyond that previously built anywhere.

Almost all new major units, except Second Baku oil refineries and chemical, aviation, and other military plants, were begun in the years 1930 to 1932, and rarely between 1933 and 1940. From 1941 to 1945 there was an increasing amount of construction behind the Urals. Construction starts bore little relationship to the dates specified in the various Five-Year Plans, and, as is already known, construction often dragged on for years after planned completion. The plans were therefore a propaganda facade, completely misleading in the quest for an understanding of the real dynamics of Soviet growth.[3]

The actual chronology of Soviet growth between 1930 and 1945 is outlined and related to the official plans and Naum Jasny's parallel conclusions in figure 22–1.

---

[2] See, for example, *Tekhnicheskii progress v chernoi metallurgii SSSR* (Moscow: 1962), p. 6.

[3] Naum Jasny made a similar suggestion. See p. 342.

Fig. 22–1　CHRONOLOGICAL RELATIONSHIP BETWEEN OFFICIAL SOVIET PLANS, JASNY'S 'MAJOR STAGES,' AND TECHNOLOGICAL TRANSFERS

OFFICIAL SOVIET PLANS

First Five-Year Plan	Second Five-Year Plan	Third Five-Year Plan	'Great Patriotic War'

1926　1928　　1932 1933　　1937　　1941 1942　　1945

NAUM JASNY'S 'MAJOR STAGES'

Warming up	All out drive	Three 'good' years	Purge era	World War II

1926　1928　early 1929　mid 1932　mid 1937　mid 1941　1945

TECHNOLOGICAL TRANSFERS

Negotiation of design and construction contracts	Actual construction by Western firms	Benefits of the new capacity	Stagnation due to decline in transfers, 1932–7	Benefits from Nazi-Soviet Pact and Lend-Lease

1926　mid 1929　mid 1932　mid 1937　1940　1945

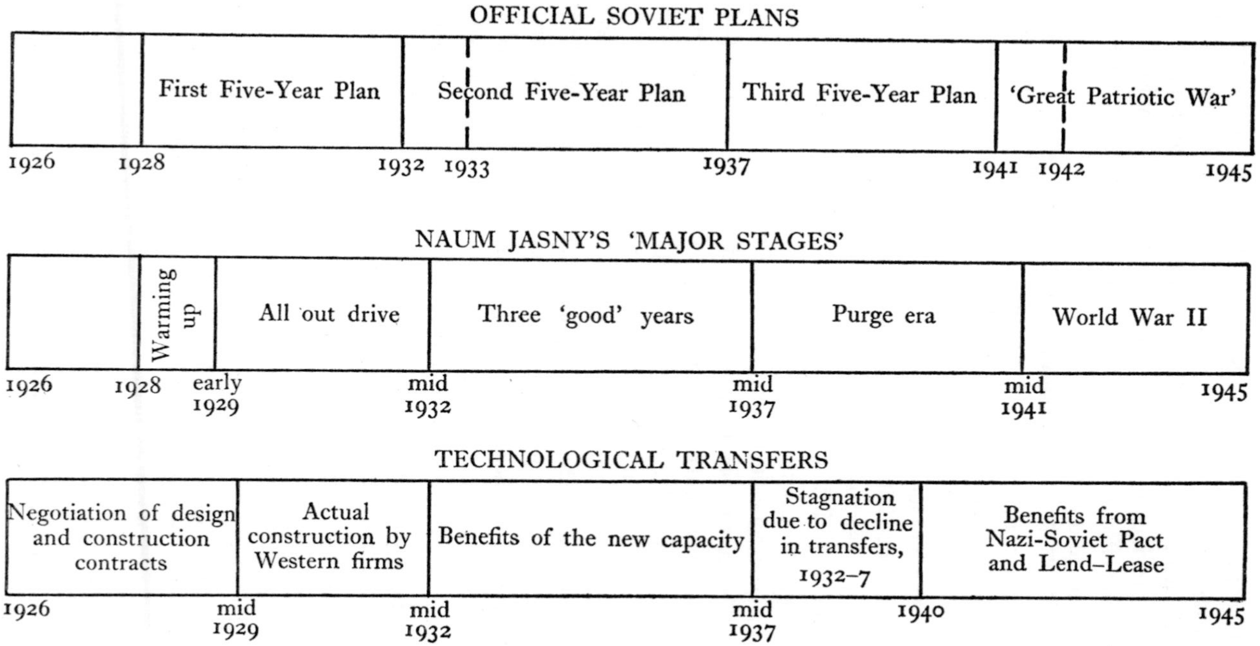

Sources: Official Soviet Plans. Naum Jasny, *Soviet Industrialization 1928–1952* (Chicago: University of Chicago Press, 1961), p. 13.

Note: Dotted lines in the 'Official Soviet Plans' indicate the terminal date of an original plan, later modified.

In brief, the year 1930 advanced the Soviets along a road begun 50 years earlier under the tsars.[4] There were numerous ineffective construction starts between about 1926 and mid-1929; this observation leads to the 'inability hypothesis.'[5] In the summer and fall of 1929, many wide-ranging technical assistance agreements were concluded with foreign firms. American engineers began arriving on site toward the end of the year. The fundamental construction agreement was that made in February of 1930 with Albert Kahn, Inc., of Detroit, builders of the Ford River Rouge, General Motors, Packard, and other large plants in the United States. The Kahn group undertook design, architectural, and engineering work for all heavy and light industrial units projected by Gosplan. Kahn's chief engineer in the U.S.S.R., Scrymgoeur, was chairman of the Vesenkha building committee.[6]

The units designed and started in 1929–32 were of truly gigantic size— usually far larger than units designed and built by the same construction firms in the rest of the world and, in addition, combining separate shops or plants for the manufacture of inputs and spare parts. The Urals Elmash combinat multiplied Soviet electrical equipment manufacturing capacity by a factor of seven; the KHEMZ at Kharkov, designed by the General Electric Company, had a turbine-manufacturing capacity two and one-half times greater than the main G. E. Schenectady plant; and Magnitogorsk, a replica of the U.S. Steel plant at Gary, Indiana, was the largest iron and steel plant in the world. When the Soviets claim these units are the 'largest in the world' they do not exaggerate; it would of course be impolitic of them to emphasize their Western origins.

Although design and layout during this period was American, probably one-half of the equipment installed was German. Of this, a large amount was manufactured in Germany to American design on Soviet account. In quantity, American-built equipment was probably second and British third.[7] Some sectors owed a great deal to other European countries; cement mills were largely from one firm in Denmark, ball bearings from one firm in Italy and another in Sweden, small ships from Italy, and aluminum technology from a French company.

In two years, then, there was a massive infusion of foreign technology, foreign engineers, and foreign equipment. Most of these engineers had gone by mid-1932, but they left behind standard designs based on Western models

---

[4] The Foss Collection at the Hoover Institution illustrates the comparatively advanced nature of tsarist industry.

[5] See pp. 284–6.

[6] See p. 250. A dozen Soviet plants were designed in Detroit in 1929 before the Kahn group went to the U.S.S.R.

[7] Before 1932–3 Soviet-made equipment was rare.

and enormous manufacturing capacity. This gigantic capacity to produce simplified standard designs was by no means fully in operation by 1933; the rest of the decade was required to master the new processes, install all the equipment, train workers, bring the subsidiary plants into phase with the main plants (a major headache), and expand operations.

First priority was given to the military departments in each of the new plants. Much of the original drive behind industrialization had been military. This goal was clearly stated in 1929 by Unashlicht, Vice President of the Revolutionary Military Soviet:

> We must try to ensure that industry can as quickly as possible be adapted to serving military needs . . . [therefore,] it is necessary to carefully structure the Five-Year Plan for maximum co-operation and interrelationship between military and civilian industry. It is necessary to plan for duplication of technological processes and absorb foreign assistance . . . such are the fundamental objectives.[8]

The requirement for interrelationship was achieved quite simply by establishing a department devoted to military products in every new works; thus every plant built in this period was producing at the same time civilian and military equipment, although the military requirements took first priority.[9] The writer has little evidence at hand, but it is possible that many of the production problems of the 1930s were caused by diversion of the best in Russian talent and materials to the military departments in each plant. It is ironic, from the Western viewpoint, that contracts viewed as serving the cause of world peace (Henry Ford, for example, elected to build the Gorki plant to advance peace) should have been utilized immediately for military end-uses.[10]

Production increases between 1933 and 1940 were not, except for petroleum refining, wood distillation, and a couple of other sectors, obtained by building new plants but by increasing the output of plants built by Western companies in 1930–3. In 1941 there were still only four large tractor plants: Putilovets Stalingrad, Kharkov, and Chelyabinsk (the Altai Tractor Plant opened in 1944, utilized equipment mostly evacuated from Kharkov); still only three major automobile-truck plants (Moscow, Yaroslavl and Gorki); and still only two giant machine-building plants (Kramatorsk and Uralmash). When units were built after 1932–3 they were subsidiary to the giants of the early 1930s. These important facts are obscured by the chronology of the Five-Year Plans.

---

[8] *Pravda*, No. 98, April 28, 1929.

[9] Search of the OKW files fails to reveal a single plant in 1937–8 that was not devoting part of its capacity to war purposes. The German intelligence lists of plants producing war equipment were at the same time, in fact, comprehensive lists of all Soviet plants.

[10] For a contemporary example, one might consider the intention announced by President Johnson to supply American equipment to the Togliatti automobile plant in the U.S.S.R. in 1966–8.

Those major new units built from 1936 to 1940 (except military plants) were again planned and constructed by Western companies. This second era has been much less publicized, but the State Department files do contain information on these contracts. Petroleum-cracking, particularly for avgas, was one such sector; all refineries in the Second Baku and elsewhere were built by Universal Oil Products, Badger Corporation, Lummus Company, Petroleum Engineering Corporation, Alco Products, McKee Corporation, and Kellogg Company. Advanced steel-rolling mills were supplied under the United Engineering agreement, and in 1938–9 the Tube Reducing Company installed a modern tube mill at Nikopol and supplied equipment for another. In 1937 the Vultee Corporation built an aircraft plant outside Moscow. These and similar agreements in half a dozen sectors ran from about 1936 to 1940 with few public news releases.

In 1940 as a reaction to the Nazi-Soviet agreement and the subsequent attack on Finland, assistance from the United States tapered off. The Nazi-Soviet pact replaced this assistance and gave another boost to the Soviet economy. The agreement makes specific reference to imports of German machinery; Soviet want lists emphasized modern machine tools, and the Germans, it would appear from the Hauptarchiv, had problems in designing, producing, and shipping the desired large quantities of advanced equipment. The Soviets kept well ahead on their raw-material deliveries, but German firms were consistently late in their machine-tool deliveries. German occupation of Czechoslovakia was indirectly beneficial to the Soviet Union, as large shipments of Czech machine tools were then channeled to the U.S.S.R.

The real bonanza was Lend-Lease; about one-half the equipment supplied under the master agreements had reconstruction potential; Nutter estimates it equalled one-third of Soviet pre-war industrial output.[11] These deliveries continued under the little-known 'pipeline agreement' of October 1945, so that Lend-Lease supplies actually continued through 1947. There is no question that the Soviets ended World War II with greater industrial capacity than in 1940—in spite of the war damage—and on a technical parity with the United States.[12]

Finally, another source of both increased capacity and technology was the World War II reparations agreements, in which the emphasis was on capital transfers, of which the Soviets received the lion's share. Germany (both zones), Austria, Manchuria, Finland, Rumania, Hungary, Italy, and other countries made a heavy contribution to the Soviet economy. This flow extended from

---

[11] G. Warren Nutter, *op. cit.*, p. 214.

[12] There are, however, State Department memoranda which minimize the technical flow under Lend-Lease.

1944 to 1955 and will be covered in the next volume.[13]

Growth between 1930 and 1945 was therefore uneven in part because it depended upon flows from the West and, indirectly, upon temporary detentes and changing political conditions. Looking at the picture as a whole, there were two massive injections of Western technology and capacity, in the periods 1930–3 and 1943–5. Even given the extensive destruction of World War II, and assuming that 25 percent of the Soviet economy was destroyed, the Soviets were far better off in terms of both capacity and technology by 1946 than before the war. Destroyed facilities were more than replaced by reparations and Lend-Lease, and, more importantly, replaced with equipment 10 to 15 years more advanced.

No major technology or major plant under construction between 1930 and 1945 has been identified as a purely Soviet effort. No usable technology originated in Soviet laboratories except in the case of synthetic rubber, and this was not up to U.S. standards in 1941. Equipment and processes transferred from the West were sufficient to fulfill *general* Soviet production claims, although their *annual* claims *are* doubtful. Acquisition of capacity and knowledge was slow and painful. There were major production and quality problems; there were problems with unskilled labor; machinery was abused; and the concept of rigid central planning in this period may itself have been contra-developmental.[14] The almost universal image of rapid development via Soviet central planning crumbles when we are confronted with the evidence. There is an obvious necessity to re-examine our assumptions concerning Soviet development in the light of the argument made in this study. On the other hand, it is to Soviet credit that they recognized the potent force of technology, identified its origins, and ruthlessly harnessed it to their own programs.

Although this requirement for assistance and technology from capitalist countries was recognized at an early date, the quantity required and the continuing nature of the demand for transfer over a long period were underestimated even by the Soviets. This is reflected in the 'inability hypothesis.' Rykov and others warned in 1929 that 'such measures as engaging only a hundred or two foreign specialists cannot solve the problem. . . .'[15] Once the

---

[13]   See p. 138 for Manchurian machine tool reparations.

[14]   If the reader doubts the assertion that central planning can be contra-developmental, the case of Japan, in relation to the U.S.S.R. and Communist China, should be examined. Using a more or less free-enterprise system, the Japanese at first copied freely and then forged ahead on their own. Today (1968) the Soviet Union is going to Japan for technical assistance, although tsarist Russia was technologically ahead of Japan in 1880–90. The comparison of Communist China and Japan is even more illuminating.

[15]   *Pravda*, No. 94, April 24, 1929.

Party became convinced of the necessity for complete infusion of foreign technology and placed its weight behind the transfer, the acquisition process became extraordinarily efficient and highly effective. Indeed, Soviet engineers have from time to time admitted as much. A one-time manager of Gipromez, Zaviniagin, has stated:

> How have the Soviet engineers benefited from cooperation with Americans? It is not immodest to say that they successfully went through an American school and with the knowledge acquired they are carrying out in our metallurgy the last word in American technique which has been derived from many years of experience. . . .[16]

If our argument for technological transfer as a prime explanation for Soviet growth is accepted, then other observations on the Soviet enigma begin to fall into place. Why, for example, increasing censorship? Why the travel bans? Why a moon trip while the domestic Soviet automobile stock is less than that of the Argentine?

Prior to 1932, descriptions of Western assistance activities can be found in Soviet sources; most of this study could at least have been outlined from Soviet sources alone. Then came the enigma of increasing censorship and the claims of spectacular economic advances. After 1932 Soviet sources are of little use and other sources must be used; thus construction of the Second Baku refineries by American companies in 1937–41 is censored in Soviet literature and hardly noted in open Western sources.

Continuous Soviet industrial espionage on a world-wide scale—in itself a subject overdue for extensive treatment—is another enigma. Soviet engineers, scientists, planners, and Party members at home and abroad have an insatiable curiosity and well-developed techniques for gaining information on all aspects of Western technology. The observation may be superficial, but it sometimes appears that the Soviets are more interested in the latest American industrial processes than in the number or sizes of our missiles or tanks. From the Soviet viewpoint, the industrial vigor of the United States is as much an enigma as any Western question over Soviet tactics. Thus economic censorship, industrial espionage, the placing of Soviet industrial plants 'off limits,' the continuing objections to specific plant visits ('under repair,' 'the bridge is out,' and so on), the establishment of 'show place' farms (where the crèches are the most-inspected units): these phenomena are explainable within the context of our argument. Free access to all industrial units throughout the Soviet Union by foreign observers would reduce the Western view of a more or less vigorous socialist technical progress to that of widespread industrial backwardness

[16] A. Zaviniagin, 'U.S.S.R. Favors American Engineers and Equipment,' *Freyn Design*, No. 11, March 1934, p. 19. This statement is consistent with those of American engineers working for Gipromez; see pp. 62–4.

(despite extensive use of Western methods and equipment) with pockets of simulated efficiency provided for foreigners. This widespread backwardness is not inconsistent with high rates of growth in many sectors of Soviet industry. Foreign technological efforts have been concentrated in sectors capable of rapid expansion (iron and steel, electricity generation) by use of simplified standardized technology. Furthermore, output in quantitative terms suggests very little about industrial or economic efficiency.

The threads of our empirical examination are pulled together in chapter twenty-one and provide the general conclusion that the greater the foreign technical assistance to a specific Soviet sector, the greater its annual average rate of growth during the period between 1928 and 1945 and beyond. Turbines, bicycles, tires, and machine-tools were the manufacturing sectors with the highest growth rates. Consumer industries such as flour manufacture and mechanical sectors such as steam locomotives received less technical assistance from abroad, and these sectors had the lowest growth rates. Considerable detail in this and the previous volume suggests these relationships are causal.

The years 1944–5 form a natural break in our discussion. Technical transfers continued after this time, as the Soviets continued to struggle for indigenous innovation, but in more varied and complex forms. Whereas concessions were the prime transfer vehicles for the period 1917–30 and technical-assistance agreements from 1930 to 1945, the method of transfer changed considerably after World War II.

Technical-Assistance Agreement Between W. L. Gorton and Sredazvodhoz, February 6, 1930

AGREEMENT MADE this sixth day of February 1930, by and between SOVIET UNION MIDDLE ASIAN WATER ECONOMY SERVICE, an organization of U.S.S.R. hereinafter called 'SREDAZVODHOZ' and W. L. Gorton of Boise, Idaho, hereinafter called 'GORTON'.

WITNESSETH

WHEREAS, Sredazvodhoz is desirous of employing the services of said Gorton in capacity of a Construction Engineer for work in Turkestan, U.S.S.R. and

WHEREAS, said Gorton is desirous of rendering his services to Sredazvodhoz in the hereinbefore described capacity,

Now, THEREFORE, the parties hereto agree as follows:

1. Sredazvodhoz agrees to employ the services of said Gorton in the capacity of Construction Engineer for the period of time as hereinafter provided, at the compensation of ONE THOUSAND DOLLARS ($1000.00) per month, payable monthly, on the first day of each calendar month, it being understood that SIX HUNDRED DOLLARS ($600.00) per month, lawful money of the United States of America, that is to say, Sixty percent (60%) of said monthly compensation, shall be deposited, to the credit of said Gorton, in a bank located in the United States of America, the name and location of said bank to be designated, in writing, by said Gorton. The remaining FOUR HUNDRED DOLLARS ($400.00) per month, that is to say, Forty percent (40%) of said monthly compensation, is to be paid in U.S.S.R. currency at the official rate of exchange then prevailing.

2. Said Gorton agrees to perform necessary construction work for Sredazvodhoz in Turkestan to the best of his ability and knowledge and in accordance with instructions of Sredazvodhoz and whenever not needed for services in

Turkestan, Gorton shall be available for assignment to construction work at any point within the jurisdiction of Sredazvodhoz.

3. It is further understood and agreed that all reports, designs, drawings as well as any other information prepared by Gorton in accordance with the performance of his duties, shall be deemed the property of Sredazvodhoz, and shall not be disclosed by said Gorton directly or indirectly to any third party or parties, or published without a written consent of Sredazvodhoz expressly given therefor.

4. Said Gorton agrees to depart from Boise, Idaho for U.S.S.R. not later than March 6, 1930, and to proceed directly to Tashkent, Turkestan and to report for duty to Sredazvodhoz immediately upon arrival.

5. Sredazvodhoz agrees to pay for actual reasonable traveling expenses of said Gorton for the entire trip each way, as well as second class steamer and railroad transportation from Boise, Idaho, U.S.A. to Tashkent U.S.S.R. and return upon expiration of the term of this agreement or its termination prior thereto, it being understood that the transportation and traveling expenses each way shall not exceed the amount of Five Hundred Dollars ($500).

6. Sredazvodhoz agrees to pay actual cost of railroad tickets, hotels and a lump sum of 10 roubles (10R.) a day for living expenses in case said Gorton is traveling in U.S.S.R. in accordance with the instructions of the administration of Sredazvodhoz.

7. Sredazvodhoz agrees to furnish said Gorton, during the time of his employment as herein provided, living quarters in the city of Tashkent, without cost to Gorton, of a character similar to living quarters used by others occupying a position similar to that occupied by said Gorton.

8. It is understood that said Gorton shall pay income tax levied in U.S.S.R., it being understood that Sredazvodhoz shall pay for and on behalf of said Gorton the difference between the amount of income tax required under the laws of U.S.S.R. and the amount of income tax which would be required at the rate existing under the laws of U.S.A.

9. Said Gorton shall abide by the laws existing in U.S.S.R. as well as by all the rules and regulations issued by Sredazvodhoz.

10. The term of employment of said Gorton shall be two years beginning with the date of departure of said Gorton from Boise, Idaho, to Tashkent, U.S.S.R.

11. Said Gorton shall have vacation consisting of two weeks during each year of his employment by Sredazvodhoz, full salary to be paid to him during such vacation.

12. Said Gorton agrees that he will not, while in the employ of Sredazvodhoz accept work from or perform services for any other enterprise or organization without consent of Sredazvodhoz expressly given in writing.

13. Sredazvodhoz shall have the right to terminate this agreement at any time in case of any contingencies beyond control of Sredazvodhoz or in case of prolonged illness of said Gorton, it being understood that Sredazvodhoz shall pay the return trip of said Gorton from U.S.S.R. to U.S.A.

14. In case said Gorton proves himself to be grossly incompetent or negligent in the performance of his duties hereunder, Sredazvodhoz shall have the right to terminate this agreement, it being understood that in such case Sredazvodhoz shall not pay for the return trip of said Gorton from U.S.S.R. to U.S.A.

15. Any differences arising between the parties to this agreement shall be settled by the court of U.S.S.R.

IN WITNESS WHEREOF, Soviet Union Middle Asian Water Economy Service has caused this instrument to be executed by Amtorg Trading Corporation, 261 Fifth Avenue, New York, its duly authorized representative, and the said Gorton has hereunto set his hand the day and year first above written.

SOVIET UNION MIDDLE ASIAN WATER
ECONOMY SERVICE

BY: Amtorg Trading Corporation

BY: A. C. Mamaeff

W. L. Gorton

Source: Willard L. Gorton Special Collection at Hoover Institution, Stanford University.

Technical-Assistance Agreement Between
Vsekhimprom and Nitrogen Engineering Corporation

CONTRACT

BETWEEN STATE TRUST OF ALL THE UNION CHEMICAL INDUSTRIES 'VSEKHIMPROM' AND NITROGEN ENGINEERING CORPORATION, JUNE 29, 1931

ON this............day of............, 1931 we, the undersigned STATE TRUST OF ALL THE UNION CHEMICAL INDUSTRIES 'VSEKHIMPROM', the legal successor to the STATE COMPANY FOR THE CONSTRUCTION OF CHEMICAL APPARATUS 'KHIMSTROI', hereinafter referred to as VSEKHIMPROM and represented by *J. L. Piatakoff (President)* of the one part, and NITROGEN ENGINEERING CORPORATION, incorporated under the laws of the State of New York in the United States of America, hereinafter called 'NITROGEN' and represented by *Frederick Pope (President)* of the other part, hereby agree to the following:

I. THE SUBJECT MATTER OF THE AGREEMENT

PAR. 1. KHIMSTROI and NITROGEN have heretofore, on or about the 11th of November 1928, entered into a written agreement, providing, among other things, for the erection and putting into operation, under NITROGEN's technical advice and direction, of a plant or plants for producing synthetic ammonia within the territory of USSR, and the grant to KHIMSTROI by NITROGEN of the right to use within such territory the methods, principles and processes of NITROGEN for the construction and operation of such plants, on the terms and conditions set forth in said written agreement; and under said written agreement NITROGEN is now engineering for VSEKHIMPROM an initial plant for the production of synthetic ammonia, located at Berezniki in the Province of Perm.

PAR. 2. VSEKHIMPROM is contemplating the construction of additional plants for the production of synthetic ammonia, and may hereafter desire to construct further plants, in connection with which NITROGEN, under the terms of said written agreement, is now obligated to render engineering service to VSEKHIMPROM, and Vsekhimprom is now obligated to employ and pay NITROGEN therefor.

PAR. 3. It is the desire of the parties hereto that the terms and conditions of the aforesaid written agreement of November 11, 1928, shall, so far as they relate to such additional plants and further plants, be modified in certain respects as hereinafter set forth.

II. WAIVER OF RIGHTS AND RELEASE OF OBLIGATION

PAR. 4. Except as hereinafter provided, NITROGEN waives any and all rights which it now has, or may hereafter have with respect to such additional and further plants, under said written agreement with KHIMSTROI, and KHIM-STROI and VSEKHIMPROM and NITROGEN hereby mutually release and discharge each other of any and all oblgations with respect to such additional and further plants, arising under said written agreement of November 11, 1928. Nothing herein contained, however, shall constitute a waiver or release of any rights or obligations with respect to said initial plant.

III. GRANT OF RIGHTS

PAR. 5. Subject to the payment of the fees and the performance of the conditions hereinafter provided, NITROGEN hereby grants to VSEKHIMPROM the exclusive rights in perpetuity for VSEKHIMPROM within the territory of USSR to build, extend, operate and transfer for operations in other state enterprises, chemical plants for the manufacture of synthetic ammonia, according to the methods, principles and processes of NITROGEN.

PAR. 6. For five years from effective date hereof NITROGEN shall assign to VSEKHIMPROM any and all patents or reserved rights in USSR covering methods or apparatus for the manufacture of synthetic ammonia said patents and reserved rights to be transferred to VSEKHIMPROM for the full period for which they are valid.

PAR. 7. NITROGEN and VSEKHIMPROM mutually agree to inform each other forthwith, without request, of all technical improvements and inventions achieved by them, or which they have learned and are free to disclose, relating to the manufacture of synthetic ammonia, to the end that VSEKHIMPROM in the territory of USSR and NITROGEN in other parts of the world, may be enabled to make use of such improvements in plants which they design, install and/or operate. NITROGEN and VSEKHIMPROM further mutually agree to deliver to each other detailed drawings, schemes, specifications and calculations such as may be in their possession. This obligation to exchange information regarding technical improvements shall continue for a period of five years from the effective date of this agreement.

IV. CONSULTATION, TECHNICAL AND ENGINEERING SERVICES

PAR. 8. NITROGEN shall render to VSEKHIMPROM, as herein provided, consultation, technical and engineering services to assist VSEKHIMPROM in projecting, constructing, installing and placing in operation synthetic ammonia plants within the territory of USSR. Such consultation, technical and engineering services shall be based upon the best methods and principles which are or may be at the disposal of NITROGEN.

PAR. 9. It is understood that VSEKHIMPROM shall have in its employ or at its disposal a competent and ample staff of engineers and competent forces of skilled and ordinary workmen for carrying out the projects and that the obligation of NITROGEN shall be to supply the special technical knowledge and information relating to the design, installation and production of synthetic ammonia plants according to its methods and processes. Nitrogen shall freely render to VSEKHIMPROM advice and assistance, when requested by VSEKHIM-PROM, in the selection and employment by VSEKHIMPROM of competent engineers of general technical training and of skilled workmen, so far as VSEKHIM-PROM shall desire to employ persons of other than Russian nationality, but such engineers and skilled workmen shall be solely employed by and responsible to VSEKHIMPROM, and NITROGEN assumes no responsibility regarding their work or the continuance of their employment. It is intended that the consultation, technical and engineering services rendered by NITROGEN for the assistance of VSEKHIMPROM shall be sufficient to enable a competent technical organization under the direction of VSEKHIMPROM to project, construct, install and operate synthetic ammonia plants.

PAR. 10. As soon as practicable, and in any event within forty days after the effective date of this Agreement, NITROGEN shall forward by mail or by personal messenger to VSEKHIMPROM five copies each of all drawings now possessed by it indicating its latest developments in the synthesis of ammonia from water gas, coke oven gas, natural gas, electrolytic hydrogen or other sources of raw material, together with explanation as to the purpose and capacity of the apparatus or equipment shown on each drawing and the operating results which have been achieved. Similarly, NITROGEN shall deliver to VSEKHIMPROM five copies of each of all future drawings of equipment or apparatus pertaining to ammonia synthesis which shall be made by NITROGEN within a period of five years from the date of this Agreement. NITROGEN shall deliver to VSEKHIMPROM all such technical and construction calculations as NITROGEN deems necessary and will upon the request of VSEKHIMPROM deliver to them other calculations useful for their purposes, if such calculations are then in the possession of NITROGEN, NITROGEN further will assist, as far as is reasonable, the engineers of VSEKHIMPROM in becoming familiar with such calculations. It is understood that the drawings referred to in this paragraph include only those which indicate the latest developments, and do not include obsolete or preliminary drawings and sketches or any drawings or sketches of special equipment made for other clients which are confidential and which NITROGEN has no right to disclose. It is further understood that the drawings referred to in this paragraph do not include drawings covering details which have been covered by drawings already delivered to KHIMSTROI under the terms of the aforesaid agreement entered into on or about the eleventh day of November, 1928. A list of such drawings as are now available for delivery to VSEKHIMPROM under this paragraph is attached hereto marked 'Exhibit A'.

PAR. 11. As soon as practicable, and in any event within forty days after the effective date of this Agreement, NITROGEN shall forward by mail or by personal messenger to VSEKHIMPROM a copy of its specifications for the purchase and manufacture of equipment and apparatus for use in the manufacture of synthetic ammonia, and NITROGEN shall similarly forward to VSEKHIMPROM copies of future specifications relating to such equipment and apparatus. It is understood that the specifications referred to in this paragraph do not include duplicates or specifications already furnished by NITROGEN to VSEKHIMPROM under the terms of the aforesaid agreement entered into on or about the eleventh day of November 1928, nor do they include specifications of special equipment for other clients which are confidential and which NITROGEN has no right to disclose. A list of the specifications now available to be furnished to VSEKHIMPROM is attached hereto marked 'Exhibit B'.

PAR. 12. NITROGEN shall forward by mail or by personal messenger to VSEKHIMPROM detailed drawings and/or specifications, instructions and formulae for the preparation of all solutions, catalysts, etc., necessary for the synthesis of ammonia according to the methods and processes of NITROGEN, including all improvements and changes in such instructions and formulae made by NITROGEN within the period of five years from the effective date of this Agreement that are applicable to the plants constructed by KHIMSTROI under this agreement, and VSEKHIMPROM may during this same period send engineers to visit any factory owned by NITROGEN making catalysts, when such plant is operating.

PAR. 13. NITROGEN shall forward by mail or by personal messenger to VSEKHIMPROM detailed written instructions for the use of its technical staff in starting and operating the synthetic ammonia plants and all departments thereof constructed by VSEKHIMPROM under this Agreement, and shall inform VSEKHIMPROM of all improvements made by NITROGEN within the period of five years from the effective date of this Agreement in methods of operation of synthetic ammonia plants so far as such improvements are applicable to the plants constructed by VSEKHIMPROM under this Agreement.

PAR. 14. During the period of five years commencing with the effective date of this Agreement, NITROGEN shall, whenever requested by VSEKHIMPROM, and with reasonable promptness, prepare and deliver to VSEKHIMPROM in Moscow (or, at the option of VSEKHIMPROM, to its representative in New York or at the office of NITROGEN in Europe):

(a) Plans, specifications, and drawings of such scale and completeness as VSEKHIMPROM requests for the installation by VSEKHIMPROM of additional plants within the territory of USSR for the manufacture of synthetic ammonia according to the methods and processes of NITROGEN.

(b) Estimates and calculations of costs of such plants and costs of production of synthetic ammonia in such plants.

(c) Projects, the substance and scope of which is shown in Exhibit C. A preliminary project is to be mailed from NITROGEN's office not later than eight weeks after the acknowledgment by NITROGEN of receipt of all necessary information. A final project is to be mailed from NITROGEN's office—complete only in its major parts—not later than six months after receipt by NITROGEN of information of acceptance of corresponding preliminary project. The rest of the final project is to be mailed from NITROGEN's office thirty days after acknowledgment by NITROGEN of receipt of all necessary information therefor.

Such plans, specifications, drawings and estimates shall be in such detail and shall be accompanied by such explanatory notes as shall be requested by VSEKHIMPROM and NITROGEN is able to prepare required for the proper planning and execution of the projects. At the request of VSEKHIMPROM, NITROTEN shall send to USSR such number of engineers as in the judgment of NITROGEN shall be necessary to explain such plans, specifications, drawings and estimates, and to take part in the defence of the projects when such projects come up for consideration before the USSR Government authorities. VSEKHIMPROM may at its option and at its own expense send its own engineers to take part in the preparation of such plans, specifications, drawings and estimates, and to inform NITROGEN regarding local conditions which will affect the building and installation of the plants.

PAR. 15. During the period of five years from the effective date of this Agreement NITROGEN shall, when requested by VSEKHIMPROM, and in the manner and to the extent in this paragraph provided, place at the disposal of VSEKHIMPROM skilled and experienced engineers for advice, competent instruction and consultation, either in the offices of NITROGEN New York or Europe, or in USSR, or elsewhere as VSEKHIMPROM may elect.

(a) VSEKHIMPROM may notify NITROGEN in writing at any time, and from time to time, of its desire to have the services of any number of Engineers of the Engineering Staff of NITROGEN up to a total of three such Engineers for any specified days in a period of twelve months commencing, so far as one Engineer is concerned, thirty days after receipt by NITROGEN at its New York office of such written notice, and so far as two other Engineers are concerned commencing three months after receipt of such written notice by NITROGEN at its New York office. Thereupon, NITROGEN shall be required to make available to VSEKHIMPROM the services of such number of engineers for such days, within the aforesaid period of twelve months, and VSEKHIMPROM shall be obliged to pay Nitrogen for the services of such engineers the remuneration provided in paragraph 17 hereof in twelve equal installments payable on the first day of each month of such period of twelve months. In giving such written notice to NITROGEN, VSEKHIMPROM shall state as definitely as possible the nature of the consultation and advice required of such engineers in order that NITROGEN may select for this purpose the engineers properly qualified to render such advice and consultation.

(b) Additional engineers may be furnished to VSEKHIMPROM by NITROGEN in accordance with agreement that may be made from time to time by the parties hereto and for remuneration as provided in paragraph 17 hereof; and regardless of any such agreement, NITROGEN shall use its best endeavours to make available its engineers to render advice and consultation to VSEKHIMPROM to the full extent desired by VSEKHIMPROM.

(c) For advice and consultation services rendered by NITROGEN to VSEKHIMPROM in the office of NITROGEN in New York or Europe or in USSR up to a total of 300 engineer days in any one year, and in addition thereto 200 engineer days in any one year, only in the offices of NITROGEN in New York or Europe, no charge shall be made by NITROGEN. It is understood, however, that for such consultation and advice in its own offices, without remuneration therefor, NITROGEN shall not be obligated to have its skilled engineers available at any particular time but shall be free to make agreements with other clients which might at various periods require the services of such engineers.

PAR. 16. During the five years from the effective date of this Agreement, NITROGEN shall, at the request of VSEKHIMPROM, send to USSR skilled engineers capable of interpreting plans, inspecting work, and advising the representatives of VSEKHIMPROM in charge of the construction, installation and operation of such additional plants, in order to assist such representatives of VSEKHIMPROM, provided, however, that NITROGEN's obligation to have such engineers available for such purpose shall for any period be limited to and included within the number of engineers that VSEKHIMPROM shall have notified NITROGEN it requires, as provided in paragraph 15 thereof. Additional engineering service of the character provided for in this paragraph may be furnished by NITROGEN to VSEKHIMPROM in accordance with agreement that may be made from time to time by the parties hereto, and NITROGEN shall at all times use its best endeavours to supply such engineering service to VSEKHIMPROM so far as it can make its skilled engineers available for such purpose.

V. REMUNERATION

PAR. 17. VSEKHIMPROM shall pay to NITROGEN for the rights and technical services to be rendered by NITROGEN to VSEKHIMPROM as herein provided, the following sums in United States Gold Dollars in New York City:

(a) Eighty Thousand dollars ($80,000) within thirty days after the effective date of this agreement.

(b) Eighty Thousand dollars ($80,000) on January 1st, 1932, or in the event that the plant now building at Berezniki is completed before that date then this payment must be made within five (5) days of such completion.

(c) Sixty thousand dollars ($60,000) one year after the effective date of this agreement.

(d) Sixty thousand dollars ($60,000) two years after the effective date of this agreement.

(e) Sixty thousand dollars ($60,000) three years after the effective date of this agreement.

(f) Sixty thousand dollars ($60,000) four years after the effective date of this agreement.

(g) Fifty dollars ($50.00) per engineer day, this is per engineer per day, for all engineers furnished by NITROGEN to VSEKHIMPROM at the request of VSEKHIMPROM, as provided in paragraphs 14, 15 and 16 hereof, except for such engineers as are furnished at no per diem cost as specified in paragraph 15, sub paragraph (c), together with the travelling and living expenses of such engineers when their services are required away from the offices of NITROGEN. The engineer days referred to herein shall include the time occupied in travelling from the offices of NITROGEN or from such other points as may be designated by NITROGEN in case such engineers are sent to the service of VSEKHIMPROM to such other points, and shall include all the days until such engineers can return to the points from which they left to go to the service of VSEKHIMPROM. The travel of engineers to and from the service of VSEKHIMPROM shall be by the quickest and most direct transportation, other than air transport, affording first-class accommodations.

(h) For the service, expenses and material consumed by draughtsmen of NITROGEN in preparation of plans, specifications, and drawings and for the other services provided in paragraph 14, hereof, the actual cost of draughtsmen to NITROGEN plus 100% (one hundred percent) for overhead.

(i) The remuneration provided in sub-paragraphs (g) and (h) hereof shall be payable upon rendering of bills therefor by NITROGEN, except to the extent that payment monthly in advance is provided by paragraph 15 hereof. Such bills shall be rendered by NITROGEN to VSEKHIMPROM monthly.

IV.* LIVING AND WORKING CONDITIONS OF NITROGEN EMPLOYEES

PAR. 18. VSEKHIMPROM shall be responsible to NITROGEN for furnishing to the engineers and representatives of NITROGEN when engaged in work in behalf of VSEKHIMPROM in USSR:

(a) First-class lodging and subsistence, or in Moscow only equivalent cash allowance therefor, equal to that furnished or available to the highest grade non-Russian technical men employed or residing in USSR, in addition suitable office accommodation and equipment shall be provided,—all of which shall be for the sole and exclusive use of such employees and be conveniently adjacent to the point at which the services of such engineers are required by VSEKHIMPROM; and private automotive transportation between place or lodging and place of work, as requested from time to time by such engineers.

(b) First-class medical and surgical and/or hospital services and medical supplied for any sickness, accident and/or disability suffered by such engineers and representatives from any cause whatsoever while in USSR. In case of disease acquired before entering the USSR, but developing only thereafter this paragraph shall be in full force and effect, but the entire expense thereof shall be a charge against NITROGEN.

(c) VSEKHIMPROM agrees to provide such engineers and representatives with a properly authenticated letter stating that he is visiting USSR at the request of VSEKHIMPROM and asking representatives of the Government to aid him wherever possible and to facilitate his compliance with all formalities especially those of entrance and exit to and from the USSR.

(d) VSEKHIMPROM agrees to do all possible to facilitate the importation of, and to pay all customs duties, fees, and/or other charges collected by the USSR on:

* Beginning this section, document misnumbered in original.

1) All equipment necessary to such engineers in the performance of their duties such as drawings, books, instruments, and

2) clothing, medicines and personal articles reasonable required by such engineers, and

3) amounts of food, all not exceeding the maximum specified in list B attached hereto.

4) Also additional amounts of any of the above for the personal use of such engineers, should such be necessary to retain the services of such engineers.

VSEKHIMPROM agrees also to do all possible to facilitate the export of any records and any of the above-mentioned things except food and to indemnify NITROGEN against loss or damage of such property and equipment, whether the property of NITROGEN or its Employees whilst in transit in USSR, and will at the time of export provide a letter duly authenticated to facilitate such export.

(e) The rights granted to NITROGEN in paragraph 18 and applicable to its engineers under these warranties shall constitute warranties to NITROGEN and shall extend to all representatives of NITROGEN.

PAR. 19. VSEKHIMPROM agrees to reimburse NITROGEN and/or NITROGEN's engineers, within ten days after receipt of claim for any expenses incurred by NITROGEN and/or NITROGEN's engineers due to failure of VSEKHIMPROM to supply any of the services and/or facilities specified in the preceding paragraph and specifically authorizes NITROGEN and/or NITROGEN's engineers to incur such expenses immediately and without any notification in the event of such failure on the part of VSEKHIMPROM.

PAR. 20. All engineers and/or employees sent into USSR under this agreement by NITROGEN are employees of NITROGEN and not of VSEKHIMPROM, and VSEKHIMPROM shall not pay any remuneration to said engineers.

PAR. 21. NITROGEN shall have the right at any time to withdraw any particular engineer from USSR and replace such engineer with another engineer, but only in unusual cases shall such withdrawal take place until the arrival of a substitute. But the traveling and living expenses incurred as the result of any such withdrawal and/or replacement at the instance of NITROGEN shall be borne by NITROGEN. VSEKHIMPROM may require the withdrawal and/or replacement within a reasonable time of any engineer, and NITROGEN will agree thereto, but such withdrawal and replacement shall be at VSEKHIMPROM's expense unless NITROGEN agrees, on submission by VSEKHIMPROM of a statement of reasons for such requirement, that such withdrawal and replacement is necessary for the fulfilment of NITROGEN's obligations under this Agreement.

PAR. 22. VSEKHIMPROM assumes and will pay or will reimburse NITROGEN or its engineers and/or representatives, if any of its engineers and/or representatives have paid any taxes and/or other obligatory expenditures specified by the laws of USSR of the engineers and/or other representatives of NITROGEN while in USSR.

V. PERIOD OF OPERATION OF AGREEMENT

PAR. 23. The period of operation of this Agreement is fixed at five years counting from the date of its making, provided, however, that where rights are specificially granted for a longer period, such rights shall not terminate with the expiration of the agreement.

PAR. 24. In case NITROGEN shall be dissolved or amalgamated with some other enterprise, all its rights and obligations under this agreement fully pass on to its successor. In case VSEKHIMPROM shall be dissolved or amalgamated with some other USSR Government enterprise, all such rights and obligations of VSEKHIMPROM under this Agreement pass in their entirety to the State enterprise which shall be designated by the Supreme Council of National Economy of USSR.

VI. FORCE MAJEURE

PAR. 25. If either party is prevented from carrying out the herein contained provisions by reason of any war, civil commotion, epidemic, fire, cyclone, flood, embargo, governmental or physical cause, existing or future, beyond the reasonable control of such party, and interfering with the performance of such party hereunder, the party so interfered with shall be excused from such performance to the extent of such interference during the period thereof; providing, however, that the party so interfered with shall use due diligence and take all reasonable steps to remove the cause or causes preventing it from carrying out its obligations hereunder, and to resume such obligations with all reasonable promptness.

VII. ARBITRATION

PAR. 26. All disputes arising out of the performance and interpretation of the present agreement are settled by the method indicated in the special annex with which the present agreement forms an integral part.

VIII. GENERAL STATEMENTS

PAR. 27. The legal addresses of the parties are: VSEKHIMPROM, Moscow, Diakoff pereulok 4, USSR.

NITROGEN, 535 Fifth Avenue, NEW YORK, U.S.A. Provided, however, that either party may change such legal address by notice in writing to the other party.

PAR. 28. This agreement becomes effective from the date of its sanction by the Supreme Economic Council attached to the Council of People's Commissaries of the Union of S.S.R., such date being referred to herein as 'the effective date,' but unless NITROGEN receives written notice of such sanction within sixty days of the signing of this agreement by NITROGEN, this agreement shall not be binding upon NITROGEN without its separate written assent.

PAR. 29. Taxes of all kinds in connection with the making and operation of the present agreement are to be borne by VSEKHIMPROM.

STATE TRUST OF ALL THE UNION
CHEMICAL INDUSTRIES "VSEKHIMPROM"

WITNESS: *by J. L. Piatakoff*

....

NITROGEN ENGINEERING CORPORATION

by Frederick Pope

WITNESS:

....

DATED: Berlin, June 29, 1931.

is

Technical-Assistance Agreements between the Soviet Union and Western Companies, 1929-45

Western Company	Country of Origin	Technical Transfer to Soviet Union
Accounting and Tabulating Machine Co.	United States	Power machines
Akron Rubber Reclaiming Co.	United States	Rubber-plant reclamation; training Soviet nationals
Aktiebolaget Vallenbygg-nadsbyran	Sweden	Construction of Svir Dam
Alco Products, Inc. (Div. of American Locomotive)	United States	Petroleum refineries
Allen & Garcia Inc.	United States	Coal mine development
Allgemeine Elektrizitäts Gesellschaft	Germany	Electrical machinery
American Can Co.	United States	Canning processes
Ansaldo	Italy	Shipbuilding
Ansonia Clock Co.	United States	Clocks and watches
Audio-Cinema, Inc.	United States	Sound film technology
Austin Co.	United States	Automobile plant construction; design of Gorki city
Babcock & Wilcox, Inc.	United States	Boiler design
Badger, E. B., & Sons	United States	Wood distillation, oil refineries
Bagley & Sewell Co.	United States	Newsprint manufacture
Baldwin Locomotive Works	United States	Locomotive repair shops
Baltimore & Ohio Railroad	United States	Railroad operations
Birdsboro Steel Foundry & Machine Co.	United States	Hydraulic presses

Western Company	*Country of Origin*	*Technical Transfer to Soviet Union*
Birmingham Small Arms Co.	England	Bicycles
Bliss, E. W., Co.	United States	Power-plant design; small arms ammunition
Blom and Kamroth	United States	Meat-packing plants
Boeing Aircraft Co.	United States	Aircraft
Borsig, A.	Germany	Refrigeration technology
Brandt, Arthur J.	United States	Reconstruction of AMO works
British Thomson-Houston Co., Ltd.	United Kingdom	Power stations
Brown-Boveri Co.	Switzerland	Gas blowers; aluminum mill equipment
Brown Instrument Co.	United States	Electrical recording instruments
Brown-Lipe Gear Co.	United States	Gear manufacture for automobile industry
Bucyrus-Erie Co.	United States	Excavating equipment
Budd Manufacturing Co.	United States	1934 auto model change (21S)
Burd Piston Ring Co.	United States	Tractors
Burrell-Mase Engineering Co.	United States	Expansion and management of Grozneft
Casale Ammonia S.A.	Italy	Nitrogen fixation; manufacture of synthetic ammonia
Caterpillar Tractor Co.	United States	Training Soviet nationals
Cellulose de Bourges	France	Chemicals
Chain Belt Co.	United States	Conveyors
Chase, Frank D., Inc.	United States	Design of foundry projects
Cheretti & Tonfani	Italy	Design and construction of conveyors
Chicago Kitchen Co.	United States	Design of community kitchens
Cie de Produits Chimiques et Electrométallurgiques Alais, Troques et Camargue	France	Aluminum
Clark, Wallace, & Co.	United States	Gantt methods
Cleveland Tractor Co.	United States	Training Soviet nationals
Cooper, H. L., & Co., Inc.	United States	Dniepr Dam
Craven Bros. (Manchester), Ltd.	United Kingdom	Special machine tools

Western Company	*Country of Origin*	*Technical Transfer to Soviet Union*
Curtiss-Wright Corp.	United States	Aircraft engine manufacturing license
Davy Bros., Ltd.	United Kingdom	Forging manipulators
Deere & Co.	United States	Agricultural equipment
Deilmann Bergbau	Germany	Design of mines at Solikamsk
Demag Aktiengesellschaft	Germany	Manufacture of cranes, hoisting equipment and blooming mills
Deutsche Tiefbohr A-G	Germany	Drilling deep water wells
Deutz Motorenfabrik A-G	Germany	Construction of Deutz diesel engines
Dewey & Almy Chemical Co.	United States	Crab meat containers
Diebold Safe & Lock Co. (Diebold, Inc.)	United States	Watch factory
Disticoque S.A.	France	Coke ovens
Douglas Aircraft Co., Inc.	United States	Aircraft: DC-3
Dow Chemical Co.	United States	Styrene
Dueber-Hampden Watch Co.	United States	Construction and equipment of watch plant
Du Pont, (E.I.) de Nemours & Co.	United States	Synthetic ammonia, nitric acid and fertilizer technology
Eastman Construction Engineering	United States	Construction
Electric Auto-Lite Co.	United States	Electrical equipment in autos and tractors
Elektrokemisk	Norway	Manufacture of Soderberg electrodes
Ericsson, L. M., A/B	Sweden	Telephone equipment
Ex-Cell-O Aircraft and Tool Corp.	United States	Stated by Soviets as agricultural implements
Fairbanks Aviation Corp.	United States	Aircraft manufacture
Farben, I. G.	Germany	Chemicals
Farrel-Birmingham Co., Inc.	United States	Sykes machines
Ferguson, Hardy S., & Co.	United States	Paper-mill technology
Fiat s.p.a.	Italy	Automobiles, aircraft, ships

Western Company	Country of Origin	Technical Transfer to Soviet Union
Ford Motor Co.	United States	Automobile plant construction and auto tire plant
Foster-Wheeler Corp.	United States	Petroleum refineries
Freyn Engineering Co.	United States	Iron and steel plants
Frolick & Knupfel	Germany	Design and construction of mines
Gaillard-Parrish	United Kingdom	Sulfuric acid
Gibbs, Harry D.	United States	Chemical processes; phthalic anhydride
Gogan Machine Co.	United States	Automobile bumpers
Goodman Manufacturing Co.	United States	Coal cutters
Graver Corp.	United States	Refineries
Great Northern Telegraph	Denmark	Telegraph operations
Grusonwerk, Friedrich Krupp	Germany	Manufacture of equipment for crushing plants
Hahn, A. W.	United States	Aluminum powder
Harburger, Eisen, and Bronzewerke, A-G	Germany	Manufacture and design of equipment for oil-crushing mills
Heinkel	Germany	Aircraft
Henshien, H. G.	United States	Meat packing plants
Hercules Motor Corp.	United States	Reconstruction of Yaroslavl truck engine plant
Hercules Powder Co.	United States	Nitrocellulose; cotton linters
Hilaturas Casablancas, S.A.	Spain	Coal cutters
Houdry Process Corp.	United States	Catalysts
Humboldt-Deutz Motoren, A-G	Germany	Diesel engines (all sizes)
Imperial Chemical Industries, Ltd.	United Kingdom	Chemical manufacture
International General Electric Co., Inc.	United States	Electrical equipment (all types)
International Harvester Co.	Canada	Agricultural implements
International Harvester Co.	United States	Training Soviet nationals
Irving Air Chute Co., Inc.	United States	Parachutes
Isacco, Vittorio	Italy	Helicopters
Jenkins Co.	United States	Petroleum refineries

Western Company	Country of Origin	Technical Transfer to Soviet Union
Kahn, Albert, Inc.	United States	Supervision of Five-Year Plan design and construction
Kallitt Products, Inc.	United States	Electrical equipment
Karlstad Mechaniska Verkstaden A/B	Sweden	Construction of turbines, Svirstroi
Kohorn, Oskar, and Co.	Germany	Production of artificial silk by viscose process
Koppers Construction Co.	United States	Coke ovens and by-products
Krupp, Friedrich, A.G.	Germany	Manufacture of special grades of steel, cement
Kugellager, Vereinigte	Germany	Ball bearings
La Compagnie Générale de Télégraphie	France	Radios
Lockwood, Greene & Co., Inc.	United States	Textile-plant construction
Loeffler	Czechoslovakia	High-pressure boilers
Longacre Engineering and Construction Co.	United States	Apartment buildings
Lucas & Luick	United States	Gas plants and pipelines
Lummus Co.	United States	Refinery construction
Lurgi Gesellschaft für Chemie und Hüttenwesen m.b.H.	Germany	Sulfuric acid process
Maatschappi	Holland	Saccharification of wood pulp for production of fodder and glucose
Macchi	Italy	Flying boats
Manchu Machine Works	Manchuria	Machine-tool plant
Manchurian Machine Tool	Manchuria	Machine-tool plant
Marietta Manufacturing Co.	United States	Carbon-black plant unit
Marshall & Sons, Ltd.	United Kingdom	Locomotives for lumber industry
Martin, Glenn L., Co.	United States	Bomber design
Maschinen und Bronze-Waren Fabrik A-G	Germany	Machine tools
Maschinenbau A-G	Germany	Manufacture of compressors

Western Company	Country of Origin	Technical Transfer to Soviet Union
Maschinenbau-Anstalt 'Humboldt'	Germany	Installation of concentrator equipment
Maschinenfabrik Augsburg-Nürnberg A-G	Germany	Construction of MAN—Diesel engines, simple 4-cycle motors, simple and double 2-cycle motors with and without compressors, and machines and equipment for cold storage plants
McClintock & Marshall Const. Co.	United States	Building erection for Stalingrad Tractor Plant
McCormick Co.	United States	Baking-plant design
McDonald Engineering Co.	United States	Industrial plants, cement, elevators
McKee, Arthur G., & Co.	United States	Magnitogorsk iron and steel plant; petroleum refineries
Mechanical Engineering (Chicago)	United States	Meat-packing plants
Merritt Engineering & Sales Co., Inc.	United States	Manufacture of rolled-steel railroad-car wheels
Messer Co. A-G	Germany	Construction of autogenous welding equipment
Metropolitan-Vickers Electrical Co., Ltd.	United Kingdom	Construction of steam turbines; power plants
Midwest Rubber Reclaiming Co.	United States	Assistance in rubber-plant construction; training Soviet nationals
Miller, Max B., and Co.	United States	Petroleum refineries
Moisseiff, Leon S.	United States	Bridge consultation
Multibestos Co.	United States	Design and technical assistance in construction of factory for asbestos products
National Rubber Machinery Co.	United States	Tire-building machines
Newport News Shipbuilding & Dry Dock Co.	United States	Turbine construction
Nickel, Arthur, Co.	United States	Iron-ore mining

Western Company	Country of Origin	Technical Transfer to Soviet Union
Nitrogen Engineering Corp.	United States	Ammonia-fertilizer plant construction and operation
Nobile, General Umberto	Italy	Airships
Nordberg Manufacturing Co.	United States and United Kingdom	Railroad equipment
Oglebay, Norton Co.	United States	Iron-ore mine development
Ohio Locomotive Crane Co.	United States	Operation and servicing of cranes
Oliver Farm Equipment Co.	United States	Tractor plows
Otis Elevator Co.	United States	Moscow subway elevators
Owens Bottle Co.	United States	Bottle-closing patent and machinery for silicate industries
Parke, Davis & Co.	United States	Pharmaceutical products
Passburg, Emil, and Berthold Block	Germany	Design of vacuum plants
Penick & Ford, Ltd., Inc.	United States	Construction of corn production and refining plants
Pennsylvania Railroad	United States	Railroad operating methods
Peterson, Hugo	Germany	Peterson sulfuric acid process
Petroleum Engineering Corp.	United States	Petroleum refineries
Pflanzennamme	Germany	Manufacture of peat products
Polakov, W. N.	United States	Management consultants
Pontiac Engineering Co.	United States	Smelter construction
Power-Gas Corp., Ltd.	United Kingdom	Gas generator plant
Pratt & Whitney Aircraft Co.	United States	Stated by Soviets as agricultural implements
Radio Corporation of America	United States	Exchange of patents and information, radio and TV
Radiore Co.	United States	Prospecting assistance
Remington Rand, Inc.	United States	Office equipment
Republic Aviation Corp.	United States	Aircraft
Richard Bros.	United States	Tractor manufacture

Western Company	Country of Origin	Technical Transfer to Soviet Union
Riedinger Maschinen- und Bronzewarenfabrik A-G	Germany	Metals manufacture
Roberts & Shaefer Co.	United States	Detailed designs and plant drawings Donetz coal trust
Rockwell, W. S., Co.	United States	Furnace technology at Stalingrad
Rosoff Subway Construction Co.	United States	Subway construction (probably not implemented)
Rust Brothers	United States	Rust cotton-picking machine
Safety Mining Co.	United States	Manufacture of CARDOX
Sauerman Bros., Inc.	United States	Equipment operation
Savoia	Italy	Flying boats
Sayer, E. Y., Engineering Corp.	United States	Steam electric plant
Scintilla A-G	Switzerland	Manufacture of magnetoes and ignition equipment
Seabrook, C. F., Co.	United States	Road construction
Seiberling Rubber Co.	United States	Sale of rubber tire plant
Seversky Aircraft Corp.	United States	Aircraft
Sharples Specialty Co.	United States	Petroleum centrifuge equipment
Siemens-Schukert	Germany	Electrical equipment
Smidth, F. L., A/S	Denmark	Cement plants
Smith, C. V., Co., Thetford	Canada	Asbestos milling
Société de Prospection Electrique Procédés, Schlumberger	France	Electrical prospecting for oil
Société Française Anonyme 'Lumière'	France	Manufacture of films
Sociétés du Duralumin	France	Duralumin
Soieries de Strasbourg S.A.	France	Production of artificial silk by viscose process
Southwestern Engineering Co.	United States	Design, construction and operation of metal plants
Sperry Gyroscope Co., Inc.	United States	Marine instruments, bomb sights
Standard Alcohol Co.	United States	Rubber technology
Standard Oil Co. of New York	United States	Operation of Batum refinery: synthetic ethyl alcohol

Western Company	Country of Origin	Technical Transfer to Soviet Union
Stockholms Superfosfat Fabriks Aktiebolaget	Sweden	Construction, equipment, and operation of plant with annual production of 20,000 tons calcium cyanamid and 3,000 tons carbide (Chernorechensk Plant); manufacture of yellow prussiate of potash; construction of equipment and operation of Karabliss Cyanamid and Carbide Plant
Stuart, James & Cooke, Inc.	United States	Coal industry; grain elevators
Sullivan Machinery Co.	United States	Mining equipment
Sulzer Gebruder A-G	Germany	Construction of 2-cycle Sulzer diesel engines
Swasey, Warner P.	United States	Tractor manufacture
Szepesi, Eugene	United States	Accounting systems in textile mills
Taft, Pierce Mfg. Co.	United States	Manufacturing of tools, jigs, etc.
Telefunken Gesellschaft A-G	Germany	Manufacture of long-distance receiving sets
Thew Shovel Co.	United States	Dragline operation
Timken-Detroit Axle Co.	United States	Automobile industry
Torfplattenwerke A-G	Germany	Construction of plant for manufacture of peat insulation plates
Tube Reducing Co.	United States	Tube mill installations
Union Construction Co.	United States	Drawings and specifications for dredges
Union Switch and Signal Co.	United States	Railroad automatic block signals
United Engineering & Foundry Co.	United States	Hot and cold wide-strip mills in steel and aluminum industries
Universal Oil Products Inc.	United States	Refinery construction
U.S. Wheel Track Layer Corp.	United States	Christie tanks

Western Company	Country of Origin	Technical Transfer to Soviet Union
Verband Deutscher Werk-zeugmaschinfabrik Ausfuhr	Germany	Organization of joint techni-cal office bureau in Berlin for execution of designs for equipment of metal manufacturing plants; organization of machine display room in Moscow
Vereinigte Carborundum & Elektritwerke A-G	Germany	Manufacture and design of plant for artificial abrasives
Vereinigte Kugellager Fabriken A-G	Germany	Manufacture of ball bearings
Veritas S.A.	France	Technical assistance on tanker construction
Vickers-Armstrongs, Ltd.	United Kingdom	Tanks
Villar-Perosa Officine (RIV) s.p.a.	Italy	Manufacture of ball bearings
Vom Bauer	United States	Electric furnaces
Vultee Aircraft (Div. of Aviation Mfg. Corp.)	United States	Bombers
Webber & Wells, Inc.	United States	Food processing
Westinghouse Electric and Manufacturing Co.	United States	Power plant design, aviation test equipment
Westvaco Chlorine Products Corp.	United States	Chemical industry
Wheeler, Archer E., Engineering Co.	United States	Non-ferrous metals
White, J. G., Engineering Corp.	United States	Technical assistance on Svir Dam
Wilson, M. L.	United States	
Winkler-Koch Engineering Co.	United States	Cracking technology
Yukon Fur Farms, Inc.	United States	Organization of animal farms
Zahn A-G	Germany	Carbon disulfide

Note: These are equivalent to the Type III concessions described in Volume I.

APPENDIX D

Guide to Sources of Material

THE official numbering system of the U.S. State Department Decimal File (the central file) is used in this volume. The records for 1910 to 1930 used in *Western Technology . . ., 1917 to 1930* have been published on microfilm and references in that volume are to the National Archives microfilm. Records dated after 1930 utilized in this volume have not, as yet, been published on microfilm and references therefore refer to the Decimal File number. Thus, for example, 861.5017—Living Conditions/100 may be found in the National Archives under this file number and, although unpublished, is available for special purchase under this number. Later references, after about 1945, are held in the State Department; some for 1945 have been published in the annual series *Foreign Relations of the United States*. The greater part of the microfilmed State Department records as well as privately collected material used in this volume has been deposited at the Hoover Institution, Stanford University.

German archival material, available at the National Archives, is referred to by microcopy number; for example T 84–122–1421674 refers to Microcopy T 84, Roll 122, Frame 1421674.

Most of the scarce periodical literature is available at the Hoover Institution or the Library of Congress. Soviet technical books cited are in most cases available only at the Library of Congress, although those used in this study have been, for the most part, deposited with the Hoover Institution.

Bibliography

UNPUBLISHED SOURCES

American Engineers in Russia (manuscript collection in the Hoover Institution, Stanford University: TS Russia A511). Collected by H. Fisher in 1934-6; called here the "Fisher data."

In particular:
Burrell, G. A., 'Life in a Soviet Town.' (Unpublished manuscript in the American Engineers collection.)
'Statement of J. S. Ferguson covering personal experiences in Russia over a period of eighteen months.' April 30, 1933. (Unpublished mimeographed material in the American Engineers Collection, folder 6.)

Bailes, Kendall E., *Stalin and Revolution from Above: The Formation of the Soviet Technical Intelligentsia 1928–1934*, Ph.D. dissertation, Columbia University, 1970.

Budd, Ralph, *Report on Railways of the U.S.S.R. 1930, Vol. I*, National Archives. (Microcopy deposited in the Hoover Institution, Stanford University.)

Butler, Charles Edward, *Productivity in Soviet Coal Mining, 1928–64*, Ph.D. dissertation, Harvard University, Economics Department, 1965-6.

Dodge, Norton T., *Trends in Labor Productivity in the Soviet Tractor Industry*, Ph.D. dissertation, Harvard University, Economics Department, February 1960.

Douglas Aircraft Company files.

Farquhar, Percival, Collection. Archives of the Hoover Institution, Stanford University.

Generalstab des Heeres, Abteilung Fremde Heere Ost, 'Stahl-Gewinnung in der U.d.S.S.R., Stand: 1943.' (Folder of tabulation of Soviet iron and steel plants of the Soviet Union.) T-78, Roll 491; begins frame 6477891.

German World War II Records (at National Archives, Washington, D.C.): Generalstab des Heeres, Abteilung Fremde Heere Ost, '33 II h Band 1 23.9.39–31.12.42.' (Folder of Gen Std/HAbt. FHO/(II) dealing with petroleum industry in the Soviet Union.) T-78, Roll 491; begins frame 6477382.

Germany, Wehrmacht Oberkommando, (OKW/Wi Rü Amt/Wi) March 1941. Miscellaneous German Records. Microcopy T-84, Roll 122.
Lists of Soviet plants giving location, product and number of employees; begins frame 1421218.
List of electric power plants in Soviet Union; begins frame 1421674.

Germany. Auswartiges Amt, *Ausfuhr-Warenwerkehr des Protektorate Böhmen und Mühren mit der U.d.S.S.R. vom 16.3.1939 bis 31, 8.1940.* (Photoblowups, Serial No. 1137, Frames 324259–324263; deposited in Hoover Institution archives.)

Gmelin-Institut. (Reports from Geheim-Archiv of the OKW/Wi Rü Amt/Wi, concerning mineral and petroleum development and industries.) T-84, Roll 127.

Russland: Die Kohlenlagerstatten des Urals. Bericht No. 66c. *Eisenhüttenindustrie.*

Gorton, Willard Collection (Special Collection of the Hoover Institution, Stanford University).

Hutchinson, Lincoln, Papers at Hoover Institution.

Thomson, J. L., 'Red Metal Mining in Red Russia.' (Unpublished manuscript in the American Engineers Collection.)

Tinkler, Charles C., (Correspondence, Feb.–July 1930. TS Russia T 589 in the Hoover Institution, Stanford University.)

U.S. State Department. *Claims made against Russia by the United States.* (National Archives microfilm T-640, deposited in the Hoover Institution, Stanford University.)

Vertreter des Auswartigen Amts beim OKH, Etzdorff. 'Das Erdöl von Maikop und des Raffinerie von Krasnodar,' August 1942. T-84, Roll 122: begins frame 1421099.

Wirtschaftsgruppe Chemische Industrie, 'Die Schwefelsäureindustrie in der Sowjet-Union,' January 1944. T-84, Roll 122: begins frame 1421674.

Witkin, Zara, Collection. Archives of the Hoover Institution, Stanford University.

JOURNALS

Aero Digest, Washington, D.C.

American Chemical Society, *Industrial and Engineering Chemistry*, Washington, 1923–39.

American Machinist, New York.

American Magazine, New York.

American Ordnance Association, *Ordnance*, Washington, D.C.

American Society of Civil Engineers, *Civil Engineering*, Easton, Pa.

American Society of Mechanical Engineers, *Mechanical Engineering*, New York.

Amtorg Trading Company (New York), *Economic Review of the Soviet Union*, New York, 1929–1934.

The Automobile Engineer, London.

Automotive Industries, Philadelphia.

Aviation, New York.

Now: *Aviation Week and Space Technology*.

Berliner Tageblatt, Berlin.

Blast Furnace and Steel Plant, Cleveland and Pittsburgh.

Brennkraft-technische gesellschaft, *Brennstoff- und Wärmewirtschaft*, Halle.

Brown-Boveri Review, Baden, Switzerland.

Business Week, Greenwich, Conn.

Case Alumni Association, *Case Alumnus*, Ohio.

Chemical Age, London.

Chemical and Metallurgical Engineering, New York.

Now: *Chemical Engineering*.

Civil Engineering, Easton, Pa.

Combustion, New York and London.

Concrete, Detroit.

Ekonomicheskaya Zhizn, Moscow, 1930–8.

The Electric Journal, Pittsburgh, Pa.

Electric Railway Traction, supplement to Railway Gazette, London, October 27, 1933.

The Electrical Review, London.

Electrical World, New York.

Electrochemical Society Transactions, Baltimore, Md.

The Engineer, London.

Engineering, London.

Engineering and Mining Journal, New York.

Engineering News Record, Chicago and New York.

Factory and Industrial Management, New York.

Far Eastern Review, Manila and Shanghai.

Fortune, New York.

Freyn Design, Chicago.

Gas and Oil Power, London.

General Electric Company, *General Electric Review*, Schnectady, N.Y.

General Electric Company, *The Monogram*, Schnectady, N.Y.

Genie Civile, Paris.

Handelsvertretund der UdSSSR in Deutschland, *Sowjetwirtschaft und Aussenhandel*, Berlin SW, Germany, IX-XII, 1930–3.

The India-Rubber Journal, London.

Industrial Spark, Stalingrad (Hoover Institution only).

Za Industrializatsiiu, Moscow.

The Iron Age, Middletown, N.Y.

Iron and Steel Industry, London.

Izvestia, Moscow.

Komiteta po standartizatsii, *Vestnik Standardizatsii*, Moscow.

Machinery, New York.

Magnitostroi, *Informatsionnyi Builletin'*, Magnitogorsk.

Le Messager de Paris, Paris.

Metallurgia, Manchester, England.

The Mining Magazine, London.

Moscow Daily News, Moscow.

Moskauer Rundschau, Moscow.

Neue Zürcher Zeitung, Berlin.

The New York Times, New York.

Oil Engine, London.

The Petroleum Times, London.

Pit and Quarry, Chicago.

Power, New York.

Pravda, Leningrad.

Pravda, Moscow.

Proceedings of the Institute of Electrical Engineers, London.

Revue des Deux Mondes, Paris.

Royal Aero Club of the United Kingdom, *Flight*, London.

Saturday Evening Post, Philadelphia.

Sevodnia, Riga.

Society of Automotive Engineers, *S.A.E. Journal*, New York.

Za Standardizatsiiu, Moscow.

State Publishing House of the RSFSR, *U.S.S.R. in Construction*, Moscow, 1930–9.

The Steam Engineer, London.

Steel, Cleveland.

Teplotekhnicheskogo Instituta, *Isvestia Teplotekhnicheskogo Instituta*, Moscow, 1924–5.

Time, New York.

The Times, London.

Torgovo-Promyshlennaya Gazeta, Moscow.

U.S. Bureau of Foreign and Domestic Commerce, *Foreign Commerce Weekly*, Washington, D.C.

U.S. Naval Institute Proceedings, Annapolis, Maryland.

U.S. State Department, *Background Notes—U.S.S.R.* (Office of Media Services, Bureau of Public Affairs: Washington, D.C., 1965).

Vestnik Komiteta po Delam Izobretenii, Leningrad.

La Vie Economique des Soviets, Paris.

World Petroleum, New York.

Zaria Vostoka, Tiflis.

Zarya, Harbin, China.

Zhurnal Industrialnoi Khimii, Moscow.

BOOKS AND JOURNAL ARTICLES

Aisenshtadt, L., *Ocherki po istorii stankostroeniya, SSSR*, Moscow, 1957.

American Council of Learned Societies devoted to Humanistic Studies, *Gosudarstvennyi plan razvitiia narodnogo khoziaistva SSSR na 1941 god*, Russian Reprint Series, 1951.

American Institute of Chemists, *Vladimir N. Ipatieff, Testimonial in Honor of Three Milestones in His Career*, Chicago, 1942.

American Iron and Steel Institute, *Steel in the Soviet Union*, New York, 1959.

American-Russian Chamber of Commerce, *Handbook of the Soviet Union*, John Day Co., New York, 1936.

Anglo-Russian Parliamentary Committee, *Possibilities of British-Russian Trade* (London: 1962).

Association of American Railroads, *Railroads of the U.S.S.R.*, Washington, D.C., n.d.

Association of American Railroads, *A Report on Diesel Locomotive Design and Maintenance on Soviet Railways*, AAR Research Center, Chicago, 1966.

Bardin, I. P., ed., *Metallurgy of the U.S.S.R.* (1917–1957), The Israel Program for Scientific Translations, 1961.

Bardin, I. P., ed., *Metallurgy of the U.S.S.R.* (1917–1957), Metallurgizdat, Moscow, 1958.

Barmine, Alexander, *One Who Survived*, G. P. Putnam, New York, 1945.

vom Baur, C. H., 'The Electric Furnace and Its Products in the U.S.S.R.,' *Electrochemical Society: Transactions*, LXIII (1933), pp. 305–8.

Beal, F. E., *Foreign Workers in a Soviet Tractor Plant*, Co-operative Publishing Society of Foreign Workers in the U.S.S.R., Moscow, 1933.

Bergson, Abram, *Economic Trends in the Soviet Union*, Harvard University Press, Cambridge, 1963.

Blinkov, B. S., *Khimicheskaya promyshlennost' SSSR*, Moscow, 1933.

Boller, Paul F., Jr., 'The "Great Conspiracy" of 1933,' *Southwest Review*, XXXIX, No. 2, Spring 1954, pp. 97–112.

Bolshaya Sovietskaya Entsiklopediya, LI, Moscow, 1945.

Bron, S., *Soviet Economic Development and American Business*, H. Liveright, New York, 1930.

Browlie, 'The Löeffler Boilers at Moscow,' *The Steam Engineer*, XXI, No. 5 (February 1933), pp. 216–8.

Budnitskii, I. M., *Ugol'naya Prom'shlennost'*, Moscow, 1958.

Bukharin, N. *Socialist Reconstruction and Struggle for Technique*, Co-operative Publishing Society of Foreign Workers in the U.S.S.R., Moscow, 1932.

Busse, W., *Bewasserungs Wirtschaft in Turan*, Jena, 1915.

Carver, W. L., 'AMO and Nizhni-Novgorod Plants Lead Soviet Plans,' *Automotive Industries*, Vol. LXVI (March 12, 1932), pp. 418–9.

Caunter, C. F., *Motor Cars. Handbook of the Collection*, Part II, H.M.S.O., London, 1959.

Chambers, Whittaker, *Witness*, Random House, New York, 1952.

Chemical and Metallurgical Engineering, *Process Industries Flow Sheets and Data Book*, McGraw-Hill Publishing Co., New York, 1942.

Chinese Association for the United Nations, *A Report on Russian Destruction of Our Industries in the North-eastern Provinces*, Hsin Sheng Printing Works, Taipei, April 1952.

Chinn, George Morgan, *The Machine Gun*, Bureau of Ordnance, Dept. of the Navy, Washington, D.C., U.S. Govt. Printing Office, 1951.

Citrine, W., *I Search for Truth in Russia*, Routledge, London, 1936.

Clark, M. Gardner, *The Economics of Soviet Steel*, Harvard University Press, Cambridge, 1956.

Clark, W., *Grafiki Ganta*, Moscow, 1931.

Cotte, Jules, *Un Ingénieur Français en URSS*, Colmann Lévy, Paris, 1946.

Dallin, David J., *Soviet Espionage*, Yale University Press, New Haven, 1956.

Dallin, David J. and B. I. Nicolaevsky, *Forced Labor in Soviet Russia*, Hollis & Carter, London, 1947.

Dalrymple, Dana G., 'American Technology and Soviet Agricultural Development, 1924–1933,' *Agricultural History*, XL, No. 3 (July 1966), pp. 187–206.

Dalrymple, Dana G., 'The American Tractor Comes to Soviet Agriculture: The Transfer of a Technology,' *Technology and Culture*, V, No. 2 (Spring 1964), pp. 191–214.

Dalrymple, Dana G., 'American Tractors and Early Soviet Agriculture,' *The Smithsonian Journal of History*, Vol. II (1967), pp. 53–62.

Dalrymple, Dana G., 'Joseph A. Rosen and Early Russian Studies of American Agriculture,' *Agricultural History*, XXXVIII, No. 3 (July 1964), pp. 157–60.

Dalrymple, Dana G., 'The Stalingrad Tractor Plant in Early Soviet Planning,' *Soviet Studies*, XVIII, No. 2 (October 1966), pp. 164–8.

Davis, A. P., 'Irrigation in Turkestan,' *Civil Engineering*, II, No. 1 (January 1932), pp. 1–5.

Dedijer, Vladimir, *Tito*, Simon and Schuster, New York, 1953.

'Double 50-inch Centre Lathe for Russia,' *The Engineer*, CLIV (September 1932), pp. 253, 258.

Dummelow, J., *1899–1949*, Metropolitan-Vickers Electrical Co., Ltd., Manchester, 1949.

Dyck, H. L., *Weimar Germany and Soviet Russia 1926–1933*, Chatto, London, 1966.

Ershler, I., and S. Stoliarov, 'The Cement Industry in the U.S.S.R.,' *Pit and Quarry*, XXX, No. 8 (February 1938), pp. 61–4.

'Facts about Russian Cement Plants Told by American Engineers,' *Concrete*, XXXIX, No. 5 (November 1931), pp. 53–5.

Fairlie, A. M., *Sulfuric Acid Manufacture*, Reinhold, New York, 1936.

Farberov, M. I. and V. N. Komarov, 'Russia's Reclaiming Process,' *The India-Rubber Journal*, LXXXVII, No. 25 (June 23, 1934), pp. 699–704.

Feuer, Lewis S., 'Travelers to the Soviet Union, 1917–1932: The Formation of a Component of New Deal Ideology,' *American Quarterly*, XIV (Summer 1962), pp. 119–49.

Fisher, Harry L., *Chemistry of Natural and Synthetic Rubbers*, Reinhold, New York, 1957.

Le Fleming, H. M. and J. H. Price, *Russian Steam Locomotives*, Marshbank, London, 1960.

Fox, Gordon and Owen R. Rice, 'Soviet Standardizes Blast Furnace Design,' *The Iron Age*, CXXXIII, No. 10 (March 8, 1934), pp. 20–4, 58.

Frankfurt, S. M., *Men and Steel*, Co-operative Publishing Society of Foreign Workers in the U.S.S.R., Moscow, 1935.

Freyn, Henry J., 'Iron and Steel Industry in Russia,' *Blast Furnace and Steel Plant*, XVII (January 1930), p. 92.

Germany, Auswärtigen amts., *Akten Zur Deutschen Auswärtigen Politik, 1918–1945*, Vandenheock und Ruprecht, Göttingen, 1967.

Gershenkron, Alexander, *Economic Backwardness in Historical Perspective*, Harvard University Press, Cambridge, 1962.

Glavnyi Kontsessionnyi komitet. *Documents Concerning the Competence of the Arbitration Court Set Up in Connection with the Questions Outstanding Between the Lena Goldfields Company Limited and the U.S.S.R.* Moscow: 1930.

Gonta, T., *The Heroes of Grozny; How the Soviet Oil Industry Fulfilled the Five Year Plan in Two and a Half Years*, Co-operative Publishing Society of Foreign Workers in the U.S.S.R., Moscow, 1932.

Gosplan, *The Second Five-Year Plan*, Lawrence and Wishart, London, n.d.

Gosplan, *Vtoroi piatiletnii plan razvitia narodnogo khoziastva SSSR (1933–1937 gg)*, I, Moscow, 1934.

Granick, David, *Soviet Metal-Fabricating and Economic Development*, University of Wisconsin, Madison, 1967.

Grady, E. G., *Seeing Red*, Brewer, Warren and Putnam, Inc., New York, 1931.

Great Britain, *Correspondence Relating to the Arrest of Employees of the Metropolitan Vickers Company at Moscow*, Command Paper 4286, London, 1933.

Great Britain, Anglo-Russian Parliamentary Committee, *Possibilities of British-Russian Trade*, London, 1926.

Grey, C. G. and Leonard Bridgman, eds., *Jane's All the World's Aircraft*, Sampson Low, Marston & Co., Ltd., London, 1932, 1933, 1939.

Gurevitch, A. I., *Zadachi chernoi metallurgii v 1932 g*, Moscow, 1932.

Gwyer, Joseph, 'Soviet Machine Tools,' *Ordnance*, XLIII, No. 231, pp. 415–9.

Handelswertretung der UdSSR in Deutschland, *Sowjetwirtschaft und Aussenhandel*, Berlin.

Hardt, John P., *Dispersal of the Soviet Electric Power Industry*, Maxwell Air Force Base, Alabama, 1957.

Hart, B. H. Liddell, *The Red Army*, Harcourt, Brace and Company, 1958.

Herman, L. M., 'Revival of Russia's Tractor Industry,' *Foreign Commerce Weekly*, XXI, No. 2 (October 6, 1945), p. 10–2.

Herman, Leon, *Varieties of Economic Secrecy in the Soviet Union*, RAND Corporation, Santa Monica, December 1963, P-2840.

Heymann, Hans, *We Can Do Business with Russia*, Ziff Davis, Chicago, 1945.

Hindus, Maurice, 'Pinch Hitter for the Soviets,' *American Magazine*, CXIII, No. 14 (April 1932), pp. 31–33, 134–136.

Hirsch, Alcan, *Industrialized Russia*, Chemical Catalog Co., New York, 1934.

Hirschman, A. O., *The Strategy of Economic Development*, Yale University Press, New Haven, 1958.

Hooftman, H., *Russian Aircraft*, Aero Publishers, Fallbrook, 1965.

Howard, Frank A., *Buna Rubber*, Van Mostrand, New York, 1947.

Institut promyshlenno-ekonomicheskikh isslodovanni NKTP, *Chernaya metallurgiya SSSR v pervoi pyatiletke*, Moscow, 1935.

Ipatieff, V. I., *Life of a Chemist*, Stanford University Press, Stanford, 1946.

Jasny, Naum, *The Socialized Agriculture of the U.S.S.R.*, Stanford University Press, Stanford, 1949.

Jones, R. E., *et al.*, *The Fighting Tanks since 1916*, National Service Publishing Company, Washington, D.C., 1933.

Jordan, George Racey, *From Major Jordan's Diaries*, Harcourt, Brace and Company, New York, 1952.

Kahn, Albert Inc., *Architecture by Albert Kahn Associates*, New York, 1948.

Kahn, Albert Inc., *Industrial and Commercial Buildings*, Detroit, 1937.

Kalmykov, N. N., *Burovaya Tekhnika i Tekhnologiya za Rubezhom*, Nedra, Moscow, 1968.

Kaufmann, P. G., 'Development of Steam Boiler Design in Russia,' *The Steam Engineer*, XIV, No. 166 (July 1945), p. 292.

Kaufmann, P. G., 'Development of Steam Boiler Design in Russia, II,' *The Steam Engineer*, XIV, No. 167 (August 1945), p. 333.

Kaufmann, P. G., 'Operating Experience with a Pulverised Fuel-Fired "Once-Through" Boiler,' *The Steam Engineer*, XIII, No. 156 (September 1944), pp. 358–64.

Keldysh, M., 'V avangarde tekhnicheskogo progressa,' *Pravda*, No. 314, November 9, 1968.

Keller, Werner, *Ost minus west=null*, Droemersche Verlagsanstalt, Munich, 1960.

Kennard, H. P., *Russian Year Book for 1912*, Macmillan, London, 1912.

Kilmarx, R. A., *A History of Soviet Air Power*, Praeger, New York, 1962.

Kolomenskii, A., *Kak my ispol'zuem zagranichnuiu tekhniku*, Gosizdat, Moscow, 1930.

Koptewskii, Sergei, *The Costs of Construction of New Metallurgical Plants in the U.S.S.R.*, East European Fund, Inc., New York, 1952.

Korobov, V. A., *Traktory avtomobili i sel'skokhozyaistvennye dvigateli*, Moscow, 1950.

Kravchenko, Viktor Andreevich, *I Chose Freedom*, Scribner's Sons, New York, 1946.

Kubek, Anthony, *How the Far East was Lost*, Regnery, Chicago, 1963.

384   Bibliography

Die Kupfererzeugung der U.d.S.S.R., Der Reichsminister der Luftfahrt und
   Oberbefehlshaber der Luftwaffe, Berlin, 1941; which is Geheim Report No.
   788, found in Microcopy T-84, Roll 127, Frame 1427764.

Lachman, Gisella R., comp., *Manufacturing and Mechanical Engineering in
   the Soviet Union*, U.S. Library of Congress, Reference Dept., Washington,
   1953.

'Large Farrel-Sykes Gear Generators for Soviet Russia,' *Machinery* (New
   York), XLIII, No. 3, pp. 211–2.

Legay, K., *Un Mineur Français chez les Russes*, Editions Pierre Tisne, Paris,
   1937.

Lenin, V. I., 'Report on Concessions to the Bolshevik Fraction of the Eighth
   Congress of Soviets,' December 21, 1920, *Dokumenty vneshnei politiki
   SSSR*, Vol. III, Gospolitizdat, Moscow, 1957.

Littlepage, John D. and Demaree Bess, *In Search of Soviet Gold*, George G.
   Harrap & Co. Ltd., London, 1939.

Lloyd's Register, *Lloyd's Register of Shipping, 1941*, London, 1942.

Lury, G. E., *50 let sovetskaya khimicheskaya nauka i promyshlennost'*, Moscow,
   1967.

Lyons, Eugene, *Assignment in Utopia*, Harcourt, Brace and Company, New
   York, 1937.

Lyons, Eugene, ed., *Six Soviet Plays*, Houghton Mifflin, Boston, 1934.

McBurney, W. G., *et al.*, *German Carbide, Cyanamide and Cyanide Industry*,
   C.I.O.S. Report No. XXVII–92 Combined Intelligence Objectives Sub-
   committee, 1946.

McMurtrie, Francis, ed., *Jane's Fighting Ships, 1946–47*, Sampson Low,
   Marston & Co. Ltd., London.

'Machine Tool Building in Russia,' *Machinery*, Vol. XLII (October 1935),
   p. 107.

Magnitostroi, *Informatsionnyi Biulleten'*, Magnitogorsk.

Mantell, C. L., *Industrial Electrochemistry*, McGraw-Hill, New York, 1950.

Miller, Ralph E., 'American Automatic Machinery Aids Soviet Reconstruction,' *The Iron Age*, CXXXI, No. 4 (January 26, 1933), pp. 162–4.

Molotov, V., *Statement at the Session of the Supreme Soviet of the U.S.S.R. on
   the Ratification of the Soviet-German Non-Aggression Pact*, Bookniga, New
   York, August 31, 1939.

Monkhouse, Allan, 'Electrical Development in the U.S.S.R.,' *Proceedings of
   the Institute of Electrical Engineers* (London), LXXVII, No. 462 (June 1935),
   p. 641.

Monkhouse, Allan, *Moscow 1911–1933*, Little, Brown and Company, Boston,
   1934.

'The Moscow Trial, New Light on the Case of 1933,' *The Times* (London),
   May 22–5, 1933.

Nelson, G., *Industrial Architecture of Albert Kahn Co., Inc.*, Architectural Book Publishing Company, Inc., New York, 1939.

Nelson, W. G., 'Waste-Wood Distillation by the Badger-Stafford Process,' *Industrial and Engineering Chemistry*, XXII, No. 4 (April 1930), pp. 312-5.

Nepomnyashcii, I. L., *Koksovye mashiny, ikh konstruktsii i raschety*, Moscow, 1963.

Nobile, Umberto, *My Polar Flights; An Account of the Voyages of the Airships Italia and Norge*, F. Muller, London, 1961.

or Putnam, New York, 1961.

Noel-Baker, Philip, *The Private Manufacture of Armaments*, Gallascz, London, 1937.

Nutt, Arthur, 'European Aviation Engines,' *S.A.E. Journal*, XLI, No. 1 (July 1937), pp. 14-5.

Nutter, G. Warren, *The Growth of Industrial Production in the Soviet Union*, Princeton University Press, Princeton, N.J., 1962.

Pauley, Edwin, *Report on Japanese Assets in Manchuria to the President of the United States, July 1946*, U.S. Govt. Printing Office, Washington, D.C., 1946.

Pauley, Edwin, *Report on Japanese Reparations to the President of the United States, November 1945 to April 1946*, U.S. Govt. Printing Office, Washington, D.C., April 1, 1946.

Penova, E. M., *Podvonoe korablestroennie v Rossii (1900–1917)*, Sudostroennie, Leningrad, 1965.

Polakov, W. N., 'The Gantt Chart in Russia,' *American Machinist*, LXXV, No. 7 (August 13, 1931), pp. 261-4.

Pose, F., *German Workers in a Moscow Factory*, Moscow, 1933.

Price-Hughes, H. A., *B.T.H. Reminiscences: Sixty Years of Progress*.

Report of the Ford Delegation to Russia and the U.S.S.R., April-August 1926, Detroit, 1926, Ford Motor Company Archives Accession No. 49.

Roberts, L., *Noranda*, Clarke, Irwin and Co., Toronto, 1956.

Rodin, N. W., *Productivity in Soviet Iron Mining, 1890–1960*, RAND Corp., Santa Monica, 1953, Report RM-1116.

'Rolling Mill Developments in the U.S.S.R.,' *Iron and Steel Industry*, X, No. 11 (June 1937), pp. 475-7.

Rossi, A. (pseud. of Angelo Tasca), *The Russo-German Alliance, 1939–1941*, Beacon Press, Boston, 1951.

Samarski, P. V., and E. K. Ziberlich, 'One Tower System for Sulphuric Acid,' *Chemical Engineering*, XLI, No. 12 (December 1934), pp. 642-3.

Saunders, M. G., ed., *The Soviet Navy*, Weidenfeld and Nicolson, London, 1958.

Saur, T., 'The Ramzin Once-Through Boiler,' *Combustion*, X, No. 1 (July 1938), pp. 35–6.

Schauder, 'Sowjetrussische notkonstruktionen,' *Beton und Eisen*, XXXII, No. 14 (July 20, 1933), pp. 213–6.

Schlaifer, R. and S. D. Heron, *Development of Aircraft Engines and Fuels*, Harvard University, Boston, 1950.

Schubert, Frank, 'Bearings for the Soviets,' *American Machinist*, LXXVII (April 12, 1933, pp. 229–32; April 26, 1933, pp. 273–6; May 10, 1933, pp. 296–9; May 24, 1933, pp. 334–7; and June 7, 1933, pp. 369–73).

Schwartz, Harry, *Russia's Soviet Economy*, Prentice Hall, New York, 1950.

Scott, John, *Behind the Urals*, The Riverside Press, Cambridge, 1942.

Shimkin, D., *Minerals: A Key to Soviet Power*, Harvard, Cambridge, 1953.

60 letters: Foreign Workers write of their Life and Work in the U.S.S.R., Moscow, 1936.

Smith, Andres, *I Was a Soviet Worker*, E. P. Dutton, New York, 1936.

'The Smoke of the Fatherland,' *Zaria Vostoka*, No. 268 (September 29, 1931), p. 3.

Sontag, Raymond J. and James S. Beddie, *Nazi-Soviet Relations, 1939–1941*, Dept. of State, Washington, D.C., 1948.

'Les Soviets et les Concessions aux étrangers,' *Revue des Deux Mondes*, XXXV (1926), p. 158.

State Law Publishing House, *Wrecking Activities at Power Stations in the Soviet Union*, II, Moscow, 1933.

Strong, A. L., *From Stalingrad to Kusbas*, International, New York, 1932.

Stroud, John, *The Red Air Force*, Pilot Press, London, 1943.

Sutton, Antony C., *Western Technology and Soviet Economic Development, 1917 to 1930*, Hoover Institution, Stanford, 1968.

Swianiewicz, S., *Forced Labour and Economic Development*, Oxford University Press, London, 1965.

Tekhnicheskii progress v chernoi metallurgii SSSR, Moscow, 1962.

'Trend of Development in Steam Generation in Russia,' *Steam Engineer*, VI, No. 72 (September 1937), pp. 502–4; VII, No. 73 (October 1937), pp. 26–8; VII, No. 76 (January 1938), pp. 160–1, 168.

Turgeon, L., *Prices of Metalworking Equipment in the Soviet Union, 1928–1951*, RAND Corp., Santa Monica, 1953, RM-1112.

U.S. House of Representatives, *Hearings before Select Committee on Export Control*, 87th Congress, 1st Session, Washington, D.C., October 25, 26, and 30 and December 5, 6, 7, and 8, 1961.

U.S. Senate, Committee on the Judiciary, *Export of Ball Bearing Machines to Russia*, 87th Congress, 1st session, Washington, 1961.

U.S. Senate, Judiciary Committee, *Exposé of Soviet Espionage*, 86th Congress, 2nd session (prepared by the FBI, U.S. Dept. of Justice), May 1960.

U.S. Senate Foreign Relations Committee, *East-West Trade*, Washington, D.C., 1964.

U.S. State Dept., *Report on War Aid Furnished by the United States to the U.S.S.R.*, Office of Foreign Liquidation, Washington, D.C., 1945.

U.S. State Dept. Decimal File, 1930–1945 (available at National Archives, Washington, D.C.).

Veingarten, S. M., *Ekonomika i planirovaniia chernoi metallurgii SSSR*, Moscow, 1939.

Veridicus (pseud.), *Suisse and Soviets: Histoire d'un Conflict*, Delpeuch, Paris, 1926.

Vneshtorgizdat, *Economic Conditions in the U.S.S.R.*, Moscow, 1931.

Voyce, Arthur, *Russian Architecture*, Philosophical Library, New York, 1948.

Wasbauer, A. M., 'Machine Tools for the Soviets,' *American Machinist*, Vol. LXXVII (February 1934), pp. 147–9.

Weinberg, Gerhard L., *Germany and the Soviet Union 1939–1941*, E. J. Brill, Leiden, 1954.

Wells, Walter, 'An American Toolmaker in Russia,' *American Machinist*, Vol. LXXV (November 26, 1931), pp. 816–8.

Westgarth, John R., *Russian Engineer*, Denis Archer, London, 1934.

Westwood, J. N., *History of Russian Railways*, George Allen and Unwin, London, 1964.

Westwood, J. N., *Soviet Railways Today*, Citadel Press, New York, 1964.

Whitcomb, Arthur J., 'Soviet Union to Build Steel Plant,' *Blast Furnace and Steel Plant*, XVIII (July 1930), p. 1135.

Woodward, David, *The Russians at Sea*, William Kimber, London, 1965.

Yeates, A. Cyril, 'Nobels' Contribution to the Early Development of the Diesel Engine,' *Gas and Oil Power*, XXXII, No. 385 (October 1937), pp. 255–6, 258.

Yugoff, A., *Economic Trends in Soviet Russia*, Smith, New York, 1930.

Zaehringer, A. J., *Soviet Space Technology*, Harper and Rowe, New York, 1961.

Zaviniagin, A., 'U.S.S.R. Favors American Engineers and Equipment,' *Freyn Design*, No. 11 (March 1934), p. 19.

Zelikin, M. B., *Proizvodstvo kauticheskoi sody khimicheskimi sposobami*, Goskhimizdat, Moscow, 1961.

To the reader: Most of the articles listed here have been reproduced and deposited in a single file at the Hoover Institution.

Index